Vancouver & Victoria For Dummies, 3rd Edition

BESTSELLING BOOK SERIES

Cheat Sheet

Vancouver

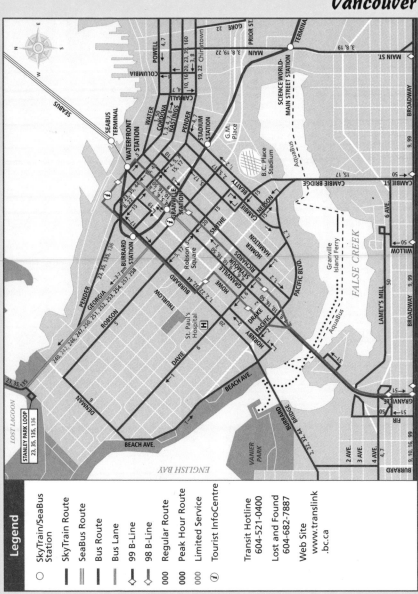

Legend

- ○ SkyTrain/SeaBus Station
- SkyTrain Route
- SeaBus Route
- Bus Route
- Bus Lane
- ◇ 99 B-Line
- ◇ 98 B-Line
- 000 Regular Route
- 000 Peak Hour Route
- 000 Limited Service
- ⓘ Tourist InfoCentre

Transit Hotline
604-521-0400

Lost and Found
604-682-7887

Web Site
www.translink
.bc.ca

Victoria

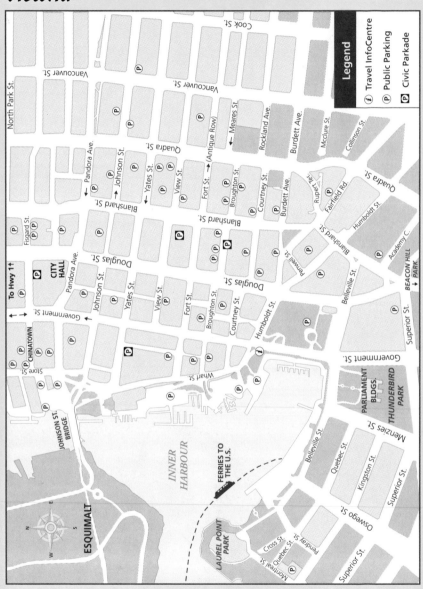

Legend

- (i) Travel InfoCentre
- (P) Public Parking
- (P) Civic Parkade

Cook St.

Vancouver St.

Vancouver St.

North Park St.

Pandora Ave.

Johnson St.

Quadra St.

Yates St.

View St.

Fort St. (Antique Row)

Meares St.

Rockland Ave.

Burdett Ave.

McClure St.

Collinson St.

Broughton St.

Courtney St.

Burdett Ave.

Rupert Ter.

Fairfield Rd.

Quadra St.

Humboldt St.

Blanshard St.

Fisgard St.

Douglas St.

Pandora Ave.

CITY HALL

To Hwy 1

Johnson St.

Yates St.

View St.

Fort St.

Broughton St.

Courtney St.

Douglas St.

Pemwell St.

Blanshard St.

Belleville St.

Academy C.

BEACON HILL PARK

Superior St.

Government St.

CHINATOWN

Store St.

Humboldt St.

Wharf St.

(i)

Government St.

PARLIAMENT BLDGS.

THUNDERBIRD PARK

JOHNSON ST. BRIDGE

ESQUIMALT

INNER HARBOUR

FERRIES TO THE U.S.

Menzies St.

Belleville St.

Quebec St.

Kingston St.

Superior St.

Oswego St.

LAUREL POINT PARK

Montreal St.

Cross St.

Quebec St.

Pendray St.

Superior St.

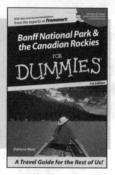
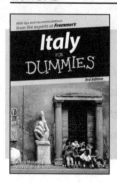

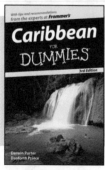

Vancouver & Victoria

FOR DUMMIES®

3RD EDITION

by Chris McBeath

John Wiley & Sons Canada, Ltd.

Vancouver & Victoria For Dummies, 3rd Edition

Published by
John Wiley & Sons Canada, Ltd.
6045 Freemont Boulevard
Mississauga, Ontario, L5R 4J3
www.wiley.ca

Library and Archives Canada Cataloguing in Publication

McBeath, Chris, 1953-

      Vancouver and Victoria for dummies / Chris McBeath. — 3rd ed.
Includes index.

ISBN-13 978-0-470-83684-2

ISBN-10 0-470-83684-9

      1. Vancouver (B.C.)—Guidebooks. 2. Victoria (B.C.)—Guidebooks.
I. Title.
FC3847.18.M23 2005   917.11'33045   C2005-902632-4

Printed in Canada

1 2 3 4 5 TRI 09 08 07 06 05

Distributed in Canada by John Wiley & Sons Canada, Ltd.

For general information on John Wiley & Sons Canada, Ltd., including all books published by Wiley Publishing, Inc., please call our warehouse, Tel 1-800-567-4797. For reseller information, including discounts and premium sales, please call our sales department, Tel 416-646-7992. For press review copies, author interviews, or other publicity information, please contact our marketing department, Tel 416-646-4584, Fax 416-236-4448.

For authorization to photocopy items for corporate, personal, or educational use, please contact CANCOPY, The Canadian Copyright Licensing Agency, One Yonge Street, Suite 1900, Toronto, ON, M5E 1E5 Tel 416-868-1620 Fax 416-868-1621; www.cancopy.com.

About the Author

Chris McBeath (greatwriter@uniserve.com) is an award-winning journalist and the author, co-author, or editor of several travel books including *Frommer's Portable Guide to Vancouver Island, The Gulf Islands & The San Juan Islands*, and *The Magic of Greater Vancouver*. With more than 25 years of experience in the tourism industry, Chris has worked aboard cruise ships, opened hotels, managed convention centers, marketed spas, and written about nearly every aspect of travel. She also owns www.greatestgetaways.com. Although based in Vancouver, she maintains strong ties to her native England and has a developing kinship with the state of Georgia. And in between her travels and penmanship, she pursues a love of acting (Chris is still a member of British Equity) — which one day might even steer her to screenwriting!

Author's Acknowledgments

Kind thanks to everyone who pitched in, but especially to Wendy Underwood of Tourism Vancouver and Kristine George of Tourism Victoria, who were quick to answer my many questions and supplied useful information at every turn; to Iona Douglas, who kept me in good cheer throughout the nitty-gritty details of the project; and to Bill Vanderford, for his loving and patient support. Finally, this book would not have happened without the guiding light of Robert Hickey, at Wiley, and the extremely fine copy editing of Joe Zingrone.

[Handwritten notes:]

Elderhostel — 51
AARP — 51
Victoria MAP — 219
Victoria Clipper hotels — 237
* Camille's — 244
Butchart Gardens — 260
Victoria Butterfly Garde — 264
Pacific Undersea God — 265
Willow Stream Spa - Hospam — 272
Theatre Inconn — 290

Publisher's Acknowledgments

We're proud of this book; please send us your comments through our Dummies online registration form located at www.dummies.com/register/.

Some of the people who helped bring this book to market include the following:

Editorial

Associate Editor: Robert Hickey

Copy Editor: Joe Zingrone

Cartographer: Mapping Specialists

Editorial Assistant: Sarah O'Brien

Front Cover Photo: Tourism Vancouver/Andy Mons

Back Cover Photo: Tourism Vancouver/Al Harvey

Cartoons: Rich Tennant (www.the5thwave.com)

Composition Services

Publishing Services Director: Karen Bryan

Publishing Services Manager: Ian Koo

Project Manager: Elizabeth McCurdy

Project Coordinator: Pamela Vokey

Layout: Carl Byers, Andrea Dahl, Lauren Goddard, Joyce Haughey, Stephanie D. Jumper, Melanee Prendergast, Julie Trippetti

Proofreader: Kelli Howey

Indexer: Belle Wong

John Wiley & Sons Canada, Ltd.

Bill Zerter, Chief Operating Officer

Robert Harris, General Manager, Professional and Trade Division

Publishing and Editorial for Consumer Dummies

Diane Graves Steele, Vice President and Publisher, Consumer Dummies

Joyce Pepple, Acquisitions Director, Consumer Dummies

Kristin A. Cocks, Product Development Director, Consumer Dummies

Michael Spring, Vice President and Publisher, Travel

Kelly Regan, Editorial Director, Travel

Publishing for Technology Dummies

Andy Cummings, Vice President and Publisher, Dummies Technology/General User

Composition Services

Gerry Fahey, Vice President of Production Services

Debbie Stailey, Director of Composition Services

Contents at a Glance

Maps at a Glance

Table of Contents

Introduction

●●●

*F*or two cities that share so much — climate, geography, heritage, the letter *v* — Vancouver and Victoria couldn't be more different; each beats to its own drummer, and captivates many with spellbinding charm. I should know — I was one of those people who, caught by their magic long ago, now call this part of British Columbia home.

To some visitors, Vancouver is California North, replete with the last vestiges of hippiedom, where you can laze on the beaches, munch organic breads, and bliss out in a no-hassle life. This view is partly true. To others, Vancouver is an international city with top-class hotels, an enviable array of restaurants, amazing shopping and sight-seeing activities, plus a taste of the Far East — all this without your ever leaving the mainland. This view also holds true. Or maybe Vancouver is a Honolulu or an Oslo — a place where you can scale mountains in the morning, sail a boat in the afternoon, and lay your head down amid spectacular scenery at night. No argument there, such is the dazzling and diverse nature of this city.

Victoria, on the other hand, carries a different reputation. As the provincial capital, and on an island unto itself, she's slightly more staid than her edgier sister. You find better weather here than in Vancouver, as well as great English beer, a plethora of antiques, double-decker buses, and gardens that are seemingly always in bloom. In addition, the city hosts a thriving arts community, and a booming eco-adventure industry that's an ever-increasing complement to the gentility of taking high tea — a wonderful juxtaposition to experience.

I wrote this book because after more than two decades here, and many travels around the world, I still enjoy these two cities more than just about any others I know. They're both extremely welcoming, refreshingly unstuffy, and have an eclectic mix of immigrant cultures. Plus, the climate is beautiful during most summers and rarely sees freezing in winter — unlike the other parts of Canada. But what really captured my heart so long ago was this: wherever you are, the sea, mountains, and forest are never out of sight. Imagine that, from right in the middle of a city.

So kick back, set those sails for Western Canada, and allow me to introduce you to the magic of my home.

Dummies Post-it® Flags

As you're reading this book, you'll find information that you'll want to double-check as you plan or enjoy your trip — whether it be a new hotel, a must-see attraction, or a must-try walking tour. Mark these pages with the handy Post-it® Flags included in this book to help make your trip planning easier.

About This Book

Treat this book as a reference, not a travel narrative. You can either read it cover to cover or dip into the sections that particularly interest you. If you already know that you'll be staying on your friend's couch, for example, you can skip the accommodations information without worrying that you're missing something crucial. If you're burning to do some serious shopping . . . well, you probably don't have your nose buried in the Introduction anyway.

In assembling the information, suggestions, and listings in this book, I've taken a greatest-hits approach. I present discriminating choices rather than encyclopedic directories. The focus is on what you need to know, not on in-case-you-were-wondering observations. Throughout, I offer plenty of insider advice to make you feel as comfortable as possible.

 Be advised that travel information is subject to change at any time — and this is especially true of prices. For this reason, I suggest that you write or call ahead for confirmation when making your travel plans. Authors, editors, and publishers cannot be held responsible for the experiences of readers while traveling. Your safety is important to us, however, so we encourage you to stay alert and be aware of your surroundings. Keep a close eye on cameras, purses, and wallets — all favorite targets of thieves and pickpockets.

Conventions Used in This Book

Vancouver & Victoria For Dummies, 3rd Edition, uses a few conventions that allow you to get the information you need quickly and easily.

I give prices in both Canadian and U.S. dollars, with all U.S. dollar amounts more than $10 rounded to the nearest dollar. I use "C$" and "US$" to let you know which currency I'm quoting. The exchange rate constantly fluctuates; for this guide, I use a rate of C$1 = US83¢.

I've included lists of hotels, restaurants, and attractions in the chapters. As I describe each, I often include abbreviations for commonly accepted credit cards. Take a look at the following list for an explanation of each:

AE: American Express

DC: Diners Club

DISC: Discover

MC: MasterCard

V: Visa

I've divided the hotels into two categories — my personal favorites and those that don't quite make my preferred list, but still get my hearty seal of approval. Don't be shy about considering these "runner-up" hotels if you're unable to get a room at one of my favorites or if your preferences differ from mine — the amenities that the not-quite-favorites offer and the services they provide make all these accommodations good choices to consider as you determine where to rest your head at night.

I also include some general pricing information to help you as you decide where to unpack your bags or dine on the local cuisine. I've used a system of dollar signs to show a range of costs for one night in a hotel (the price refers to a double-occupancy room) or a meal at a restaurant (based on main courses only). Check out the following table to decipher the dollar signs:

Cost	Hotel	Restaurant
$	Less than C$100 (US$83)	Less than C$10 (US$8.30)
$$	C$101–C$200 (US$84–US$166)	C$10–C$20 (US$8.30–US$17)
$$$	C$201–C$300 (US$167–US$250)	C$21–C$30 (US$17–US$25)
$$$$	C$301 and up (US$250)	C$30 and up (US$25 and up)

 Canadians often use the term "First Nations" to refer to the various indigenous peoples that U.S. residents call "Native Americans." Canadians also use the correct term "Inuit" to designate those far-northern people whom some in the United States call "Eskimos."

Foolish Assumptions

In writing this book, I made some assumptions about you and what your needs might be as a traveler. Here's what I assumed about you:

> ✔ You may be an experienced traveler who hasn't had much time to explore Vancouver and Victoria and wants expert advice when you finally get a chance to enjoy this particular locale.

✔ You may be an inexperienced traveler looking for guidance when determining whether to take a trip to Vancouver and Victoria and how to plan for it.

✔ You're not looking for a book that provides all the information available about Vancouver and Victoria or that lists every hotel, restaurant, or attraction available to you. Instead, you're looking for one that focuses on the places that will give you the best or most unique experience in the area.

If you fit any of these criteria, *Vancouver & Victoria For Dummies*, 3rd Edition, gives you the information you're looking for!

How This Book Is Organized

This book consists of five parts that lead you through the process of arriving in and navigating through Vancouver and/or Victoria, finding a great place to stay, searching out the restaurants that cater to your tastes, discovering the worthwhile attractions and shopping areas, and, well, having a great time.

Part 1: Introducing Vancouver and Victoria

This part gives you a thumbnail sketch of what these two cities are all about — a snapshot as to what makes them tick, the best time to go, the type of weather you can expect and some fun annual events you might want to consider. I even throw in some local lingo just to get you ready for the "British" in British Columbia.

Part 11: Planning Your Trip to Vancouver and Victoria

Here's where you'll find help in planning your trip: learn how to create a realistic budget, manage your money, and get an overall idea as to what things cost. These chapters cover all the nitty-gritty details you need to worry about such as your passport, travel insurance, and other paperwork. I look at your various options for travel, and discuss the pros and cons of booking a trip through a travel agent, joining a package tour, surfing the net for the best deals, and what to do if you have special needs.

Part 111: Vancouver

This part focuses on Vancouver, first orienting you to the city and then diving in to what makes it unique. This is where you find my recommendations of the city's top hotels, restaurants, and attractions. I tell you about the various guided tours of the city as well as the shopping districts, bars, dance clubs, and performing arts venues. I've included some sample itineraries for people with special tastes and interests in case you don't have time to draw up your own plan. You'll also find three ideas for daylong excursions away from the city, so you can experience the wonderful islands, mountains, and beaches that make living here such a pleasure.

Part 1V: Victoria

Like Vancouver, Victoria has its own special feeling. These chapters introduce you to this picturesque city and its offerings. I give you my top picks for where to stay and dine, and tell you all about Victoria's top sights. I describe guided tours to the city and surrounding area, as well as the best shopping streets, pubs, dance clubs, and theater performances. Finally, I offer a sample itinerary for discovering the city's English roots and for keeping up with family fun.

Part V: The Part of Tens

Just for fun, this is my chance to share a little bit more about the cities I love. With tongue planted firmly in my cheek, I share a list of items that will help acclimatize you quickly to the local environment. I also reveal the names of ten celebrities who hail from here — you might even bump into some of them during your stay.

In the back of *Vancouver & Victoria* I've included an appendix — your Quick Concierge — containing lots of handy information you may need when traveling in Vancouver and Victoria, like phone numbers and addresses of emergency personnel or area hospitals and pharmacies; lists of local newspapers and magazines; protocol for sending mail or finding taxis; and more. You can find Quick Concierge easily, because it's printed on yellow paper.

Icons Used in This Book

To help save you time — something no one has enough of — I use five icons to help guide you quickly to key points.

 Keep an eye out for the Bargain Alert icon as you seek out money-saving tips and/or great deals.

 This icon highlights the best that Vancouver and Victoria have to offer in all categories — hotels, restaurants, attractions, activities, shopping, and nightlife.

 Take note of the Great Northwest icon to point the way to what's particularly special about this part of the world: foods, mountains, museums, and other British Columbia–specific stuff.

 Watch for the Heads Up icon to identify annoying or potentially dangerous situations, such as tourist traps, unsafe neighborhoods, budgetary rip-offs, and other things to beware.

 Look to the Kid Friendly icon for attractions, hotels, restaurants, and activities that are particularly hospitable to children or people traveling with kids.

Find out useful advice on things to do and ways to schedule your time when you see the Tip icon.

Points out secret little finds or useful resources that are worth the extra bit of effort to get to or find.

Where to Go from Here?

Now you're primed. You're as ready to go to Vancouver and Victoria as you're ever going to be. So, what do you do next?

Dive into this book — tonight. Read a few chapters, whatever strikes your fancy, to start getting the flavor (only locals spell it "flavour") of these two cities. That should get you sufficiently excited to take a minute at lunch tomorrow to contact a travel agent, package operator, or online ticket broker to price your tickets — maybe even buy them. And before you know it, you're already halfway to these exciting cities.

Part I

Introducing Vancouver and Victoria

The 5th Wave   By Rich Tennant

Just for the record, it was _your_ idea to book the Yoga/Meditation package tour to Vancouver.

In this part . . .

1 guide you through those first important steps in preparing your trip to Vancouver and Victoria. Discover the best of the cities in Chapter 1, and then dig a bit deeper in Chapter 2 with an outline of their history, culture, and overall flavors. I even give you the lowdown on the local lingo. Now all you need to do is decide when to take your trip — check out Chapter 3 for advice on this score.

Chapter 1

Discovering the Best of Vancouver and Victoria

*W*elcome to the best of the best — a compilation of what I view to be at the very top of the list when it comes to giving you a no-holds-barred, top-notch experience in Vancouver and Victoria. But, let me tell you, it was no easy task. These cities brim with so many exciting adventures that, for me, it's a delight just to walk around and discover what's new. Which reminds me, did I mention that good shoes are an absolute must when you're here? These cities are safe, clean, and very walkable, and nothing beats hitting the streets to appreciate fully the texture and vibrancy of what Vancouver and Victoria have to offer.

Vancouver's Best

Vancouver owns its "spectacular" boast in so many areas. I guess I'm just going to jump on that bandwagon by sharing my favorites for the ultimate dining experiences and the best hotels, attractions, adventures, and shops. Although you'll probably come up with your own list, I promise this is a great place to start!

Best hotels

For more information on all the hotels listed, refer to Chapter 9.

Best Downtown Hotels: With each boasting a AAA, five-diamond rank, **The Sutton Place** and **Pan Pacific Hotel** have to take this honor, with the **Four Seasons** hotel not far behind (the latter recently lost, and is striving to regain, its fifth diamond). Canada has only two hotels with five-diamond status, and both of these are in Vancouver. Need I say more?

Best Trendy Hotel: The **Opus Hotel** has to take the cake. It's in the trendiest neighborhood, has the most risqué advertising campaign (young urbanites frolicking around in bed, no less), the most avant-garde room amenities (oxygen anyone?), and a place at the Oscars (see Chapter 9).

Best Romantic Hotel: The **Wedgewood Hotel** is not only a hot downtown location for everything, it lavishes you with attention: whether it takes the form of decadent chocolates at your bedside (no mere truffles, these) or oversized tubs that encourage togetherness. The Wedgewood also pulls out the stops on candlelit dinners and smoochy tête-à-têtes in the Bacchus Lounge and Restaurant.

Best Family-Value Hotel: Rosedale on Robson Suite Hotel — because it's so central, has a pool, and lets kids up to 16 years of age stay for free in the same suite, which are configured in a way that makes sharing with teens bearable. Families like the free toys for younger ones, and the fact that it's pet friendly.

Best restaurants and food experiences

With so many excellent restaurants in and out of hotels, I've chosen to share only the best of the independents — places that are eating icons within the community. For more information on the restaurants listed, check out Chapter 10.

Best Fusion Restaurant: ViJ's is hybrid cooking at its most unexpected — Indian with a West Coast–kick. Translate that into exotic spice blends that put a creative twist on traditional dishes, and menus that change more times than Madonna changes her look.

Best Vegetarian: There's a reason why **The Naam** is bohemian, organic, and always busy. It grew out of Vancouver's hippy enclave in Kitsilano and thrives with a mixed clientele of aging hippies, fifty-something boomers who've "discovered organic," and diehard vegans.

Best Restaurant Chef: Rob Feenie is today's sizzling hot commodity, in large part because he's the Iron Chef extraordinaire (see Chapter 25) and because his restaurant, **Lumière,** was the first freestanding restaurant in Canada to receive the prestigious *Relais Gourmand* designation. Plus, it's been voted Vancouver's best restaurant for an unprecedented seven years.

Best West Coast Fare: Bishop's has understated simplicity, sumptuous fare, and prices for the deep-pocketed brigade. But folks keep coming back, again and again. Once tried, forever hooked.

Best Breakfast: The **Elbow Room** wins by a hair, because any restaurant that can be this saucy in the morning, and dish it up all day long, deserves you as a customer. When it's busy, which is frequently, you're sitting elbow to elbow with other fans all giving as good as they get.

Best Burger: Hamburger Mary's is in the pulsating heart of Denman Village (a.k.a. gay country) and while the staff is far less colorful than it used to be, the place's stylish burgers still attract a mixed and entertaining crowd.

Best Chocolate Dessert: Fleuri's chocolate buffet is a chocoholic's nirvana, fulfilling every (well, perhaps not *every*) fantasy choco-fiends might imagine.

Best Native Restaurant: Liliget Feast House serves up the real McCoy of Native cuisine with fresh and traditional West Coast ingredients. The food and atmosphere add up to a terrifically authentic experience, one that's peppered with local folklore.

Best Market: Granville Island has long been considered one of North America's most successful urban redevelopments and the market is a large part of this success. Fresh produce from the surrounding valleys, land, and sea are here in abundance, alongside freshly baked breads, gourmet delis (think homespun pasta and crafted cheeses), and the studio wares of local artists.

Best Delicatessen: Urban Fare, in hip Yaletown, is like a fashionable warehouse of local and imported flavors. Steps away from the water, and set amid the ever-increasing number of skyscrapers along False Creek, this is a destination shop for something special. That idyllic picnic perhaps?

Best Ice Cream: La Casa Gelato is in a slightly grungy part of town but the ice creams are . . . well . . . out of this world. More specifically, the almost 200 flavors are out there; I mean waaaay out there. Hot chili ice cream anyone? How about wasabi sorbetto?

Best attractions

For more information on the following attractions, take a look at Chapter 11.

Best Mountain: I'm not even going to breathe Whistler (that would be no contest — besides, it's a two-hour drive north). So, the local award goes to **Grouse Mountain,** because it's a veritable playground in the summer and, being that much closer to the sun, always a couple of degrees hotter than down by the water. Bring a picnic, bring your camera, bring your hiking boots, bring the family.

Best Museum: The **Museum of Anthropology** is likely one of the finest museums for Native culture in North America. The location on the cliffs of Point Grey is stunning, as are its longhouse, totem poles, and other artifacts. If you're into Native history, you must include this museum on your schedule.

Best Park: Stanley Park is a 1,000-acre wilderness on the edge of the downtown core. What other North American city can boast that? No, not even Central Park comes close. It's not just the wild side of the park that's so extraordinary, it's all the other things you can do there: cycling around the seawall, retreating to one of its beaches, dining in a couple of excellent restaurants, meandering through impromptu art shows. And its **Aquarium and Marine Science Centre?** Just a gold mine of fishy adventure, especially for youngsters.

Best adventures

If you're feeling brave, you can read more about these attractions in Chapters 11 and 15.

Best Bridge: Capilano Suspension Bridge is not for the faint of heart, swinging some 450 feet above a perilous gorge, but it's Vancouver's oldest running tourist attraction that just keeps getting better. You have to try the crossing, and if you make it to the other side, you're rewarded by a maze of easy walking trails through ancient rain forest as well as new tree walks — a series of bridges that cross the canopy from one tree to the next. Very cool.

Best City Escape: A kayaking trip up Indian Arm with the First Nations outfitter, **Takaya tours** — an opportunity to see the city skyline from an awe-inspiring vantage point before heading through the busy port to hidden coves, forested shorelines, and waterfalls.

Best Laugh: *Tony n' Tina's Wedding* is an adventure in improvisational comedy, in which you play an integral part. Unlike any theater show you might expect, this can get as fun and involved as you're willing to venture.

Best shopping

For more information on the stores listed, head on to Chapter 12.

Best Shopping Streets: Robson Street for fashionistas, **Main Street** for antiquing, **Water Street** in **Gastown** for tacky souvenirs, virtually any street in **Chinatown** for photographing "what on earth is *that*" stuff.

Best First Nations Art: Art for your person is at **Dorothy Grant**'s studio, where she has incorporated Haida designs into top-flight fashions; art for your home is best sought at **Hill's Native Art** in Gastown.

Best Hat: A hat from **Tilley Endurables** has become to hats what Kleenex is to tissues. And it's a worldwide phenomenon.

Best *Homes & Gardens*–Style Designer: Martha Sturdy's initials are the same as another domestic diva, and it's her "initials" jewelry line that, in fact, first got this former sculptor into the home fashion and furniture business.

Best Escapes

Best (aaaah . . .) Spa: Le Miraj Hammam, the only one of its kind in North America, is a Turkish delight that combines an exotic steam on cool Jerusalem marble with a black Moroccan soap body scrub and a relaxing body massage.

Victoria's Best

Victoria is so swaddled in Brit-like charm, it would be easy just to rattle off every English thing in town and leave it at that. But because this city is really coming into its own, any best-of list has to reflect the rich texture of its experience, what with its hotels, eateries, galleries, high teas, pubs, and shops. So read and enjoy. This is a Victoria you might not be expecting.

Best hotels

For more information, jump to Chapter 17.

Best Colonial Hotel: The Fairmont Empress Hotel takes the whole British thing to the hilt, from ivy-covered brickwork to over-the-top high tea served with much pomp and circumstance. The Empire is well served here.

Best Renaissance Hotel: The Swans Suite Hotel was the Cinderella story of downtown hotels, but recent renos have seen her shed her threads — you might even say she's now showy enough for royalty.

Best B&B: I can't decide whether it's the four-poster beds or the lavish chandeliers that put Abigail's Hotel in this list. It's a lovely Tudor mansion that exudes old England; the breakfasts are pretty impressive, too.

Best Family Value: Royal Scot Suite Hotel has everything from pool tables for teens to self-serve laundry facilities for when kiddie T-shirts get splattered with ice cream. And it's so central to everything, you can park the car (for free) and either walk or take the courtesy shuttle to your points of interest.

Best restaurants

To further whet your restaurant appetite, skip to Chapter 18.

Best Fish and Chips: Barb's Place on Fisherman's Wharf. It might be a shack, but on a sunny day you can't beat the camaraderie of eating greasy, ketchup-covered chips out of newspaper, amid the bobbing masts of commercial fish boats and houseboats.

Best-Dressed Seafood: Blue Crab Bar & Grill puts out great seafood all day long. Cited by *The Wine Spectator* for its excellence, you can watch the fiery action in the open kitchen, though the stunning harbor views will likely win out.

Best Breakfast: At the **Blue Fox Café,** you would miss the doorway if it weren't for the lineups and the steamy windows. The waits are never long; besides, they work up the appetite that you'll need just to be able to conquer the generous portions.

Best Italian Restaurant: Il Terrazzo Ristorante is consistently rated among the best Victoria has to offer. Stepping inside is like being enveloped by a little piece of Tuscany. The food just further trans-ports you.

Best Romantic Restaurant: Camille's Fine West Coast Dining not only embraces local ingredients for stylish West Coast fare, it does so with such romantic panache, it's *the* place for honeymooners and anniversary couples.

Best Fusion Restaurants: Or is that confusion? **Pablo's Dining Lounge** for Spanish-French; **Café Brio** for Canadian-Italian; **Santiago's** for a hybrid of Latin American flavors.

Best Vegetarian: Green Cuisine is a Victoria institution when it comes to vegan fare that's so good and extensive, it might even convert the most diehard carnivore.

Best teas

For more information, steep yourself in Chapter 18.

Best Tea Blend: The **Empress Blend,** created by Murchies especially for the teas served at The Empress — souvenir packets are provided along with the scones and clotted cream.

Best Real McCoy: The **White Heather Tea Room,** because, quite simply, the service comes with a broguish Scottish accent and warm familial hospitality. Cozy up!

Best pubs

For more information, head over to Chapter 18.

Best Pub Crawl: Start at **Canoe,** a huge rambling warehouse space right on the water; from here it's an easy walk to **Swans Pub** (see Chapter 22) for its Bavarian-style beer; then carry on to **Spinnakers Brewpub,** the first microbrewery in Canada, that now serves up music, darts, and dozens of home brews. End up either at **Hugo's** at the Magnolia Hotel or the very rowdy **Sticky Wicket.**

Best Mood: Away from the downtown core in quieter Oak Bay Village, the **Penny Farthing Pub** is intimate, atmospheric, and a great place (especially in front of the fire) to have a good chitchat over a half-bitter. Reminiscent of what you would find in England's countryside.

Best attractions

For more information on these attractions, take a look at Chapter 19.

Best Garden: By the time you read this, world famous **Butchart Gardens** will have welcomed their 50,000,000th visitor. However you do the math, it takes a sky-high pile of flowers and blooming displays to keep up those kinds of numbers. Impressively beautiful — I can't even begin to describe what you'll see.

Best Museum: The **Royal British Columbia Museum** isn't your cliché museum at all. It's all about enveloping you with historical sensation, not just presenting artifacts in glass cases (though it does do this as well). The RBCM shines particularly bright with its interpretation of specialty exhibits.

Best for Kids: The **Victoria Bug Zoo** brings bugs up close and personal. Be prepared for crawlies, such as a 400-leg millipede that stretches the length of your arm or glow-in-the-dark scorpions.

Best walks

For more information, stroll over to Chapter 19.

Best Hill: Mile Zero at **Beacon Hill Park** sits right above the Pacific Ocean and has been the start of many a cross-Canada trek. Any walk through this park is a delight; kite flying near the bluffs is the best.

Best Historical Walk: John Adams from **Discover the Past Tours** puts on some well-informed, terrific walks in and around the city. His **Ghostly Walks** are laced with spooky anecdotes.

Best shopping

For more information on the stores listed, see Chapter 20.

Best Read: Munro's Books might be the most heralded bookstore, but **Chronicles of Crime** is the most intriguing — customers include lawyers, forensic experts, and FBI folks (ahem, spies!).

Best Studio Shop: Starfish Glassworks, because you get to see the goods in action, being blown, shaped, and crafted before your eyes.

Best Packable Antiques: Any store along **Antique Row** (Fort Street) is bound to rustle up something of interest. **Vanity Fair** may not have the poke-around ambience, but practically everything in its 40-plus showcases is small enough to pack into a suitcase.

Best Tea Wares: Murchie's Tea and Coffee is a local, family-run company that's been peddling tea for almost 100 years — I think they know what they're doing, right? Jolly good teas and tea paraphernalia.

Best Candies: Did you know that toffee was once considered an aphrodisiac? In addition to this, the **English Sweet Shop** delivers jars of penny candies, by the pound if you want. Some you can't get elsewhere in North America. The best news is that if you get hooked on one, mail order is available.

Best of the Best: The name says it all: **Simply the Best** has all manner of exclusive, tough-on-the-wallet items, Egyptian cotton shirts, silk ties from Ermenegildo Zegna, private-label wines, and pens that cost more than a year's mortgage payments.

Best escapes

Best (aaaah . . .) Spa: Maria Manna Life Spa (see Chapter 20) is Victoria's only Euro-Ayurvedic spa (it even has an Ayurvedic doctor on staff), and the only place to experience the traditions of a Shirodhara (warm oil) treatment with a Swedana (steam cabinet) and an Abhyanga (full-body massage) with two therapists.

Best Natural Wow: Botanical Beach (see Chapter 21) is one of the jewels of Juan de Fuca Provincial Park, as much for its shoreline as its tidal pools. The drive there is also breathtaking; in places, it follows the dramatic Juan de Fuca Trail (a much easier version of the famed and rugged West Coast Trail).

Chapter 2

Digging Deeper into Vancouver and Victoria

A buzz fills the air in British Columbia — and it's not just from the shade-grown organic coffee you can get anywhere in downtown Vancouver. Or from the younger, shifting demographics that are infusing vitality into Victoria's quieter mode.

No, the buzz comes from a province that's being discovered for its spectacular beauty, hospitality, and cosmopolitan nature. And by 2010, when Vancouver and Whistler host the Winter Olympic and Paralympic Games, B.C. will become a hotter commodity (even in the cooler weather!).

Nowhere is this better seen than in Vancouver and Victoria. They are, quite simply, two fabulous cities in which to live and work. Everyone from expat Brits to stressed-out Toronto lawyers to Japanese students, Chinese businessmen, and even Hollywood types have decided that Vancouver is *the place* to raise a family. Victoria, too, is experiencing its own renaissance, as young families and longtime Vancouver residents relocate there in search of that perfect combination of small town and big city that Vancouver once was.

Safe, clean, and consistently ranked as top places to visit by *Condé Nast Traveler* and other leading travel magazines, Vancouver and Victoria offer the best of all worlds, both very different from just about any place else in North America. I won't tell you everything to do in these destinations just yet — that's what the rest of this book is for. But this chapter provides a quick snapshot of each city.

Discovering Vancouver's Highlights

Variety may be Vancouver's best asset. Its colorful past, fascinating ethnic communities, interesting structures and even more impressive natural attractions, and world-class culinary and arts scenes all make for a city well worth getting to know.

Vancouver history 101

For thousands of years, the Greater Vancouver Area was just a quiet and beautiful backwater where small, salmon-fishing Native settlements (including one in present-day Stanley Park) moved from one inlet to the other, trading along the Fraser River and beyond. That all changed late in the 18th century, however, when Spanish and English navigators, in search of routes between Asia and Europe, stumbled across the region's network of tidal inlets, rivers, islands, and sounds.

After some sparring between the two nations, Captain George Vancouver staked a British claim in 1792. Then, as interest in lumber (the region's naturally tall timber became sought after for masts), fishing, trapping, and trading began to build throughout the British Empire, the Hudson's Bay Company established a post here. When gold was discovered in the Cariboo, backcountry to the north of Vancouver, hundreds of prospectors rolled through the area during the mid–19th century, solidifying Vancouver's future as a port of call.

Although the gold veins soon played out, people still came; when Canadian Pacific Railroad surveyors showed up to lay out a terminal station for a new transcontinental railroad line, things would never be the same again. In fact, finding a way through the Rockies and bringing people and business to the West Coast was the linchpin for British Columbia becoming a part of Canada. The trains began rolling in from the East Coast in 1887, and from that moment on, Vancouver — having survived a disastrous citywide fire that nearly stopped the entire project in its tracks — grew exponentially.

Vancouver's many cultures: Exploring the mosaic

Where the United States describes itself as a melting pot, Canada likes to describe itself as a mosaic — a place where all the different immigrant cultures retain their unique identities while, at the same time, they form a cohesive nation. That idea is nowhere more apparent than in Vancouver. First, you see examples of the region's Native origins, from the huge, ornately carved totem poles in Stanley Park to the impressive Museum of Anthropology to the quality selection of Native-Canadian foods, arts, and crafts. Because Vancouver grew through immigration, starting with British traders and Chinese railroad workers, you quickly get a sense of that heritage, too. Although Vancouver is painfully yuppie in certain parts, the city does possess surprising diversity in others. Take, for example, the prominent **Chinatown** district — where you can sample Asian cuisine that easily rivals San Francisco's — and the smaller

Japanese and **Indian** enclaves. For dining, attractions, and shopping in Vancouver's ethnic neighborhoods, see Chapters 10, 11, and 12, respectively.

Building Blocks: Local architecture

Vancouver is a relatively young city so historical buildings are few and far between, although what does stand is quite fascinating. Stroll through **Gastown** and into Chinatown and you may note some odd-shaped buildings, the result of having to follow the once-wavy shoreline when Vancouver was a rough-and-tumble town. Or head into Shaughnessy to see the mansions which once housed the railroad "lords" who helped shape much of this province.

Wild Vancouver: Finding the nature of the business

First and foremost, you come to Vancouver for city amenities amid a breathtaking setting. Name another major city in the world, that's surrounded by sparkling ocean beaches and rocks, huge mountains that constantly create their own weather, and intensely green parks — few cities come close.

You undoubtedly want to experience Vancouver's natural treasures by land, water, and even air. Hiking **Stanley Park** within sight of the city's skyscrapers, ascending in a gondola to the top of **Grouse Mountain** (which overlooks all), walking along the **Spanish Banks,** or cruising the harbor while tasting the salt air on your tongue, you begin to understand why everyone here seems so relaxed. (For more on these attractions, see Chapter 11.)

Taste of Vancouver: Local cuisine

As you might expect from a mosaic city, the quality, authentic, and diverse foods are, well, almost too yummy for words. First you have all the ethnic flavors; then you have the West Coast spin on traditional recipes; then you have all the seafood and fresh produce that comes from the region (just check out **Granville Island** or **Robson Street Market** and you'll see what I mean — see Chapter 10). Add to this the innate creativity that the coastal environment seems to engender, and you have restaurants that are among the finest you'll find anywhere in the world.

Feeding culture vultures: Arts in Vancouver

Vancouver's cultural scene is going great guns. The musical offerings run the gamut from ponytailed, strumming folkies to serious jazz players to alternative rockers to a top-flight orchestra, **Vancouver Symphony Orchestra** (see Chapter 15). Theater, too, ranges from offbeat alternative to major musicals. And the **Vancouver Art Gallery,** along with other galleries and museums, provides an intriguing visual arts scene (see Chapter 11). You also find nightlife aplenty in several different areas, including thriving — even surging — **coffeehouse and dining scenes** (see Chapter 10).

Background check: Recommended books

Vancouver certainly has its fair share of esteemed authors: a shortlist includes George Bowering (Canada's first poet laureate), Peter C. Newman, David Suzuki, Lynn Johnston (of "For Better or For Worse" comic strip fame), Nick Bantock (Griffin and Sabine series), and W.P. Kinsella, whose novel *Shoeless Joe* went on to become the popular and acclaimed movie *Field of Dreams*.

Books that reflect the cultural rhythm of the city include

- *The Greater Vancouver Book: An Urban Encyclopedia,* edited by Chuck Davis: The most comprehensive sourcebook of information about the city and its history, as well as an excellent glimpse of life in Vancouver at the end of the 20th century.

- *Vancouver Short Stories,* edited by Carole Gerson, a Vancouver literature professor: This book includes selections from the work of Pauline Johnson, Dorothy Livesay, and Alice Munro.

- *City of Glass: Douglas Coupland's Vancouver:* Written by the author of *Generation X*, this book is both a personal memoir and history, packaged with arty photographs and a compelling layout.

Sampling England in Victoria

In comparison to Vancouver, Victoria, located at the southern tip of Vancouver Island (a huge island sitting just offshore from the B.C. mainland, not far from Vancouver), is pretty small, more intimate, and probably more civil, as well. That's because Victoria is intensely British (the city was named, after all, for Queen Victoria), from its colonial roots to its prim architecture to its refined gardens.

Victoria history 101

Victoria, once a small *Salish* (Native) fishing and farming village, was established as a British city in 1843 after James Douglas, a representative of the Hudson's Bay Company, landed in the harbor, looked around, began using epithets like "Eden," and sent word back to London. The Hudson's Bay Company went on to build a fur-trading post and fort here, and Britain's navy — realizing at once the strategic advantages of the island port over Vancouver's harbor — also soon moored its own fleet of ships here. It was only a matter of time before gold-panners and fishermen arrived, stayed, and banded together to formally charter a city.

Victoria was named capital of the province of British Columbia in 1866 and remains B.C.'s top tourist draw today.

Stately estates: Victoria's architecture

Stand on the Inner Harbour and you are virtually enveloped by Frances Rattenbury, the Victorian architect who was responsible for the imposing and ornate Legislative Buildings and The Empress Hotel. These really steal the show by epitomizing the architecture of the era. The surrounding streets are sprinkled with some grand old houses, including some like Craigdarroch Castle (see Chapter 19) that were built by Victoria's gentry — the coal and land barons.

Walking about: Victoria on foot

Victoria is heavier on historical sights — including museums, old houses, hotels, and maritime attractions — than highrise-dominated Vancouver, and as a bonus, the city is refreshingly compact and walkable. Getting from **The Fairmont Empress Hotel** to scenic **Beach Drive** or other sights is only a few minutes' stroll. Despite a population of more than half a million, the city does not have traffic jams. You can even step from downtown right onto a boat that will whisk you to Vancouver or Washington State — the city is closer to the U.S. mainland than to Canada's. (See Chapter 19 for more on touring Victoria.)

Strolling through gardens

Victoria is world-renowned for its **Butchart Gardens.** Carved out of an abandoned quarry 100 years ago, the gardens represent the dream of a single person, Jenny Butchart, who sought to reclaim a wasteland. She achieved her goal, and today thousands of visitors marvel at the great variety of flowers here and their artful arrangements. But Butchart Gardens isn't the only piece of greenery in town — this is, after all, the land of horticulturalists. You can view numerous other gardens, parks, and conservatories, such as the nearby **Victoria Butterfly Gardens** and **The Fairmont Empress Hotel and Rose Gardens.** (See Chapter 19 for more on Victoria's gardens.)

Turning in Early in Vancouver and Victoria

The only truly critical word that you ever hear about Vancouver and Victoria is that, well, they're a bit . . . how shall I put this? . . . *dull.* Local youths and artsy types try hard to create a "scene" — they're the ones hanging around in the streets looking disaffected after 9 p.m.; in fact, in Victoria, they're the *only* ones out after 9 p.m. — the truth is that most locals are in bed by then. And if you're an early riser, you'll understand why. Jogging, going to the gym, tai chi, and other activities are common sights at sunrise.

Face it: Most of the nightlife was created for tourists. Ah, well, what price paradise?

Word to the wise: Victoria's local lingo

Despite the close proximity of the United States — the border is less than an hour's drive away — Victoria is closer, culturally speaking, to London than it is to Seattle. As a result, you find more than your share of fish-and-chip shops, afternoon high teas, umbrellas, golf courses . . . and polite expressions that you may not quite understand. Herewith, a (very) short primer on what the locals mean when they say something you've never quite heard before:

Victoria Expression	U.S. Meaning
biscuit	cookie
bonnet	hood of a car
boot	trunk of a car
chip	French fry
chippie	fish-and-fries shop
crisp	potato chip
dear	expensive
loonie	one-dollar Canadian coin
lorry	truck
lovely	good
mac (short for macintosh)	raincoat
MIF	Milk In First (as in serving tea)
MIL	Milk In Last (see above)
miffed	annoyed
parkade	parking lot
petrol	gasoline
Tilley	brand describing the epitome of useful travel hats
toonie	two-dollar Canadian coin
tromp	walk with deliberation

Chapter 3

Deciding When to Go

· ·

In This Chapter

▶ Facing the rain

▶ Finding out about the seasons

▶ Flipping through Vancouver's and Victoria's event calendars

· ·

*V*ancouver and Victoria are fine any time of year — this part of the world never gets very hot or cold — but, given a choice, I'd come in late summer or fall. Why? Oceanside Vancouver has a maritime climate, characterized by beautiful summers and falls, separated by cool, damp winters with strong storms blowing in off the Pacific and springs of variable, though relatively mild, weather.

 Summer is by far the busiest season for Vancouver and Victoria tourism. Book accommodations (see Chapter 9 for Vancouver accommodations, Chapter 17 for Victoria accommodations) as far in advance as possible if you plan to visit during July, August, or September.

Chasing the Rain Away

No travel plans to Vancouver and Victoria can begin without discussing the weather. Yes, rain will probably fall during your visit, but you won't get too wet — the rain tends to be a (sometimes steady) drizzle, rarely a downpour.

More interestingly, however, *where* you stay can make a big difference in the amount of precipitation that you see. Facing the open Strait of Georgia, Vancouver has little protection from storms moving west to east, and so tends to get the coastal rains that have also made Seattle famous.

But Victoria, set on the easternmost spit of land on Vancouver Island, is a little different. A high range of coastal mountains to the east guards the city from the rains. This *rain shadow* effect means that a bit less rain falls here each year than on its neighbor, Vancouver, across the strait.

The mainland area just northwest of Vancouver — beginning at Gibsons Landing — is so well guarded by the same sorts of mountains that the region calls itself the "Sunshine Coast." That name's a bit euphemistic, perhaps, but meteorological records do bear out the boast: This coastal area receives less rain than the city.

In fall and winter, rain becomes sleet and snow at higher altitudes. And as you drive north toward Whistler from Vancouver on Route 99, known as the Sea to Sky Highway, you gradually ascend into honest-to-goodness high mountains. That means that a rainy or even merely overcast day in Vancouver can become a bad snowstorm, without warning, by the time that you reach the ski resorts. (Why do you think they're located there?) To keep accidents to a minimum, the provincial government sometimes closes the Sea to Sky Highway when heavy snows are possible.

Figuring Out the Secret of the Seasons

Vancouver is green and beautiful any time of year, but certain times are better than others. Most locals do their heavy-duty enjoyment of the outdoors in summer and fall, when the weather is mild and sunshine actually makes regular appearances.

This section takes a look at the pros and cons of each season. For information on average temperature and rainfall, see Table 2-1.

Table 2-1	Vancouver's Average Temperatures and Precipitation	
Month	*Temperature °F/°C*	*Rainfall (in./cm.)*
January	42/5	5.1/13.2
February	44/7	4.5/11.6
March	50/10	4.1/10
April	58/14	2.9/7.5
May	65/18	2.4/6.2
June	69/21	1.8/4.6
July	74/23	1.4/3.6
August	74/23	1.5/3.8
September	65/18	2.5/6.4
October	58/14	4.5/1.5
November	48/9	4.5/1.5
December	43/6	6.5/16.7

Blooming in spring

Spring in Vancouver and Victoria has several high points.

- ✔ Crowds are still thin.
- ✔ Gardens in Vancouver and, especially, in Victoria are in full bloom.
- ✔ Days are long, with up to 16 hours of sunlight.

But, spring can have its drawbacks, too.

- ✔ The weather is still a crapshoot — mighty fine one year and rain, rain, rain the next.
- ✔ The temperature is not warm enough yet to sunbathe or skinny-dip.

Shining in summer

Summer's a great time to visit this corner of Canada.

- ✔ Summer is Vancouver's sunniest season. Some days, you can actually leave your umbrella in the hotel room.
- ✔ Hiking trails aren't muddy, thanks to that shining sun.
- ✔ The beach water is as close to warm and swimmable as it's ever going to get.
- ✔ Many attractions stay open longer than during the rest of the year.

Keep in mind, however, that summer has its pitfalls.

- ✔ An army of tourists descends on the area.
- ✔ Because this is high season, airfares to Vancouver shoot sky high.

Glowing in autumn

You have several reasons to plan a fall trip to the area.

- ✔ The weather remains wonderful; a Vancouver fall can be brighter and drier than the summer.
- ✔ Salmon run in the rivers.
- ✔ The leaves glow with autumn colors in Stanley and Pacific Spirit Parks.
- ✔ The number of tourists thins noticeably.

- ✔ Airfares drop from their summertime highs.

But, you want to keep in mind a few downfalls.

- ✔ Conventions, business trade shows, and international conferences kick into high gear come September, so finding a hotel room at an affordable price can be surprisingly difficult.
- ✔ Daylight hours become shorter.

Welcoming in winter

Vancouver and Victoria can be a winter wonderland.

- ✔ The tourists disappear, eliminating lines at museums and other popular attractions.
- ✔ Airlines and tour operators often offer exceptionally good deals on flights and packages.
- ✔ Hotel prices drop; expect considerable discounts.
- ✔ The skiing at Whistler and Grouse is exceptional; snow is guaranteed.

However, winter does have its downsides.

- ✔ Rain falls any time from November through February, sometimes drizzling for weeks on end.
- ✔ Although the temperature stays above freezing, the gray skies bring bone-chilling dampness — pack a thick sweater.
- ✔ Daylight hours are short.

Getting the Lowdown on Vancouver's Main Events

Vancouver's calendar becomes most crowded during the pleasant summer. Spring and fall bring fewer events and festivals, while winter is trade-show and exhibition time.

January/February

The big, colorful **Chinese New Year Festival** culminates in the annual dragon parade through the city, followed by fireworks. For information, call ☎ 604-658-8850. Late January or early February.

March/April

The **International Wine Festival,** at the Vancouver Convention and Exhibition Center (200–999 Canada Place), is North America's biggest wine-tasting soirée, with fine snacks to match. Call ☎ 604-873-3311 or visit playhousewinefest.com for information. Late March or early April.

June

Colorful teams compete in races right on the water in the **Alcan Dragon Boat Festival,** a unique and eye-catching celebration of the city's vital Chinese community. The festival takes place at the Plaza of Nations on False Creek (750 Pacific Boulevard). For information, call ☎ 604-688-2382 or visit www.addf.com. The second or third week in June. Victoria hosts a similar event in August (☎ 250-704-2500).

One of the best jazz festivals going, the popular **International Jazz Festival Vancouver** features some of the world's top acts performing on a combination of open-air (often free) stages and indoor venues. Call ☎ 604-872-5200 or visit www.jazzvancouver.com. Late June to early July.

July and August

Ceremonial gunshots kick off **Canada Day,** Canada's national holiday, celebrated in several locations around the city including Canada Place and Granville Island. For information, contact the Greater Vancouver Convention and Visitors Bureau (☎ 604-682-2222; www.tourism vancouver.com). July 1.

Sea Vancouver is a new festival celebrating the city's kinship to the sea. You can expect to see tallships, watersport activities such as outrigger, kayak, and canoe races, wooden boats, fishing demonstrations, and various zones for arts, food, and entertainment. Call ☎ 604-688-2382 or visit www.seavancouver.ca for information. Early July.

One of North America's best folk festivals, the **Vancouver Folk Music Festival** takes place over a variety of venues around town — especially pretty Jericho Beach Park. Special musical programs and face-painting booths help occupy children. For information, call ☎ 800-985-8363 or 604-602-9798; you can also visit www.thefestival.bc.ca. Second or third weekend in July.

Summer's climax is the two-week **Celebration of Light,** a series of fireworks displays over English Bay every three or four nights beginning at 10 p.m.; special cruises and tour boats provide waterside views. Visit www.celebration-of-light.com for information. Late July through early August.

September and October

Vancouver International Film Festival, the last pearl in Canada's string of three fall film festivals (try saying *that* five times fast), takes place at theaters around the city over a two-week period, drawing more than 100,000 film buffs. Tickets cost about C$9 (US$7.50) per flick, with day and festival passes available. For information, call ☎ 604-685-0260 or visit www.viff.org. Late September through early October.

Checking Out Victoria's Main Events

Victoria is also festival-happy on a year-round basis, celebrating everything from beer to Shakespeare. Summer is busiest, when street performers fill the parks and town squares and event after event marches through the downtown area, but fall also brings a number of harvest and fishing festivals to surrounding Vancouver Island communities.

June and July

The city's **International Jazz Festival** draws headliners from all over the world including names such as Dave Brubeck, Diana Krall, Holly Cole, Jimmy Scott, and others. It is also a one-of-a-kind showcase of local talent. With more than 350 musicians performing over 80 performances in 10 days, jazz aficionados need to pencil this one in. For information, call the Victoria Jazz Society (☎ **250-388-4433**).

For nine days, folk and world music acts take over the inner harbor for the much-appreciated **ICA Folkfest.** The main venues are Inner Harbour and Market Square, where you find a beer garden and food. The C$3 (US$2.50) festival button is an incredible bargain. Call ☎ **250-388-4728** or visit www.icafolkfest.com. Late June and early July.

August and September

Modeled after Edinburgh's summer festival, the **Fringe Festival** — a mix of avant-garde comedy, music, dance, and performance art, among other things — is rapidly becoming a Canadian institution. For information, call ☎ **250-383-2663** or visit www.intrepidtheatre.com. (Another very good version of this festival also happens in Vancouver during this month. For information, call ☎ **604-257-0366**.) Late August through early September.

Part II

Planning Your Trip to Vancouver and Victoria

The 5th Wave   By Rich Tennant

"The closest hotel room I could get you to the Inner Harbour for that amount of money is in Seattle."

In this part . . .

*I*f you're laid-back, you may want to show up in this corner of Canada without any planning, but the truth is that a little bit of advance work goes a long way toward saving you money and ensuring an enjoyable trip. Part II helps you through the stickier details. In Chapter 4, you find money tips and budgeting advice. In Chapter 5, you can check out options on how to get here, and in Chapter 6, I offer guidance for seniors, gay travelers, those with disabilities, and families. Finally, in Chapter 7, I tackle some of the least exciting (but critical) matters — airport customs, travel insurance, health care, car rentals, activity reservations, and packing — in what I hope is a straightforward enough way to keep your eyes from glazing over.

Chapter 4

Managing Your Money

· ·

In This Chapter

▶ Preparing your budget
▶ Cutting corners to save bucks
▶ Deciding on a form of payment
▶ Handling a money emergency

· ·

*V*ancouver and Victoria have so many great parks, restaurants, and other attractions that not immersing yourself in the experience is foolish. On the other hand, the illusory pleasures of a good exchange rate can turn sour when your credit card bill shows up later, with your indulgences — and Canadian taxes — spelled out in black and white. Believe me, I've seen many a tourist come to these cities vowing to hold to a budget, only to overspend on totem poles, horse-drawn tours, Native art, gifts of smoked salmon, teacups, tartans, and all the rest.

But don't despair. After you devise a strategy, you can have a blast without sinking your bottom line.

 I give the prices in this guide in both Canadian and U.S. dollars, with all U.S. dollar amounts more than $10 rounded to the nearest dollar. The good news is that, thanks to a favorable exchange rate, most everything costs less in Vancouver and Victoria than in a comparable U.S. city.

At press time, C$1 was roughly equal to US83¢.

Adding Up the Costs of Your Trip

A well-constructed budget is like a tricky jigsaw puzzle, and making it work can be as satisfying as dropping that 1,000th piece into place. By running through several expense categories, this section helps you begin to pull your budget together.

Lodging

Without question, lodging will be your biggest expense, but the amount really depends on where you choose to stay. In the downtown or West End of Vancouver, or the Victoria waterfront, figure at least C$150

(US$125) a night in high summer season — more (upwards from C$300 (US$250)) for a swankier place, less (but not much less) for a bland chain, family-style hotel. Bed-and-breakfasts may cost a shade less, as little as C$75 (US$62), or more, especially in Victoria where you can easily drop C$300 (US$250) a night on a really nice B&B — but at least one of those Bs stands for "breakfast." See Chapters 9 and 17 for exact hotel prices in each city.

Transportation

You don't need a rental car in Vancouver or Victoria, but getting one is a good idea if you want to explore the parks, gardens, and beaches on the outskirts. A rental car costs about C$35 to C$60 (US$29–US$50) per day — higher on summer weekends, but watch for deals and promotions — plus about C$12 to C$15 (US$10–US$12) a day for insurance, which you may be able to waive, thanks to your own coverage. (See Chapter 7 for more about renting a car.)

Gas in Canada is expensive — not as expensive as in Europe, maybe, but still pretty costly. Canadian newspapers and television are always lamenting the hikes in gas prices, and when they drop a few cents from the average of C$4 a gallon — well, there's mayhem at the pumps. Even when converted to U.S. dollars, that's a hefty US$3.35 a gallon. Clearly, any sort of extended driving tour — even in the city, where the miles eat up gas much more quickly — will add significantly to your budget.

Other transportation costs to keep in mind include

- ✔ **Ferry transport:** If you plan on visiting islands in your car, you'll have to pay to transport the car on the ferry in addition to the fee for yourself and others traveling with you. Transport for a car varies, according to ferry and distance, from C$20 to C$50 (US$17–US$42) per one-way hop from within British Columbia — more from the United States.

- ✔ **Parking fees:** Metered parking in downtown Vancouver can be difficult to find. When this happens, you'll want to use one of the downtown's many garages, which charge between C$2.50 and C$4 (US$2.10–US$3.35) per hour or approximately C$12 to C$15 (US$10–US$12) a day. If you park early, you may receive a discount for the whole day.

My advice on transportation? Hoof it around central Vancouver or use the good public transit system or taxicabs to get from point to point. The cost per day for a transit pass or one downtown cab ride is a bargain at about C$7 (US$5.80). Check the hotel listings in Chapters 9 and 17: Some offer free shuttle service in the downtown core. If you do rent a car, restrict its usage to longer trips and stay in a hotel and/or B&B that provides complimentary guest parking.

Restaurants

When eating out, you can save or splurge — the choice is really up to you. To cut costs, I usually recommend dining out at fine restaurants for lunch, and then eating at family-oriented places for dinner. That way, you can splurge on lunch — which ranges from C$5 (US$4.15) per person in a Chinatown eatery to no more than C$20 (US$17) per person at the very finest restaurants — and trim the fat at dinner, which costs from C$5 to C$10 (US$4.15–US$8.30) per person at a chain restaurant, C$10 to C$25 (US$8.30–US$21) per person at most local restaurants, and C$25 to C$100 (US$21–US$83) per person at the *really* exclusive places. See Chapters 10 and 18 for exact meal prices in each city.

Attractions

For most major attractions, the cost is somewhere around C$24 (US$20) per couple, but prices vary wildly and can escalate to as much as C$45 (US$37) for a couple to visit, say, Butchart Gardens in Victoria. Or, prices can drop to as little as C$10 to C$15 (US$8.30–US$12) for two adults to visit a small museum. Always figure about half as much for teens and keep in mind that attractions are normally free for children under the age of 6. Figure two to three of these attractions per day in your calculations. See Chapters 11 and 19 for exact prices in each city.

Shopping

Souvenirs cost anywhere from two bucks in Chinatown to several thousand dollars for a piece of Native-Canadian art; shops on Robson Street and similar areas of Vancouver are definitely going to put a dent in your wallet. Still, I'd personally figure no more than C$100 (US$83) per day (and that's a hefty amount), but you'll have to determine the final amount yourself.

Nightlife

The cost of stepping out to a bar or club varies according to how much you drink — and where. Clubs rarely charge covers — well, the ones that think they're important do — and drink prices vary from the C$3 (US$2.50) well drink at happy hour to the C$6 (US$5) microbrew in an Irish pub to the C$15 (US$12) drink at a gentleman's club or hotel lounge.

For the culturally minded, theater and opera tickets start at around C$15 (US$12) per person and swiftly climb to as much as C$75 (US$62) per person for a major orchestral performance. Sometimes prices will be more for special visiting artists and touring off-Broadway shows. For more guidance on nightlife prices, see Chapters 15 and 22.

What stuff costs in Vancouver and Victoria

Taxi from the airport to downtown Vancouver	C$30–C$36 (US$25–US$30)
Taxi from ferry in Swartz Bay to downtown Victoria	C$50 (US$42)
SeaBus to Lonsdale Quay, Vancouver	C$3.25 (US$2.70)
Local telephone call, both cities	C$0.25 (US$0.20)
Double room at Granville Island Hotel and Marina, Vancouver	C$199 (US$166)
Double room at Wedgewood Hotel, Vancouver	C$400 (US$333)
Double room at English Bay Inn B&B, Vancouver	C$225 (US$187)
Double room at Strathcona Hotel, Victoria	C$120 (US$100)
Double room at Abigail's Hotel, Victoria	C$279 (US$232)
Double room at Victoria Marriott	C$300 (US$250)
Dinner for one (without alcohol) at CinCin, Vancouver	C$50 (US$42)
Dinner for one (without alcohol) at Spinnakers Brewpub, Victoria	C$20 (US$17)
Pint of microbrewed beer, both cities	C$4.50–C$7 (US$3.75–US$5.80)
Double cappuccino, both cities	C$2.95–C$3.50 (US$2.45–US$2.90)
Adult admission to the Vancouver Art Gallery	C$15 (US$12)
Adult admission to the Royal British Columbia Museum, Victoria	C$12.50 (US$10.50)
Movie ticket, both cities	C$8.95 (US$7.45)

Taxes

Canada's high quality of life doesn't come cheaply: You pay two, and often three, taxes on everything you buy in Vancouver and Victoria.

First, a 7 percent *goods and services tax* (GST) applies to every purchase except liquor, to which a special 10 percent provincial tax is added. Next, another 7 percent *provincial sales tax* (PST) is applied. Every hotel in Vancouver and Victoria also tacks on a 10 percent lodging tax (which is composed of an 8 percent provincial hotel tax and a 2 percent tourism tax).

The good news is that the GST is refundable for non-Canadian residents if it adds up to more than C$14 in tax (or C$200 in hotel bills). Of course, you have to fill out some impressive government paperwork to get it — and part with your original receipts forever when you send them. The necessary forms are available at border customs offices or, more conveniently, at some hotels and merchants.

If you want the GST refund for your hotel bills while still in Canada, you can bring your hotel receipts, two forms of photo identification, and a return transit ticket to a company called **Maple Leaf Tax Refunds,** which will pay you the instant refund. Maple Leaf has an office in Vancouver in the lower lobby of Hotel Vancouver (☎ **604-893-8478**). If you visit Whistler (see Chapter 14), you'll find an office in the Spirit of the North store (☎ **604-905-4977**).

Be aware, however, that Maple Leaf Tax Refunds, a private company, keeps 18 percent of each refund for its services.

To receive your refund for any purchased items — or to get a hotel refund without the service charge — you must send the appropriate forms and all original receipts to the government's **Visitor Rebate Program,** Summerside Tax Centre, Canada Revenue Agency, 275 Pope Rd., Suite 104, Summerside, PEI, C1N 6C6, Canada. For more details, contact Canada Revenue Agency (☎ **902-432-5608** or 800-668-4748 toll-free from within Canada only). The processing of your refund will take some time, but the money will arrive eventually.

If you want the GST refund for any item, you *must* get the receipt for that item stamped by a customs officer as you're departing Canada.

Tips

The average tip for most service providers, such as waiters and cab drivers, is 15 percent, rising to 20 percent for particularly good service. A 10 to 15 percent tip is sufficient if you just drink at a bar. Bellhops get C$1 or C$2 a bag, hotel housekeepers should receive at least C$1 per person per day, and valet-parking and coat-check attendants expect C$1 to C$2 for their services.

Check your restaurant bill carefully before laying down a tip on the table. Some pricier establishments may include the cost of service as an automatic 15 percent tip in the bill, although this practice isn't as widespread in Vancouver as it is in many other tourist towns.

Cutting Costs — But Not the Fun

So you want to save a few dollars, but not skimp on your vacation fun? No problem. What follows are cost-saving tips that you can use for any vacation, as well as some specific tips for Vancouver and Victoria:

✔ **Go in the off-season.** If you can travel at non-peak times (October through April, for example), you'll find hotel prices that are as little as half the cost of peak months listed in this book.

✔ **Try a package tour.** For many destinations, you can book airfare, hotel, ground transportation, and even some sightseeing just by making one call to a travel agent or packager, and the entire package will cost a lot less than if you try to put the trip together yourself. (See Chapter 5 for more on package tours.)

✔ **Always ask for discount rates.** Membership in AAA, CAA, frequent-flier plans, trade unions, AARP, CARP, or other groups may qualify you for savings on car rentals, plane tickets, hotel rooms, and even restaurant meals. Ask about discounts; you may be pleasantly surprised.

✔ **Reserve a room with a kitchen.** Doing your own cooking and dishes may not be your idea of a vacation, but you save a lot of money by not eating in restaurants three times a day. Even if you make only breakfast and pack an occasional bag lunch, you'll save in the long run.

✔ **Ask if your kids can stay in the room with you.** A room with two double beds usually doesn't cost any more than one with a queen-size bed. And many hotels won't charge you the additional person rate if the additional person is pint-sized and related to you. Even if you have to pay $10 or $15 extra for a rollaway bed, you'll save hundreds by not taking two rooms.

✔ **Think twice about upgrading your rental car.** Some of Vancouver's central-city car rental companies deal almost exclusively in mini-vans. Sure, you may end up getting a van for the price of a midsize, but do you really want the hassle of driving and parking it, not to mention the increased cost of gas from a vehicle that gets poor gas mileage?

✔ **Avoid exchange bureaus.** I cannot stress enough that exchange bureaus are no longer a necessary evil; if you have an ATM card, you can get Canadian cash at your bank's rates, guaranteed to be much better than any currency exchange bureau's. (See the "Using ATMs and carrying cash" section later in this chapter.) The only time that you need an exchange bureau is when

- You can't find an ATM (unlikely in downtown Vancouver or Victoria)

- You have lost your ATM card, or it suddenly won't work.

In either case, be prepared to pay an exchange bureau a commission or fee that will deduct perhaps 10 percent from the value of what you get back in return.

Handling Money

You're the best judge of how much cash you feel comfortable carrying or what alternative form of currency is your favorite. That's not going to change much on your vacation. True, you'll probably be moving around more and incurring more expenses than you generally do (unless you happen to eat out every meal when you're at home), and you may let your mind slip into vacation gear and not be as vigilant about your safety as when you're in work mode. But, those factors aside, the only type of payment that won't be quite as available to you away from home is your personal checkbook.

Canadian currency isn't hard to figure out — it looks a lot like U.S. money, only with different pictures (prime ministers, queens, loons, and so on). The bills and coins come mostly in the same denominations as America's — in C$100, C$50, C$20, C$10, and C$5 bills, and C25¢, C10¢, C5¢, C1¢ coins — with two notable exceptions: Canada uses handy one- and two-dollar coins. A "loonie" is worth C$1 (US83¢) and is gold colored. The slightly bigger "toonie," worth C$2 (US$1.65), consists of a silver outer ring and a golden inner disk.

Using ATMs and carrying cash

The easiest and best way to get cash abroad is from an ATM (automated teller machine). The **Cirrus** (☎ **800-424-7787;** www.mastercard.com) and **PLUS** (☎ **800-843-7587;** www.visa.com) networks span the globe; look at the back of your bank card to see which network you're on, then call or check online for ATM locations at your destination. Be sure you know your personal identification number (PIN) before you leave home and be sure to find out your daily withdrawal limit before you depart. Also keep in mind that many banks impose a fee every time your card is used at a different bank's ATM, and that fee can be higher for international transactions (up to $5 or more) than for domestic ones (where they're rarely more than $1.50). On top of this, the bank from which you withdraw cash may charge its own fee. To compare banks' ATM fees within the U.S., use www.bankrate.com. For international withdrawal fees, ask your bank.

The major banks in Vancouver and Victoria (along with their networks), are as follows:

- ✔ **Bank of Montreal:** Cirrus
- ✔ **Bank of Nova Scotia (Scotia Bank):** Plus
- ✔ **Canada Trust:** Cirrus and Plus
- ✔ **Canadian Imperial Bank of Commerce (CIBC):** Plus
- ✔ **Hong Kong Bank of Canada:** Cirrus

> ✔ **Royal Bank of Canada:** Cirrus and Plus
> ✔ **Toronto Dominion (TD):** Plus

For exact locations of ATMs, see the Appendix.

 Popping up around Vancouver and Victoria are several ATMs not affiliated with any bank, and these charge the highest fees in exchange for the convenience of their locations in supermarkets, pharmacies, corner stores, and the like. Fees can be C$2.50 (US$2.10) or more for a single withdrawal at these little monsters. Avoid them if at all possible.

Charging ahead with credit cards

Credit cards are a safe way to carry money: They also provide a convenient record of all your expenses, and they generally offer relatively good exchange rates. You can also withdraw cash advances from your credit cards at banks or ATMs, provided you know your PIN. If you've forgotten your PIN, or didn't even know you had one, call the number on the back of your credit card and ask the bank to send it to you. It usually takes five to seven business days, though some banks will provide the number over the phone if you tell them your mother's maiden name or some other personal information.

 Some credit card companies recommend that you notify them of any impending trip to a foreign country so that they don't become suspicious when the card is used numerous times in a foreign destination and block your charges. Even if you don't call your credit card company in advance, you can always call the card's toll-free emergency number if a charge is refused — a good reason to carry the phone number with you. But perhaps the most important lesson here is to carry more than one card with you on your trip; a card might not work for any number of reasons, so having a backup is the smart way to go.

Toting traveler's checks

These days, traveler's checks are less necessary because most cities have 24-hour ATMs that allow you to withdraw small amounts of cash as needed. However, keep in mind that you will likely be charged an ATM withdrawal fee if the bank is not your own, so if you're withdrawing money every day, you might be better off with traveler's checks — provided that you don't mind showing identification every time you want to cash one.

You can obtain traveler's checks at almost any bank. **American Express** offers denominations of C$10, C$20, C$50, C$100, and (for cardholders only) C$1,000. You pay a service charge ranging from 1 to 4 percent. You can also get American Express traveler's checks over the phone by calling ☎ **800-221-7282;** Amex gold and platinum cardholders who use this number are exempt from the 1 percent fee. For the locations of the American Express and AAA offices in Vancouver and Victoria, see the Appendix.

Visa offers traveler's checks at Citibank locations across the U.S., as well as at several other banks. The service charge ranges between 1.5 percent and 2 percent; checks come in denominations of C$20, C$50, C$100, C$500, and C$1,000. Call ☎ **800-732-1322** for information. AAA members can obtain Visa checks without a fee at most AAA offices or by calling ☎ **866-339-3378**. MasterCard also offers traveler's checks. Call ☎ **800-223-9920** for a location near you.

Dealing with a Lost or Stolen Wallet

Be sure to contact all of your credit card companies the minute you discover your wallet has been lost or stolen and file a report at the nearest police precinct. Your credit card company or insurer may require a police report number or record of the loss. Most credit card companies have an emergency toll-free number to call if your card is lost or stolen; they may be able to wire you a cash advance immediately or deliver an emergency credit card in a day or two. The issuing bank's toll-free number is usually on the back of the credit card, but that won't help you much if the card was stolen. Write down on a piece of paper the number listed on the back of your card before you leave, and keep the transcribed number in a safe place just in case. The Canadian toll-free, emergency numbers for the major credit cards are

- ✔ **American Express** ☎ 800-268-9824
- ✔ **MasterCard** ☎ 800-826-2181
- ✔ **Visa** ☎ 800-336-8472

If you opt to carry traveler's checks, be sure to keep a record of their serial numbers so that you can handle just such an emergency.

If you need emergency cash over the weekend when all banks and American Express offices are closed, you can have money wired to you via **Western Union** (☎ **800-325-6000**; www.westernunion.com).

Identity theft and fraud are potential complications of losing your wallet, especially if the wallet contained your driver's license along with your cash and credit cards. Notify the major credit-reporting bureaus immediately; placing a fraud alert on your records may protect you against liability for criminal activity. The three major U.S. credit-reporting agencies are **Equifax** (☎ **800-766-0008**; www.equifax.com), **Experian** (☎ **888-397-3742**; www.experian.com), and **TransUnion** (☎ **800-680-7289**; www.transunion.com). Finally, if you've lost all forms of photo ID, call your airline and explain the situation; they might allow you to board the plane if you have a copy of your passport or birth certificate and a copy of the police report you've filed.

Chapter 5

Getting to Vancouver and Victoria

• •

In This Chapter
▶ Arriving by plane
▶ Getting to Vancouver and Victoria by train, ferry, or car
▶ Selecting an escorted or package tour

• •

*I*f the details of trip planning start to bog you down, you may begin to suspect that the *longest* distance between two points is a straight line. You don't have to feel that way. This chapter outlines your options, from hands-off to hands-on, for flying, driving, or boating to Vancouver and Victoria.

Flying to Vancouver and Victoria

Look on the map — these cities aren't exactly the hub of North America (although Vancouver does pride itself as being the Gateway to the South Pacific). Most major airlines have direct flights to Vancouver and most flights to Victoria are via Vancouver, and unless you like driving the highway (the drive up the West Coast and through the Rocky Mountains is spectacular), flying to this corner of the world is your best bet. If you're traveling from anywhere in North America, check out flights to Seattle. The hop across the border can add hundreds to your ticket price that you may prefer to spend in car rentals, particularly if you like to do your own thing.

Finding out which airlines fly here

Vancouver International Airport (abbreviation: YVR; ☎ **604-207-7077**), which serves as a major hub to Asia, Australia, and New Zealand, is well connected to most U.S. flight routes. Although the airport's major players are Air Canada and United, a number of other airlines fly directly to Vancouver from Chicago, San Francisco, Los Angeles, and New York, as well as from all major Canadian cities. For a complete list of the airlines flying into Vancouver, see the Appendix.

All passengers departing from YVR must pay an Airport Improvement Fee — C$5 (US$4.15) if you're flying elsewhere in British Columbia, and C$15 (US$12) to all other destinations. There was a time when you needed cash in hand at boarding, but, thankfully, they've now made the fee a part of the many up-front tax add-ons to your ticket price.

Victoria International Airport (abbreviation: CYYJ; ☎ **250-953-7500**) is about a 30-minute drive or bus ride north of Victoria, 5 miles outside Sidney on the Saanich Peninsula. More than 50 flights a day connect it with Vancouver International Airport, Seattle-Tacoma Airport, and several others in Canada and the United States. For a list of airports serving Victoria, see the Appendix.

Getting the best deal on your airfare

Competition among the major U.S. airlines is unlike that of any other industry. Every company offers virtually the same product (basically, a coach seat is a coach seat is a . . .), yet prices can vary by hundreds of dollars.

Business travelers who need the flexibility to buy their tickets at the last minute and change their itineraries at a moment's notice — and who want to get home before the weekend — pay (or at least their companies pay) the premium rate, known as the "full fare." But if you can book your ticket far in advance, are able to stay over Saturday night, and are willing to travel midweek (Tuesday, Wednesday, or Thursday), you can qualify for the least expensive price — usually a fraction of the full fare. On most flights, even the shortest hops within the United States, the full fare is close to US$1,000 or more, but a 7- or 14-day advance purchase ticket may cost less than half of that amount. Obviously, planning ahead pays.

The airlines also periodically hold sales in which they lower the prices on their most popular routes. These fares have advance purchase requirements and date-of-travel restrictions, but you can't beat the prices. As you plan your vacation, keep your eyes open for these sales, which tend to take place in seasons of low travel volume — for Vancouver and Victoria, from mid-October through May. You almost never see a sale around the peak summer vacation months of July and August, or around Thanksgiving or Christmas, when many people fly regardless of the fare they have to pay.

Consolidators, also known as "bucket shops," are great sources for international tickets, although they usually can't beat the Internet on fares within North America. Start by looking in Sunday newspaper travel sections; U.S. travelers should focus on the *New York Times*, *Los Angeles Times*, and *Miami Herald*. For less-developed destinations, small travel agents who cater to immigrant communities in large cities often have the best deals.

Bucket shop tickets are usually non-refundable or rigged with stiff cancellation penalties, often as high as 50 percent to 75 percent of the ticket price, and some put you on charter airlines with questionable safety records.

Several reliable consolidators are worldwide and available on the Net. **STA Travel** (☎ **800-781-4040**; www.statravel.com), the world's leader in student travel, offers good fares for travelers of all ages. **ELTExpress** (☎ **800-TRAV-800**; www.flights.com) started in Europe and has excellent fares worldwide, but particularly to that continent. **Flights.com** also has "local" Web sites in 12 countries. **FlyCheap** (☎ **800-FLY-CHEAP**; www.1800flycheap.com) is owned by package-holiday megalith **MyTravel** and so has especially good access to fares for sunny destinations. **Air Tickets Direct** (☎ **800-778-3447**; www.airticketsdirect.com) is based in Montreal and leverages the rate of exchange for low fares.

Booking your flight online

The "big three" online travel agencies, **Expedia** (www.expedia.com), **Travelocity** (www.travelocity.com), and **Orbitz** (www.orbitz.com) sell most of the air tickets bought on the Internet. (Canadian travelers should try www.expedia.ca and www.travelocity.ca; U.K. residents can go for www.expedia.co.uk and www.opodo.co.uk.) Each has different business deals with the airlines and may offer different fares on the same flights, so shopping around is wise. Expedia and Travelocity will also send you an **e-mail notification** when a cheap fare becomes available to your favorite destination. Of the smaller travel agency Web sites, **SideStep** (www.sidestep.com) receives good reviews from users. It's a browser add-on that purports to "search 140 sites at once," but in reality only beats competitors' fares as often as other sites do.

Great **last-minute deals** are available through free weekly e-mail services provided directly by the airlines. Most of these deals are announced on Tuesday or Wednesday and must be purchased online. Most are only valid for travel that weekend, but some (such as Southwest's) can be booked weeks or months in advance. Sign up for weekly e-mail alerts at airline Web sites or check mega-sites that compile comprehensive lists of last-minute specials — **Smarter Living** (smarterliving.com) is one such site. For last-minute trips, www.site59.com in the U.S. and www.lastminute.com in Europe often have better deals than the major-label sites.

If you're willing to give up some control over your flight details, use an "opaque fare service" like **Priceline** (www.priceline.com) or **Hotwire** (www.hotwire.com). Both offer rock-bottom prices in exchange for travel on a "mystery airline" at a mysterious time of day, often with a mysterious change of planes en route. The mystery airlines are all major, well-known carriers — and the possibility of being sent from Philadelphia to Chicago via Tampa is remote. But your chances of getting a 6 a.m. or 11 p.m. flight are pretty high. Hotwire tells you flight prices before you buy; Priceline usually has better deals than Hotwire, but you have to play their "name our price" game. ***Note:*** In 2004, Priceline added non-opaque service to its roster. You now have the option to pick exact flights, times, and airlines from a list of offers — or to bid on opaque fares as before.

Great last-minute deals are also available directly from the airlines themselves through a free e-mail service called E-savers. Each week, the airline sends you a list of discounted flights, usually leaving the upcoming Friday or Saturday and returning the following Monday or Tuesday. You can sign up for all the major airlines at one time by logging on to **Smarter Living** (www.smarterliving.com), or you can go to each individual airline's Web site. Airline sites also offer schedules, flight booking, and information on late-breaking bargains.

Arriving by Other Means

Sometimes, flying just won't do. Maybe you have mobility issues, you're on a big road-trip vacation, or every flight is booked. Or maybe you just want to know about other options. If this sounds like you, read on for the scoop on traveling by train, ferry, and car.

By train across Canada

VIA Rail (☎ 888-842-7245; www.viarail.ca), Canada's national passenger rail network, offers a romantic and luxurious way to get to Vancouver from the East Coast while seeing the spectacular countryside that lies between — if you have the time it takes, that is. The cross-country train service known as "the Canadian" runs three times a week, departing Toronto on Tuesday, Thursday, and Saturday mornings and passing through Winnipeg, Saskatoon, Edmonton, and Jasper before arriving in Vancouver three mornings later. Costs vary depending on how far you go and whether or not you get a sleeping compartment and/or meal package.

The summer cross-country trains are especially popular and usually need to be booked weeks, even months, ahead to ensure a seat.

By train from Seattle

Amtrak (☎ 800-USA-RAIL; www.amtrak.com) offers a much shorter rail journey from Seattle. It runs a slow, once-daily service at a cost of US$24 to US$37 in each direction (seniors get a 15 percent discount off the adult fare; kids are at 50 percent of the adult fare). The train leaves Seattle at 7:45 a.m. and rolls into Vancouver about four hours later; the return trip leaves Vancouver each night at 6 p.m. and arrives just before 10 p.m.

Although the train schedule looks as if there are several departures, be aware that they include train and bus travel between cities; the time listed above is the only departure that travels the rails all the way through.

By ferry from Washington State

Taking a conventional car ferry or fast-moving catamaran (passengers only; that is, no cars allowed) from the state of Washington to Victoria is convenient and probably less expensive than you'd expect. On a clear, summer day, the ride can even be delightful — you pass pretty islands, towering mountains, and perhaps even seals and whales. The companies providing this service include the following:

- ✓ **Black Ball Transport** (☎ 360-457-4491 (information only) or 250-386-2202 (reservations and information); www.cohoferry.com), a cruise ship–sized ferry, departs from Port Angeles, Washington, on the Olympic Peninsula west of Seattle. The ferry takes about 90 minutes and runs 4 times daily from June to September; twice daily in May, October, and November; and just once daily during the winter months. Call for departure times. The ferry, one way, costs US$9.50 per adult, US$4.75 per child ages 5 to 11; children under 5 ride free. This is the only ferry that carries cars; the cost is US$36.50 per car and driver, one way, with additional charges for passengers. Bicycles cost US$4 (plus passenger fare), motorcycles US$20.50 including rider.

  Reservations are not accepted so arrive at least an hour early for departures, especially in summer; this is first come, first served.

- ✓ **Victoria Clipper** (☎ 800-888-2535, 206-448-5000 in Seattle, or 250-382-8100 in Victoria; www.victoriaclipper.com) carries foot passengers only from Pier 69 on the Seattle waterfront. A boat departs four times a day in summer and once a day in winter. The trip generally takes about three hours — longer depending on ocean and wave conditions and the route. The round-trip cost is US$110 to US$133 for adults (summer weekends being the most expensive), US$100 to US$123 for seniors over 65, and US$55 to US$66 for children ages 1 to 11 (children under 1 are admitted for free).

  In summer, the second sailing of the day (at 7:45 a.m.) stops at other islands along the way, greatly slowing the ride. If you have the time, the trip is wonderful. Otherwise, take the high-speed, direct ferry at 8:45 a.m.

- ✓ **Washington State Ferries** (☎ 206-464-6400; www.wsdot.wa.gov/ferries) makes three-hour trips from Anacortes, Washington, to the Sidney docks about 20 miles north of Victoria for US$14 for adults, US$7 for seniors, and US$11 for children ages 5 to 18 each way. Cars cost from US$37 to US$47, including the driver. BC Transit buses #70, #72, and #75 run from Sidney to Victoria; call Victoria Transit (☎ 250-382-6161) for information.

Bear in mind that summertime lineups for these ferries can be very long. You may even be bumped from one sailing time to the next if the first boat sells out. Also, you'll be inspected by a customs or immigration officer on the Victoria docks; have your driver's license and any declaration forms at the ready, and don't joke around with the inspectors. Just answer their questions patiently and truthfully. (For more on crossing the border, see Chapter 7.)

By car from Seattle

An attractive option for some travelers is to fly to Seattle, rent a car at the airport, and drive the 140 miles north to Vancouver. Most of the major rental agencies are at Seattle–Tacoma International Airport (see the Appendix for the agencies' toll-free numbers).

The route to Vancouver is relatively straightforward. From the airport, follow signs to Interstate 5, and simply proceed north; at the border, the route number changes to Highway 99. It eventually crosses a series of bridges and becomes a two-way road, at which point the going slows considerably. Remember to make a left at 70th Avenue and proceed a few blocks west to Granville Street, make a right onto Granville and continue straight downtown.

 As you get closer to Vancouver, Route 99 tends to become clogged at its bridges after 3 or 4 in the afternoon. If possible, try to leave Seattle early in the day to avoid this congestion.

 Under normal conditions, this drive should take about three hours. On summer weekends, or when the border post is understaffed, the backup of cars and resulting wait can seem interminable. Also, Vancouver's rush-hour traffic can be heavy; Friday and Sunday afternoons are especially congested. So what's my recommendation? Allow an extra hour for the border congestion and possible city traffic.

Joining an Escorted Tour

You may be one of the many people who love escorted tours. The tour company takes care of all the details, and tells you what to expect at each leg of your journey. You know your costs up front and, in the case of the tame tours, you don't get many surprises. Escorted tours can take you to the maximum number of sights in the minimum amount of time with the least amount of hassle.

 If you decide to go with an escorted tour, I strongly recommend purchasing travel insurance, especially if the tour operator asks you to pay up front. But don't buy insurance from the tour operator! If the tour company doesn't fulfill its obligation to provide you with the vacation you paid for, there's no reason to think that they'll fulfill their insurance obligations either. Get travel insurance through an independent agency. (I tell you more about the ins and outs of travel insurance in Chapter 7.)

When choosing an escorted tour, along with finding out whether you have to put down a deposit and when final payment is due, ask a few simple questions before you buy:

✔ **What is the cancellation policy?** Can they cancel the trip if they don't get enough people? How late can you cancel if you are unable to go? Do you get a refund if you cancel? If they cancel?

✔ **How jam-packed is the schedule?** Does the tour schedule try to fit 25 hours into a 24-hour day, or does it give you ample time to relax by the pool or shop? If getting up at 7 a.m. every day and not returning to your hotel until 6 or 7 p.m. at night sounds like a grind, certain escorted tours may not be for you.

✔ **How large is the group?** The smaller the group, the less time you spend waiting for people to get on and off the bus. Tour operators may be evasive about this, because they may not know the exact size of the group until everybody has made reservations, but they should be able to give you a rough estimate.

✔ **Is there a minimum group size?** Some tours have a minimum group size, and may cancel the tour if they don't book enough people. If a quota exists, find out what it is and how close they are to reaching it. Again, tour operators may be evasive in their answers, but the information may help you select a tour that's sure to happen.

✔ **What exactly is included?** Don't assume anything. You may have to pay to get yourself to and from the airport. A box lunch may be included in an excursion, but drinks may be extra. Beer may be included, but not wine. As a traveler, how much flexibility do you have? Does the tour let you opt out of certain activities, or does the bus leave once a day, with no exceptions? Are all your meals planned in advance? Can you choose your entree at dinner, or does everybody get the same chicken cutlet?

Depending on your recreational passions, I recommend one of the following local tour companies:

✔ **Bell Tours** (☎ **800-665-8488** or 604-535-2587; www.belltours.ca) has been in business for more than 40 years and is a local favorite. Their specialty is customized tours, tailoring itineraries to small groups of four to six people — families would fall into this category — and whisking them around in a minivan-style vehicle. Costs vary depending on what's included, but example services would be a "meet and greet" (C$135/US$112 per two hours) that gets you from the airport or cruise ship to your hotel, to fully escorted tours that start at C$350 (US$291) per group for four hours. The cost just keeps going up from there depending on what hotels, attractions, and mileage is involved, but if you have a budget these folks will do their darnedest to make it work for you.

✔ **Collette** (☎ **800-340-5158** or 604-635-0902; www.collettetours.com) offers two tours, including Vancouver and/or Victoria as well as a variety of Canadian Rockies tours that combine time in Banff and Jasper with visits to Vancouver or Victoria. The most popular is their nine-day stint in the Canadian Rockies via Rocky Mountaineer Railtours; these start at C$2,709 (US$2,254) per person with a Vancouver/Victoria add-on from C$379 (US$315) per person.

Choosing a Package Tour

For lots of destinations, package tours can be a smart way to go. In many cases, a package tour that includes airfare, hotel, and transportation to and from the airport costs less than the hotel alone on a tour you book yourself. That's because packages are sold in bulk to tour operators, who resell them to the public. It's kind of like buying your vacation at a buy-in-bulk store — except the tour operator is the one who buys the 1,000-count box of garbage bags and resells them ten at a time at a cost that undercuts the local supermarket.

Package tours can vary as much as those garbage bags, too. Some offer a better class of hotels; others provide the same hotels for lower prices. Some book flights on scheduled airlines; others sell charters. In some packages, your choice of accommodations and travel days may be limited. Some let you choose between escorted vacations and independent vacations; others allow you to add on just a few excursions or escorted day trips (also at discounted prices) without booking an entirely escorted tour.

To find package tours, check out the travel section of your local Sunday newspaper or the ads in the back of national travel magazines such as *Travel & Leisure*, *National Geographic Traveler*, and *Condé Nast Traveler*. **Liberty Travel** (call ☎ 888-271-1584 to find the store nearest you; www.libertytravel.com) is one of the biggest packagers in the Northeast, and usually boasts a full-page ad in Sunday papers.

Another good source of package deals is the airlines themselves. Most major airlines offer air–land packages, including **American Airlines Vacations** (☎ 800-321-2121; www.aavacations.com), **Delta Vacations** (☎ 800-221-6666; www.deltavacations.com), **Continental Airlines Vacations** (☎ 800-301-3800; www.covacations.com), and **United Vacations** (☎ 888-854-3899; www.unitedvacations.com). Several big **online travel agencies** — Expedia, Travelocity, Orbitz, Site59, and Lastminute.com — also do brisk business in packages. If you're unsure about the pedigree of a smaller packager, check with the Better Business Bureau in the city where the company is based, or go online at www.bbb.org. If a packager won't tell you where it's based, don't fly with it.

The following companies are good sources for package tours to Vancouver and Victoria:

- ✔ **Air Canada Vacations** (☎ 888-247-2262; www.aircanada.com) is the single largest carrier flying into Vancouver. Contact this company directly to find out about its many package options.

- ✔ **Alaska Airlines** (☎ 800-252-7522; www.alaskaair.com) and its busy shuttle service **Horizon Air** (☎ 800-547-9308; www.horizonair.com) offer a selection of tours to both Vancouver and Victoria, mostly from Western U.S. cities, including air–hotel–sightseeing packages.

✔ **Globus** (no telephone; www.globusandcosmos.com) is the budget-travel half of an operator offering 12-day tours of Western Canada ending in Victoria and Vancouver. After seeing Calgary, the Rockies, and Whistler, you get about 1½ days in Victoria (including Butchart Gardens) and then from 1½ to nearly 3 days in Vancouver, mostly at your leisure. **Cosmos** (which has the same Web site) is the upscale half of the same operation and offers 10- to 13-day tours of British Columbia, including time in Vancouver.

✔ **Gray Line of Seattle** (☎ **800-426-7505** or 206-624-5077; www.gray lineofseattle.com) operates several Vancouver and Victoria tours out of Seattle, a good way to sample all three cities. The three-day, two-night Vancouver–Victoria Adventure, offered from May through September, includes an Amtrak trip to Vancouver, bus tours of the city, a ferry ride to Victoria, a tour of Butchart Gardens, a ferry to Seattle, and a city tour. You spend one night in each city. The cost is from US$650 per person (double occupancy). You can also do a single-day tour (from Seattle) of either city; cost is from US$135 per person.

Several local operators also put together escorted day tours of both cities. See Chapters 11 and 19 for more information on these.

Picking a package tour

Loads of package-tour operators — big and small — offer tours of Vancouver and Victoria. Unfortunately, that means you have to do a lot of weeding out of the bad deals. When grabbing the weed-whacker, keep these points in mind:

✔ Most of the all-inclusive packages to Vancouver and Victoria encompass a wider swath of Western Canada. They typically last about ten days, and you spend only a day or two in each of these cities; the rest of the time is spent in other beautiful places — Alaska, Banff, Seattle, Calgary, usually on a train or cruise ship — but *not* in Vancouver or Victoria. Be aware that any tour with "British Columbia" or "Canadian Rockies" in its title is probably of this variety.

✔ Small, under-the-radar tour operators know the cities better and give you a more local flavor than the big names can ever hope to capture. On the other hand, these tour companies also tend to go out of business more frequently than established firms do. Check into trip-cancellation provisions when inquiring about bookings, and remember that nothing the company tells you is technically true until it's in writing.

✔ Because flying into Seattle from a U.S. departure point is usually cheaper than flying into Vancouver, I recommend looking into a package tour that begins in Seattle. (Package tours do not typically include air travel to Seattle; you have to get there yourself.)

Chapter 6

Catering to Special Travel Needs or Interests

. . . .

In This Chapter

▶ Making the most of your family vacation

▶ Traveling as a senior

▶ Moving beyond disabilities

▶ Finding gay and lesbian resources

. . . .

*A*mazingly welcoming, Vancouver and Victoria are prime vacation spots for just about anyone — and that includes families with kids, older folks, travelers with disabilities, and gay or lesbian travelers.

Bringing the Brood: Advice for Families

Safe, clean, and filled with kids, dogs, festivals, and open spaces, Vancouver is extremely family-friendly. Victoria has an older population, so although that city is not as geared toward youngsters, plenty of family-oriented activities let you bring the kids to the city with little trouble.

Familyhostel (☎ 800-733-9753; www.learn.unh.edu/familyhostel) takes the whole family, including kids ages 8 to 15, on moderately priced domestic and international learning vacations. Lectures, field trips, and sightseeing are guided by a team of academics.

You can find good family-oriented vacation advice on the Internet from sites like **Family Travel Forum** (www.familytravelforum.com), a comprehensive site that offers customized trip planning; **Family Travel Network** (www.familytravelnetwork.com), an award-winning site that offers travel features, deals, and tips; **Traveling Internationally with Your Kids** (www.travelwithyourkids.com), a comprehensive site that offers customized trip planning; and **Family Travel Files** (www.thefamily travelfiles.com), which offers an online magazine and a directory of off-the-beaten-path tours and tour operators for families.

What follows are my tips for getting the most out of your family trip:

- ✔ **Involve the kids in planning.** Before you travel, let the kids help you plan the trip — send away for brochures that you can view together or click onto the Web sites of family-friendly destinations you're likely to visit.

  You can also surf the Web sites of **_Monday Magazine_** (www.monday mag.com) or **Tourism Victoria** (www.tourismvictoria.com) for information on special children's events and exhibits.

  If you come in May, one happening you shouldn't miss is the big **Vancouver International Children's Festival** (☎ 604-280-4444 for tickets) in Vanier Park, an event with storytellers, mimes, clowns, music, and other events geared to kids of all ages — even teens.

- ✔ **Locate kid-friendly attractions. Kid friendly!** (☎ 604-541-6192; www.KidFriendly.org), a not-for-profit organization, reviews local businesses for their family-friendliness and accredits those offering useful programs for kids and families.

- ✔ **Contact a travel agent.** If you don't have much time to plan, turn to **Infinity Travel Concepts** (☎ 604-926-8511 or 604-986-2262; www.trvlconcepts.com), which creates specialized family-oriented vacations in the Vancouver area.

- ✔ **Rent kid-friendly wheels.** If you're bringing a large family, know that several of Vancouver's downtown car rental agencies stock a good supply of passenger vans. The spacious vehicles are convenient for accommodating families and all their gear. Try **National** (☎ 604-609-7150), centrally located at 1185 West Georgia St., for starters.

- ✔ **Pack kid-friendly diversions.** Keep children entertained while traveling by carrying travel games, books, or puzzles.

- ✔ **Pick up a kid-oriented guide.** On arrival in Vancouver, the very first thing you should do is drop by the Vancouver **TouristInfo Centre,** 200 Burrard St. (☎ 604-683-2000; www.tourismvancouver.com), and stock up on reading material. Be sure to pick up a free copy of the city's kid-oriented guide, _Kids' Guide to Vancouver_, which includes coupons, information, and a local map. Just ask for the _Kids' Guide_ at the visitor's center, and they'll know what you mean.

You may adore your young ones, but sometimes you want to leave them behind — under careful, trustworthy supervision, of course. Several baby-sitting and child-care services, accredited by the tourist office, are located in Vancouver's downtown area. For recommended agencies, see the Appendix.

Making Age Work for You: Tips for Seniors

People over the age of 60 are traveling more than ever before. And why not? Being a senior citizen entitles you to some terrific travel bargains. If you're not a member of **AARP** (formerly the American Association of Retired Persons), 601 E St. NW, Washington, DC 20049 (☎ **800-424-3410** or 202-434-2277; www.aarp.org), do yourself a favor and join. You'll get discounts on car rentals and hotels, a subscription to *AARP: The Magazine*, a monthly newsletter, and other benefits. Anyone over 50 can join.

Many reliable agencies and organizations target the 50-plus market. **Elderhostel** (☎ **877-426-8056;** www.elderhostel.org) arranges study programs for people ages 55 and over (and a spouse or companion of any age) in the United States and in more than 80 countries around the world. Many packages include airfare, accommodations in university dormitories or modest inns, meals, and tuition.

Recommended publications offering travel resources and discounts for seniors include the quarterly magazine *Travel 50 & Beyond* (www.travel50andbeyond.com); *Travel Unlimited: Uncommon Adventures for the Mature Traveler* (Avalon); *101 Tips for Mature Travelers*, available from Grand Circle Travel (☎ **800-221-2610** or 617-350-7500; www.gct.com); *The 50+ Traveler's Guidebook* (St. Martin's Press); and *Unbelievably Good Deals and Great Adventures That You Absolutely Can't Get Unless You're Over 50* (McGraw-Hill).

In addition, in most cities, people over the age of 60 get reduced admission at theaters, museums, and other attractions, and you can often get discount fares on public transportation. Carrying identification with proof of age can pay off in all these situations.

To get the skinny on the latest Vancouver seniors' activities, consult the **Seniors' Services Directory** online at www.seniorsservingseniors.bc.ca, a kind of community resource handbook listing everything from government and community services to events and gathering places. Also see the "At your hotel" section later in this chapter for information on Access Canada, which rates hotels on their accessibility for seniors.

Accessing Canada: Resources for Travelers with Disabilities

A disability needn't stop you from traveling. More options and resources exist now than ever before.

Worldwide resources

Many travel agencies offer customized tours and itineraries for travelers with disabilities. **Flying Wheels Travel** (☎ **507-451-5005;** www.flyingwheelstravel.com) offers escorted tours and cruises that emphasize sports and private tours in minivans with lifts. **Access-Able Travel Source** (☎ 303-232-2979; www.access-able.com) offers extensive access information and advice for traveling around the world with disabilities. **Accessible Journeys** (☎ 800-846-4537 or 610-521-0339) caters to wheelchair travelers and their families and friends.

Avis Rent a Car has an "Avis Access" program that offers such services as a dedicated 24-hour toll-free number (☎ 888-879-4273) for customers with special travel needs; special car features such as swivel seats, spinner knobs, and hand controls; and accessible bus service.

Organizations that offer assistance to disabled travelers include the **MossRehab** (www.mossresourcenet.org), which provides a library of accessible-travel resources online; **SATH (Society for Accessible Travel and Hospitality)** (☎ 212-447-7284; www.sath.org; annual membership fees: US$45 adults, US$30 seniors and students), which offers a wealth of travel resources for all types of disabilities and informed recommendations on destinations, access guides, travel agents, tour operators, vehicle rentals, and companion services; and the **AFB (American Foundation for the Blind)** (☎ 800-232-5463; www.afb.org), a referral resource for the blind or visually impaired that includes information on traveling with seeing-eye dogs.

For more information specifically targeted to travelers with disabilities, the community Web site **iCan** (www.icanonline.net/channels/travel/index.cfm) has destination guides and several regular columns on accessible travel. Also check out the quarterly magazine *Emerging Horizons* (US$14.95 per year, $19.95 outside the U.S.; www.emerginghorizons.com); **Twin Peaks Press** (☎ 360-694-2462; http://disabilitybookshop.virtualave.net/blist84.htm), offering books for travelers with special needs; and *Open World Magazine,* published by SATH (subscription: US$13 per year, US$21 outside the U.S.).

Vancouver resources and information

Vancouver itself has the reputation of being one of the most accessible cities in the world for people with disabilities. Everything, from its public transit and airport counters to crosswalks and public bathrooms, has been designed with travelers with disabilities in mind.

If you want someone else to worry about your travel plans, **Pacific Coach Lines** (☎ 604-662-7575) runs handicapped-accessible bus trips between Vancouver and Victoria.

At the airport

Vancouver International Airport, your most likely arrival point, is very handicapped-accessible. The ticket and service counters have amplified hand sets; flight departure and arrival information boards are mounted low and printed with high-contrast typefaces to facilitate easy reading; the airport maintains visual paging monitors and public address systems displayed in written form; and the information kiosks are equipped with closed-captioned decoders. Other amenities include tactile guidance maps of the terminal building for the visually impaired, and fully accessible public telephones and services for the hearing impaired. If you need to know more, call the airport's operations department at ☎ **604-207-7077** (TTY☎ **604-207-7070**).

A special service, the **Airporter** (☎ **800-668-3141** or 604-946-8866), arranges transit from the city airport for visitors with disabilities. Call to arrange a ride, which costs C$12 (US$10). Handicapped-accessible taxis and a handicapped-accessible shuttle bus are available at the arrivals terminal.

At your hotel

Access Canada (☎ **250-387-6309**) is a government program that rates hotels on their accessibility for seniors and travelers with disabilities. It divides hotels into four categories:

- ✔ **A1:** Suitable for active seniors and people with minor disabilities.

- ✔ **A2:** Suitable for seniors and people with moderate disabilities.

- ✔ **A3:** Suitable for people with advanced hearing, mobility, and vision disabilities, and independent wheelchair users.

- ✔ **A4:** Suitable for people with severe disabilities.

You can call the organization to check the handicapped accessibility of certain Vancouver and Victoria hotels.

In transit

In Vancouver, most local buses are now handicapped-accessible. Handicapped-accessible buses and bus stops are identified by a wheelchair symbol. Or look for the letter "L" next to a route on a bus timetable. (For details on Vancouver's transportation systems, see Chapter 8.)

The **SkyTrains** are also wheelchair-accessible, with help buttons and elevators at all but those stations in the Granville neighborhood (where you find a free shuttle to the next stop). If you're disabled, board the trains through the doors with wheelchair symbols.

BC Ferries' vessels are fully equipped with elevators, bathrooms, and decks that can accommodate handicapped travelers; be sure to ask the ticket seller for a parking spot near the elevator. **SeaBus** terminals and boats are also wheelchair-accessible.

For a handicapped-accessible taxi in Vancouver, contact **Vancouver Taxi** (☎ **604-255-5111** or 604-871-1111). To rent a lift-equipped van, call the **BC Paraplegic Association** (☎ **604-324-3611**).

Even walking or wheeling around Vancouver is a snap: Thousands of sidewalk ramps exist for wheelchairs, and the "Walk/Don't Walk" crosswalk signs downtown beep or chirp when they change.

Victoria resources and information

Compared to Vancouver, Victoria has fewer amenities for handicapped visitors. Many city buses now include wheelchair lifts or other design considerations to allow disabled access. Call ☎ **205-382-6161** for transit information. The city's **handyDART** (☎ **205-727-7811**) vans are also available if you're not able to find an accessible bus. The downtown area also has beeping crosswalk signs.

Other Canadian resources

The following groups, agencies, and offices provide information for disabled travelers to the area:

- ✔ **BC Paraplegic Association** (☎ **604-324-3611**)
- ✔ **Canadian National Institute for the Blind** (☎ **604-431-2121**)
- ✔ **Coalition of People with Disabilities** (☎ **604-875-0188,** TDD 604-875-8835; Fax: 604-875-9227)
- ✔ **UBC Disability Resource Centre** (☎ **604-822-5844,** TTY/TDD 604-822-9049)
- ✔ **Western Institute for the Deaf and Hard of Hearing** (☎ **604-736-7391,** TTY/TDD 604-736-2527)

Handicapped-accessible attractions

Many Vancouver and Victoria attractions are handicapped-accessible. The following list is just a small sampling; call ☎ **604-576-5075** (in Vancouver) or visit any tourism office in Victoria for further details, listings, and information.

- ✔ You can take a free wheelchair-accessible trolley ride around Vancouver's **Stanley Park.** Call ☎ **604-801-5515** for information.
- ✔ All **horse-drawn carriage tours** of Stanley Park are wheelchair-accessible. These depart from the Coal Harbour parking lot next to the information booth on Park Drive, east of the Rowing Club.
- ✔ Grouse Mountain's blue **Skyride** gondola in North Vancouver is handicapped-accessible with 24 hours' notice. Call ☎ **604-984-0661** for information.
- ✔ The **BC Sport and Fitness Council for the Disabled** (☎ **604-737-3039**), based in Vancouver, runs a host of competitive events and recreational outings, including (but not necessarily limited to) skiing, horseback riding, sailing, sledge hockey, and track and field.
- ✔ Vancouver's **Mobility Opportunities Society** (☎ **604-688-6464**) is under the wing of the BC Disability Foundation, and offers handicapped-accessible sailing and other outdoor activities.

Following the Rainbow: Advice for Gay and Lesbian Travelers

British Columbia was among the first provinces to legislate same-sex marriage, so this corner of the world is about as gay-friendly as any North American city can be. Vancouver has an exceptionally tolerant attitude, a concentrated population of activist gays and lesbians, and a network of services, such as bookstores, clubs, and other organizations. Victoria's scene is less developed. Despite its more straight-laced attitude (in comparison to Vancouver), however, a tolerant attitude and plenty of resources exist here also.

The International Gay and Lesbian Travel Association (IGLTA) (☎ 800-448-8550 or 954-776-2626; www.iglta.org) is the trade association for the gay and lesbian travel industry, and offers an online directory of gay- and lesbian-friendly travel businesses; go to their Web site and click on "Members."

Many agencies offer tours and travel itineraries specifically for gay and lesbian travelers. **Above and Beyond Tours** (☎ 800-397-2681; www.abovebeyondtours.com) is the exclusive gay and lesbian tour operator for United Airlines. **Now, Voyager** (☎ 800-255-6951; www.nowvoyager.com) is a well-known San Francisco–based gay-owned and operated travel service. **Olivia Cruises & Resorts** (☎ 800-631-6277 or 510-655-0364; www.olivia.com) charters entire resorts and ships for exclusive lesbian vacations and offers smaller group experiences for both gay and lesbian travelers.

The following travel guides are available at most travel bookstores and gay and lesbian bookstores: *Out and About* (☎ 800-929-2268 or 415-644-8044; www.outandabout.com), which offers guidebooks and a newsletter (US$20/yr; 10 issues) packed with solid information on the global gay and lesbian scene; *Spartacus International Gay Guide* (Bruno Gmünder Verlag; www.spartacusworld.com/gayguide) and *Odysseus,* both good, annual English-language guidebooks focused on gay men; the *Damron* guides (www.damron.com), with separate, annual books for gay men and lesbians; and *Gay Travel A to Z: The World of Gay & Lesbian Travel Options at Your Fingertips* by Marianne Ferrari (Ferrari International; Box 35575, Phoenix, AZ 85069), a very good gay and lesbian guidebook series.

Local resources

The main nerve center for gay, lesbian, bisexual, and transsexual activity in Vancouver is, named appropriately enough, **The Centre,** 1170 Bute St. (☎ 604-684-5307; www.lgtbcentrevancouver.com), in the heart of the West End. The group hosts discussion groups; maintains a library; and runs health, legal, and youth clinics. The Centre also runs the **Prideline** (☎ 604-684-6869), a free telephone hot line with volunteer operators working nights from 7 to 10 p.m., Monday through Saturday.

In Vancouver, you may want to pick up *Xtra West,* a free biweekly gay and lesbian newspaper with community news, event listings, and the latest report on the bar scene. You can find the newspaper — and other gay and lesbian resources — at **Little Sister's,** 1238 Davie St. (☎ **604-669-1753;** www.littlesistersbookstore.com), a bookstore that maintains a bulletin board and sells tickets to gay and lesbian events. Look out, also, for the guide *Gay Friendly Vancouver,* available from Tourism Vancouver InfoCentre, and many bars, lounges and, coffee shops in the West End. In Victoria, start with www.gayvictoria.ca.

Gay and lesbian events

Several annual events are worth catching. The **Pride Festival,** hosted by the **Vancouver Pride Society** (☎ 604-687-0955; www.vanpride.bc.ca) during the first weekend of each August, is a series of parties, dances, cruises, and other events; a Sunday parade beginning at Denman Street and live concerts in the park beside Sunset Beach cap off the festivities. Happening at almost the same time, in early August, is the annual **Out On Screen Queer Film and Video Festival** (www.outonscreen.com).

Where to eat, stay, and play

Ground zero for the gay/lesbian scene in Vancouver is probably the stretch of Davie Street that runs between Burrard and Jervis Streets: Cafes, restaurants, and stores with a gay tilt are plentiful in this area. A secondary stretch, a bit more upscale, runs along Denman Street from Davie to Robson Streets; this area isn't exclusively gay, but gay travelers certainly feel comfortable here with the many gay-friendly eating, shopping, and beach options.

Some of Vancouver's most popular night haunts of the moment include **Numbers Cabaret** (1042 Davie St.; ☎ 604-685-4077) and **The Odyssey** (1251 Howe St.; ☎ 604-689-5256). **Delany's** (1105 Denman St.; ☎ 604-662-3344) is a quieter spot with a heavily gay clientele. **Hamburger Mary's** (1202 Davie St.; ☎ 604-687-1293) is a legendary diner popular with straights, gays, and lesbians alike. For more gay-friendly bars, see Chapters 15 and 22. Most any accommodation in Vancouver is suitably gay-friendly, but those especially friendly include the **Hotel Royal** (1025 Granville St.; ☎ 604-685-5335) and the **Sylvia Hotel** (see Chapter 9 for full details).

What gay nightlife exists in Victoria probably centers on **Hush** (☎ 250-385-0566), a bar at 1325 Government Street. It's so "hush" that there's no sign on the door. Around the corner, at 642 Johnson Street, lies **Prism Lounge** (☎ 250-388-0505). It's another non-advertised space, open seven days a week, and featuring theme nights such as Karaoke Monday and Drag Bingo on Wednesday. For gay-friendly accommodations, try the **Prior House B&B** (see Chapter 17 for full details) or the **Oak Bay Guest House** (1052 Newport Ave.; ☎ 250-598-3812).

Chapter 7

Taking Care of the Remaining Details

*W*hat's worse than the nagging feeling that you forgot something, but you don't know what it is? I'd nominate the sensation of remembering it just as your plane leaves the ground.

This chapter attempts to relieve that sense of impending doom (or at least inconvenience) with a round-up of topics that can simplify your final trip planning. How do you get a passport? What can you bring with you into the country, and, more importantly for the shopaholics, what can you take back? What's the story with rental cars? Do you need insurance? What if you get sick? How do you check your e-mail? And what exactly are those airport security guards going to do to you?

Getting a Passport

A valid passport is the only legal form of identification accepted around the world. You can't cross an international border without it. Getting a passport is easy, but the process takes some time. For an up-to-date, country-by-country listing of passport requirements around the world, go to the "Foreign Entry Requirement" Web page of the U.S. State Department at http://travel.state.gov/foreignentryreqs.html.

Applying for a U.S. passport

If you're applying for a first-time passport, follow these steps:

1. Complete a **passport application** in person at a U.S. passport office; a federal, state, or probate court; or a major post office. To find your regional passport office, either check the **U.S. State Department** Web site, http://travel.state.gov/passport_services.html, or call the **National Passport Information Center** (☎ 877-487-2778) for automated information.

2. Present a **certified birth certificate** as proof of citizenship. (Bringing along your driver's license, state or military ID, or social security card is also a good idea.)

3. Submit **two identical passport-sized photos,** measuring 2 x 2 inches in size. You often find businesses that take these photos near a passport office. *Note:* You can't use a strip from a photo-vending machine because the pictures aren't identical.

4. Pay a **fee.** For people ages 16 and over, a passport is valid for ten years and costs $85. For those 15 and under, a passport is valid for 5 years and costs $70.

Allow plenty of time before your trip to apply for a passport; processing normally takes three weeks but can take longer during busy periods (especially spring).

If you have a passport in your current name that was issued within the past 15 years (and you were over age 16 when it was issued), you can renew the passport by mail for $55. Whether you're applying in person or by mail, you can download passport applications from the U.S. State Department Web site at http://travel.state.gov/passport_services.html. For general information, call the **National Passport Agency** (☎ 202-647-0518). To find your regional passport office, either check the U.S. State Department Web site or call the **National Passport Information Center** toll-free number (☎ 877-487-2778) for automated information.

Applying for other passports

The following list offers more information for citizens of Australia, New Zealand, and the United Kingdom.

- **Australians** can visit a local post office or passport office, call the **Australia Passport Information Service** (☎ 131-232 toll-free from Australia), or log on to www.passports.gov.au for details on how and where to apply.

- **New Zealanders** can pick up a passport application at any **New Zealand Passports Office** or download it from their Web site. For information, contact the **NZPO** or download it from their Web site. Contact the **NZPO** at ☎ 0800-225-050 in New Zealand or 04-474-8100, or log on to www.passports.govt.nz.

✔ **United Kingdom** residents can pick up applications for a standard ten-year passport (five-year passport for children under 16) at passport offices, major post offices, or travel agencies. For information, contact the **United Kingdom Passport Service** (☎ **0870-521-0410;** www.ukpa.gov.uk).

Navigating Your Way through Passport Control and Customs

Upon arrival in Canada, you first have to pass through Customs and Immigration. Canada is known as an exceptionally welcoming country, but immigrations officers are still likely to grill you on the length and purpose of your trip — particularly since the tragic events of 9/11.

Technically, for entry into Canada, U.S. citizens don't yet need a passport; instead, you can show a birth certificate, baptismal certificate, or voter registration card plus some other form of photo ID. If you have a valid passport, bringing it can't hurt. (A driver's license isn't considered proof of citizenship, but may help in a tight spot.) In very rare cases, these officers may also ask for proof that you carry enough cash to support yourself during your stay; thus, exchanging some money beforehand isn't a bad idea.

If you're not a U.S. citizen, you need, at the very least, a valid passport.

If you travel with a passport, keep it with you at all times and make sure it's secure in your money belt. The only times to give up your passport are at the bank for tellers to photocopy when they change your traveler's checks and at the border for guards to peruse. If you lose your passport while in Canada, go directly to the nearest U.S. embassy or consulate, or that of your own country. (See the Appendix for consulate and embassy locations.)

Crossing into Canada

If you're bringing something into Canada besides clothing or personal effects, you're supposed to fill out a declarations form. Here are the limits of what you can bring into Canada: 50 cigars, 400 cigarettes, and 350 grams (14 ounces) of tobacco; and either 1.14 liters (40 ounces) of liquor or wine or 8.5 liters/288 ounces (one case of 12-ounce bottles) of beer.

Revolvers, pistols, and fully automatic firearms — not that you were thinking about it — are definitely *not* allowed. Neither are narcotics. Hunting rifles and shotguns are allowed, although they must be declared. A Customs official may sometimes ask to search your car or person. I don't recommend cracking jokes about a stash of drugs, explosives, or whatnot; you're likely to be taken seriously and you don't want to spend your vacation time in custody.

For more information on Canadian Customs regulations, contact **Canada Revenue Agency** (☎ **800-461-9999** or 204-983-3500) or **U.S. Customs** (☎ **604-278-1825**), both located at Vancouver International Airport.

Returning home

If you're a citizen of the United States, you may bring home US$800 worth of goods duty free, provided you've been out of the country at least 48 hours and haven't used the exemption in the past 30 days; anything more is charged a flat 4 percent duty. This includes 1 liter of an alcoholic beverage, 200 cigarettes, and 100 cigars. On mailed gifts, the duty-free limit is US$200.

For more information, contact the **U.S. Customs Service,** 1300 Pennsylvania Ave., NW, Washington, DC 20229 (☎ **877-287-8867;** www. customs.gov), and request the free pamphlet, *Know Before You Go.*

If you're a citizen of the United Kingdom, Australia, or New Zealand, contact the following agencies for information on returning to your country:

- ✔ **HM Customs & Excise** (for the United Kingdom); ☎ **0181-910-3744;** www.open.gov.uk.

- ✔ **Australian Customs Services,** GPO Box 8, Sydney NSW 2001; ☎ **02-6275-6666** from Australia or 202-797-3189 from the U.S.; www.customs.gov.au.

- ✔ **New Zealand Customs,** 50 Anzac Ave., P.O. Box 29, Auckland; ☎ **09-359-6655.**

Renting (Or Not Renting) a Car

Renting a car and driving in Vancouver or Victoria is an extremely easy undertaking. If you plan on spending most of your trip in the downtown core with some journeys to other parts of the metropolitan area, I suggest you take advantage of the excellent public transportation network in the city. If your trip includes likely journeys to Whistler or Vancouver Island, however, consider renting a car for the duration of your stay.

When trying to decide whether to rent a car, keep this in mind: Gasoline costs a lot more in Canada than in the United States. At this writing, gas prices in Vancouver and Victoria were around C$4 (US$3.35) a gallon.

Several rental car companies are located in Vancouver and Victoria. At the Vancouver International Airport, you'll find the car rental desks on Parkade Level B. At Victoria International Airport, they're located just inside the entrance to the arrivals area. See the Appendix for a list of rental car companies and their toll-free numbers and Web sites.

Many rental car firms offer vehicles with CD or tape players. Remember to pack a few of your favorite CDs or tapes if you intend to cruise around a lot. (Just remember to eject them before you return the car.) As a safety precaution, make sure your rental car has a secure trunk; be wary of hatchback cars, in which all your belongings are in plain view. And, of course, remove all valuables from the car when you're not driving. Parking in garages may seem safe, but all those parked cars are a temptation to thieves, and even in relatively safe Vancouver and Victoria, break-ins do happen.

Ensuring the best deal for yourself

Car rental rates vary even more than airline fares. The price depends on the size of the car, the length of time you keep it, where and when you pick it up and drop it off, where you take it, and a host of other factors.

The following is a list of things to keep in mind to get the best deal:

✔ **Weekend rates may be lower than weekday rates.** Ask whether the rate is the same for pickup Friday morning as it is for Thursday night.

✔ **Check the weekly rate.** If you keep the car five or more days, a weekly rate may be cheaper (per day) than the daily rate.

✔ **Don't rent your car at the airport.** If possible, try to do it at a location away from the airport to avoid paying the airport concession recovery fee, which adds almost 15 percent to your bill.

✔ **Rent a car with unlimited kilometers.** Always opt for this kind of deal, because planning how far you'll drive when you're on vacation is difficult. Even if the daily rate is slightly higher, you'll probably come out ahead, because the charge for each kilometer over your limit can be anywhere from C18¢ to C38¢ (US15¢ to US32¢) — and remember that kilometers are shorter than miles.

✔ **Avoid over-upgrades.** Some of Vancouver's car rental companies deal almost exclusively in minivans, which can be a hassle to park and tend to guzzle gas — and gas here ain't cheap. Make sure to ask about this when you call.

✔ **If you see an advertised price in your local newspaper, be sure to ask for that specific rate.** If not, you may be charged the standard (higher) rate. Don't forget to mention membership in AAA, AARP, and trade unions. These memberships usually entitle you to discounts ranging from 5 to 30 percent.

✔ **Check your frequent-flier accounts.** Not only are your favorite (or at least most-used) airlines likely to send you discount coupons, but most car rentals add at least 500 miles to your account.

✔ **Use the Internet to comparison shop for a car rental.** All the major travel sites — **Frommer's** (www.frommers.com), **Travelocity** (www.travelocity.com), **Expedia** (www.expedia.com), **Orbitz** (www.orbitz.com), and **Smarter Living** (www.smarterliving.com) have search engines that can dig up discounted car rental rates. Just enter the car size you want, the pickup and return dates, and location, and the server returns a price. You can even make the reservation through any of these sites.

Identifying the additional charges

In addition to the standard rental prices (about C$35 to C$60 (US$29–US$50) a day in Vancouver and Victoria), you have to pay several additional charges.

All rental car bills in Canada include a **7 percent goods and services tax** (known as the GST), a **7 percent provincial sales tax** (PST), and the C$1.50 (US$1.25) **environmental tax.** If you rent your car from an airport location, you also have to add on a **15.5 percent airport recovery fee.**

You'll also encounter a few optional charges. Many credit card companies cover the **collision damage waiver (CDW),** which requires you to pay for damage to the car in a collision. Check with your credit card company before your trip to avoid paying this hefty fee (as much as US$15 a day).

The car rental companies also offer additional **liability insurance** (if you harm others in an accident), **personal accident insurance** (if you harm yourself or your passengers), and **personal effects insurance** (if your luggage is stolen from your car). Your insurance policy on your car at home probably covers most of these unlikely occurrences. However, if your own insurance doesn't cover you for rentals or if you don't have auto insurance, definitely consider the additional coverage (ask your car rental agent for more information). Unless you're toting around the Hope diamond — and you don't want to leave that in your car trunk anyway — you can probably skip the personal effects insurance, but driving around without liability or personal accident coverage is never a good idea. Even if you're a good driver, other people may not be, and liability claims can be complicated.

Some companies also offer **refueling packages,** in which you pay for your initial full tank of gas up front and return the car with an empty gas tank. The prices can be competitive with local gas prices, but you don't get credit for any gas remaining in the tank. If you reject this option, you pay only for the gas you use, but you need to return your rental car with a full tank or face charges (usually at a per-liter rate twice that of Canadian gas stations) for the shortfall. So, I usually forgo the refueling package and allow plenty of time for refueling en route to the car rental return. However, if you usually run late and a refueling stop may make you miss your plane, you're a perfect candidate for the fuel-purchase option.

If you refuse the refueling option and you're traveling south of Vancouver, consider making a detour to Blaine or Point Roberts, Washington, to refuel. This short hop over the border can translate into big savings at the pump.

Playing It Safe with Travel and Medical Insurance

Three kinds of travel insurance are available: trip-cancellation insurance, medical insurance, and lost-luggage insurance. The cost of travel insurance varies widely, depending on the cost and length of your trip, your age and health, and the type of trip you're taking, but expect to pay between 5 percent and 8 percent of the vacation itself. Here is my advice on all three.

✔ **Trip-cancellation insurance** helps you get your money back if you have to back out of a trip, if you have to go home early, or if your travel supplier goes bankrupt. Allowed reasons for cancellation can range from sickness to natural disasters to the State Department declaring your destination unsafe for travel. (Insurers usually won't cover vague fears, though, as many travelers discovered who tried to cancel their trips in October 2001 because they were wary of flying.)

A good resource is **Travel Guard Alerts,** a list of companies considered high risk by Travel Guard International (www.travelinsured.com). Protect yourself further by paying for the insurance with a credit card — by law, consumers can get their money back on goods and services not received if they report the loss within 60 days after the charge is listed on their credit card statement.

Note: Many tour operators, particularly those offering trips to remote or high-risk areas, include insurance in the cost of the trip or can arrange insurance policies through a partnering provider, a convenient and often cost-effective way for the traveler to obtain insurance. Make sure the tour company is a reputable one, however: Some experts suggest you avoid buying insurance from the tour or cruise company you're traveling with, saying it's better to buy from a third-party insurer than to put all your money in one place.

✔ Buying **medical insurance** for your trip doesn't make sense for most travelers. Your existing health insurance should cover you if you get sick while on vacation (although if you belong to a health maintenance organization (HMO), check to see whether you're fully covered while in Canada).

If you require additional medical insurance, try **MEDEX Assistance** (☎ **410-453-6300;** www.medexassist.com) or **Travel Assistance International** (☎ **800-821-2828;** www.travelassistance.com; for general information on services, call the company's **Worldwide Assistance Services, Inc.,** at ☎ 800-777-8710).

✔ **Lost-luggage insurance** is not necessary for most travelers. On domestic flights, checked baggage is covered up to US$2,500 per ticketed passenger. On international flights (including U.S. portions of international trips), baggage coverage is limited to approximately US$9.07 per pound, up to approximately US$635 per checked bag. If you plan to check items more valuable than the standard liability, see if your valuables are covered by your homeowner's policy, get baggage insurance as part of your comprehensive travel insurance package, or buy Travel Guard's BagTrak product. Don't buy insurance at the airport, as it's usually overpriced. Be sure to take any valuables or irreplaceable items with you in your carry-on luggage, as many valuables (including books, money, and electronics) aren't covered by airline policies.

If your luggage is lost, immediately file a lost-luggage claim at the airport, detailing the luggage contents. For most airlines, you must report delayed, damaged, or lost baggage within four hours of arrival. The airlines are required to deliver luggage, once found, directly to your house or destination free of charge.

For more information, contact one of the following recommended insurers:

- **Access America** (☎ 866-807-3982; www.accessamerica.com);

- **Travel Guard International** (☎ 800-826-4919; www.travelguard.com);

- **Travel Insured International** (☎ 800-243-3174; www.travelinsured.com); and

- **Travelex Insurance Services** (☎ 888-457-4602;www.travelex-insurance.com).

Staying Healthy When You Travel

Getting sick will ruin your vacation, so I *strongly* advise against coming down with something (of course, last time I checked, the bugs weren't listening to me any more than they probably listen to you).

For domestic trips, most reliable health-care plans provide coverage if you get sick away from home. For travel abroad, you may have to pay all medical costs up front and be reimbursed later. For information on purchasing additional medical insurance for your trip, see the previous section.

Talk to your doctor before leaving on a trip if you have a serious and/or chronic illness. For conditions such as epilepsy, diabetes, or heart problems wear a **MedicAlert identification tag** (☎ 888-633-4298; www.medicalert.org), which immediately informs doctors of your condition and gives them access to your records through MedicAlert's 24-hour hotline. Contact the **International Association for Medical Assistance to Travelers (IAMAT)** (☎ 716-754-4883 or, in Canada, **416-652-0137;** www. iamat.org) for tips on travel and health concerns in the countries you're visiting, and lists of local, English-speaking doctors. The United States **Centers for Disease Control and Prevention** (☎ **800-311-3435;** www. cdc.gov) provides up-to-date information on health hazards by region or country and offers tips on food safety.

If you need a doctor, ask your hotel's concierge or front desk. Most large hotels can recommend someone at any hour. This recommendation may be more reliable than what you'd receive from a national consortium of doctors available through an 800 number.

If you can't get a doctor to help you right away, try a walk-in clinic. You may not get immediate attention, but you won't pay the high price of an emergency-room visit. Vancouver has a number of clinics that stay open late. Fees generally range from C$55 to C$75 (US$46–US$62), compared to a minimum of C$300 (US$250) for most emergency-room visits. But bear in mind that just gets you in the door. Having a doctor attend to you in the emergency room starts at around C$130 (US$108)!

For the locations of hospitals, doctors, and dentists in Vancouver and Victoria, see the Appendix.

Staying Connected by Cellphone or E-mail

These days, people go through withdrawal when they're disconnected from their cellphones or e-mail accounts for even a moment. Here is some useful information that'll help you stay wired while you're on vacation — just remember to look up and enjoy the scenery every once in a while, okay?

Using a cellphone outside the U.S.

Just because your cellphone works at home doesn't mean it'll work elsewhere. Surprisingly, some U.S.-based servers do not work in Canada, so take a look at your wireless company's coverage map on its Web site before heading out. If you need to stay in touch at a destination where you know your phone won't work, rent a phone that does from **InTouch USA** (☎ **800-872-7626;** www.intouchglobal.com) or a rental car location, but beware that you'll pay C$1 (US85¢) a minute or more for airtime.

If you're not from the U.S., you'll be appalled at the poor reach of North America's GSM (Global System for Mobiles) wireless network, which is used by much of the rest of the world. Your phone will probably work in Vancouver and Victoria, as it will in most major cities, but you may not be able to send SMS (Short Messaging Service) text messages home — something North Americans tend not to do anyway, for various cultural and technological reasons. And it definitely won't work if you start to travel to rural areas farther afield. So, assume nothing when it comes to using your cellphone in another city — call your wireless provider and get the full scoop.

Accessing the Internet away from home

Travelers have any number of ways to check their e-mail and access the Internet on the road. Of course, using your own laptop — or even a PDA (personal digital assistant) or electronic organizer with a modem — gives you the most flexibility. But even if you don't have a computer, you can still access your e-mail and even your office computer from cyber-cafes as well as from many hotel lounges and guest rooms.

It's hard nowadays to find a city that *doesn't* have a few cybercafes. Although there's no definitive directory for cybercafes — these are inde-pendent businesses, after all — two places to start looking are at www.cybercaptive.com and www.cybercafe.com.

Aside from formal cybercafes, most **youth hostels** now have at least one computer for you to search the Internet. And most **public libraries** across the world offer Internet access free or for a small charge. Avoid **hotel business centers** unless you're willing to pay exorbitant rates.

Most major airports now have **Internet kiosks** scattered throughout. These kiosks, which you'll also see in shopping malls, hotel lobbies, and tourist information offices around the world, give you basic Web access for a per-minute fee that's usually higher than cybercafe prices. The kiosks' clunkiness and high price mean they should be avoided when-ever possible.

To retrieve your e-mail, ask your **Internet service provider (ISP)** if it has a Web-based interface tied to your existing e-mail account. If your ISP doesn't have such an interface, you can use the free **mail2web** service (www.mail2web.com) to view and reply to your home e-mail. For more flexibility, you may want to open a free, Web-based e-mail account with **Yahoo! Mail** (http://mail.yahoo.com). (Microsoft's **Hotmail** is another popular option, but Hotmail has severe spam problems.) Your home ISP may be able to forward your e-mail to the Web-based account automatically.

If you need to access files on your office computer, look into a service called **GoToMyPC** (www.gotomypc.com). The service provides a Web-based interface for you to access and manipulate a distant PC from anywhere — even a cybercafe — provided your "target" PC is on and has an always-on connection to the Internet (such as with Road Runner cable). The service offers top-quality security, but if you're worried about hackers, use your own laptop rather than a cybercafe computer to access the GoToMyPC system.

If you are bringing your own computer, the buzzword in computer access to familiarize yourself with is **wi-fi** (wireless fidelity), and more hotels, cafes, and retailers are signing on as wireless "hot spots" from where you can get high-speed connection without cable wires, networking hardware, or a phone line. You can get a wi-fi connection one of several ways. Many laptops sold in the last year have built-in wi-fi capability (an 802.11b wireless Ethernet connection). Macintosh owners have their own networking technology, **Apple AirPort.** For those with older computers, an 802.11b/**wi-fi card** (around US$50) can be plugged into your laptop. You sign up for wireless access service much as you do cellphone service, through a plan offered by one of several commercial companies that have made wireless service available in airports, hotel lobbies, and coffee shops, primarily in the U.S. (followed by the U.K. and Japan). **T-Mobile Hotspot** (www.t-mobile.com/hotspot) serves up wireless connections at more than 1,000 Starbucks coffee shops nationwide. **Boingo** (www.boingo.com) and **Wayport** (www.wayport.com) have set up networks in airports and high-class hotel lobbies. **iPass** providers also give you access to a few hundred wireless hotel lobby set-ups. Best of all, you don't need to be staying at the Four Seasons to use the hotel's network; just set yourself up on a comfy couch in the lobby. The companies' pricing policies can be Byzantine, with a variety of monthly, per-connection, and per-minute plans, but in general you pay around $30 a month for limited access — and as more and more companies jump on the wireless bandwagon, prices are likely to get even more competitive.

There are also places that provide **free wireless networks** in cities around the world. To locate these free hot spots, go to www.personaltelco. net/index.cgi/WirelessCommunities.

If wi-fi is not available at your destination, note that most business-class hotels throughout the world offer dataports for laptop modems, and a few thousand hotels in the U.S. and Europe now offer free high-speed Internet access using an Ethernet network cable. You can bring your own cables, but most hotels rent them for roughly $10. Call your hotel in advance to see what your options are.

In addition, major Internet service providers (ISPs) have **local access numbers (LANs)** around the world, allowing you to go online by simply placing a local call. Check your ISP's Web site or call its toll-free number and ask how you can use your current account away from home, and how much it will cost. If you're traveling outside the reach of your ISP, the **iPass** network has dial-up numbers in most of the world's countries. You'll have to sign up with an iPass provider, who will then tell you how to set up your computer for your destination(s). For a list of iPass providers, go to www.ipass.com and click on "Individual Purchase." One solid provider is **i2roam** (www.i2roam.com; ☎ **866-811-6209** or 920-235-0475).

Wherever you go, bring a **connection kit** of sufficient power, phone adapters, a spare phone cord, and a spare Ethernet network cable — or find out whether your hotel supplies them to guests.

Keeping Up with Airline Security Measures

With the federalization of airport security, security procedures at U.S. and many other airports are more stable and consistent than ever. Generally, you'll be fine if you arrive at the airport **one hour** before a domestic flight and **two hours** before an international flight; if you show up late, tell an airline employee and he or she will probably whisk you to the front of the line.

U.S. citizens used to travel to Canada on only a driver's license or other government-issued photo ID, but my advice is, bring your passport (see earlier in this chapter for entry details). Keep your ID at the ready to show at check-in, the security checkpoint, and sometimes even the gate. (Children under 18 do not need government-issued photo IDs for domestic flights, but they do for international flights to most countries.)

In 2003, the Transportation Security Administration (TSA) phased out **gate check-in** at all U.S. airports. And **e-tickets** have made paper tickets nearly obsolete. Passengers with e-tickets can beat the ticket-counter lines by using airport **electronic kiosks** or even **online check-in** from your home computer. Online check-in involves logging on to your airline's Web site, accessing your reservation, and printing out your boarding pass — and the airline may even offer you bonus miles to do so! If you're using a kiosk at the airport, bring the credit card you used to book the ticket or your frequent-flier card. Print out your boarding pass from the kiosk and simply proceed to the security checkpoint with your pass and a photo ID. If you're checking bags or looking to snag an exit-row seat, you will be able to do so using most airline kiosks. Even the smaller airlines are employing the kiosk system, but always call your airline to make sure these alternatives are available. **Curbside check-in** is also a good way to avoid lines, although a few airlines still ban it; call before you go.

 Security lines are getting shorter than they were the last couple of years, but some doozies remain. If you have trouble standing for long periods of time, tell an airline employee; the airline will provide a wheelchair. Speed up security by **not wearing metal objects,** such as big belt buckles or clanky earrings. If you have metallic body parts, a note from your doctor can prevent a long chat with the security screeners.

Federalization has stabilized **what you can carry on** and **what you can't.** The general rule is that sharp things are out, nail clippers are okay, and food and beverages must be passed through the X-ray machine; security screeners can't make you drink from your coffee cup to prove that your beverage is free of small weapons and not poisonous. Bring food in your carry-on rather than checking it, as explosive-detection machines used on checked luggage have been known to mistake food (especially chocolate, for some reason) for bombs. Travelers in the U.S. are allowed one carry-on bag, plus a personal item such as a purse, briefcase, or laptop bag. Carry-on hoarders can stuff all sorts of things into a laptop bag — as long as it has a laptop in it, it's still considered a personal item. The TSA has issued a list of restricted items; check its Web site (www.tsa.gov/public/index.jsp) for details.

Airport screeners may decide that your checked luggage needs to be searched by hand. You can now purchase luggage locks that allow screeners to open and re-lock a checked bag if hand searching is necessary. Look for Travel Sentry–certified locks at luggage or travel shops and **Brookstone** stores (you can buy them online at www.brookstone.com). These locks, approved by the TSA, can be opened by luggage inspectors with a special code or key. For more information on the locks, visit www.travelsentry.org. If you use something other than TSA-approved locks, your lock will be cut off your suitcase if a TSA agent needs to hand search your luggage.

Part III
Vancouver

The 5th Wave — By Rich Tennant

"Sorry I was late...but the next time, be more specific than 'I'll meet you at the coffee shop on Robson Street.' This was the 48th place I checked."

In this part . . .

Welcome to the lovely Pacific Northwest! So that you can easily get your bearings, I begin Part III with your orientation to Vancouver in Chapter 8. Next, I guide you through Vancouver's many highlights, including the best hotels (Chapter 9), restaurants (Chapter 10), attractions (Chapter 11), shopping (Chapter 12), and nightlife (Chapter 15). If you want some tips on how to plan your time, I include four great itineraries in Chapter 13, and follow up with a few recommended day trips in Chapter 14, just in case you're hungry for more.

Chapter 8

Arriving and Getting Oriented

● ●

In This Chapter

▶ Getting your bearings

▶ Exploring the neighborhoods

▶ Finding information

▶ Transporting yourself around the city

● ●

*V*ancouver stretches out on all sides, but the central area is fairly compact. After I help you figure out how to get from the airport or highway to where you're staying, I show you around the city's neighborhoods, and tell you where to pick up bagfuls of tourist information. Navigating around the city to sights, restaurants, and all the rest doesn't have to be a hassle, either: Vancouver's public transit is actually clean and efficient, and in this chapter I take you through the nuts and bolts of it.

Arriving in Vancouver

Easy to access, Vancouver welcomes visitors by plane, car, and train.

Flying into the airport

Vancouver International Airport (YVR) (☎ **604-207-7077;** www.yvr.ca) is big and busy, with daily flights to every continent except Antarctica. The facility has won numerous awards both for its design and operation so you can expect to find it easy to navigate, relatively uncrowded, and clean. YVR is located in Richmond, a community of land-filled islands in the middle of the Fraser River about 8 miles south of Vancouver.

The airport has two terminals: an older one, exclusively for Canadian departures and arrivals, and a slick, newer one for international travel. You'll probably arrive at the newer one, which has Customs and Immigration checkpoints, ATMs, a bank, currency exchange facilities, and car rental agencies. All these facilities are easy to find and are handicapped accessible. You can use your laptop wirelessly in the lounges if your computer's equipped for it, and 22 pay phones around the airport have e-mail and browsing capabilities, too; access costs C35¢ (US23¢) per minute.

The international terminal also hosts the **Tourist InfoCentre** (☎ 604-207-0953), open daily from 8:30 a.m. to 11:30 p.m. and located on level two. The facility sells bus and shuttle tickets, calls cabs and limousines, and can put you on the right bus to Victoria or Whistler if you're heading there first. Staff can also book accommodations for any night (at no extra fee for walk-ins; those who call pay a small fee). You can also call some downtown hotels for free on special phones. Plenty of baggage carts, skycaps, and Green Coat travel assistants are available to answer questions about the airport, the city, and Canada.

Getting from the airport to your hotel

You have plenty of options for getting into town from Vancouver International Airport: taxi and limousine services, the Airporter shuttle, and a wide choice of rental cars.

Taxis and limousines, the easiest option and quite affordable for two or more travelers arriving together, can be hailed curbside in front of the airport's two terminals. The ride into the central downtown area takes roughly 25 minutes. Taxis should cost between C$30–C$36 (US$25–US$30). The more comfortable **Limojet Gold Express** limousine service (☎ 604-273-1331) runs a flat C$41.75 (US$35) — a good deal. An appropriate tip for the taxi or limousine driver is 15 percent.

The next easiest option, and a less expensive one for a single traveler, is the green shuttle bus, **Airporter** (☎ 800-668-3141 or 604-946-8866). Beginning at 6 a.m., the shuttle runs every 30 minutes from a spot right outside the international arrivals terminal (the first stop is the domestic arrivals terminal) and drops off at a number of central downtown hotels about 30 or 40 minutes later. One-way fares are C$12 (US$10) for adults; buy tickets either inside or outside the terminal.

You find **rental car facilities** on the ground floor of the new parking deck beside the international arrivals terminal, just a short shuttle ride from domestic arrivals. (For information about renting a car, see Chapter 7.) To get downtown from the airport (which is well signposted), drive out of the parking lot and follow Great McConachie Way over the Arthur Laing Bridge. Turn onto SW Marine Drive and continue along West 72nd Avenue to Granville Street. Turn right and follow Granville several miles north to the foot of the Granville Bridge, where you need to make a decision, depending on where you plan to stay. For directions after the Granville Bridge, see the following section.

Driving into town

If you drive north from Seattle to Vancouver, take Route 99 (it becomes Granville Street) right to the foot of the Granville Bridge. Your next move depends on where you plan to stay.

To reach **Gastown,** continue all the way to the end of the street and turn right. To reach **Stanley Park,** make the second exit off the bridge (to Pacific Street), then turn right on Pacific and drive west to the beach. To reach **Kitsilano,** you need to exit and head west on 4th Avenue. If you're staying in **North Vancouver,** you make an even more spectacular approach: drive through Stanley Park and right onto the Lion's Gate Bridge, which deposits you in North Vancouver.

Riding the rails

If you take the train from Seattle or another Canadian city, you arrive at **Pacific Central Station** (no phone), 1150 Station St., which has vendors, an ATM, luggage lockers, and ticket windows open daily from 9:30 a.m. to 6 p.m., a bit earlier and later on Tuesdays, Fridays, and Sundays. Exit the front of the station. If you're staying downtown or in the West End, hail a cab right there — it's the most convenient way to travel with luggage, and the ride shouldn't set you back more than C$8 (US$6.65).

To reach North Vancouver, cross the street and climb to the SkyTrain platform, buy a ticket from the machine (C$2.25; US$1.85), and take the SkyTrain to Waterfront Station. Walk across the covered walkway to the SeaBus terminal, buy another ticket for the SeaBus ferry, take the ferry to Lonsdale Quay, then walk or hail a cab, depending on the location of your hotel.

Getting to Know Vancouver's Neighborhoods

Half the battle when determining where to stay in Vancouver is figuring out where you are; every neighborhood in town seems to sport the name "West," even some that aren't west at all. Plus, downtown sights and eats are concentrated on a surprisingly small peninsula, which is connected by bridges, ferries, and highways (but no high-speed expressway) to much larger areas with differing characters to the north (suburban), the south (hip), and the east (grungy).

In this section, I tell you what you need to know about the neighborhoods that usually interest visitors. To figure out their exact locations — west or otherwise — see the Greater Vancouver map in this chapter.

West End to the waterfront

Any lodging in the residential **West End** is central to Robson Street shopping, Denman Street cafe life, and a small beach. Even Stanley Park is at most an easy 15-minute stroll away. West End is your best bet for staying in the center of the action, and although prices reflect this convenience as well as the stupendous views, the area may be worth the splurge. Some of the hotels are high-rise monstrosities, but others are attractive B&Bs or suite-style hotels.

Greater Vancouver

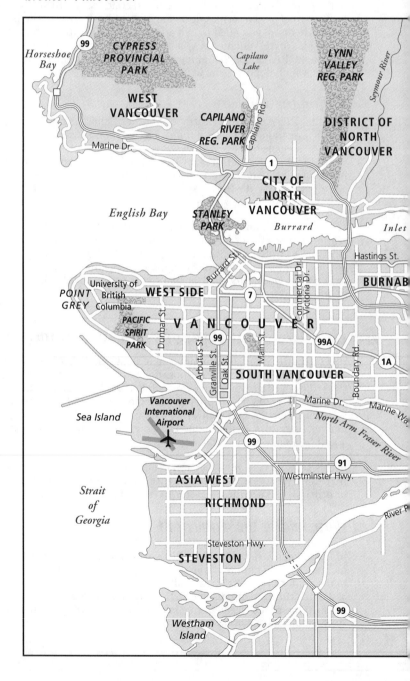

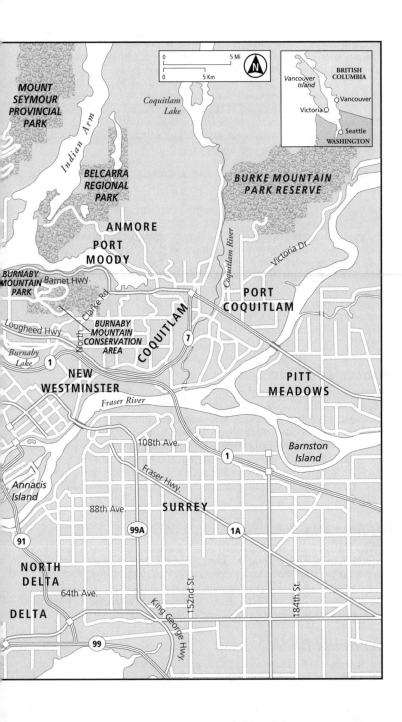

As you move north through the **downtown** area, business hotels predominate. These places jack up their rates during weekdays for the business travelers who will pay them. Weekends should be cheaper, but in summertime, this may not be the case. Expect either blandness or luxury, but don't expect to save money.

Finally, the **waterfront** area is tourist central, and the offerings here are huge, bland, and convenient. Expect to pay too much, once again, just for the convenience of being steps from a convention center or having a view of the water. This area books up well in advance, so you're unlikely to find a bed in high season on short notice.

For a map of Vancouver's West End and downtown, see the inside front cover of this book.

Yaletown

At the eastern edge of downtown, **Yaletown's** turn-of-the-century brick warehouses are undergoing a renaissance as New York–styled apartments, elegant galleries, restaurants, and boutiques. This urban-cool neighborhood is hot to trot with high-rise towers and chic townhouses; so, while dot-com companies and fashionistas create the buzz by day, the district also bustles with dining and club activity at night. The north side has a lovely seawall along False Creek, and the Roundhouse Community Centre, once a railway marshaling yard, is a funky performance space for special events.

Gastown and Chinatown

Moving east from the downtown waterfront, this district starts out in **Gastown,** the oldest section of Vancouver. The cobblestone streets and late-Victorian architecture make this quaint and cool area well worth a visit. Here you find interesting shops and delis amid souvenir stands. The next area to the east is **Chinatown,** which offers great markets and restaurants. The neighborhood may be small, but the bustling atmosphere is intense. Although you should walk through both Gastown and Chinatown, I don't recommend staying in them, because the accommodations tend to be shabby.

Kitsilano and West Side

Perhaps the quietest and most attractive location, this area is largely residential, free of heavy traffic, and blessed with both parks and even better weather than downtown Vancouver. You're also close to many of the city's top restaurants. However, you face a half-hour bus ride or 10- to 20-minute drive to reach most of the central attractions, such as Robson Street, Vancouver Art Gallery, or the waterfront.

Commercial Drive

Once the center of Vancouver's Portuguese and Italian immigrant population, **Commercial Drive** is heavy on coffee shops and has a funky vibe with clothing stores, health food restaurants, and alternative music clubs. What it *isn't* heavy on are accommodations, although this is slowly changing. The area isn't especially quiet, either, because all the commercial activity tends to draw lots of traffic.

North Vancouver

North Vancouver — usually referred to by locals as simply "North Van" — is an area that actually includes two suburban cities that are administratively separate from Vancouver: North Vancouver and West Vancouver. Go figure. Anyway, all you need to know is that North Van is a quiet lodging choice — if a little far from the action, requiring a SeaBus ride or a commute over the steep, narrow Lions Gate Bridge to get to the downtown peninsula.

Finding Information After You Arrive

The city of Vancouver maintains a handy network of four information booths known as **Tourist InfoCentres.** You can find two of them at the airport, in the international terminal between the Customs and Immigration checkpoints and the rest of the terminal, and in the domestic terminal on arrivals level two. Both offices are open daily from 8:30 a.m. until almost midnight (international terminal), or 9:30 p.m. (domestic terminal).

The main **Tourist InfoCentre** (☎ **800-663-6000** or 604-683-2000) is on the harbor at 200 Burrard St., in the Waterfront Centre near Canada Place. This large office is open Monday through Friday, 8:30 a.m. to 6 p.m.; and Saturday, 8:30 a.m. to 5 p.m.

The fourth **Tourist InfoCentre** (☎ **604-666-5784**), in the middle of Granville Island at 1398 Cartwright St., tends to focus on island attractions but is still useful. In summer, this branch is open daily, 9 a.m. to 6 p.m.; and in winter, Thursday through Sunday, 9 a.m. to 5 p.m.

Getting Around Vancouver

When friends ask my advice, I always recommend using public transit or walking while visiting Vancouver. This city has all the traffic and parking headaches you'd expect at home but wish to avoid on vacation.

By public transportation

Vancouver planned its public transit well. The transit authority, **TransLink** (☎ **604-953-3333;** www.translink.bc.ca), operates a smoothly integrated network of buses, elevated trains, and ferries, and all are pleasant, clean, and punctual. (Find out more about fares for public transportation in the following section.)

✔ **Traveling by bus:** Buses travel the widest network of routes through the city and beyond, and for that reason you may end up riding one at some point or another. City buses in Vancouver run from 4 a.m. until about 2:30 a.m. daily — certainly long enough to get all but the busiest night owls home before bedtime. Some late-night routes to the suburbs run even later, leaving downtown at 3 a.m.

Remember that you need a ticket or exact change to ride a Vancouver city bus — the drivers don't carry change. Also, figuring out routes and stops can be a hassle, because bus lines fan out in all directions in complicated, changing patterns. You can pick up a free bus map at the Tourist InfoCentre, from a FareDealer (see the "Buying tickets" section), or at the main city library (350 West Georgia St.) or any branch library.

✔ **Taking the SkyTrain:** Look up! It's a bird! It's a plane! It's a train! No, actually, it's an elevated light-rail system driven by computers and magnetic levitation, better known as *SkyTrain*. This relentlessly efficient system gets you from Main Street Station or Chinatown to the waterfront in no more than about 6 minutes.

The advantages of SkyTrain — the closest thing Vancouver has to a subway system — are its speed (50 miles per hour) and its ease of use (no ticket takers or gates). And, as is so often true in Canada, the cleanliness is beyond reproach, and could even rival Singapore's transit.

On the downside, only two train lines carry the SkyTrain, and most of it barely skirts the downtown peninsula. So its usefulness is limited. The bottom line? Check a map before making plans to SkyTrain around town. If you need to get to Kitsilano or even the West End, you have to forgo the train except in combination with other transit methods. (For example, from the SkyTrain Waterfront Station, you can catch bus #1 to English Bay (West End), bus #2 or #22 to Kitsilano, or bus #5 up Robson Street.)

The line runs west to east from distant suburbs to the city's water-front, leaving every 3 to 5 minutes from about 5:30 a.m. until roughly 1 a.m. You can ride from about 32 SkyTrain stations in all, but for practical purposes, you can forget all but the easternmost six or so. These are, in order, **Broadway Station** (you can transfer to downtown or Kitsilano buses here, or to the second train line's **Commercial Drive Station**), **Main Street** (near Chinatown, where the cross-country VIA Rail train arrives, and close to Science World), **Stadium** (the stop for B.C. Place Stadium at the edge of Yaletown, the lost-and-found office of the bus company, and — with a hike — Chinatown), **Granville** (close to several shopping areas), **Burrard** (beside the Hyatt Regency hotel), and **Waterfront** (connected to Canada Place, the ferry to North Vancouver, and close to Gastown). Most stations connect with handy bus routes, but bear in mind that none, with the exception of Burrard, and perhaps Waterfront, is really located in what's considered the central downtown area of Vancouver.

Buy tickets at any station (you don't need exact change) before boarding. You ride on the honor system, although inspectors occasionally show up to check your honesty. (They claim to make some three-quarters of a million spot-checks each month — that's 24,000 a *day* — and although I'm not sure about that number, buying a real ticket rather than risking your luck is still a good idea.)

✔ **Riding the SeaBus ferry:** To shuttle you quickly between Vancouver and North Van — where a few attractions and accommodations await you — the city has taken full advantage of its waterside position with something called *SeaBus,* a scenic way to get across Burrard Inlet in a hurry.

I recommend riding the SeaBus for a quick first introduction to the local scenery — few of the big-bucks cruise boats can offer better views than these do.

The two catamaran SeaBus ferries, known as the *Burrard Beaver* and the *Burrard Otter,* dock two to four times per hour and carry up to 400 passengers each. They take about 12 minutes to cross the sometimes placid, sometimes rolling surface of the inlet; doors open and close automatically to let you in and out, and views are splendid. As a bonus, this service can get you where you're going even when bad weather has closed down the buses, bridges, and roads.

SeaBus has two terminals: one on the Vancouver waterfront and the other at North Vancouver's Lonsdale Quay. The boats sail from Vancouver every 15 minutes from about 6:15 a.m. to approximately 6:45 p.m., then every half-hour afterward until about 12:45 a.m.; from North Vancouver, they begin around 6 a.m. and sail every 15 minutes until 6:30 p.m., then every half-hour until about 12:30 a.m. Saturday sailings are roughly the same times, although less frequently during the early-morning hours. Sundays and holidays, the boats sail half-hourly from around 8 a.m. until about 11 p.m. (Note that during the summer — defined here as early June to Labour Day — SeaBuses sail more frequently on Sundays and holidays, departing every 15 minutes during most of the day.)

Fares are the same as those for city buses and SkyTrains. But note that the trip across Burrard Inlet takes you from one fare zone to another, which increases the cost — figure an extra C$1 (US85¢) each way. (See "Understanding the fare system" section later in this chapter for more on prices.)

Bringing a bike on the SeaBus? Bikes ride free — but the attendant can, at his or her discretion, refuse to allow it to board if the SeaBus is full at rush hour. Keep that in mind and keep your cool if it happens.

TransLink claims that the system covers some 700 square miles, which probably includes just about everywhere you want to go. Privately operated, short-hop ferries (see the "By AquaBus ferry" section) also supplement the system quite usefully, along with a commuter-train service that can transport you even farther afield. (See Chapter 6 for more information on using public transportation if you have a disability.)

The TransLink network is seamlessly integrated. Buy a ticket for the bus, say, and the transfer you get from the driver will get you onto other parts of the system. You have only 90 minutes after the moment you stamp that first ticket to use a transfer, however; after that, it turns into a pumpkin and you have to start over again. For more on buying tickets, see the aptly named "Buying tickets" section.

The city maintains a **lost-and-found office** (☎ 604-682-7887) specifically for items found on city buses, trains, and ferries. Located at the SkyTrain's Stadium Station, the office is open weekdays only, from 8:30 a.m. until 5 p.m.

Timetables, including the comprehensive *BC Transit Guide* and the flyer *Discover Vancouver on Transit,* are available free of charge at the Tourist InfoCentre at 200 Burrard St. For answers to any other questions you may have about how to use Vancouver's public transportation, call the city's **Transit Hotline** ☎ 604-953-3333 from 6:30 a.m. until 11 p.m. daily. Operators are *extremely* helpful. You can also log on to the agency's somewhat helpful Web site at www.translink.bc.ca.

Understanding the fare system

Fares are the same for all Vancouver buses, elevated trains, and public ferries, although they do vary according to time of day, distance traveled, and age of the traveler. Here's a quick guide:

✔ Greater Vancouver is divided into three fare zones. **Zone one** includes all central areas, including the downtown peninsula and the Point Grey peninsula; it ends at the line known as Boundary Road (same as the Second Narrows Bridge). **Zone two** includes the airport, North Van, West Van, and suburbs out to Port Moody in the east and the Fraser River in the south. **Zone three** is everything else — Horseshoe Bay, Bowen Island, Tsawwassen, and more.

✔ To travel within one zone any time of the week costs C$2.25 (US$1.85) for adults and C$1.50 (US$1.25) for seniors and children.

✔ To travel from one zone to another costs C$3.25 (US$2.70) for adults and C$2 (US$1.65) for seniors and children during weekdays until 6:30 p.m. The price drops to C$2.25 (US$1.85) for adults weekdays after 6:30 p.m. or on weekends, and down to C$1.50 (US$1.25) for seniors and children weekdays after 6:30 p.m. or on weekends.

✔ To travel among all three zones costs C$4.50 (US$3.75) for adults and C$3 (US$2.50) for seniors and children — but, again, the rate drops all the way down to C$2 (US$1.65) for adults and C$1.50 (US$1.25) for seniors or children weekdays after 6:30 p.m. and on weekends.

 Fares for children (ages 5 to 13) and seniors (over 65) represent a savings of 35 to 40 percent off the adult fares. Children under age 5 ride free.

Buying tickets

To use public transit, you need either a ticket (for bus, boat, and train rides) or exact change (for bus rides). Then you must validate (punch) each ticket at a machine before boarding the bus, SkyTrain, or SeaBus. You keep the ticket and show it to a transit officer if one requests to see it. (They do occasionally check, and the fine isn't cheap if you don't have one — about C$40 (US$33).)

Transit tickets are dispensed singly, in books of ten (called FareSavers), or as a DayPass. Tickets are good for all forms of public transportation — bus, boat, or train. You can buy tickets at fare machines inside SkyTrain stations or from a **FareDealer,** designated by a FareDealer decal placed prominently on the door or window of a business that participates. FareDealers are in all major malls and at convenience and grocery stores such as 7-Eleven, Safeway, and Save-On-Foods.

Fare machines give change and accept C$20 bills, C$10 bills, C$5 bills, C$2 coins (called *toonies*), and C$1 coins (*loonies*). Remember these terms when using fare machines:

✔ *Regular fare* is for an adult during weekday hours.

✔ *Discount fare* applies on weekends and after 6:30 p.m. on weekdays.

✔ *Concession fare* is only for senior citizens or children ages 5 to 13.

You can save money on transit costs by buying books of tickets called **FareSavers.** They come in booklets of ten tickets each and cost C$18 (US$15) for one-zone travel (children and seniors pay C$15 (US$12)), C$27 (US$22) for two-zone travel, and C$36 (US$30) for three-zone travel. (Discounts aren't available for booklets for two- and three-zone travel.)

 If you plan on doing a lot of riding in a single day, the **DayPass** is the best deal both in terms of cost savings and the avoided hassle of standing in lines to buy ticket after ticket. A DayPass costs C$8 (US$6.65) per day of unlimited SeaBus, SkyTrain, and city-bus travel; seniors and children pay C$6 (US$5). DayPasses are valid seven days a week.

 The days of the week are preprinted on the DayPass; you must cross off the present day so that the conductor can see when you started using the pass. Officially, the pass is good until midnight; however, if you're riding past midnight, the pass is still valid — you won't get kicked off the bus or have to pay extra.

By AquaBus ferry

Not to be confused with the city's SeaBus (and that's easy to do), the privately run **AquaBus** (☎ **604-689-5858;** www.aquabus.bc.ca) and Granville Island Ferries (☎ **604-684-7781;** www.granvilleisland ferries.bc.ca) are two coordinated systems of a dozen tugboat-like ferries that are *not* part of the official city transit system. But these 12-passenger vessels are handy for getting to Granville Island and some other places, and you'll likely catch a ride on one at some point. This is definitely the most enjoyable transit option in the city, although the price you pay for such a short ride is relatively high — and for a family, it can add up fast. Tickets for short downtown hops cost C$2.50 to C$6 (US$2.10–US$5) for adults, C$1.25 to C$3 (US$1.05–US$2.50) for seniors and children ages 4 to 12; longer tours of the waterfront cost C$6 (US$5) for adults and C$3 to C$4 (US$2.50–US$3.35) for seniors and children.

The ferries leave from the southern end of Hornby Street (almost beneath the Granville Bridge) and arrive right at the island market; the several-minute ride across False Creek is pleasant and festive with anticipation. Other routes run up the Creek and to English Bay. The boats run daily from 7 a.m. to 10:30 p.m. most of the year, but stop at 8:30 p.m. in winter.

By foot

The first thing you need to know about getting around Vancouver is that you can see many of the best sights on foot. Assuming that you're staying in a downtown or West End hotel — the two most central areas — you can walk without much trouble to Stanley Park (20 minutes at most), Robson Street (10 minutes), Yaletown (15 minutes), Gastown (10–20 minutes), and Chinatown (15–30 minutes). Granville Island is a longer hike, but certainly doable if you have plenty of time.

Walking in Stanley Park is wonderfully scenic. Notice all the locals who make coming here part of their daily routine. Some merely walk to the nearest point — the seawall at English Bay — and hang out, maybe eating an ice cream, while others make the full circuit, a trip more easily done by bicycle.

Gastown, Robson Street, and Yaletown are best explored on foot, simply poking from shop to shop, and stopping where you like. The same is true of Chinatown, although you have to walk farther to get here. If you don't like wandering at will, a number of companies and individuals offer walking tours of city neighborhoods and attractions. See Chapters 11 and 13 for my recommendations.

By taxi

Vancouver cabs are reasonably clean and punctual; maybe that's because the drivers are trained by something called the TaxiHost Centre, under the auspices of the Justice Institute of British Columbia, and operations are tightly regulated by the city.

Find a cab by heading for any taxi stand or by flagging down one with its light on in the street. Cabs also linger outside or cruise past the major downtown hotels, the convention center, Granville Island, Robson Street, and other areas frequented by visitors. Cabs cost C$2.50 (US$2.10) to start the meter, then an additional C$1.45 (US$1.20) per kilometer. It's roughly $24 per hour (US$20) to sit and wait at stoplights or outside your swanky hotel or cruise around the city taking in the sights. An appropriate tip is 15 percent.

The two largest cab companies are **Black Top Cabs** (☎ **604-731-1111**) and **Yellow Cabs** (☎ **604-681-1111**). If you leave something in a taxi, call its lost-and-found department at ☎ **604-681-3201** for Black Top Cabs or ☎ **604-258-4702** for Yellow Cab. Another company is **Vancouver Taxi** (☎ **604-255-5111** or 604-871-1111), which has wheelchair-accessible cabs. The **Canadian Paraplegic Association** (☎ **604-324-3611**) rents lift-equipped vans.

By car

Drivers here are exceedingly polite; road rage simply isn't a factor. (***Note:*** This doesn't mean that you have a free pass to do your best Mario Andretti impression.) In fact, the mechanics, traffic cops, parking enforcement officers — and just about anyone else car-related you may meet — are also polite. Really.

Figuring out the basics

Traffic rules are mostly the same as they are in the United States: You drive on the right and stop at red lights. Plus, you can turn right on most red lights (watch for the "strictly forbidden" signs) if no traffic is coming. **Blinking green arrows,** however, can be confusing: Usually, they are pedestrian controlled and mean "proceed with caution," not "go ahead . . . turn left, I dare ya." Your car's headlights must be on at all times, although on Canadian rental cars this happens automatically. Seat belts are always required. And be alert for cyclists; there are a fair number. Some cyclists weave in and out of traffic as if they own the road and may creep up on your curbside just as you're about to turn right.

Don't run red lights or stop signs here. Vancouver was one of the first cities in North America to test out *camera cops* — basically, camcorders that record the plates of traffic offenders — and you never know when you're being watched.

Traffic jams can be a problem during rush hour — in Vancouver, that's roughly from 7:30 to 9 a.m. and again from 3:30 to 6 p.m. The biggest trouble spots are the Burrard, Lions Gate, and Granville Bridges; any stretch of Granville Street; and the Trans-Canada Highway (Highway 1). Other parts of town can be jammed any time of day, depending on construction, local events, sudden bad weather, road closures and detours, and a number of other factors. The Lions Gate Bridge occasionally closes for short periods of time.

Parking the car

Parking is a hassle in downtown Vancouver — what with all the off-limits neighborhood streets and rush-hour restrictions — and it's not cheap, even when the exchange rate is considered. Plenty of **garages and lots** are available, however. For example, you can find several lots on Thurlow Street, another facility at The Bay on Richards Street, one near the public library, and a huge underground garage at Pacific Centre. After business hours, a number of private lots open up to the general public. These are usually cheap, although sporting or other special events sometimes jack up the all-night rates.

Metered parking can be convenient and cheap, but it does have its downside. First, a spot can be difficult to find any time of year, but especially during summer. Second, parking-meter attendants vigilantly scrutinize the meters and mark the tire of your car with chalk to discourage you from feeding the meter. Finally, many of downtown's metered parking spots disappear at 3 p.m., not to reappear for several hours. The city does this to free up extra lanes for rush hour — and if you park in one of these spots a moment past 3 p.m., you'll surely get towed. Check street signs carefully when parking in the afternoon.

In the West End and in much of the West Side of Vancouver, **on-street parking** is for residents with permits only; you will be towed and ticketed. If you have a rental car, the ticket is automatically sent to the car rental company that will, in turn, charge you for it.

For more information on parking bylaws, fines, and penalties, visit Vancouver's official Web site at www.city.vancouver.bc.ca.

Chapter 9

Checking In at Vancouver's Best Hotels

The hotels in this chapter are the ones I suggest when friends call to ask for recommendations. Although I list my top picks, by no means are these lodgings the only acceptable selections. Toward the end of this chapter, I also include other options, just in case the top choices are booked. If you're still having difficulty finding a room, I make some suggestions on how to find something at the last minute.

Getting to Know Your Options

As with most major cities, chain hotels are prevalent, particularly the pricier ones in the downtown core — the ones that can afford the rocketing taxes. (See the Quick Concierge Appendix for the toll-free numbers and Web sites of Vancouver and Victoria's hotel chains.)

But Vancouver is not central Manhattan, and happily, some reasonably priced options exist, especially if you're prepared to walk two blocks or more. For example, stay anywhere near ritzy Robson and Burrard Streets and come armed with moulah. Stay on Robson Street, but nearer to the West End, and the price difference is appreciable. And, bear this in mind: Yaletown is hot and hip (and more expensive each year); the West Side and North Shore mean you need to cross a bridge to get to the downtown peninsula — translate that into savings. And ignore the savings you'll find near or east of Main Street. It's bordering on the poorest postal code district in Canada — not a good neighborhood.

Look for the Kid Friendly icon to find hotels that are especially welcoming to families. Many of these accommodations have swimming pools, some offer family packages (usually on weekends), and all offer plenty of patience and good advice. A listing without this symbol does not necessarily mean "kid unfriendly." Keep in mind, though, that a lot of B&Bs in Vancouver explicitly state that they don't take children under the age of around 12 — make sure to ask about this when you call.

Vancouver is healthy — many places are non-smoking, period. If you need to light up, ask if smokers are accommodated.

See the map in this chapter for hotel locations, except for those in the areas of the North Shore. For a key to the dollar sign ratings used in each listing, see the Introduction.

Finding the Best Room at the Best Rate

If you must travel in high season (see Chapter 3), then you can expect to pay top dollar. Travel has rebounded in the last couple of years and hotels in both Vancouver and Victoria no longer need any promotional rates to lure summer visitors. So what does this mean in terms of rates?

The **rack rate** is the maximum rate a hotel charges for a room. It's the rate you get if you walk in off the street and ask for a room for the night. You sometimes see these rates printed on the fire/emergency exit diagrams posted on the back of your door.

Hotels are happy to charge you the rack rate, but you can almost always do better. Perhaps the best way to avoid paying the rack rate is surprisingly simple: Just ask for a cheaper or discounted rate. You may be pleasantly surprised.

Using a travel agent

In all but the smallest accommodations, the rate you pay for a room depends on many factors — chief among them being how you make your reservation. A travel agent may be able to negotiate a better rate with certain hotels than you can get by yourself. (That's because the hotel often gives the agent a discount in exchange for steering his or her business toward that hotel.) Similarly, a package operator or consolidator (see Chapter 5) gets some great hotel rates because they buy in bulk, and pass those savings on to their customers.

Booking direct

Reserving a room through the hotel's toll-free number may also result in a lower rate than calling the hotel directly. On the other hand, the central reservations number may not know about discount rates at specific locations. For example, local franchises may offer a special group rate for a wedding or family reunion, but they may neglect to tell the central booking line. Your best bet is to call both the local number and the toll-free number and see which one gives you a better deal.

Because room rates (even rack rates) change with the season, and sometimes even within the season as occupancy rates rise and fall, prices are subject to change without notice. Hence the rates quoted in this book may be different from the actual rate you receive when you make your reservation. Be sure to mention membership in AAA, CAA, AARP, CARP, frequent-flier programs, and any other corporate rewards programs you can think of — your Uncle Travis's Elk Lodge in which you're an honorary inductee, for that matter — when you call to book.

Surfing the Web for hotel deals

Shopping online for hotels is generally done one of two ways: By booking through the hotel's own Web site or through an independent booking agency (or a fare-service agency like Priceline). These Internet hotel agencies have multiplied in mind-boggling numbers of late, competing for the business of millions of consumers surfing for accommodations around the world. This competitiveness can be a boon to consumers who have the patience and time to shop and compare the online sites for good deals — but shop they must, for prices can vary considerably from site to site. And keep in mind that hotels at the top of a site's listing may be there for no other reason than that they paid money to get the placement.

Of the "big three" sites, **Expedia** offers a long list of special deals and "virtual tours" or photos of available rooms so you can see what you're paying for (a feature that helps counter the claims that the best rooms are often held back from bargain-booking Web sites). **Travelocity** posts unvarnished customer reviews and ranks its properties according to the AAA rating system. For travelers within Canada, both Travelocity and Expedia offer Canadian sites.

Also reliable are **Hotels.com** and **Quikbook.com.** An excellent free program, **TravelAxe** (www.travelweb.com) is partly owned by the hotels it represents (including the Hilton, Hyatt, and Starwood chains) and is therefore plugged directly into the hotels' reservations systems — unlike independent online agencies, which have to fax or e-mail reservation requests to the hotel, a good portion of which get misplaced in the shuffle. More than once, travelers have arrived at the hotel only to be told that they have no reservation. To be fair, many of the major sites are undergoing improvements in service and ease of use, and Expedia will soon be able to plug directly into the reservations systems of many hotel chains — none of which can be bad news for consumers. In the meantime, it's a good idea to **get a confirmation number** and **make a printout** of any online booking transaction.

In the opaque Web site category, **Priceline** and **Hotwire** are even better for hotels than for airfares; with both, you're allowed to pick the neighborhood and quality level of your hotel before offering up your money.

Priceline's hotel product is much better at getting five-star lodging for three-star prices than at finding anything at the bottom of the scale. On the down side, many hotels stick Priceline guests in their least desirable rooms. Be sure to go to the BiddingforTravel Web site (www.biddingfortravel.com) before bidding on a hotel room on Priceline; it features a fairly up-to-date list of hotels that Priceline uses in major cities. For both Priceline and Hotwire, you pay up front, and the fee is nonrefundable.

Note: Some hotels do not provide loyalty program credits or points or other frequent-stay amenities when you book a room through opaque online services.

Reserving the best room

After you make your reservation, asking one or two more pointed questions can go a long way toward making sure you get the best room in the house. Always ask for a corner room. They're usually larger, quieter, and have more windows and light than standard rooms, and they don't always cost more. Also ask if the hotel is renovating; if it is, request a room away from the renovation work. Inquire, too, about the location of the restaurants, bars, and discos in the hotel — all sources of annoying noise. And if you aren't happy with your room when you arrive, talk to the front desk. If they have another room, they should be happy to accommodate you, within reason.

Arriving without a Reservation

Arriving without a reservation can be risky business, and definitely not recommended if you want to stay downtown in high season.

If you're arriving by air, both the Vancouver and Victoria airports have a bank of telephones, each a direct line to the hotel the phone is promoting. This is as good a place to start as any. The visitor centers are also pretty helpful. For locally based agencies, try these:

- ✔ **Best Canadian Bed & Breakfast Network** (☎ 604-738-7207; www.bestcanadianbb.com)

- ✔ **Canada-West Accommodations** (☎ 800-561-3223 or 604-990-6730; www.b-b.com)

- ✔ **Vancouver Bed & Breakfast** (☎ 800-488-1941 or 604-298-8815; www.vancouverbandb.bc.ca)

Or, you can try the following bureaus:

- ✔ **Hotel Discounts** (☎ 800-715-7666; www.hoteldiscounts.com): another good source for last minutes reservations; it is particularly strong on searching out locally based chains.

- ✔ **Quikbook** (☎ 800-789-9887; www.quikbook.com): covers dozens of quality downtown hotels; discounts can reach 60 percent.

> ✔ **Turbotrip.com** (☎ 800-473-7829; www.turbotrip.com): provides comprehensive lodging and travel information for destinations throughout North America, and worldwide.

Vancouver's Best Hotels

Best Western Vancouver Downtown
$$–$$$ Downtown

Sure, it's a chain property, but a pretty decent one and goes out of its way for both repeat-customer, business people and independent travelers who value flexibility. This Best Western features 30 efficiency units with full kitchens in addition to standard hotel rooms — all with free Internet access. For true star treatment, the penthouse suite is very comfortable (at a through-the-roof price). The hotel's near the hip Yaletown neighborhood, so finding a spot to dine or shop is easy. You can also opt for a whirlpool room for a little extra dough. The hotel thoughtfully provides a free shuttle service to downtown.

See map p. 93. 718 Drake St. ☎ *888-669-9888 or 604-669-9888. Fax: 604-669-3440.* www.bestwesterndowntown.com. *Parking: Valet C$6 (US$5). Rates: C$199– C$209 (US$166–US$174) double. AE, DISC, MC, V.*

Blue Horizon Hotel
$$ West End

This high-rise on the upper end of Robson Street near Stanley Park has the advantage of offering all corner rooms with private balconies that are more spacious than at a typical hotel. Rooms come in a variety of configurations, the most plush (and expensive) being the suites with one or two beds on the top 15 floors: Each comes with two bathrooms, a living room, two televisions, and other amenities. The bottom 12 floors have smaller rooms but require shorter elevator rides. Bonus points: Rooms are Internet access–friendly and because this is a *green* hotel (despite the name), management employs energy-saving practices such as super-efficient lighting, low-flow shower heads, and recycling bins in all the rooms.

See map p. 93. 1225 Robson St. ☎ *800-663-1333 or 604-688-1411. Fax: 604-688-4461.* www.bluehorizonhotel.com. *Parking: Garage C$10 (US$8.30). Rates: C$129– C$199 (US$107–US$166) double. AE, DISC, MC, V.*

Buchan Hotel
$–$$ West End

An older hotel by Vancouver standards, the Buchan (pronounced BUCK-in) isn't for everyone — especially if you dislike sharing a bathroom. It *is* an affordable alternative to big-bucks digs on a quiet residential street with views of the park. It's European-style, from the antique photos throughout the place to the size of the rooms: rather small, unless you request one of

Vancouver Accommodations

Best Western Vancouver
Downtown **13**
Blue Horizon Hotel **10**
Buchan Hotel **5**
Century Plaza Hotel and Spa **17**
Coast Plaza Hotel and Suites **2**
Comfort Inn Downtown **16**
Crowne Plaza Hotel Georgia **24**
Delta Vancouver Suites **32**
English Bay Inn **3**
The Fairmont Hotel Vancouver **23**
Four Seasons **25**
Georgian Court Hotel **34**
Granville Island
Hotel and Marina **12**
Holiday Inn
Vancouver Centre **37**
Holiday Inn
Vancouver Downtown **14**
Hyatt Regency Vancouver **22**
Kenya Court Guest House **11**
La Grande Residence **19**
Le Soleil Suites **27**
Listel Hotel **9**
Lonsdale Quay Hotel **30**
Metropolitan Hotel **26**
"O Canada" House **18**
Opus Hotel **35**
Pan Pacific Hotel **28**
Pillow Suites **39**
Plaza 500 Hotel **38**
Rosedale on Robson Suite
Hotel **33**
Rosellen Suites **4**
Shaughnessy Village **36**
Sheraton Wall Centre Hotel **15**
Sutton Place Hotel **20**
Sylvia Hotel **1**
Thistledown B&B **31**
Times Square Suites **6**
Waterfront Centre Hotel **29**
Wedgewood Hotel **21**
West End Guest House **8**
Westin Bayshore Resort
& Marina **7**

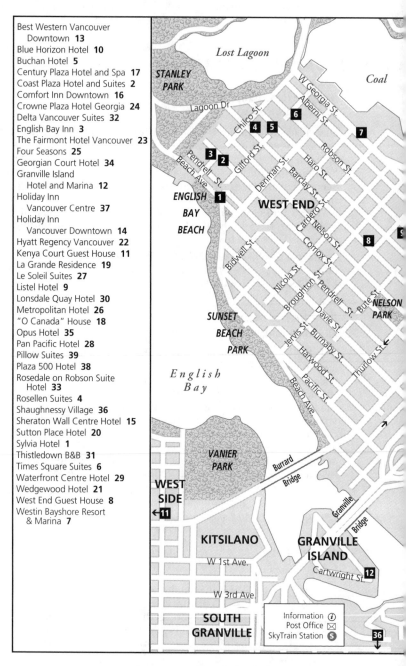

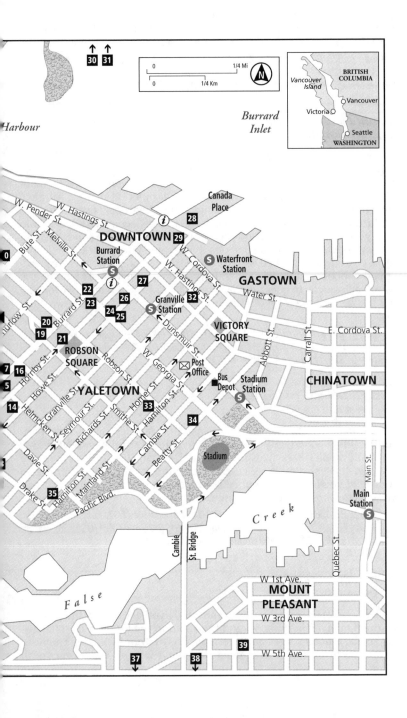

the four executive corner rooms, which do have their own private baths. In keeping with its backpacker-like clientele, the hotel offers bike, ski, and luggage storage, as well as on-site coin laundry. ***Note:*** It's entirely non-smoking.

See map p. 92. 1906 Haro St. ☎ ***800-668-6654*** *or 604-685-5354. Fax: 604-685-5367.* www.buchanhotel.com. *Parking: Free on street 6 p.m. to 11 a.m., otherwise none. Rack rates: C$85–C$135 (US$71–US$112) double. AE, DISC, MC, V.*

Century Plaza Hotel and Spa
$$–$$$$ **Downtown**

The exterior and public areas are nothing to write home about; in fact, one of the best reasons to stay at the all-suites Century Plaza is its famous spa, which, paradoxically, is difficult to get into — unless you're a stressed-out celeb, of course. Guestrooms, though, are a different matter: All have kitchen facilities with handsome dining tables; bedrooms come with big, comfortable beds and the majority have a newly renovated, bright and cheery ambience. The 30th-floor penthouse suite looks like something out of *House Beautiful* with its spacious living room and separate bedroom with a customized king bed. Guests in the Honeymoon Suite receive hand-dipped chocolate strawberries and private room service. The hotel graciously allows you to check out as late as 3 p.m. — just remember to hang that "Privacy Please" sign on the door. Yuk Yuks comedy club downstairs is good for a laugh.

See map p. 93. 1015 Burrard St. ☎ ***800-663-1818*** *or 604-687-0575. Fax: 604-682-5790.* www.century-plaza.com. *Parking: Garage C$10 (US$8.30). Rates: C$169–C$350 (US$141–US$291) double. AE, DISC, MC, V.*

Coast Plaza Hotel and Suites
$$$ **West End**

A fave with both Hollywood film crews and their families, this former apartment building is perfectly located within a stone's throw of English Bay beach and Stanley Park. It also sits just off Denman Street, one of the city's best and busiest dining areas, although most of the suites here have kitchens if you feel overwhelmed by the dining options. Some also have Jacuzzis. Be sure to ask for a room with a view.

See map p. 92. 1763 Comox St. ☎ ***800-663-1144*** *or 604-688-7711. Fax: 604-688-5934.* www.coasthotels.com. *Parking: Valet C$15 (US$12), self C$10 (US$8.30). Rates: C$279–C$319 (US$232–US$265) double. AE, DC, DISC, MC, V.*

Comfort Inn Downtown
$$ **Downtown**

An older (1912) property that was renovated to reflect a new attitude in the surrounding neighborhood — and then sold to the Comfort Inn chain — this smallish hotel serves an in-between crowd: those who don't want to spend a fortune on a swanky place, but don't want to head for a youth hostel, either. The smallish rooms are tasteful enough, with beds covered in thick duvets and modern artwork gracing the walls. Smoking is forbidden on entire floors, and no — the bathrooms aren't shared. Some rooms even have Jacuzzis. You also get continental breakfast with your room and a ride to the airport if need be, as well as room-access to high-speed Internet, voice mail, and a dataport for your laptop computer. Doolins Irish Pub next door can get a bit rowdy, but — boy — the Guinness sure is good.

See map p. 93. 645 Nelson St. ☎ *888-605-5333 or 604-605-4333. Fax: 604-605-4334.* www.comfortinndowntown.com. *Parking: None on-site; lot next door, C$11 (US$9.15) per 24 hours. Rates: C$139–C$199 (US$116–US$166) double. Rates include continental breakfast. AE, DC, MC, V.*

Crowne Plaza Hotel Georgia
$$–$$$ Downtown

This grand hotel, polished up and prettified to its finest, offers a stunning array of amenities, plus great views of the Frances Rattenbury–designed Vancouver Art Gallery. All furnishings here show off a snazzy, 1920s art deco look; standard guest rooms feature king, queen, or double (but full-size) beds and two-line phones, while king suites include a spacious sitting area. Executive Club Floor rooms include extras such as bathrobes, evening turn-down service, CD players, speakerphones, and breakfast. Traffic noise can be a problem on the gallery side, however. The Casablanca Lounge, off the lobby, is a lovely retreat for afternoon high tea.

See map p. 93. 801 West Georgia St. ☎ *800-663-1111 or 604-682-5566. Fax: 604-642-5579.* www.hotelgeorgia.bc.ca. *Parking: Valet C$22 (US$18). Rates: C$189–C$239 (US$157–US$199) double. AE, DC, DISC, MC, V.*

Delta Vancouver Suites
$$–$$$ Downtown

Smack in the middle of Vancouver's bustling financial district, this plush, all-suite business hotel is almost like home — except, surprisingly, there are no kitchenette facilities, possibly to lure guests downstairs to the trendy New York–style restaurant on the ground floor. All guestrooms have spacious work areas with movable (even expandable) desks, CEO-type chairs, speakerphones, and high-speed Internet access, and most of the bedrooms are separated from work areas by a door. Other personal touches include bathrobes, Nintendo games for children, and irons and ironing boards. To get more Vancouver views for your buck, ask about the king corner suites that have windows on two sides. A fitness center, indoor pool, and sauna are part of the package. Also, don't neglect the hotel restaurant: It's very good.

See map p. 93. 550 West Hastings St. ☎ *877-814-7706 or 604-689-8188. Fax: 604-605-8881.* www.deltahotels.com. *Parking: Valet C$19.50 (US$16). Rates: C$209–C$305 (US$174–US$254) suites. AE, DC, DISC, MC, V.*

English Bay Inn
$$–$$$ **West End**

This hideaway in the cozy West End is romantic and well located: close to Stanley Park and the beach at English Bay, and with a delightful garden to take time out between sight-seeing. The inn has seven guest rooms in all, each decked out in period antiques and including two suites. The upstairs suite, more luxurious, comes with its own fireplace and costs about C$100 (US$83) extra. All guests receive comfy bathrobes and a full breakfast and are treated to a complimentary evening aperitif.

See map p. 92. 1968 Comox St. ☎ *866-683-8002 or 604-683-8002.* www.englishbay inn.com. *Parking: Free. Rates: C$190–C$225 (US$158–US$187) double. AE, MC, V.*

The Fairmont Hotel Vancouver
$$$$ **Downtown**

The bland name doesn't begin to describe the luxury inside. Part of the original, and venerable Canadian Pacific Hotel Chain (which includes The Fairmont Empress Hotel in Victoria), the hotel's big and comfortable rooms come in dozens of configurations. Courtyard suites offer more privacy, space, and televisions, while the Entrée Gold floor is super exclusive and includes dedicated staff and your own private lounge. The Premier Rooms are more like suites designed for longer stays, with full kitchens, dining rooms, entertainment areas, and extra beds — plus sweeping views of the city; some rooms have extra-deep tubs, too. The exotic pool and intimate fitness center (and a quality spa) help keep the calories in check; the hotel's restaurant, Griffins, is excellent. Fairmont also has the exceptionally plush Waterfront Hotel near Canada Place.

See map p. 93. 900 West Georgia St. ☎ *800-441-1414 or 604-684-3131. Fax: 604-662-1929.* www.fairmont.com. *Parking: Valet C$27 (US$22). Rates: C$389–C$579 (US$324–US$482) double. AE, DC, MC, V.*

Four Seasons
$$$$ **Downtown**

One of the city's very best (and most expensive) hotels, the Four Seasons shows its caring side by going out of its way to attract both families with children and travelers who can't go anywhere without man's best friend. Kids feel right at home as they slip into mini bathrobes, munch freshly baked cookies, and hop up onto the stool thoughtfully placed in bathrooms to help them reach the sink; there's also a teddy bear provided to help the kids drop off to sleep, and upper-floor rooms add Sony PlayStations (along with better views). Adults seem to like the place, too: Rooms are huge and beyond plush, while the staff is attentive. Even dogs are given the royal treatment: Special water bowls, designer dog biscuits, and dog beds mean Rover won't ever want to leave. The hotel has one of the city's premier restaurants, Chartwell (see Chapter 10) — a place to see and be seen among power brokers.

See map p. 93. 791 West Georgia St. ☎ ***800-332-3442*** *or 604-689-9333. Fax: 604-684-4555.* www.fourseasons.com. *Parking: Valet parking in underground garage, C$27 (US$22). Rates: C$350–C$470 (US$291–US$391) double. AE, DC, DISC, MC, V.*

Georgian Court Hotel
$$$–$$$$ Yaletown

This place, a member of the Golden Tulip family, is something of a find — as good as some much higher-priced hotels and right in the city's hippest district. (It's also well located for sports fans, not far from BC Place and GM Place stadiums.) Lots of mahogany, brass, beveled glass, and even a grandfather clock in the lobby sets the tone. The handsomely appointed rooms have been designed with business travelers in mind: Think spacious work areas, multi-line telephones, and complimentary high-speed Internet. You're steps from plenty of clubs and bars. Perhaps the most compelling reason to stay, though, is the popular and excellent William Tell Restaurant (see Chapter 10) right in the hotel, with its hearty Swiss cuisine.

See map p. 93. 773 Beatty St. ☎ ***800-663-1155*** *or 604-682-5555. Fax: 604-682-8830.* www.georgiancourt.com. *Parking: Garage C$9 (US$7.50). Rates: C$240–C$300 (US$200–US$250) double. AE, DC, MC, V.*

Granville Island Hotel and Marina
$$–$$$ Granville Island

Located at the opposite end of Granville Island to the very busy Public Market (and therefore a shade more peaceful), this is quite simply a fun place to stay — and the views are fantastic. Little touches such as in-room coffee-makers and high-speed Internet access, a free morning newspaper delivered to your door, and the on-site microbrewery make up for the sometimes raucous atmosphere in the halls. Pets are made to feel very welcome, too, with the Island's store, Woofles, providing dog toys, treats, and even pet-sitting services! Pets are C$25 (US$21) extra per night. You can find room to relax in the rooftop health club (more great views), or you can rent a canoe or ocean kayak from the hotel marina. Yes, a kayak. Is that quintessentially Vancouver, or what?

See map p. 92. 1253 Johnson St. ☎ ***800-663-1840*** *or 604-683-7373. Fax: 604-683-3061.* www.granvilleislandhotel.com. *Parking: Garage C$7 (US$5.80). Rates: C$199–C$249 (US$166–US$207) double. AE, DC, MC, V.*

Hyatt Regency Vancouver
$$$–$$$$ Downtown

After an $18 million renovation, the hotel reopened its doors in 2002 with a completely fresh and dynamic West Coast look. The rooms are bigger than at most any other downtown hotel (with Internet access, of course) and as with all of downtown's big-name hotels, there's even a special category of stay where — for big bucks — you receive a private elevator, personal concierge, afternoon snacks, and access to a private lounge complete with stereo and big-screen television. Shoppers and tour groups flock to the Hyatt, because it offers loads of space and terrific views. This spot is also quite popular with conventioneers, making weekday rates rather high, although weekend rates can be lower.

See map p. 93. 655 Burrard St. ☎ *800-532-1496 or 604-683-1234. Fax: 604-689-3707.* www.vancouver.hyatt.com. *Parking: Valet parking C$24 (US$20). Rates: C$229–C$384 (US$191–US$319) double. AE, DC, DISC, MC, V.*

Kenya Court Guest House
$$ **Kitsilano**

This three-story apartment building out in Kitsilano has been completely renovated to provide short-term suite accommodations just a few paces from Kits Beach and the good collection of restaurants lining Cornwall Avenue. Each room is a suite, and has a living room, separate bedroom, fully equipped kitchen, and bathroom. Advertising is primarily by word of mouth between savvy travelers. It doesn't even have a Web site, but the four rooms fill well in advance.

See map p. 92. 2230 Cornwall Ave. (from downtown, follow Burrard St. across Burrard Bridge). ☎ *604-738-7085. Parking: Free on street. Rates: C$155–C$175 (US$129–US$146) suite. Rates include full breakfast. Credit cards not accepted.*

Le Soleil Suites
$$$$ **Downtown**

For a taste of the high life, Le Soleil Suites doesn't disappoint. Its fashionable design, ripped from the pages of upscale interior design magazines, can seem a bit overdone; but the services and little touches definitely make you feel pampered. For example, not-tested-on-animals Aveda cosmetics are in the bathrooms, and yummy Godiva chocolates wait on feather pillows nestled into silk brocade coverlets. Rooms aren't enormous, but some suites do have big balconies to give the illusion of more space. Other amenities include the usual business-set perks — speakerphones, dataports, TV, Internet, and a business center. You also find 'round-the-clock room service and one of Vancouver's hottest restaurants among the younger power elite, Oritalia. Although the hotel has no on-site health club, you can use fitness equipment at the nearby YWCA at an additional C$11 (US$9.15) per day.

See map p. 93. 567 Hornby St. ☎ *877-632-3030 or 604-632-3000. Fax: 604-632-3001.* www.lesoleilhotel.com. *Parking: Valet C$22 (US$18) Rates: C$395–C$455 (US$329–US$379) suites. AE, DC, MC, V.*

Listel Hotel
$$$–$$$$ **Downtown**

More than just a marketing ploy, this hotel has teamed up with two of the city's most prestigious art emporiums (one of which is the Museum of Anthropology) to create a unique art environment — in public areas and guest rooms — that showcases original art and sculptures. Rooms are spacious and comfortable, with the upper floors offering peek-a-boo views of the mountains. The latest partnership in this "think-out-of-the-box" hotel is with the Association of Magazine Publishers; guests are offered an eclectic selection of locally published magazines. In the evenings, head for the hotel's restaurant and bar: O'Doul's has live jazz playing seven nights a week.

*See map p. 92. 1300 Robson St. ☎ **800-663-5491** or 604-684-8461. Fax: 604-684-7092. www.listel-vancouver.com. Parking: C$19 (US$16) valet. Rates: C$240–C$320 (US$200–US$266).*

Lonsdale Quay Hotel
$$ North Shore

Located right inside the Lonsdale Quay Public Market complex (where the SeaBus from Vancouver lands), this modern and unpretentious hotel has unbeatable views of the city, plus well-appointed, affordable rooms. Just don't expect the same sorts of do-everything service (turndown, valets, and the like) that the big names across the inlet offer; you won't find them here. But, you are well-positioned for treks on this side of the Burrard Inlet to attractions such as Grouse Mountain, the Capilano Suspension Bridge, and some wonderful jaunts to other mountains such as Seymour and Cypress. Besides, the market itself (which closes around 6 p.m.) is great fun to experience with its restaurant stalls, gourmet food shops, and fresh produce.

*See map p. 93. 123 Carrie Cates Court, North Vancouver (attached to SeaBus terminal). ☎ **604-986-6111**. Fax: 604-986-8782. www.lonsdalequayhotel.bc.ca. Parking: C$7 (US$5.80); free weekends/holidays. Rates: C$125–C$180 (US$104–US$150) double. AE, DISC, DC, MC, V.*

Metropolitan Hotel
$$$$ Downtown

One of the most stylish hotels in all Vancouver, rooms here have almost a modern B&B look, rather than the typical hotel blah room that you often find. For example, rooms include fresh flowers, a retro-looking bed-stand lamp, lively red throw pillows and homey duvets, and floor plants. The hotel lists 18 luxury suites, including a trio that contain whirlpools, but every room in the place features large bathrooms, fluffy down comforters, voicemail, free Internet access, and (almost always) a private balcony or two. The business center is especially good, with everything from laser printers, fax machines, and speakerphones to limousines and secretarial services on call, while the health club includes squash courts (a rarity) along with a heated indoor pool, sauna rooms with built-in televisions, and massage service. Another plus, the hotel restaurant Diva at the Met (see Chapter 10) is one the city's very finest. ***Note:*** Depending on availability, you can save almost $100 by booking rooms directly via their Web site.

*See map p. 93. 645 Howe St. ☎ **800-667-2300** or 604-687-1122. Fax: 604-643-7267. www.metropolitan.com. Parking: Valet C$25 (US$21). Rates: C$399–C$599 (US$332–US$498) double. AE, DC, DISC, MC, V.*

"O Canada" House
$$–$$$ **West End**

A gracious Victorian home a little more than a century old, this B&B offers a quiet space and proximity to downtown. All six guest rooms are big enough to accommodate a separate sitting area, and all have modern bathrooms, televisions, free Internet access, VCRs, refrigerators, and a telephone — you don't usually find *those* in a B&B. Opt for the Penthouse Suite and you add more space and a decent view of downtown; there's also a small cottage with gas fireplace and an outdoor patio. During evenings, the inn serves a complimentary aperitif in the nicely furnished common area or (in good weather) outside on the porch. The name? Why, this is the very place where the Canadian national anthem was written — the one you hear before hockey games.

See map p. 93. 1114 Barclay St. ☎ *877-688-1114 or 604-688-0555. Fax: 604-488-0556.* www.ocanadahouse.com. *Parking: Free at inn. Rates: C$195–C$265 (US$162–US$220) double. MC, V.*

Opus Hotel
$$$ **Yaletown**

From the moment it opened in late 2002 with a risque advertising campaign featuring urban couples in bed at noon, Opus has been a trendsetter — very appropriate for its location in a neighborhood of dot-com companies and movie production houses. Perhaps that's why Opus has twice been featured as part of the Academy Awards ceremonies, offering presenters a chance to stay in one of their stylish, visually rich (and high-wired) rooms. Bathrooms even come equipped with hand-held oxygen dispensers if you need to catch your breath for any reason. Hmmm . . . now doesn't that let the imagination run amok? Guest services also include a chauffer-driven limo for downtown gadabouts, an on-site fitness room, and 24-hour room service. The Opus Bar is adjacent to hotel's reception area, making it feel as if you're checking in at a lounge; the Elixir is a small and lively brasserie that's always hopping with activity.

See map p. 93. 322 Davie St. ☎ *866-642-6787 or 604-642-6787. Fax: 604-642-6780.* www.opushotel.com. *Valet parking: C$25 (US$21). Rates: C$269–C$479 (US$224–US$399) double. AE, DC, MC, V.*

Pan Pacific Hotel
$$$$ **Downtown**

The Pan Pacific is one of the city's most luxurious hotels, with fantastic views, meticulous service, and sky-high prices to match. Rooms are modern and well appointed, but really more notable for their size and views than any unusual decorative touches; the corner (Premier) suites, with more of an eyeful of the outdoors, cost up to an extra C$100 (US$83). The services of the hotel's *amazing* new spa (see Chapter 12) also cost extra. A favorite of conventioneers and Japanese tourists, the hotel is located right in Canada Place, Vancouver's most visually interesting building (it's topped by white Teflon "sails") and home of the gourmet **Five Sails** restaurant (see Chapter 10).

See map p. 93. 999 Canada Place. ☎ *800-937-1515 from the U.S., 800-663-1515 or 604-662-8111 from Canada. Fax: 604-685-8690.* www.vancouver.panpacific.com. *Parking: Valet C$27 (US$22), self-park C$20 (US$17). Rates: C$490–C$590 (US$408–US$491) double. AE, DC, MC, V.*

Rosedale on Robson Suite Hotel
$$–$$$$ Yaletown

Tour groups, primarily from Australia and the U.K., judging from the accents, love this hotel — as do families. Its one- and two-bedroom suites come in various configurations, complete with pullout beds and kitchenettes. The family suites even have bunk beds for the kids plus toy chests. Now you can't get much more child friendly than that! The hotel has a small pool and gym, and the on-site restaurant, Rosie's, is reasonably priced and fun (and the corned beef on rye is as good as you'll find in any New York deli), but it can get packed if there's a sporting event or show happening in nearby Queen Elizabeth Theatre or BC Place Stadium. *Note:* Internet specials can sometimes save you C$100 (US$83) or more on rooms.

See map p. 93. 838 Hamilton St. (at Robson St.) ☎ *800-661-8870 or 604-689-8033.* www.rosedaleonrobson.com. *Fax: 604-689-4426. Parking: Garage C$8 (US$6.65). Rates: C$270–C$335 (US$225–US$279) double. AE, DC, DISC, MC, V.*

Rosellen Suites
$$–$$$ West End

A secluded, all-suite, bungalow type of place on a quiet street very near Stanley Park, the Rosellen is one of Vancouver's suite deals. It's an older property and has been known to house celebrity types (Katharine Hepburn loved it). A good arrangement for families, each suite is completely furnished with kitchens, one or two bedrooms, and a living/dining area; some have in-room dishwashers and laundry facilities. You even get your very own telephone number with voicemail during your stay.

See map p. 92. 2030 Barclay St. ☎ *888-317-6648 or 604-689-4807. Fax: 604-684-3327.* www.rosellensuites.com. *Parking: C$7.50 (US$6.25). Rates: C$199–C$299 (US$166–US$249) apartment suites. AE, DC, MC, V.*

Sheraton Wall Centre Hotel
$$–$$$$ Downtown

This opulent Sheraton wins the prize in Vancouver for tallest human-made structure (though a fast-rising Shangri-La will soon topple that claim) — and the higher you go, the more opulent the rooms become. The Crystal Club rooms allow guests access to the suave Crystal Club lounge, where they can savor breakfast, snacks, and drinks, and gaze out windows at the too-close-to-believe mountains to the north. The hotel doesn't shortchange on rooms, either; expect comfortable linens, fluffy duvets, heated bathroom floor tiles, and exquisite room furnishings. You can carry on six telephone conversations at one time with the three two-line phones in the room, or leave in a hurry using the express video-checkout system. The extensive health club includes a very good spa wellness center, and the on-site restaurant is modern with a bistro flair.

See map p. 93. 1088 Burrard St. ☎ *800-663-9255 or 604-331-1000. Fax: 604-897-7200.* www.sheratonvancouver.com. *Parking: Garage C$20 (US$17). Rates: C$199–C$329 (US$166–US$274) double. AE, DC, MC, V.*

Sutton Place Hotel

$$$–$$$$ **Downtown**

Downtown Vancouver certainly doesn't lack for luxury hotels, but most folks agree this is among the top. Whether you want fresh flowers or an in-room ice dispenser, Sutton has you covered. The hotel also provides business-hotel niceties, such as computer dataports, Internet access and multi-line phones, as well as bathrobes, king-size beds in every room, complimentary umbrellas, and shoe shines. If you're a non-smoker, you'll be thankful for the 11 floors that forbid all forms of tobacco, and if you use a wheelchair, you'll appreciate the extra spacious rooms. It wouldn't be a top hotel without a great spa. Heck, even pets are well looked after, with gourmet room service, designer dish water (!), and massage services — maybe this is taking luxury a little *too* far. Ah, well, I guess it's a dog's life, eh? Sip that cognac in the Gérard Lounge and check out the crowd for celebs. You're not going anywhere. Fleuri (see Chapter 10) is Sutton's contribution to the vibrant Vancouver dining scene. ***Note:*** If you're planning a long-term stay, and can afford top-quality digs, ask about La Grande Residence apartments next door.

See map p. 93. 845 Burrard St. ☎ *800-961-7555 or 604-682-5511. Fax: 604-682-5513.* www.vancouver.suttonplace.com. *Parking: Garage C$21.75 (US$18). Rates: C$267–C$478 (US$222–US$398) double. AE, DC, DISC, MC, V.*

Sylvia Hotel

$–$$ **West End**

Despite its obviously well-loved rooms (some would say *too* well-loved — they're a bit tired), the Sylvia steadfastly remains one of the most popular budget hotels in the city, mainly for its prime location next to English Bay Beach and Stanley Park — and the great service provided by an attentive and unharried staff. Too bad its rooms are fairly threadbare and that furniture is an afterthought at best; consider this place only if you want to rough it for a night. The hotel consists of two buildings: a vine-covered structure built in 1912 (which back then was the tallest in the West End), and a second, newer building. The advantage to the older property is the top floor, where views are spectacular; rooms in the newer building have better heating and less-worn rugs. The older building also has some suites with full kitchens, good for a family or small group. The hotel's tacky lounge (see Chapter 15) is legendary among locals — it's hard to imagine why, though. To stay at this hotel, plan on making reservations several months in advance.

See map p. 92. 1154 Gilford St. ☎ *604-681-9321. Fax: 604-682-3551.* www.sylvia hotel.com. *Parking: C$7 (US$5.80). Rates: C$95–C$155 (US$79–US$129) double. AE, DC, MC, V.*

Times Square Suites
$$–$$$ West End

A home away from home is what these spacious studio, one- and two-bedroom suites offer. The 42 units are tucked away in a Victorian-style building, each offering fully equipped kitchens that include a dishwasher and a microwave, a washer and dryer, expanded cable TV, DVD players, and CD stereo systems. Housekeeping comes by twice a week, and you can grill your salmon (or whatever else that's grillable) on the rooftop barbecue. The location is ace, too: Denman Street is just around the corner, and Stanley Park is only a few more minutes away. This is a great spot for families.

See map p. 92. 1821 Robson St. ☎ *877-684-2223 or 604-684-2223. Fax: 604-684-2225.* www.timessquaresuites.com. *Parking: Garage C$10 (US$8.30). Rates: C$149–C$229 (US$124–US$191) suites. AE, MC, V.*

Wedgewood Hotel
$$$–$$$$ Downtown

A small, exquisite boutique hotel catering to different types of guests depending on the day of the week, this is perhaps the city's most intriguing upscale option. During the week, business people line up to book this place for its proximity to the heart of the city's financial district and plentiful amenities, such as the new ultra-chic, in-room soaker-tubs and 'round-the-clock room service. On weekends, couples arrive to cozy up in the sumptuous rooms filled with elegant antiques, toasting each other in the hotel's highly touted restaurant Bacchus (see Chapter 10), pampering themselves in the spa, or just gazing out at the city lights from their flower-decked balconies. As you may guess, this hotel goes all out to provide extra touches, like turndown service and bathrobes, and a personality gradually emerges — something well worth the cost, given the number of other equally luxurious but *far* blander business hotels in Vancouver's city center.

See map p. 93. 845 Hornby St. ☎ *800-663-0666 or 604-689-7777. Fax: 604-608-5348.* www.wedgewoodhotel.com. *Parking: Valet parking in underground garage, C$19 (US$16). Rates: C$295–C$900 (US$245–US$749) double. AE, DC, MC, V.*

West End Guest House
$$–$$$ West End

Guests appreciate the quiet West End residential neighborhood in which this small, eight-room inn is located — not to mention the personal attention lavished on them by the inn's hardworking owner. You can splurge on the spacious top-floor suite with a queen-size brass bed, gas fireplace, and huge bathroom with an antique claw-foot bathtub. Or choose smaller rooms featuring queen or double beds; it doesn't matter. All the accommodations retain a cozy, Victorian feel, thanks to lots of antiques and duvets, along with a dose of modern conveniences such as televisions and phones. Hot breakfast and complimentary refreshments are included with the price of your stay, and throughout the day you're also allowed to help yourself to snacks in the kitchen. Still not convinced? Free bicycles will get you to Stanley Park in a jiffy, parking is free, and there's no smoking on the premises. Ask about the resident ghost. And if that scares you off, ask about their new guesthouse, on the North Shore, called Inn Penzance.

See map p. 92. 1362 Haro St. ☎ *888-546-3327 or 604-681-2889. Fax: 604-688-8812.* www.westendguesthouse.com. *Parking: Valet free. Rates: C$135–C$255 (US$112–US$212) double. Rates include full breakfast. AE, MC, V.*

Westin Bayshore Resort & Marina
$$$$ West End

One of the best located of Vancouver's upscale accommodations, the Westin Bayshore is the only true resort anywhere near downtown; it teeters right at the entrance to glorious Stanley Park and staying here could spoil you for any other Vancouver hotel. A serious splurge, the Westin's a hit among vacationing families and has a loyal repeat clientele who come back for its *very* comfortably furnished rooms, each and every one of them with unhindered water and mountain views, and still glowing with fresh appeal from the hotel's major refurbishment a few years ago. A picturesque marina is on its doorstep where guests can moor their own boats or pick up a charter; a helpful information desk can also arrange all sorts of other sight-seeing excursions and expeditions. Additional amenities include child-sitting, business and concierge services, bicycle rentals, special movie nights for kids, and a free shuttle drop-off and pick-up to your choice of downtown locations.

See map p. 92. 1601 Bayshore Dr. (from downtown, follow West Georgia St. toward Stanley Park; hotel is on right, at the foot of Cardero St.). ☎ *800-228-3000 or 604-682-3377. Fax: 604-687-3102.* www.westinbayshore.com. *Parking: self-park C$18 (US$15), Valet C$18.50 (US$15.50). Rates: C$460–C$530 (US$383–US$441) double. AE, DC, DISC, MC, V.*

Runner-up Hotels

Holiday Inn Vancouver Centre

$–$$ West Side You know exactly what you're getting at this well-known chain. The hotel's Web site often runs special rates. *See map p. 93. 711 West Broadway.* ☎ *604-879-0511. Fax: 604-872-7520.* www.holiday innvancouver.com.

Holiday Inn Vancouver Downtown

$$ Downtown   Yes, another chain choice, but if you have kids, this is a good, centrally located option, thanks to its play area for children and kitchenettes in some units. *See map p. 93. 1110 Howe St.* ☎ *800-663-9151 or 604-684-2151. Fax: 604-684-4736.* www.hi-vancouver.bc.ca.

Pillow & Porridge Suites

$$ West Side   You get the best of both worlds at this place — beautiful and residential surroundings, plus many of the amenities of downtown suite hotels without the parking or traffic hassles. *See map p. 93. 2859 Manitoba St.* ☎ *604-879-8977. Fax: 604-879-8966.* www.pillow.net.

Plaza 500 Hotel

$$ West Side   Clean, comfortable, and just over the bridge from Yaletown and on a great bus route to get you elsewhere, there's nothing spectacular about this hotel other than its value. *See map p. 93. 500 West 12th Ave.* ☎ *800-473-1811 or 604-873-1811. Fax: 604-873-5103.* www.plaza500.com.

Shaughnessy Village

$ West Side   A bargain hunter's dream, if you don't mind the oddly tiny rooms, this highrise has all the facilities of a full-service hotel without the price tags or attitude. *See map p. 92. 1125 West 12th Ave.* ☎ *604-736-5511. Fax: 604-737-1321.* www.shaughnessyvillage.com.

Thistledown Bed & Breakfast

$$–$$$ North Shore   Romantic, adult-oriented, and full of charm, this comfortable guesthouse lies in a great residential area. The warm and hospitable hosts dish up a terrific breakfast alongside insider tips on what to see and do. *See map p. 93. 3910 Capilano Rd.* ☎ *888-633-7173 or 604-986-7173. Fax: 604-980-2939.* www.thistle-down.com.

Index of Accommodations by Neighborhood

English Bay Inn ($$–$$$)
"O Canada" House ($$–$$$)
Parkhill Hotel ($$)
Rosellen Suites ($$–$$$)
Sylvia Hotel ($–$$)
Times Square Suites ($$–$$$)
West End Guest House ($$–$$$)
Westin Bayshore Resort & Marina ($$$$)

West Side (Granville Island, Kitsilano, Point Grey, South Granville)

Granville Island Hotel and Marina ($$–$$$)
Holiday Inn Vancouver Centre ($$)

Kenya Court Guest House ($$)
Pillow & Porridge Suites ($$)
Plaza 500 Hotel ($$)
Shaughnessy Village ($)

Yaletown

Georgian Court Hotel ($$$–$$$$)
Opus Hotel ($$$)
Rosedale on Robson Suite Hotel ($$–$$$$)

Index of Accommodations by Price

$$$$

Century Plaza Hotel and Spa (Downtown)
Crowne Plaza Hotel Georgia (Downtown)
The Fairmont Hotel Vancouver (Downtown)
Four Seasons (Downtown)
Georgian Court Hotel (Yaletown)
Hyatt Regency (Downtown)
Le Soleil Suites (Downtown)
Listel Hotel (Downtown)
Metropolitan Hotel (Downtown)
Pan Pacific Hotel (Downtown)
Rosedale on Robson Suite Hotel (Yaletown)
Sheraton Wall Centre Hotel (Downtown)
Sutton Place Hotel (Downtown)
Wedgewood Hotel (Downtown)
Westin Bayshore Resort & Marina (West End)

$$$

Best Western Vancouver Downtown (Downtown)
Century Plaza Hotel and Spa (Downtown)
Coast Plaza Hotel and Suites (West End)
Crowne Plaza Hotel Georgia (Downtown)

Delta Vancouver Suites (Downtown)
English Bay Inn (West End)
Georgian Court Hotel (Yaletown)
Granville Island Hotel and Marina (West Side)
Hyatt Regency Vancouver (Downtown)
Listel Hotel (Downtown)
"O Canada" House (West End)
Opus Hotel (Yaletown)
Rosedale on Robson Suite Hotel (Yaletown)
Rosellen Suites (West End)
Sheraton Wall Centre Hotel (Downtown)
Sutton Place Hotel (Downtown)
Thistledown B&B (North Vancouver)
Times Square Suites (West End)
Wedgewood Hotel (Downtown)
West End Guest House (West End)

$$

Best Western Vancouver Downtown (Downtown)
Blue Horizon Hotel (West End)
Buchan Hotel (West End)
Century Plaza Hotel and Spa (Downtown)
Comfort Inn Downtown (Downtown)
Crowne Plaza Hotel Georgia (Downtown)

Delta Vancouver Suites (Downtown)
English Bay Inn (West End)
Granville Island Hotel and Marina
(West Side)
Holiday Inn Vancouver Centre
(West Side)
Holiday Inn Vancouver Downtown
(Downtown)
Kenya Court Guest House (West Side)
Lonsdale Quay Hotel (North Shore)
"O Canada" House (West End)
Pillow Suites & Porridge (West Side)
Plaza 500 Hotel (West Side)
Rosedale on Robson Suite Hotel
(Yaletown)

Rosellen Suites (West End)
Sheraton Wall Centre Hotel
(Downtown)
Sylvia Hotel (West End)
Times Square Suites (West End)
Thistledown B&B (North Vancouver)
West End Guest House (West End)

$

Buchan Hotel (West End)
Pillow & Porridge Suites (West Side)
Shaughnessy Village (West Side)
Sylvia Hotel (West End)
West End Guest House (West End)

Chapter 10

Dining and Snacking in Vancouver

• •

In This Chapter

▶ Getting the dish on the local scene
▶ Trimming the fat from your budget
▶ Finding Vancouver's best restaurants
▶ Dining and snacking on the go

• •

*W*ith a reportedly more than 3,000 eateries in the Vancouver area, you can sample more kinds of cuisine here, probably, than almost anywhere else on the continent. Malaysian? Hawaiian? Indian? Japanese? Cuban? It's just one gastronomic, culinary adventure after another, including a great selection of vegetarian options. And it's all healthy — the region's organic farms help supply fresh ingredients, and keep innovative chefs, cooks, and menu-planners on their toes with tastes that are fresh and stylish.

Discovering What's New, What's Hot, and Who's in the Kitchen

First things first: Asian cuisine is still strong. Vancouverites love their sushi, and there's been no appreciable slowdown in the move toward *nouvelle* Japanese cuisine that began in the '80s. You can get authentic fish soup and raw fish that may have spent the morning in Japan.

The Yaletown and Commercial districts are the two hot dining spots of the moment, with growing concentrations of microbreweries and bistros.

Other trends happening now:

  ✔ Locally caught salmon is still — and will probably always be — a perennial favorite amongst West Coasters. On just about every menu in town, you find salmon raw (as sushi), grilled, or smoked. No matter how you eat it, it has been fresh caught (not farmed) somewhere in the province and is undoubtedly delicious.

✔ Vancouver's "tapasing" out! Not all good things come in small, dim sum–style packages; Spanish tapas-style restaurants have blossomed in the city, a bonus if you like to nibble on delicacies such as grilled Japanese eggplant, deep-fried calamari, and other treats at places like **La Bodega** or **Bin 942 Tapas Parlour** (see the "Vancouver's Best Restaurants" section later in the chapter).

✔ Also red-hot (literally) on the dining scene is the hot pot. Not the handy heating device so popular in the '80s, but a scheme by which you pay to cook your own meal. Each table comes equipped with a little stove, and you select a broth and fillings. The menu is Chinese or Japanese; most folks opt for live *prawns* (basically, big shrimp) or *geoduck* (jumbo clams native to the Pacific, pronounced GOO-eeey-duck). Then you dunk the fillings in the hot broth until they don't move any more, and it's time to eat. A great place for this is **Landmark Hot Pot House** (see the "Vancouver's Best Restaurants" section).

✔ Everybody thought rich, classic French food was a thing of the past when *nouvelle* French hit in the health-conscious early '80s. Well, guess what? What's old is new again. At such places as **Le Crocodile** and **Fleuri,** Vancouverites are enjoying traditional French cuisine — mega-calories and all, with buttery cream sauces, cheese for dessert (Camembert, chèvre, and Brie), and meat carved right at the table. Bring on the cherries jubilee! (See the "Vancouver's Best Restaurants" section for both places.)

Searching Out Where the Locals Eat

Most locals seem to agree that eating "local" in Vancouver doesn't mean any one thing — in fact, it can mean just about anything. Locals are made up of just about every ethnic group on the planet, so eating sushi or biryani is just as typically Vancouver as noshing on fish 'n' chips. See the "Vancouver's Ethnic Eats" section later in this chapter for my top spots for ethnic cuisine.

Anglo favorites (after all, this is *British* Columbia) include, you guessed it, fish 'n' chips, as well as pub grub (see the "Fish and pub grub" section later in this chapter). And, not to be outdone by Victoria, you'll find traditional high tea (basically, tea with sweets, scones, and dainty sandwiches) in one or two hotels such as the **Sutton Place Hotel** (see the listing for Fleuri later in this chapter), **Hotel Vancouver** (see Chapter 15), and the **Crown Plaza Georgia Hotel** (see Chapter 9); tea aficionados should check out the cute little specialty tea restaurant, the **Secret Garden Tea Room** (see the "Sweets to eat" section in this chapter).

Most local foods associated with Vancouver come from the sea. Beyond fried fish, try alder-grilled salmon at the **Liliget Feasthouse** or the hot-smoked fish known as "Indian Candy." Dungeness Crab, geoduck, rock cod, and West Coast oysters all grace the menus of hot spots like

Vancouver Dining and Snacking

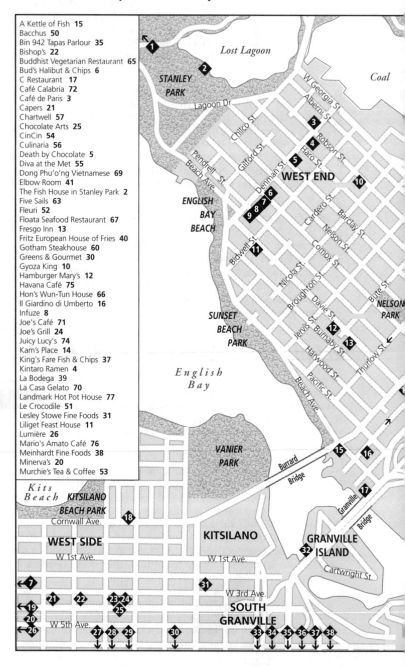

A Kettle of Fish **15**
Bacchus **50**
Bin 942 Tapas Parlour **35**
Bishop's **22**
Buddhist Vegetarian Restaurant **65**
Bud's Halibut & Chips **6**
C Restaurant **17**
Café Calabria **72**
Café de Paris **3**
Capers **21**
Chartwell **57**
Chocolate Arts **25**
CinCin **54**
Culinaria **56**
Death by Chocolate **5**
Diva at the Met **55**
Dong Phu'o'ng Vietnamese **69**
Elbow Room **41**
The Fish House in Stanley Park **2**
Five Sails **63**
Fleuri **52**
Floata Seafood Restaurant **67**
Fresgo Inn **13**
Fritz European House of Fries **40**
Gotham Steakhouse **60**
Greens & Gourmet **30**
Gyoza King **10**
Hamburger Mary's **12**
Havana Café **75**
Hon's Wun-Tun House **66**
Il Giardino di Umberto **16**
Infuze **8**
Joe's Café **71**
Joe's Grill **24**
Juicy Lucy's **74**
Kam's Place **14**
King's Fare Fish & Chips **37**
Kintaro Ramen **4**
La Bodega **39**
La Casa Gelato **70**
Landmark Hot Pot House **77**
Le Crocodile **51**
Lesley Stowe Fine Foods **31**
Liliget Feast House **11**
Lumière **26**
Mario's Amato Café **76**
Meinhardt Fine Foods **38**
Minerva's **20**
Murchie's Tea & Coffee **53**

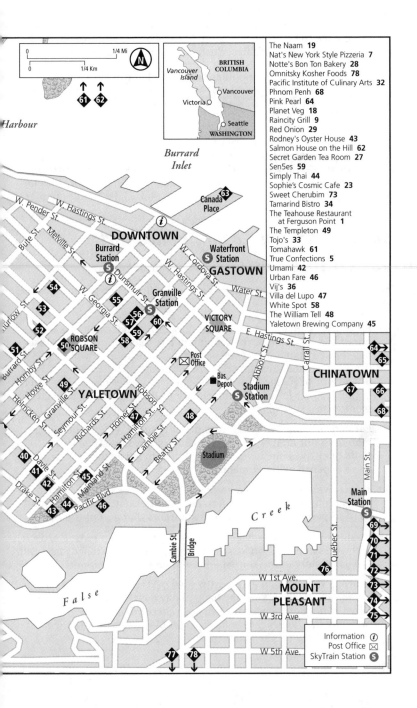

The Naam **19**
Nat's New York Style Pizzeria **7**
Notte's Bon Ton Bakery **28**
Omnitsky Kosher Foods **78**
Pacific Institute of Culinary Arts **32**
Phnom Penh **68**
Pink Pearl **64**
Planet Veg **18**
Raincity Grill **9**
Red Onion **29**
Rodney's Oyster House **43**
Salmon House on the Hill **62**
Secret Garden Tea Room **27**
Sen5es **59**
Simply Thai **44**
Sophie's Cosmic Cafe **23**
Sweet Cherubim **73**
Tamarind Bistro **34**
The Teahouse Restaurant
  at Ferguson Point **1**
The Templeton **49**
Tojo's **33**
Tomahawk **61**
True Confections **5**
Umami **42**
Urban Fare **46**
Vij's **36**
Villa del Lupo **47**
White Spot **58**
The William Tell **48**
Yaletown Brewing Company **45**

Information (i)
Post Office ✉
SkyTrain Station Ⓢ

C Restaurant. Trendy locals — or stars in town shooting movies and pretending to be locals — also prefer the upscale ambience of **CinCin,** where you have to be up on the latest clothing and music to even *think* of eating. (See "Vancouver's Best Restaurants" for all three places.)

Burgers remain enduringly popular here as well, both at chains (check out the beloved **White Spot**) and a host of drive-ins and diners. See the "Burgered and fried" section later in this chapter for my recommendations.

But just as there's a yin for every yang, vegetarians also make up a huge part of the population — especially in the once-hippy, now-yuppy Kitsilano district — and are well served by places such as **The Naam** on West 4th Avenue (see "Vancouver's Best Restaurants"). For more vegetarian options, see "Restaurant rescue for vegetarians" later in this chapter.

Eating Out without Losing Your Shirt: Tips for Cutting Costs

Here are some of my favorite insider's tips for dining inexpensively while in Vancouver:

- ✔ **Picnic.** Vancouver's year-round mild weather makes picnicking a possibility any time of year; inquire if a restaurant provides a take-out service (sometimes even an expensive restaurant will do this). Picnicking eliminates the pressure to tip and order appetizers, dessert, or beverages. See "Urban-guerrilla power picnicking" later in this chapter for my recommendations on where to pick up great picnic fare.

- ✔ **Eat your big meal at lunch rather than dinner.** Often, you can get more for your money this way, because many mid-range restaurants offer the same items on their lunch menu as they do on a more expensive dinner menu.

- ✔ **Take advantage of club memberships.** Use your membership in an automobile club such as AAA to receive discounts (usually around 10 to 15 percent of your bill) at restaurants that accept the card.

- ✔ **Double up.** Take advantage of two-for-one specials often advertised in the free weekly *Georgia Straight* newspaper or the daily *Vancouver Sun.* Or inquire at the Tourist InfoCentre for other coupons.

- ✔ **Share.** Either split an entree with your partner or, if eating alone, ask for a half-order. You may have to pay a little extra for the additional plate, but the vast majority of Vancouver's mid- or budget-priced restaurants seem to have no problem with the practice. (I wouldn't try this in a fancy place.)

Dressing to dine

In Vancouver, almost anything goes. Almost. This is the West Coast, after all, so most restaurants are pretty casual. You see everything from in-line skaters noshing on wrap sandwiches at a chic sidewalk cafe on Denman Street to sailors throwing back microbrews at waterfront bars on False Creek.

That's not to say you shouldn't dress up on occasion, however. You may see the pre-theater crowd dining elegantly in the latest designer creations, for example, at the many fabulous downtown hotel restaurants. My general rule? If you plan to dine at a place where reservations are either required or recommended — I tell you which do in "Vancouver's Best Restaurants" — call ahead to find out whether they have a dress code. Most places accept "refined casual," a fuzzy term that seems to have expanded generously to mean anything from Armani threads to pressed designer jeans with a $150 T-shirt. Otherwise, don't sweat it.

✔ **Pay one price for an unlimited meal.** At all-you-can-eat buffets, you can eat more than your fill — and you won't have to tip, either, if the restaurant doesn't have table service. Many East Indian and other Asian restaurants in the city offer these buffets at lunchtime and on the weekends. Ask, too, about fixed-price menus. Many restaurants offer these three- and four-course meals as early-bird-special dinners which, if you go easy on the wine, represent terrific value.

✔ **Go lowbrow.** Despite its glitzy profile, Vancouver still has lots of cheap diners where real people eat plain meals at low prices — you just need to get away from the main tourist areas to find them. The food is hearty and crazy cheap, cooked breakfast being the biggest bargain. For recommendations, see "Grease is the word: The best diners" later in this chapter.

✔ **Eat in.** Some suite-style hotels provide in-room refrigerators, microwaves, or both, and you can prepare small meals in these rooms when you don't feel like going out to eat. Around the city you find plenty of supermarkets and natural food stores, as well as farmer's markets on Granville Island, Robson Street, and Lonsdale Quay.

✔ **Eat your vegetables.** Vancouver offers a healthy quantity of vegetarian restaurants to pick from, and one more hidden benefit of these good-for-you places is meals at a fraction of the cost of meat-oriented menus. Some Chinese restaurants in the city are also completely vegetarian, and offer shockingly realistic *faux* meat, poultry, and shellfish entrees that nearly outshine the real thing. Again, you pay less while eating healthfully.

> ✔ **Go to school.** The Pacific Institute of Culinary Arts (1505 2nd Ave., Granville Island, ☎ **800-416-4040** or 604-734-4488) offers two-for-one lunch and dinner specials on Mondays and Tuesdays (and all week long from January through March). Executive-chefs-in-training provide gourmet meals at low prices. **Culinaria** (609 Granville St. ☎ **604-639-2055**), the school restaurant run by Dubrelle Culinary Arts, also offers some decent deals.

Vancouver's Best Restaurants

This section includes my recommendations of the best places to dine. For a quick listing of restaurants by neighborhood, cuisine, and price, check out the index at the end of the chapter. For a key to the dollar sign ratings, see the Introduction to this book.

As in any large city, the finest restaurants are popular, and reservations are not only sensible but also often required. In each listing, I tell you which restaurants require you to call ahead to guarantee a table.

A Kettle of Fish
$$$–$$$$ **Downtown   SEAFOOD**

This cheerful restaurant near the Burrard Bridge urges guests to "Eat Lotsa Fish," and here you can do it — easily. Naturally, the star attractions on the changing menu are locally caught: British Columbia salmon, Dungeness crab, spotted prawns (you may know them as tiger shrimp), sea scallops, and Sunshine Coast red snapper, all prepared with care and creativity. The combination seafood medley plate offers a chance to stretch your taste buds and try a little of everything. Tired of fish? The kitchen also grills steak, and roasts items such as chestnut-stuffed lamb. The atmosphere is surprisingly casual in spite of the prices, and as a result, the crowd can get a little tourist-heavy. Save room for something off the lengthy dessert menu.

See map p. 110. 900 Pacific St. ☎ *604-682-6661. Reservations recommended. Main courses: C$22–C$40 (US$18–US$33). AE, DC, MC, V. Open: Dinner daily.*

Bacchus
$$$–$$$$ **Downtown   CONTINENTAL**

One of the top picks in town for a splurge, this place isn't for the faint of culinary heart. Sequestered in the terrific Wedgewood Hotel (see Chapter 9), it's designed with romance in mind with a limestone fireplace, lots of silk and velvet drapes, gorgeous wood paneling, and an intimate piano bar. The food itself blends classic French and Italian cuisine with West Coast influences — venison with warm parsnip mouseline, for example, or Chardonnay-steamed local clams, or butternut squash ravioli. Dessert includes some exquisite French pastries, and you'll find a *very* complete wine list. Bacchus is lovely respite for afternoon tea after a hard day's shopping along Robson Street.

See map p. 111. 845 Hornby St. (in the Wedgewood Hotel). ☎ *604-608-5319. Reservations required. Main courses: C$29–C$40 (US$24–US$33). AE, DC, MC, V. Open: Breakfast, lunch, and dinner daily.*

Bin 942 Tapas Parlour
$$–$$$$ **South Granville PACIFIC NORTHWEST/FUSION**

Small, funky, and always lively until closing time at 2 a.m., "the bins" as they are affectionately called (there's another location at 941 Davie St. ☎ **604-683-1246**) deliver a variety of tapas-tizers alongside an equally impressive wine list. Every plate is C$12 (US$10), which sounds reasonable until you realize how good they are and you start to create an entire dinner from them. Items include skilleted smoked Alaska black cod, scallop and tiger prawn tournedos, and confit of duck. As for bin's dessert tapas (all at C$7 (US$5.80)), try this on for size: Baked double cream pistachio crusted French Brie wedge, warm blackberry honey-rosemary nectar, blackberry coulis, and gingerbread biscotti. Phew . . . all that and so much more on such a small plate.

See map p. 110. 1521 West Broadway. ☎ *604-734-9421. Reservations not accepted. Main courses: C$12 (US$10). AE, DC, MC, V. Open: Dinner daily.*

Bishop's
$$$$ **Kitsilano PACIFIC NORTHWEST/FUSION**

This Kitsilano star has been drawing big-ticket actors, politicians, and the like almost since the moment it opened during the mid 1980s. Despite his A-list clientele, however, owner John Bishop prides himself on warm personal service and welcomes all to his minimalist room. The kitchen features the best in fresh local ingredients; appetizers are straightforward (a romaine salad topped with warm goat cheese, toasted pecans, and drizzled with a tangy blackberry vinaigrette, or a smoked-salmon salad), while the main dishes are hearty yet refined: roasted duck breast with cider-braised cabbage and potato croquette, pan-seared scallops with inventive sauces, and grilled lamb. All receive rave reviews — and return visits. The pastry staff is solid, too, fashioning a selection of crème brulées, ginger cake with toffee sauce, and homemade Irish whiskey ice cream.

See map p. 110. 2183 West 4th Ave. ☎ *604-738-2025. Reservations required. Main courses: C$30–C$38 (US$25–US$32). AE, DC, MC, V. Open: Dinner daily.*

C Restaurant
$$$–$$$$ **Downtown SEAFOOD**

This waterside seafood restaurant is constantly raising the bar with its cutting-edge take on the genre. Quebec-born chef Robert Clark (who also owns Raincity Grill) takes the high road on fish and chips: Caviar is one of C's signature appetizers (served in a gold-leaf pouch), as do his lobster bisque and delicious maple-glazed sardines. Main courses incorporate a dazzling Asian influence as well as some rather unexpected Indian and even Middle Eastern touches; expect mind-blowing pairings such as soft-shell crabs with samosas of peas and sweet potato, scallops with smoked-bacon hash and a birch syrup, and pan-roasted scallops with gnocchi and fried capers. Clark also offers a vertical bento *tasting box* (C$35 (US$29)) that lays out a rich quartet of small portions packed with taste punch — it includes signature smoked salmon, side-striped shrimp, yellowfin tuna tartare and a Dungeness crab salad. The wine list here is heavy on Alsatian whites, while desserts show a light touch — or, if you want to finish heavily, select from a cart of French cheeses.

See map p. 110. 1600 Howe St. ☎ *604-681-1164. Reservations recommended. Main courses: C$28–C$50 (US$23–US$42). AE, DC, MC, V. Open: Lunch and dinner daily.*

Café de Paris
$$$–$$$$ West End   FRENCH

Stuck right amid the full-throttle activity along busy Denman Street, this bistro really does feel like one in 1920s Paris or Montreal, from the wall art to the smoky music in the air. In fact, it's the oldest traditional French eatery in town. Yet you won't have to worry about pronouncing menu items correctly; service is refreshingly unpretentious. Everything is steadfastly Franco: densely cheesy onion soup, beef tartare, escargot, fish stew, steak and excellent *pommes frites,* and all the rest. Wash it down with something from the wine list (plenty of big bouncy reds and bubbly whites). Of course, it wouldn't be a French dining experience without a delectable dessert — say, the discomfortingly comforting chocolate cake. And don't forget an aperitif or a coffee. Feeling full? Pull those in-line skates out, strap 'em on, and race your pals around Stanley Park. If you dare.

See map p. 110. 751 Denman St. ☎ *604-687-1418. Reservations recommended. Main courses: C$25–C$40 (US$21–US$33). AE, MC, V. Open: Lunch Mon–Fri, dinner daily.*

Chartwell
$$$$ Downtown   PACIFIC NORTHWEST/FUSION

This superb restaurant inside the expensive Four Seasons Hotel (see Chapter 9) has the ambience of an upper-crust British club — put it this way, the fireplace is accented with lovely landscapes, beautifully framed, and is surrounded by leather chairs — yet without the stuffy service you may expect. This is a good spot for pre-theater meals, with staff delivering timely and unharried service to ensure that you make the curtain call. The food is stellar, from deliciously simple filet mignon or rack of lamb to a teasing of the expected — suckling wild boar, seared halibut, and honey mussel ragout salmon. The wine list is among the best in the city — a good place to try something local.

See map p. 111. 791 West Georgia St. (in the Four Seasons Hotel). ☎ *604-689-9333. Reservations required for dinner. Main courses: C$24–C$45 (US$20–US$37). AE, DC, DISC, MC, V. Open: Dinner daily.*

CinCin
$$$–$$$$ **Downtown   ITALIAN**

Robson Street doesn't suffer from a lack of glitz and glamour, but the Italian-fusion CinCin is the icing on the cake. A decidedly hip and trendy (and famous) crowd comes in search of inventive pizzas and pastas concocted in the open-concept kitchen's roaring, wood-fired ovens. Begin with complimentary out-of-the-ordinary fresh bread and olive tapenade spread, perhaps an appetizer of hand-formed *bocconcini* (that's fresh mozzarella) and organic tomato salad; then go for the gusto with a pizza of smoked salmon, caramelized onions, capers, and *crème fraîche*. Or try veal tenderloin scalloppini baked with white polenta cup stuffed with mixed mushrooms, young Gorgonzola and sweet marsala sauce. The restaurant features quite a good vegetarian menu, as well, and the sweets afterward include melt-in-your mouth *panna cotta* or a three-nut caramel tart. Just remember to display your peanut-sized cellphone prominently at your table at all times, or you're nobody.

See map p. 111. 1154 Robson St. ☎ 604-688-7338. Reservations recommended. Main courses: C$18–C$44 (US$15–US$37). AE, DC, MC, V. Open: Lunch Mon to Fri; dinner daily.

Diva at the Met
$$$$ **Downtown   PACIFIC NORTHWEST/FUSION**

A pre- and post-theater hotspot inside a hotel, Diva at the Met is quite simply one of the best meals Vancouver has to offer. The menu takes cuisines from France, Italy, and Asia and shakes them up with fresh, local ingredients: lobster gnocchi, ahi tuna tartare and marinated sashimi, smoked salmon caviar with Yuza soya vinaigrette, cinnamon smoked duck breast with parsnip risotto, poached wecle pear wedge, and lapin cherry jus. Whatever you do, don't forget to order from the extensive cellar of British Columbian wines, and don't leave without a slice of English cheesecake. Brunch is terrific, as well.

See map p. 111. 645 Howe St. (in the Metropolitan Hotel). ☎ 604-602-7788. Reservations recommended. Main courses: C$26–C$40 (US$22–US$33). AE, DC, MC, V. Open: Breakfast, lunch, and dinner daily.

The Fish House in Stanley Park
$$–$$$$ **West End   SEAFOOD**

This venerable institution capitalizes on its equally venerable location — planted firmly in the heart of Stanley Park, away from tour buses and in-line skaters — then serves up great West Coast meals. Chef Karen Barnaby has created some *nouvelle* combinations, such as risotto with seared sablefish, clams, mussels, and chorizo sausages, as well as low-carb choices and guilt-free desserts. The fresh sheet changes constantly, the oyster bar and a dish of flaming prawns add some spark, and favorites (a hearty portion of clam chowder; fresh salmon cakes and a mean rib-eye steak) are comfort-food standbys. In good weather, enjoy your meal out on the porch.

See map p. 110. 2099 Beach Ave. ☎ 877-681-7275 or 604-681-7275. Reservations recommended. Main courses: C$10–C$28 (US$8–US$23). AE, DC, MC, V. Open: Lunch and dinner daily.

Five Sails
$$$–$$$$ **Downtown** **PACIFIC NORTHWEST/FUSION**

The mountain and water views alone would be reason enough to dine here, but the food is spectacularly fancy — pricey, though not pretentious. The excellent, restrained menu runs mostly to Canadian meat, seafood, and vegetables; think spiced hazelnut-crusted halibut finished with white and green asparagus, wild mushrooms and watercress emulsion, chilled lobster salad, a local rack of lamb crusted with macadamia nuts, Alberta steaks, or a seafood sampler (scallops, prawns, and fresh fish of the day). They take the whiskey and wine lists very seriously, and the chocolate ice-cream bonbons served afterward are sublime. Whatever your reasons to come here, you won't leave hungry or disappointed — or wealthy.

See map p. 111. 999 Canada Place. ☎ 604-891-2892. Reservations required. Main courses: C$26–C$45 (US$22–US$37). AE, DC, MC, V. Open: Dinner daily.

Fleuri
$$$–$$$$ **Downtown** **PACIFIC NORTHWEST/FUSION**

Located inside the Sutton Place Hotel (see Chapter 9), the restaurant continues to be a magnet for the celebrity clientele who stay at the hotel. While the menu is certainly good (a combination of French and Italian tastes with a British Columbia twist), what's really worth noting is the preponderance of rather lavish buffets: daily afternoon high teas with scones, clotted cream, and all the fixings; a seafood buffet on Friday and Saturday nights; a Sunday brunch widely applauded as one of the town's best; and a weekend dessert bar that turns every Thursday, Friday, and Saturday into chocoholic madness with anything from chocolate mousse to truffles to daring creations such as a chocolate fruit pizza or non-chocolate crêpes with ice cream. Definitely a place to see and be seen — and eat well.

See map p. 111. 845 Burrard St. (in the Sutton Place Hotel). ☎ 604-642-2900. Reservations recommended. Main courses: C$15–C$30 (US$12–US$25). AE, DC, DISC, MC, V. Open: Lunch and dinner daily.

Floata Seafood Restaurant
$$–$$$$ **Chinatown** **CHINESE**

Some of the city's best dim sum is served at this enormous Chinatown favorite, which actually has its roots in Hong Kong. The lunchtime cuisine, served from those ubiquitous dim sum carts, is just what you'd expect — a wide variety of steamed buns filled with pork, stir-fries, roasted duck or pork, fried or steamed spring rolls, and much more — and the dinner entrees are better than you may expect. All in all, expect about 80 items to choose from. Don't come for a quiet meal; this place gets mobbed at lunch.

They have another location in the southern suburb of Richmond (☎ 604-270-8889), but parking there can be difficult (unlike the six-story parkade in Chinatown).

See map p. 111. 180 Keefer St. (restaurant located on 3rd floor). ☎ 604-270-0368. Reservations recommended. Main courses: C$5–C$30 (US$4.15–US$25). AE, DC, MC, V. Open: Breakfast, lunch, and dinner daily.

Gotham Steakhouse
$$$–$$$$ Downtown STEAK

Now that eating red meat is hip again, restaurateurs are capitalizing on the latest carnivore carnival — and Gotham Steakhouse delivers the goods in spades, albeit at top dollar. Diners are young, urban, and wealthy and appreciate management's single-minded efforts to create an upscale ode to maleness and meat. The bar is long and picks up volume as the night progresses. Steak is the star (only the best aged beef from the United States and Canada makes it here), grilled in huge, tender cuts and paired with plenty of good red wine choices to match; sides are more filling then inventive, with creamed spinach, sautéed mushrooms, fries, and more. Given the size and expense, sharing a meal between two people is not out of the question.

See map p. 111. 615 Seymour St. ☎ 604-605-8282. Reservations recommended. Main courses: C$27–C$50 (US$22–US$42). AE, DC, MC, V. Open: Breakfast, lunch, and dinner daily.

Gyoza King
$–$$ West End JAPANESE

Gyoza, a Japanese take on potstickers or ravioli, are practically the only menu item at this wildly popular West End eatery, which offers about two dozen moderately priced variations. To make them, half-moon dumplings are filled with pork, veggies, or shellfish, tarted up with spices, and then deep-fried. Also on the board: a few sushi items and daily specials such as *udon* and *o-den* soups. Beer and wine are available to drink, and the place sucks a constant stream of patrons in from Robson Street's busy stretch — anyone from Japanese students and tourists to residents of the local neighborhood. Be patient with the staff, though, as some speak rather limited English.

See map p. 110. 1508 Robson St. ☎ 604-669-8278. Reservations not necessary. Main courses: C$6–C$12 (US$5–US$10). AE, DC, MC, V. Open: Lunch and dinner daily.

Havana Café
$$ Commercial Drive CUBAN

Long-renowned as one of the city's finest authentic, ethnic restaurant/ art gallery combos, Havana's decor is an ocular feast — the walls are garnished with a seemingly limitless array of cigar boxes, Cuban flags, communist manifestos, sepia photos, and perhaps even locks of Castro's. The food, too, hits your senses with its Latin flair: Cuban-style black bean soup,

Creole prawns sautéed in Cajun spice and baby back ribs in a lime-chili BBQ sauce. The Cuban-fried chicken wrap is delicious. Yes, it sells Cuban cigars (smoke 'em 'round the back on the outside patio). The adjoining gallery and tiny 60-seat theater are both very avant-garde and sometimes downright weird in their presentations.

See map p. 111. 1212 Commercial Dr. ☎ *604-253-9119. Reservations not accepted. Main courses: C$11–C$20 (US$9–US$17). AE, MC, V. Open: Lunch and dinner daily; breakfast Sat and Sun.*

Hon's Wun-Tun House
$-$$ Chinatown CHINESE

Love it or hate it, the original Hon's is a legend in Vancouver — real Chinese served in a really crazy, communal atmosphere. It's fast, cheap, and tasty, and although some of the foods may be foreign to your palate, you have to try them; the menu runs to more than three hundred dishes. Specialties include stir-fried shrimp — sorry, prawns — in black bean sauce, Shanghai fried noodles with shredded beef, a range of *congee* (rice porridge) dishes, and much more. Side dishes keep things interesting as well, with items such as curry beef brisket and potato, steamed sticky rice wrap, and mini flour buns — fun just to say, not to mention eat! Finish off with a sweet dessert such as chilled coconut-and-red-bean cake. Hon's has become a local chain in recent years, and has another, more upscale branch at 1339 Robson St. (☎ **604-685-0871**), which lacks the authentic, gritty feel of the original. The Robson location does, however, do takeout.

See map p. 111. 268 Keefer St. ☎ *604-688-0871. Reservations not accepted. Main courses: C$5–C$15 (US$4.15–US$12). Credit cards not accepted at this location. Open: Lunch and dinner daily.*

Il Giardino di Umberto
$$$-$$$$ Downtown ITALIAN

Umberto Menghi is the proud founder of this Tuscan star, with a menu of simple yet satisfying cuisine and a restaurant itself resembling a villa from that fair land — all wood-beamed ceilings, garden flowers, and hushed tones. The menu focuses on classic pasta *primi piatti* (first courses), such as linguine with pesto, tortellini *con panna,* cannelloni filled with game meats, or spaghetti carbonara. The *secondi* (main courses) are heavy on game and other meat dishes such as roasted pheasant breast with wild mushrooms, roasted reindeer loin, and veal in a rosemary-accented wine jus. The wine list is pretty darned good, too. When you call to reserve, try for a choice seat in the garden terrace — likely the prettiest in the city.

See map p. 110. 1382 Hornby St. ☎ *604-669-2422. Main courses: C$15–C$35 (US$12–US$29). Reservations recommended. AE, DC, MC, V. Open: Lunch Mon–Fri, dinner daily except Sun.*

La Bodega
$–$$$ Downtown   SPANISH

Tapas, small plates of exquisite dishes that are Spanish in origin, have taken Vancouver by storm — and La Bodega offers some of the best. Most places fuse the form with Pacific Rim styles. However, *this* tapas bar stays the course and remains traditionally Spanish: Menu items — over half of which are under C$10 (US$8.30) — run to rabbit, blood sausage, chicken livers, garlic prawns, pan-fried squid, and plenty of salty olives. The room is rather low lit — on the upside, a good place to snuggle, although you can't exactly make out all the foods or faces. Be sure to try a glass of Spanish or Portuguese wine.

See map p. 111. 1277 Howe St. ☎ *604-684-8814. Reservations accepted. Main courses: C$7–C$15 (US$5.80–US$12). AE, MC, V. Open: Lunch Fri only; dinner daily.*

Landmark Hot Pot House
$$–$$$ Shaughnessy   CHINESE

Few places in town do hot pots better than Vancouver's original hot pot hotspot, south of the city center but pretty close to Queen Elizabeth Park and its conservatory. You get to do the cooking for a change; yes, you. You're presented with a choice of soup bases — chicken and seafood are popular — that are heated on a gas burner at your table. Then you dip raw meat, seafood, or live shellfish into the hot stock and hold it there until it's done, and pop it into your mouth. Simple, trendy, healthy — but why do I have to tip? Shouldn't *they* be tipping *me?*

See map p. 111. 4023 Cambie St. ☎ *604-872-2868. Reservations not necessary. Main courses: C$10–C$20 (US$8–US$17). MC, V. Open: Dinner daily.*

Le Crocodile
$$$–$$$$ Downtown   FRENCH

Run by a transplanted Alsatian, this bright, award-winning restaurant features classic French cuisine with a slight nod to that region's German-tinged food as well. That means the menu is heavy on fatty, filling food; best bets are the onion tart, sautéed Dover sole, and game dishes. You'll want to complement the meal with a glass of wine, mostly (of course) French, and it goes without saying that dessert will be a memorable chocolatey or cheesy something.

See map p. 111. 909 Burrard St. ☎ *604-669-4298. Reservations recommended. Main courses: C$15–C$38 (US$12–US$32). AE, DC, MC, V. Open: Lunch Mon–Fri, dinner Mon–Sat.*

Liliget Feast House
$$$–$$$$ West End   NATIVE CANADIAN

If there's one restaurant you've simply got to see while in Vancouver, this is it: an authentic Native-Canadian house right in the city's hip West End with big platters of Native cuisine. You sit at wooden tables in a dining room decorated with Coast Salish touches, including a pebbled floor and cedar walls. The meal begins with a warmed flatbread called *bannock,* then crisped kelp, salmon soup, or wind-cured almond. The main dishes are simple yet full of flavor — grilled halibut, smoked cod, grilled salmon, and platters of seafood. The Liliget Feast is made for sharing between two people: a sampler of buffalo, venison, duck, and oysters, plus sides of whatever's in season: fern shoots, sweet potatoes, hazelnuts, wild rice. You can also order various poached fish dishes with interesting sauces, or wild caribou with Saskatoon berry sauce. Owner Dolly Watts is always pleased to guide you through the menu so that you'll leave with a first-hand knowledge of Native West Coast foodways, as well as a full stomach.

See map p. 110. 1724 Davie St. ☎ *604-681-7044. Main courses: C$18–C$28 (US$15–US$23). Reservations recommended. AE, DC, MC, V. Open: Dinner daily (closed Mon and Tues in winter).*

Lumière
$$$$ Kitsilano FRENCH

The sunny cuisine of Provence is featured at this excellent West Side bistro, which also tosses in the occasional Asian or Pacific accent. Chef Rob Feenie is so dedicated to his craft that he regularly visits the region to bone up on techniques and get fresh ideas. In fact, he's so darn good that he recently won the coveted title of Iron Chef (see Chapter 25). Everything's good, but sample the tasting menus if you can — they include vegetarian, seafood, and other combinations designed to give a range of tastes (most cost C$60–C$90/US$50–US$75 apiece); they're so changeable and eclectic that I can't even begin to describe them. Just trust Feenie's judgment, and come armed to discover challenging and thrilling new food combinations. If you're not feeling quite so flush, eat at the bar — you can sample simpler plates for C$12 (US$10) a throw or check out his relatively new bistro, **Feenies,** 2563 West Broadway (☎ 604-739-7115), a few doors along.

See map p. 110. 2551 West Broadway. ☎ *604-739-8185. Reservations recommended. Main courses: C$25–C$35 (US$21–US$29). AE, DC, MC, V. Open: Dinner daily except Mon.*

The Naam
$–$$ Kitsilano VEGETARIAN

The city's undisputed top vegetarian nosh, this Kitsilano standby has been serving up salads, sandwiches, and breakfast — and maintaining its hippie vibe — for 30 years now. Despite the yuppification of the neighborhood, you'll still feel the laid-back (maybe *too* laid-back) charm that this always-open health food emporium delivers. People come for a variety of meatless variations on ethnic cuisines, plus interesting side dishes, always served in big, tasty portions; top sellers include the sesame-spiced fries (to which you can add miso gravy or cheese) and quesadillas on grilled whole-wheat tortillas. The breakfasts of French toast, fruit, baked goods, and the like are also terrific. Slow service has been a problem plaguing this institution since the early years — and it isn't getting any faster. My advice? Don't show up starving.

See map p. 110. 2724 West 4th Ave. ☎ *604-738-7151. Reservations not accepted. Main courses: C$4–C$11 (US$3.30–US$9). AE, MC, V. Open: Breakfast, lunch, and dinner daily; open 24 hours.*

Phnom Penh
$–$$ Chinatown   VIETNAMESE

Considered the most authentic of the many Vietnamese restaurants in Vancouver, Phnom Penh serves up delicious — dare I say, Phnom-enal? — and cheap food in a pleasant setting. You'll be amazed at the flavor of dishes such as marinated butter beef, deep-fried squid or prawns, garlic chili squid, or hot-and-sour soup. Other standards for updated taste buds include beef brochettes and deep-fried spring rolls; vegetarian offerings are imaginative and tasty, as well. All of it should be accompanied by sweet Vietnamese coffee, either hot or iced, and a subtly sweetened dessert such as white bean pudding with coconut milk.

See map p. 111. 244 East Georgia St. ☎ *604-682-5777. Reservations not accepted. Main courses: C$5–C$15 (US$4.15–US$12). DC, MC. Open: Lunch and dinner Wed–Mon.*

Pink Pearl
$–$$$ Chinatown   CHINESE

A great place for dim sum, seafood or just something a little different, the Pink Pearl is the kind of place where big Chinese families congregate for both daily meals and big occasions such as weddings — those can get pretty raucous, especially when you consider it can seat 700 diners. Try to ignore the clamor, though, and focus on the food, you'll be well rewarded. Good bets are dishes such as sizzling prawns with ginger and green onions, sautéed scallops with cream-filled crisps, sautéed crab, braised abalone in oyster sauce, or rainbow lettuce wrap. Are you sensing a more playful hand than is normal at a Chinese joint? Well, you're right — there is.

See map p. 111. 1132 East Hastings St. ☎ *604-253-4316. Reservations accepted. Main courses: C$5–C$25 (US$4.15–US$21). AE, DC, MC, V. Open: Breakfast, lunch, and dinner daily.*

Raincity Grill
$$$$ West End   PACIFIC NORTHWEST/FUSION

Locals and tourists love this pleasant restaurant with its great food and million-dollar view of English Bay; they love the place so much that you may not get to enjoy that quiet romantic meal as quietly as you had planned. The chef makes sure ingredients are fresh and interesting — try seared and roasted giant sea scallops, or roasted fish cakes with fennel-carrot slaw, or grilled bison tenderloin. The wine list couldn't be fuller with locally produced bottles. Desserts are rich — a pumpkin tart, chocolate soufflé, and maple-apple-caramel tart are just a few of the caloric offerings. A C$25 (US$21) early-bird, three-course dinner, served between 5 p.m. and 6 p.m., is great value. Weekend brunch features the usual items, with upscale twists: duck sausage, brioche French toast, and the like.

See map p. 110. 1193 Denman St. ☎ *604-685-7337. Reservations recommended. Main courses: C$19–C$33 (US$16–US$27). AE, DC, MC, V. Open: Dinner daily, brunch Sat–Sun.*

Rodney's Oyster House
$$–$$$ Yaletown SEAFOOD

Although other shellfish grace the menu, you come for the oysters and the atmosphere, which gets pretty lively on weekends. The staff is upbeat and knowledgeable, shucking a dozen shells in the blink of an eye. The early evenings are quiet enough to really enjoy the terrific bluesy-jazz music, canned though it is, and if one of the up to 18 varieties of oyster doesn't appeal, then any one of the deeee-licious chowders is bound to hit the spot. The Louisiana wild white shrimp and Fundy scallops might tempt your palate, too.

See map p. 111. 1228 Hamilton St. ☎ *604-609-0080. Main courses: C$12–C$28 (US$10–US$23). AE, DC, MC, V. Open: Lunch and dinner daily.*

Salmon House on the Hill
$$$–$$$$ West Vancouver (North Shore) SEAFOOD

A great place to top off a day of sight-seeing on the North Shore, this restaurant serves up mostly seafood — in fact, mostly salmon, no surprise there — prepared in a variety of ways, most often grilled over alder wood. The ambience is West Coast all the way, with indigenous art lining the cedar walls and an upscale menu. Lunch items are mostly chowders and sandwiches, but come for dinner — even the appetizers are exciting. The Salmon House Sampler flanks three different preparations of the buttery, succulent fish with a variety of salsas and relishes. Main courses also run to grilled fish, lamb, steak, and sesame-encrusted tuna seared rare. Desserts are recommended, too. Sunday brunch is popular for celebratory family affairs, but for my money, the awesome views of the Strait of Georgia, Vancouver's skyline, and the Burrard Inlet just before sundown are the best; there's hardly a better viewpoint.

See map p. 111. 2229 Folkestone Way. ☎ *604-926-3212. Reservations recommended. Main courses: C$25–C$28 (US$21–US$23). AE, DC, MC, V. Open: Lunch and dinner daily.*

Simply Thai
$$–$$$ Yaletown THAI

The decor incorporates a very artsy concept with traditional Thai motifs for a light, fresh, and clean ambience. Located in the heart of Yaletown, and across from Bar None, a popular night spot, the clientele tends to be young and hip. But the appeal goes beyond the two dozen martinis that this restaurant serves up — the food is fabulously prepared by an open kitchen using all the evocative flavors of lemon grass, sweet basil, kaffir lime leaf, pandun leaf, and others to create some of the best, authentic Thai food to come along in a while. The pad thais are numerous and delicious; vegetarians are well-catered-to and the multiple-course set menus (ranging from C$25–C$40 (US$21–US$33)) encourage experimentation to dishes that otherwise you may not have considered.

See map p. 111. 1211 Hamilton St. ☎ 604-642-0123. Reservations recommended. Main courses C$13–C$26 (US$11–US$22). AE, MC, V. Open: Lunch Mon to Fri; dinner daily.

Tamarind Bistro
$–$$ South Granville INDIAN

This funky bistro restaurant is one of the latest arrivals near South Granville, though the cooks behind it have been on Vancouver's dining scene for almost 25 years. Simply stated, the menu is as wild as the decor and so unconventional that it fuels your palate for more. Forget your ho-hum samosas, these tapas-centric plates are filled with lamb korma sutra, mango almond scallops, Bombay blast chicken, char-roasted aubergine crush, masala cheese papadums, and the best spinach panir ever. Salads and desserts are even on the menu, but with a twist. Ever had potato salad spiked with almonds, peanuts, and chickpeas, and a tamarind dressing? Or a chocolate fondue Indianized with cayenne, nutmeg, and cinnamon? The wine list is decent, too, as are the hot chili-inspired martinis.

See map p. 110. 1626 West Broadway. ☎ 604-733-5335. Reservations not accepted. Main course: C$5–C$12 (US$4.15–US$10) AE, DC, MC, V. Open: Dinner daily.

The Teahouse Restaurant at Ferguson Point
$$$$ West End PACIFIC NORTHWEST/FUSION

Dining at the Teahouse is a classic Vancouver experience. First, the setting within the greenery of Stanley Park is simply stunning; second, despite the hordes of tour buses unloading at the door, the food still rates highly. The best seats in the house — even on cloudy day — are inside the all-glass conservatory. I suggest you start your meal with the signature Teahouse button mushrooms packed with crab, prawns, scallions, and Emmenthal cheese; or else try the organic carrot, chive, and Chantilly cream soup. The main menu runs to steak, coffee-roasted duck, and a spicy rack of lamb as well as contemporary West Coast cuisine such as lobster ravioli and sake-marinated scallops. And, if only for the fun of it, you *must* try the signature dessert: Delight of the King — a pastry swan filled with rum custard and cream, all gliding along in a pool of chocolate sauce.

See map p. 110. 7501 Stanley Park Dr. ☎ 800-280-9893 or 604-669-3281. Reservations required. Main courses: C$19–C$29 (US$16–US$24). AE, MC, V. Open: Lunch and dinner daily.

Tojo's
$$–$$$$ South Granville   JAPANESE

A perennial winner as one of the best Japanese eateries in town, you'll be hard pressed to secure a coveted seat at the sushi bar. But it's well worth the effort — these guys are maestros. Sure, the traditionals are here, but they're liberally sprinkled with creations such as steamed Japanese eggplant salad in chilled dashi with green onion, ground ginger, and bonito shavings; and Dungeness crab meat with julienne vegetables and mushrooms topped with white miso sauce and broiled in the shell. Guests sometimes read like a who's who of Hollywood; bring some extra shekels if you're hungry.

See map p. 110. 202–777 West Broadway. ☎ 604-872-8050. Reservations accepted. Main courses: C$17–$45 (US$14–US$37). AE, DC, MC, V. Open: Dinner Mon through Sat.

Umami
$$–$$$ Downtown   JAPANESE

Owned by sommelier Hiro Shintaku, this hidden-away wine bar and restaurant is tiny and inventive — it's the Japanese take on tapas, delivered in duo and trio tapas sized dishes as gastronomic works of art. You may have to wait for this artistry but since the person sitting at the next table is only inches away, you can't help but strike up conversation. Almost half the wines listed are from B.C.

See map p. 111. 572 Davie St. ☎ 604-696-9563. Reservations not accepted. Main courses: C$15–C$30 (US$12–US$25). Open: Dinner daily.

Vij's
$$–$$$ South Granville   INDIAN

Whatever you choose from the ever-changing menu, your choice will be an inspired fusion of Anglo-Indian tastes. Lamb chops are grilled to perfection and come with fenugreek sauce atop, or the selection might feature the duck breast and coconut-green chili rice pilaf in lime leaf curry. The appetizers are equally delicious and can be made into a meal, tapas style. And if you have to line up for a table (a high probability), the wait is bearable as the host circulates tumblers of steaming chai and tidbits to nibble on — tiny potato poori and naan with mint mango chutney, or corn on semolina halva. Next door, Vij's Rangoli opens at noon, offering excellent take-out.

See map p. 110. 1480 West 11th Ave. ☎ 604-736-6664. Reservations not accepted. Main courses: C$18–C$25 (US$15–US$21). AE, DC, MC, V. Open: Dinner daily.

Villa del Lupo
$$$–$$$$ Downtown   ITALIAN

Located in a beautiful heritage house, one of the few remaining in downtown Vancouver, this award-winning restaurant is cosy, elegant, and intimate. Food is Italian with a West Coast twist; chefs create dishes such as ahi tuna loin vegetable ragot, braised wild boar fettuccine, and lemon fish filet with bay scallops. Service really makes you feel, well, at home. Check out their most popular item — the lamb osso bucco — and the three- and four-course dinners (C$67–C$80 (US$56–US$67)).

See map p. 111. 896 Hamilton St. ☎ 604-688-7436. Reservations recommended. Main courses: C$22 –C$35 (US$18–US$29). AE, DC, MC, V. Open: Dinner daily.

The William Tell
$$–$$$$ **Downtown   CONTINENTAL**

Swiss food in Vancouver? Who'd have thunk it. Yet it's true — this opulent hotel restaurant serves anything from *rösti* (a Swiss potato pancake) to *raclette* (French cheese, melted and spread on split potatoes), plus a good deal more continental cuisine. Everyone from the resident glitterati to local office workers sing the praises of the top-notch menu, which includes stunners such as veal and mushrooms in wine sauce with *rösti;* breast of duck with baked layered yams in a maple sauce; and a very good steak tartare. Desserts are no holds barred, including an exceptional array of flaming table desserts (think crêpes and cherries jubilee), chocolate fondue, and crème brûlée.

See map p. 111. 765 Beatty St. (in the Georgian Court Hotel). ☎ 604-688-3504. Reservations accepted. Main courses: C$12–C$35 (US$10–US$29). AE, DC, MC, V. Open: Breakfast, lunch, and dinner daily; closed daily 2–5 p.m.

Yaletown Brewing Company
$$–$$$ **Yaletown   PUB FARE**

One of the more popular, and boisterous, brewpubs that have sprouted in the formerly working-class Yaletown district, this one serves good meals such as pizza, burgers, ribs, and salmon — all done with a slightly upscale touch to match the yuppified surroundings. It almost goes without saying that you come here more for the beer than for the food, so make sure to try a draft — they even have a classy sampler rack of a half-dozen tiny beers.

See map p. 111. 1110 Mainland St. ☎ 604-681-2739. Reservations: Recommended for dinner. Main courses: C$10–C$30 (US$8–US$25). AE, MC, V. Open: Lunch and dinner daily.

On the Lighter Side: Snacks and Meals on the Go

Vancouver's chockablock with eats, treats, and food on the go. Whether it's swimming in grease, covered in ketchup — sorry there, old chap, I meant malt vinegar — sliced into wedges, wrapped in tortilla shells, or packed in a picnic basket, you'll find it somewhere in town. This section shows you where.

Asian invasion

Asian food remains the chief ethnic influence. Whether you go to the large Hong Kong–style restaurants popping up in southern exurban shopping malls or the tiny, crammed-to-the-gills joints in Chinatown, you'll have no problem finding an authentic dim sum or *congee* (rice porridge) at any number of Chinese eateries.

However, Chinatown has lately been seeing more Vietnamese *pho* noodle shops and Thai eateries move in on its turf. Southeast Asian restaurants are also moving east to the Commercial Drive area, where rents are lower — as is the price of a good meal. Japanese restaurants are mostly concentrated downtown near the Robson Street shopping strip, and they tend to be more expensive as a result, although Japanese food is also gaining a foothold in the Yaletown district. Finally, on both the eastern side of the city and on the West Side, you find East Indian Punjabi merchants with their spice markets and curry houses.

Given all these concentrated pockets of Asian food and ample choices, for me to even attempt any kind of definitive list is foolhardy. Nonetheless, I recommend a number of ethnic restaurants in the "Vancouver's Best Restaurants" section earlier in this chapter. Some cheap and cheerful standouts to watch for include

- ✔ **Kam's Place,** 1043 Davie St. (☎ **604-669-3389**), serves food with a primarily Singaporean accent, although other influences are present, as well. Lunches are cheap here.

- ✔ **Dong Phu'o'ng Vietnamese Restaurant,** 1188 Kingsway (☎ **604-873-6666**), is rather scruffy and its mini-mall location is easily bypassed, but authentic Vietnamese food and friendly service have made this a hot spot for those "in the know."

- ✔ **Kintaro Ramen,** 788 Denman St. (☎ **604-682-7568**), can fill you to the gunnels with delicious Japanese-styled noodles for less than C$10 (US$8.30). The Forest Fire ramens (Saturdays only) are the best in the city.

Zooropa: European eats

Germans and other Eastern Europeans immigrated to downtown Vancouver in the 19th century. In fact, Robson Street was once so full of old European delis featuring sausages, sauerkraut, and schnitzel that it was known as Robsonstrasse (*strasse* is German for "street"). Glitzy stores catering to moneyed tourists have largely replaced these shops, but you can still find European delis and eateries in other corners of the city.

If you're a serious foodie, you can also locate numerous additional pockets of Euro-cooking in the city. Spanish and Portuguese communities are well served by authentic Spanish tapas bars and Portuguese grilled-meat specialists, while Greek immigrants still congregate at authentic *tavernas* on the city's West Side. The city holds other surprises: Commercial

Drive, long the bastion of Italian *trattorias*, has Central Americans filtering into the area and bringing a unique food style with them; as a result, you can now nosh on *tacos*, *papusas*, and barbecued chicken at stands and joints up and down the drive.

Whew! That's a lot of ground — and a lot of calories — to cover. Here are some of the ethnic eateries I like.

- ✔ **Bavaria Restaurant and Deli,** 203 Carrall St. (☎ 604-687-4047), is one of many Eastern European delis in the Gastown area; a good bet for solid German fare.

- ✔ **Fritz European House of Fries,** 718 Davie St. (☎ 604-684-0811), is just what it sounds like: an emporium dedicated to the art of the fry, much like you'd find in any town square in Belgium, with a choice of flavored ketchups and mayonnaise-based sauces.

- ✔ **Minerva's,** 3207 West Broadway (☎ 604-733-3956), is a Greek deli on Broadway that's good for aficionados of moussaka and dolmathes.

- ✔ **Omnitsky Kosher Foods,** 5866 Cambie St. (☎ 604-321-1818), is, quite simply, an old-world Hebrew deli with caloric specials such as corned beef on marble rye, matzoh ball soup, gefilte fish, and brisket. The portions are bigger than enormous.

Gimme a pizza that pie

It's hard to believe you would head all the way to Vancouver on vacation and then eat pizza. Then again, sometimes the urge just strikes. For those times, the C99¢ (US66¢) pizza slice phenomenon is a real bargain, and it's something of a fad among young people in Vancouver right now. Just remember the quality isn't all that consistent.

Still, if you're looking for a quick, cheap bite, dozens of competing places downtown are falling over each other to offer you a drink and a slice for the lowest price. One of my favorite pizzerias has to be **Nat's New York Style Pizzeria,** 1080 Denman St. (☎ 604-642-0777) and 2684 West Broadway (☎ 604-737-0707) — they're the real thing. Thin crust New York Style. Not too much sauce, not too much cheese and dished up in a New York ambiance, without the New York attitude.

Burgered and fried

Vancouver loves its thick and juicy burgers, and you'll be a burgermeister in no time if that's your thing. Naturally, fries and milkshakes are always offered on the side.

The concession stand at Third Beach in Stanley Park is reputed to make some of the best french fries in the city.

✔ **Fresgo Inn,** 1138 Davie St. (☎ **604-689-1332**), a lowbrow West End cafeteria, grills up hamburgers, eggs, and other greasy-spoon fare, and it's open quite late, and 'round-the-clock Friday and Saturday.

✔ **Hamburger Mary's,** 1202 Davie St. (☎ **604-687-1293**), is the burger queen of Vancouver, with a hopping West End location in the midst of the Davie Street action, great fries and shakes, a genuine diner feel, and very late hours. The food's less greasy here than at the more divey places, and it's open from 8 a.m. until 2 a.m. daily.

✔ **Red Onion,** 2028 West 41st Ave. (☎ **604-263-0833**), is a true local's pick, buried in the otherwise toney Kerrisdale neighborhood, not far from the University of British Columbia campus. They make burgers, fries, and sandwiches, but everyone comes for the *double dogs:* two sausages packed into one bun, dripping with toppings, cheese, and sauce.

✔ The one-of-a-kind **Tomahawk,** 1550 Philip Ave. (☎ **604-988-2612**), simply can't be ignored when you're up in North Vancouver. They've gone way over the top with the Native-motif decoration, the menu names, and especially the food, which leans heavily toward stacked burgers and huge wedges of good pie. It's also a solid breakfast option — if you like heavy, cooked breakfasts, that is. Note that this place isn't as cheap as a fast-food burger joint.

✔ **White Spot,** 2518 West Broadway (☎ **604-731-2434**) and 1616 West Georgia St. (☎ **604-681-8034**), is the most locally famous place of all. This tasty provincial hamburger chain was born in the '20s and now boasts dozens of locations around the city; the one on West Broadway still does carhop-at-your-window service. The legendary burger is justly famous for its secret sauce.

Fish and pub grub

Lowbrow chip shops are easy to find around town. Some chippies even still go so far as to swaddle this meal in the traditional newspaper wrapping — find that, and you've probably unearthed a winner.

✔ **Bud's Halibut & Chips,** 1007 Denman St. (☎ **604-683-0661**), is okay, although perhaps a little more famous than it deserves to be. Still, portions are huge.

✔ **King's Fare Fish & Chips,** 1320 West 73rd St., in South Vancouver (☎ **604-266-3474**), is practically out at the airport but makes for a good bite if you're incoming or outgoing; they're smart enough to serve English beers alongside the food, only they don't open 'til 4 p.m.

Grease is the word: The best diners

Greasy-spoon cafes around the city serve up cheap, popular breakfasts and other meals, too. You can find concentrations of these high-fat dives along Granville and Davie Streets; also look for diners in the somewhat down-at-the-heels neighborhood of East Hastings, east of Gastown. Don't like grease? Don't despair. Another kind of healthier, upscale diner is popping up in Vancouver in increasing numbers — a higher-end sort that serves burgers and malts, but also offers eggs Benedict, granola, pecan-encrusted French toast, actual squeezed juice, and sumptuous brunches. **Hamburger Mary's** (see the preceding "Burgered and fried" section) is one classic example; **Sophie's** (see its listing in this section) is another.

- ✔ The cleverly named **Elbow Room,** 560 Davie St. (☎ 604-685-3628), is your quintessential sassy, hard-nosed (but ultimately soft-hearted) diner where breakfast rules, no matter the time of day or night. Servers aren't shy to treat you as one of the family and give as good as they get: Exchanges can get good-naturedly feisty.

- ✔ **Joe's Grill,** 2061 West 4th Ave. (☎ 604-736-6588), in Kitsilano, offers a refreshingly non–New Agey take on food: big portions, tasty breakfasts, and low prices — all of which are hard to find thereabouts.

- ✔ Practically next door to Joe's Grill, **Sophie's Cosmic Cafe,** 2095 West 4th Ave. (☎ 604-732-6810), is your classic yuppie diner: rib-sticking food, but some concessions to taste, spicing, and health, too. Prices tend to be a little higher here, and weekend brunch is wildly popular.

- ✔ **The Templeton,** 1087 Granville St. (☎ 604-685-4612), in Yaletown, may be more of the same food-wise — a diner that's tough with the talk and low in fiber — but its atmosphere is a throwback in time: jukeboxes, soda fountain booths (and great sodas, too), good kiddies' menus and gargantuan breakfasts, served until 3 p.m. daily.

Restaurant rescue for vegetarians

If you're a vegetarian who just skipped the three preceding sections, you're in luck: In Vancouver, for once, you're *very* well looked after. Any Asian restaurant offers plenty of tasty tofu entrees, and the local hippie population has outfitted itself with a range of self-defense eateries to keep out the meat. One of these restaurants, **The Naam,** is so famous and good that I include it earlier in the "Vancouver's Best Restaurants" section. Here are a few more possibilities if you're a meat-, fish- and fowl-avoiding traveler.

- ✔ **Buddhist Vegetarian Restaurant,** 137 East Pender St. (☎ 604-683-8816), is totally vegan, cooking up everything from dim sum to mock lemon chicken, mock shark fin soup and dishes that cater to special diets: no wheat, no soy, no salt, no oil, and no MSG.

- ✔ **Greens & Gourmet Natural Food Restaurant,** 2582 West Broadway (☎ 604-737-7373), is a comfortable spot in Kitsilano. The most fun are its pay-by-the-weight hot and cold buffets. I mean, how much can a lettuce leaf weigh?

- **Juicy Lucy's,** 1420 Commercial Dr. (☎ 604-254-6101), is smack dab in the middle of Commercial Drive's activity and serves inventive veggie Indian — and more mainstream — meals.

- **Sweet Cherubim,** 1105 Commercial Dr. (☎ 604-253-0969), is a multicultural vegan and vegetarian restaurant where dishes include Greek moussaka, Italian lasagna, Indian dahl, and American pumpkin pie! Low fat, non-dairy, and wheat-free options are plentiful. Saturday afternoons even include free consultations with a master herbalist.

- **Planet Veg,** 1941 Cornwall Ave. (☎ 604-734-1001), sates the veggie-happy of Kitsilano by serving cheapo Indian meals, wraps, samosas, and similar fare.

The coffee connection

Vancouver has so much good coffee, I hardly know where to begin — I know only what to avoid (more on that in the following paragraph). For starters, the best coffee *bars* — many with Italian names — line the old Italian neighborhood along Commercial Drive; these are good places for an espresso, cappuccino, or panino. Ultra-hip Robson and Denman Streets are also packed with more beans per square foot than any other neighborhood in the city; you really can't go wrong.

Whatever you do, though, avoid the encroaching U.S. chains from that city just to the south. They can't make good coffee: Good coffee does not come flavored with . . . What was that? Fake hazelnuts? Yuck. (And coffee shouldn't come in a cistern-sized cup, either.)

- **Café Calabria,** 1745 Commercial Dr. (☎ 604-253-7017), is a family-run, dyed-in-the-wool Italian coffee bar, which means it knows exactly how to make a real cappuccino, macchiata, and espresso. Decor is pretty over the top, which just adds to the flavor.

- **Infuze,** 1114 Denman St. (☎ 604-688-3170), looks more like an experimentation laboratory for its 50 or so teas than a coffee bar. Translate that as being a *very* contemporary style tea house. Its Matcha green tea is rated 137 times more potent than the regular stuff.

- **Joe's Café,** 1150 Commercial Dr. (☎ 604-255-1046), unrelated to Joe's Grill (mentioned earlier in "Grease is the word: The best diners"), was *the* place for coffee (pre-Starbucks), and still holds its own against some of the best in the city. It's very "boho," and the young staff has created some funky-hipster alternative coffee-based drinks. Dare I say it? The coffee is exciting.

- **Murchie's Tea & Coffee,** 970 Robson St. (☎ 604-669-0783), is an importer of some of the world's finest teas, plus java, too, and a mouth-watering dessert selection. Established in 1894, Murchie's is one of Vancouver's most enduring family-run businesses, which today has several retail branches around town (and in Victoria).

Sweets to eat

Chocoholics abound in Vancouver, and you're never very far from a fix if you're also a member of the choc-club. Kitsilano, in particular, seems to have become Chocolate Central. Don't worry if you're more of an ice cream fan. Vancouver has what you're looking for, too.

✔ **Chocolate Arts,** 2037 West 4th Ave. (☎ 604-739-0475), is pretty unique: A partnership between a master chocolatier and Robert Davidson, a well-known, local artist. The result? Chocolate masks and other intricate, First Nations–designed treats that look too good to eat — but you'll want to anyway.

✔ **Death by Chocolate,** 1598 West Broadway (☎ 604-730-2462), may force you to pry open your wallet. So what? This is perhaps the best locally made chocolate in Vancouver. Simply amazing.

✔ Martha Stewart's a fan of **La Casa Gelato,** 1033 Venables St. (☎ 604-251-3211), which may be way off the beaten path, east of East Hastings, but if you're an ice cream freak, you'll want to stop by here. These folks, like some madly experimenting Willy Wonkas, crank out some of the weirdest ice creams known to humankind (wasabi and wild asparagus, for example); try something. Other branches are around town.

✔ Nearer to downtown is **Mario's Amato Café,** 78 East 1st Ave. (☎ 604-879-9011) showcases more than 70 flavors of gelati, sorbetti, ice cream, and frozen yogurt. Tastes are are imaginative — even wild, from basic vanilla to funky ones like viagra, red bean, durian (stinky!), or green tea. The cafe also offers desserts, pastries, panini, and beverages for those who aren't in the mood for gelato.

✔ **Notte's Bon Ton Bakery,** 3150 West Broadway (☎ 604-681-3058), is a Vancouver institution, though not at this relatively new location. The decadent range of fancy pastries is still the same, though, especially its famous, richly layered Diplomat Cakes. Tarot and teacup readings are on a first-come, first-served basis every afternoon.

✔ **Secret Garden Tea Room,** 5559 West Boulevard (☎ 604-261-3070), serves elaborate high teas (as well as lighter versions) complete with homemade scones with Devon cream, savory pastries, lemon tarts, and egg-salad finger sandwiches. Breakfasts are pretty good, too — go for the fruit-laden flapjacks or egg strudels, made from grandma's recipes.

✔ The sweets at **True Confections,** 866 Denman St. (☎ 604-682-1292), aren't anywhere near cheap level, but boy, are they good! So good that lineups begin at 8 p.m. and extend to the wee hours just to get in on one of their 50 or so desserts.

Urban-guerrilla power picnicking

Vancouver is a picnicker's kind of town, the rainy weather not withstanding. At the **Granville Island Public Market** or other markets on Robson Street and the Lonsdale Quay SeaBus landing in North Vancouver, you can stock up on fresh fruit and veggies, smoked fish, desserts, and maybe a boxed iced tea or juice drink. Here are some of the city's other premiere picnic providers, most located off the downtown peninsula in either Kitsilano or adjacent South Granville. After picking up your supplies, head to nearby Wreck Beach, Kits Beach, Pacific Spirit Park, or the UBC campus.

- ✔ **Capers,** 2285 West 4th Ave. (☎ **604-739-6676**), is a combination gourmet food store and health food store, with a substantial gourmet takeout business on the side. Salmon, roasted chicken, exotic salads, pastas, and soups? No problem; they're all here, ready to go, from 8 a.m. until 10 p.m. daily.

- ✔ **Lesley Stowe Fine Foods,** 1780 West 3rd Ave. (☎ **604-731-3663**), is a superior caterer with a justifiably high reputation for sweets, take-'em-and-eat-'em entrees, and high-quality beverages.

- ✔ **Meinhardt Fine Foods,** 3002 Granville St. (☎ **604-732-4405**), in South Granville is known for its ready-to-go goodies and great deli-styled foods. Grocery staples are from all over the world.

- ✔ **Sen5es,** 801 Georgia St. (☎ **604-633-0138**), right downtown, specializes in gourmet takeouts — sandwiches, baguettes, and decadent pastries.

- ✔ **Urban Fare,** 177 Davie St. (☎ **604-975-7550**), is Yaletown's upscale neighborhood grocery store, where you find great produce, French breads — from France — and plenty of meals that are ready to roll. This is a real winner, open 8 a.m. to 11 p.m. daily.

Index of Restaurants by Neighborhood

Five Sails (Pacific Northwest/Fusion, $$$–$$$$)
Fleuri (Pacific Northwest/Fusion, $$$–$$$$)
Fritz European House of Fries (European Deli, $)
Gotham Steakhouse (Steak, $$$–$$$$)
Il Giardino di Umberto (Italian, $$$–$$$$)
Infuze (Coffee, $)
Kam's Place ($, Singapore)
La Bodega (Spanish, $–$$$)
Le Crocodile (French, $$$–$$$$)
Murchie's (Coffee, $)
Nat's New York Style Pizzeria (Italian, $–$$)
Sen5es (Picnic, $)
Templeton (Diner, $)
True Confections (Sweets, $)
Umami (Japanese, $$–$$$)
Villa del Lupo (Italian, $$$–$$$$)
The William Tell (Continental, $$–$$$$)

East Vancouver

Dong Phu'o'ng Vietnamese Restaurant (Vietnamese, $–$$)
La Casa Gelato (Sweets, $)

Kitsilano

Bishop's (Pacific Northwest/Fusion, $$$$)
Capers (Picnic, $)
Chocolate Arts (Sweets, $)
Greens & Gourmet Natural Food Restaurant (Vegetarian, $)
Joe's Grill (diner, $)
Lesley Stowe Fine Foods (Picnic, $)
Lumière (French, $$$$)
Minerva's (European Deli, $)
The Naam (Vegetarian, $–$$)
Nat's New York Style Pizzeria (Italian, $–$$)
Notte's Bon Ton Bakery (Sweets, $)
Planet Veg (Vegetarian, $)
Sophie's Cosmic Café (Diner, $)
White Spot (Burgers, $)

North Shore

Salmon House on the Hill (Seafood, $$$–$$$$)
Tomahawk (Burgers, $)

South Granville

Bin 942 Tapa Parlour (Pacific Northwest, $$–$$$)
Death by Chocolate (Sweets, $)
Meinhardt Fine Foods (Picnic, $)
Tamarind Bistro (Indian, $–$$)
Tojo's (Japanese, $$–$$$$)
Vij's (Indian/Fusion, $$–$$$)

South Vancouver

King's Fare Fish & Chips (Seafood, $)
Omnitsky Kosher Foods (European Deli, $)

West End

Bud's Halibut & Chips (Seafood, $)
Café de Paris (French, $$$–$$$$)
Fish House in Stanley Park (Seafood, $$–$$$$)
Fresgo Inn (Burgers, $)
Gyoza King (Japanese, $–$$)
Hamburger Mary's (Burgers, $)
Kintaro Ramen (Japanese, $)
Liliget Feast House (Native Canadian, $$$–$$$$)
Raincity Grill (Pacific Northwest/Fusion, $$$$)
The Teahouse Restaurant at Ferguson Point (Pacific Northwest/Fusion, $$$$)
White Spot (Burgers, $)

West Side

Landmark Hot Pot House (Chinese, $$–$$$)
Red Onion (Burgers, $)
Secret Garden Tea Room (Sweets, $)

Yaletown

Elbow Room (Diner, $)
Mario's Amato Café (Cambie Bridge, Sweets, $)

Rodney's Oyster House (Seafood, $$–$$$)

Simply Thai (Thai, $$–$$$)

Urban Fare (Picnic, $)

Yaletown Brewing Company (Pub Fare, $$–$$$)

Index of Restaurants by Cuisine

Burgers

Fresgo Inn (West End, $)

Hamburger Mary's (West End, $)

Red Onion (Kerrisdale, West Side, $)

Tomahawk (North Shore, $)

White Spot (West End/Kitsilano, $)

Chinese

Floata Seafood Restaurant (Chinatown, $$–$$$$)

Hon's Wun-Tun House (Chinatown, $–$$)

Landmark Hot Pot House (Shaughnessy, $$–$$$)

Pink Pearl (Chinatown, $–$$$)

Coffee Connection

Café Calabria (Commerical Dr., $)

Infuze (Downtown, $)

Joe's Café (Commercial Dr., $)

Murchie's (Downtown, $)

Continental

Bacchus (Downtown, $$$–$$$$)

900 West (Downtown, $$$–$$$$)

The William Tell (Downtown, $$–$$$$)

Cuban

Havana Café (Commercial Dr., $$)

Diner

Elbow Room (Yaletown, $)

Joe's Grill (Kitsilano, $)

Sophie's Cosmic Café (Kitsilano, $)

Templeton (Downtown, $)

European Deli

Bavarian Restaurant Deli (Downtown, $)

Fritz European House of Fries (Downtown, $)

Minerva's (Kitsilano, $)

Omnitsky Kosher Foods (South Vancouver, $)

French

Café de Paris (West End, $$$–$$$$)

Le Crocodile (Downtown, $$$–$$$$)

Lumière (Kitsilano, $$$$)

Indian

Tamarind Bistro (South Granville, $–$$)

Vij's (South Granville, $$–$$$)

Italian

CinCin (Downtown, $$$–$$$$)

Il Giardino di Umberto (Downtown, $$$–$$$$)

Nat's New York Style Pizzeria (Downtown/Kitsilano, $–$$)

Villa del Lupo (Downtown, $$$–$$$$)

Japanese

Gyoza King (West End, $–$$)

Kintaro Ramen (West End, $)

Tojo's (South Granville, $$–$$$$)

Umami (Downtown, $$–$$$)

Native Canadian

Liliget Feast House (West End, $$$–$$$$)

Pacific Northwest/Fusion

Bin 942 Tapas Parlour (South Granville, $$–$$$)

Bishop's (Kitsilano, $$$$)

Chartwell (Downtown, $$$$)

Diva at the Met (Downtown, $$$$)

Five Sails (Downtown, $$$–$$$$)

Fleuri (Downtown, $$$–$$$$)

Raincity Grill (West End, $$$$)
The Teahouse Restaurant at Ferguson Point (West End, $$$$)

Picnic

Capers (Kitsilano, $)
Lesley Stowe Fine Foods (Kitsilano, $)
Meinhardt Fine Foods (South Granville, $)
Sen5es (Downtown, $)
Urban Fare (Yaletown, $)

Pub Fare

Yaletown Brewing Company (Yaletown, $$–$$$)

Seafood

A Kettle of Fish (Downtown, $$$–$$$$)
Bud's Halibut & Chips (West End, $)
C Restaurant (Downtown, $$$–$$$$)
Fish House in Stanley Park (West End, $$–$$$$)
King's Fare Fish & Chips (South Vancouver, $)
Rodney's Oyster House (Yaletown, $$–$$$)
Salmon House on the Hill (North Shore, $$$–$$$$)

Singapore

Kam's Place (Downtown, $)

Spanish

La Bodega (Downtown, $–$$$)

Steak

Gotham Steakhouse (Downtown, $$$–$$$$)

Sweets

La Casa Gelato (East Vancouver, $)
Chocolate Arts (Kitsilano, $)
Death by Chocolate (South Granville, $)
Mario's Amato Café (Cambie Bridge, Yaletown, $)
Notte's bon Ton Bakery (Kitsilano, $)
Secret Garden Tea Room (Kerrisdale, West Side, $)
True Confections (Downtown, $)

Thai

Simply Thai (Yaletown, $$–$$$)

Vegetarian

Buddhist Vegetarian Restaurant (Downtown, $)
Greens & Gourmet Natural Food Restaurant (Kitsilano, $)
Juicy Lucy's (Commercial Dr., $)
The Naam (Kitsilano, $–$$)
Planet Veg (Kitsilano, $)
Sweet Chrubim (Commercial Dr., $)

Vietnamese

Dong Phu'o'ng Vietnamese Restaurant (East Vancouver, $–$$)
Phnom Penh (Chinatown, $–$$)

Index of Restaurants by Price

Floata Seafood Restaurant (Chinese, Chinatown)
Gotham Steakhouse (Steak, Downtown)
Il Giardino di Umberto (Italian, Downtown)
Liliget Feast House (Native Canadian, West End)
Lumière (French, Kitsilano)
Raincity Grill (Pacific Northwest/Fusion, West End)
Salmon House on the Hill (Seafood, North Shore)
The Teahouse Restaurant at Ferguson Point (Pacific Northwest/Fusion, West End)
Tojo's (Japanese, South Granville)
Villa del Lupo (Italian, Downtown)
The William Tell (Continental, Downtown)

$$$

A Kettle of Fish (Seafood, Downtown)
Bacchus (Continental, Downtown)
Bin 942 Tapas Parlour (Pacific Northwest, South Granville)
C Restaurant (Seafood, Downtown)
Café de Paris (French, West End)
CinCin (Italian, Downtown)
Fish House in Stanley Park (Seafood, West End)
Five Sails (Pacific Northwest/Fusion, Downtown)
Fleuri (Pacific Northwest/Fusion, Downtown)
Floata Seafood Restaurant (Chinese, Chinatown)
Gotham Steakhouse (Steak, Downtown)
Il Giardino di Umberto (Italian, Downtown)
Landmark Hot Pot House (Chinese, Shaughnessy)
La Bodega (Spanish, Downtown)
Le Crocodile (French, Downtown)
Liliget Feast House (Native Canadian, West End)
Pink Pearl (Chinese, Chinatown)

Rodney's Oyster House (Seafood, Yaletown)
Salmon House on the Hill (Seafood, North Shore)
Simply Thai (Thai, Yaletown)
Tojo's (Japanese, South Granville)
Umami (Japanese, Downtown)
Vij's (Indian/Fusion, South Granville)
Villa del Lupo (Italian, Downtown)
The William Tell (Continental, Downtown)
Yaletown Brewing Company (Pub Fare, Yaletown)

$$

Bin 942 Tapas Parlour (Pacific Northwest, South Granville)
Dong Phu'o'ng Vietnamese Restaurant (Vietnamese, East Vancouver)
Fish House in Stanley Park (Seafood, West End)
Floata Seafood Restaurant (Chinese, Chinatown)
Gyoza King (Japanese, West End)
Havana Café (Cuban, Commercial Dr.)
Hon's Wun-Tun House (Chinese, Chinatown)
La Bodega (Spanish, Downtown)
Landmark Hot Pot House (Chinese, Shaughnessy)
The Naam (Vegetarian, Kitsilano)
Nat's New York Style Pizzeria (Italian, Downtown/Kitsilano)
Phnom Penh (Vietnamese, Chinatown)
Pink Pearl (Chinese, Chinatown)
Rodney's Oyster House (Seafood, Yaletown)
Simply Thai (Thai, Yaletown)
Tamarind Bistro (Indian, South Granville)
Tojo's (Japanese, South Granville)
Umami (Japanese, Downtown)
Vij's (Indian/Fusion, South Granville)
The William Tell (Continental, Downtown)
Yaletown Brewing Company (Pub Fare, Yaletown)

$

Bavarian Restaurant Deli (European Deli, Downtown)

Buddhist Vegetarian Restaurant (Vegetarian, Downtown)

Bud's Halibut & Chips (Seafood, West End)

Café Calabria (Coffee, Commercial Dr.)

Capers (Picnic, Kitsilano)

La Casa Gelato (Sweets, East Vancouver)

Chocolate Arts (Sweets, Kitsilano)

Death by Chocolate (Sweets, South Granville)

Dong Phu'o'ng Vietnamese Restaurant (Vietnamese, East Vancouver)

Elbow Room (Diner, Yaletown)

Fresgo Inn (Burgers, West End)

Fritz European House of Frieds (European Deli, Downtown)

Greens & Gourmet Natural Food Restaurant (Vegetarian, Kitsilano)

Gyoza King (Japanese, West End)

Hamburger Mary's (Burgers, West End)

Hon's Wun-Tun House (Chinese, Chinatown)

Infuze (Coffee, Downtown)

Joe's Café (Coffee, Commercial Dr.)

Joe's Grill (Diner, Kitsilano)

Juicy Lucy's (Vegetarian, Commercial Dr.)

Kam's Place (Singapore, Downtown)

King's Fare Fish & Chips (Seafood, South Vancouver)

Kintaro Ramen (Japanese, West End)

La Bodega (Spanish, Downtown)

Lesley Show Fine Foods (Picnic, Kitsilano)

Mario's Amato Café (Sweets, South Yaletown)

Meinhardt Fine Foods (Picnic, South Granville)

Minerva's (European Deli, Kitsilano)

Murchie's (Coffee, Downtown)

The Naam (Vegetarian, Kitsilano)

Nat's New York Style Pizzeria (Italian, Downtown/Kitsilano)

Notte's Bon Ton Bakery (Sweets, Kitsilano)

Omnitsky Kosher Foods (European Deli, South Vancouver)

Phnom Penh (Vietnamese, Chinatown)

Pink Pearl (Chinese, Chinatown)

Planet Veg (Vegetarian, Kitsilano)

Red Onion (Burgers, Kerrisdale, West Side)

Secret Garden Tea Room (Sweets, Kerrisdale, West Side)

Sen5es (Picnic, Downtown)

Sophie's cosmic Café (Diner, Kitsilano)

Sweet Cherubim (Vegetarian, Commercial Dr.)

Tamarind Bistro (Indian, South Granville)

Templeton (Diner, Downtown)

Tomahawk (Burgers, North Shore)

True Confections (Sweets, Downtown)

Urban Fare (Picnic, Yaletown)

White Spot (Burgers, West End/ Kitsilano)

Chapter 11

Exploring Vancouver

●●

In This Chapter

▶ Checking out the most popular destinations and rewarding activities
▶ Exploring other excellent options
▶ Taking a guided tour

●●

Considered as a whole, Vancouver presents a lot of territory to cover, but I'm here to help. Whether you're interested in strapping on your walking shoes and checking out the coolest neighborhoods and historic sites, or you just want to sit in a tour bus and let someone else narrate away, I tell you how to find the sights that make this city special. In Chapter 13, I also devise several specific itineraries targeted at travelers with special interests. Ready? Let's go!

Discovering Vancouver's Top Sights from A to Z

Bloedel Floral Conservatory
Shaughnessy-Cambie

You'll be thankful for the warm, dry Plexiglas dome of this floral conservatory on a rainy Vancouver day. Under the dome, away from the elements, a spectacular array of plant (5,000 species) and animal life thrives in different types of climates. You find a desert oasis complete with prickly cacti and a lush tropical jungle of banana trees, colorful plants, and free-flying parrots (plus hundreds of exotic birds). These sights, along with a pond stocked with colorful fish, will entertain the kids. The rest of the large Queen Elizabeth Park is also worth some time, too, for its walking trails and fun pitch-and-putt golf course (see "Finding More Cool Things to See and Do" later in this chapter). Allow one hour.

See map p.145. Queen Elizabeth Park (33rd at Cambie St.). ☎ **604-257-8584.** www. city.vancouver.bc.ca/parks. *Admission: Adults C$4.25 (US$3.55), seniors and children 13–18 C$3.20 (US$2.65), children 6–12 C$2 (US$1.65). Open: Apr–Sept weekdays 9 a.m.–8 p.m.; weekends 10 a.m.–9 p.m.; Oct–March daily 10 a.m.–5 p.m.*

Capilano Suspension Bridge and Park
North Vancouver

This is *the* quintessential Vancouver experience if you don't mind parting with a bundle of dough just to say you walked a narrow, swinging bridge high above a raging river. You certainly won't be alone — this place gets busy with tourists. More than just a bridge attracts visitors, however; you also find out about First Nations culture by watching traditional dancers perform or Native carvers turn humble logs into noble totem poles. The neatest and newest attraction is its network of suspended treetop bridges that lead from one Douglas fir to another. Other activities include a new cliffhanger walk (almost as dramatic as it sounds), lovely gardens, a forestry exhibit, and a center explaining the history of the bridge, plus hiking trails and the obligatory restaurant and gift shop. Allow one to two hours.

See map p. 145. 3735 Capilano Rd. (To get there by car, take Hwy. 1 to exit 14 and follow the road for approximately 1.2 miles (2 km). By bus from downtown Vancouver, take bus #246 directly to the bridge; from North Vancouver, take bus #236 from Lonsdale Quay.) ☎ *604-985-7474.* www.capbridge.com. *Admission: Adults C$21.95 (US$18), seniors C$16.50 (US$14), students with ID C$10.95 (US$9.10), children 6–12 C$5.50 (US$4.60). Open: Mid-May–Sept daily 8:30 a.m. to dusk; Oct–mid-May daily 9 a.m.–6 p.m.; closed Christmas Day.*

Chinatown

The most authentic of Vancouver's ethnic neighborhoods, Chinatown — bawling, boisterous, crowded, a little odd smelling — simply must be experienced. It's so small that a tour doesn't take much time at all. Begin on Keefer Street, the center of the action and the location of any number of eateries, herb shops, and seafood markets. Here, you find the Chinese Cultural Centre and the Dr. Sun-Yat Sen Classical Chinese Garden (see the two following listings). Don't forget to try a steamed bun or something more exotic at a place such as Hon's Wun-Tun House (see Chapter 10). Finally, the 5-foot-wide Sam Kee Building, at 8 West Pender St., is the so-called narrowest building in the world, and travelers make sure to take a look. Allow one to two hours.

See map p. 143. Located along Keefer and Pender streets, from Abbott Street to Gore Avenue.

Chinese Cultural Centre
Chinatown

The Chinese Cultural Centre is a nice complement to the adjoining Dr. Sun Yat-Sen Classical Chinese Garden (see the following listing). Through the center's extensive library, educational displays, archives, and even classes, you can discover the interesting history of Chinese immigrants who settled in this bustling neighborhood. A great time to visit is during the two-week Chinese New Year festivities in late January and early February, which are sponsored and coordinated by the cultural center. Allow 30 minutes.

See map p. 143. 50 East Pender St. ☎ *604-658-8880.* www.cccvan.com. *Admission: Adults C$4 (US$3.35), seniors and students C$2.50 (US$2.10). Open: Tues–Sun 11 a.m.–5 p.m.*

Vancouver Attractions

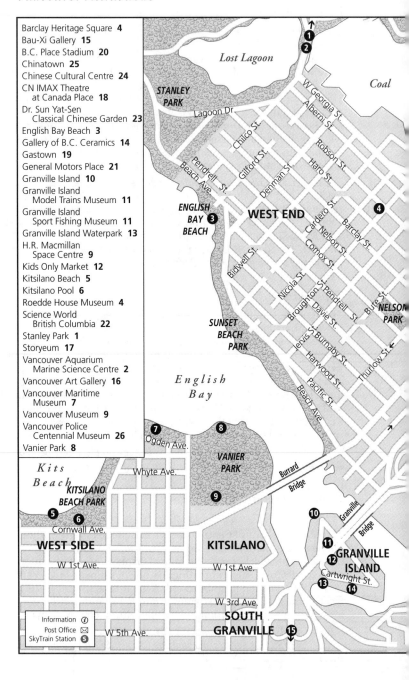

Barclay Heritage Square **4**
Bau-Xi Gallery **15**
B.C. Place Stadium **20**
Chinatown **25**
Chinese Cultural Centre **24**
CN IMAX Theatre
    at Canada Place **18**
Dr. Sun Yat-Sen
    Classical Chinese Garden **23**
English Bay Beach **3**
Gallery of B.C. Ceramics **14**
Gastown **19**
General Motors Place **21**
Granville Island **10**
Granville Island
    Model Trains Museum **11**
Granville Island
    Sport Fishing Museum **11**
Granville Island Waterpark **13**
H.R. Macmillan
    Space Centre **9**
Kids Only Market **12**
Kitsilano Beach **5**
Kitsilano Pool **6**
Roedde House Museum **4**
Science World
    British Columbia **22**
Stanley Park **1**
Storyeum **17**
Vancouver Aquarium
    Marine Science Centre **2**
Vancouver Art Gallery **16**
Vancouver Maritime
    Museum **7**
Vancouver Museum **9**
Vancouver Police
    Centennial Museum **26**
Vanier Park **8**

Lost Lagoon

STANLEY
PARK

Lagoon Dr.

Coal

W Georgia St.
Alberni St.
Chilco St.
Robson St.
Haro St.
Pendrell St.
Gilford St.
Denman St.
Beach Ave.

ENGLISH
BAY **3**
BEACH

WEST END **4**

Cardero St.
Nelson St.
Barclay St.
Comox St.
Bidwell St.
Nicola St.
St. Pendrell St.
Bute St.
NELSON
PARK
Broughton St.
Davie St.
Jervis St.
Burnaby St.
Harwood St.
Thurlow St.

SUNSET
BEACH
PARK

*English
Bay*

Pacific St.
Beach Ave.

7
8

Ogden Ave.

*Kits
Beach*

KITSILANO
BEACH PARK

Whyte Ave.

VANIER
PARK

Burrard
Bridge

9

5   **6**
Cornwall Ave.

WEST SIDE

W 1st Ave.

KITSILANO

W 1st Ave.

10

Granville
Bridge

11

12 GRANVILLE
    ISLAND
Cartwright St.
13   **14**

W 3rd Ave.

SOUTH
GRANVILLE **15**

Information *i*
Post Office ✉
SkyTrain Station **S**

W 5th Ave.

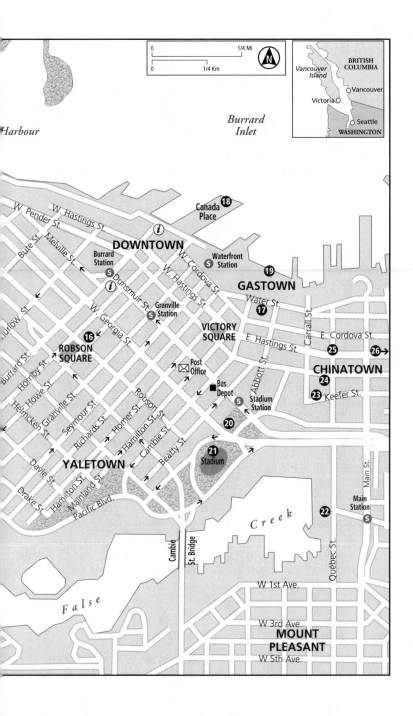

Harbour

Burrard Inlet

BRITISH COLUMBIA

Vancouver Island

Victoria ○ ○ Vancouver

○ Seattle

WASHINGTON

Canada Place **18**

W. Hastings St.

W. Pender St.

DOWNTOWN

Burrard Station

Waterfront Station

19

GASTOWN

Water St. **17**

Granville Station

VICTORY SQUARE

E. Cordova St.

Carrall St.

25 **26**

E. Hastings St.

CHINATOWN

24

Post Office

16

ROBSON SQUARE

W. Georgia St.

Bus Depot

23 Keefer St.

Stadium Station

Robson St.

20

21
Stadium

YALETOWN

Pacific Blvd.

Creek

22

Main St.

Main Station

Cambie

St. Bridge

Québec St.

False

W 1st Ave.

W 3rd Ave.

MOUNT PLEASANT

W 5th Ave.

Dr. Sun Yat-Sen Classical Chinese Garden
Chinatown

The first authentic classical Chinese garden built outside of China, this serene spot offers a place for contemplation right in the heart of busy Chinatown. All the materials used in the garden — including the plants and building supplies — were shipped from China in nearly a thousand separate boxes. The aim of the garden is to present visitors with a vision of Taoist philosophy — a quiet place to contemplate the harmony in nature. The garden features architecture with exquisitely carved windows and moon-shaped doors, twisting walkways, waterfalls, and trees, all of it carefully symbolic of something — ask an employee to explain the code to you. Ironically, this island of serenity is one of the most visited attractions in Vancouver and may not be so serene when you get here; try for early morning or just before closing to get the most out of the experience. Allow one hour.

See map p. 143. 578 Carrall St. (east side of downtown core). ☎ **604-662-3207.** www. vancouverchinesegarden.com. *Admission: Adults C$8.25 (US$6.85), seniors C$6.75 (US$5.62), children 5–17 C$5.75 (US$4.80), family C$18 (US$15). Open: Mid-June–Sept daily 9:30 a.m.–7 p.m.; Oct–Apr daily 10 a.m.–4:30 p.m.; Apr–mid-June daily 10 a.m.–6 p.m.*

Gastown

The original historic center of Vancouver, Gastown was once presided over by the garrulous barkeeper nicknamed (for his oration) "Gassy Jack" Deighton. His statue now stands in Maple Leaf Park, a slightly decrepit area that edges on a part of this part-touristy, part-seedy neighborhood. Attractions include the Vancouver Police Centennial Museum (see the "Finding More Cool Things to See and Do" section later in this chapter); plenty of 19th-century architecture and historic place names such as Gaolhouse Mews and Blood Alley; the old-fashioned ambience of shops, restaurants, and bars; and the closeness of downtown and the waterfront. The biggest draw, however, is a steam clock — which doesn't actually run on steam, although it does *emit* steam every 15 minutes for effect — at the corner of Water and Cambie Streets. The Landing, a restored heritage building that has been transformed into an upscale mall at 375 Water St., is worth a moment, as are excellent bars, cafes, and vintage clothing stores. Allow one hour; allow two hours or more if dining or visiting a bar.

East Hastings Street, which connects Gastown and Chinatown, is one of the city's worst — home to plenty of drug addicts and the like. Find another route to walk, or take a cab, if you visit at night.

See map p. 143. Located along Water and Cordova Streets, just east of the SkyTrain's Waterfront station and just west of Chinatown.

Granville Island

Granville Island, teeming with houseboats, studios, and shop stalls, is a public-space success story that has become one of the most visited areas

Greater Vancouver Attractions

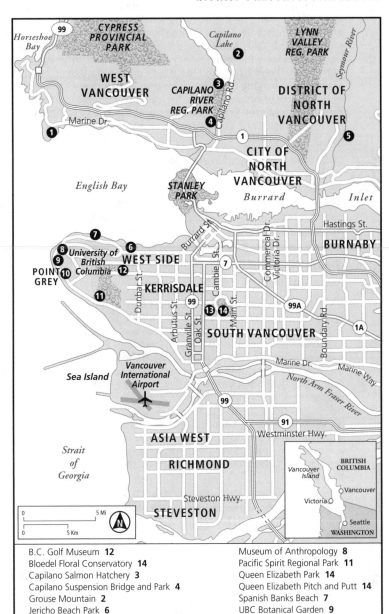

B.C. Golf Museum **12**
Bloedel Floral Conservatory **14**
Capilano Salmon Hatchery **3**
Capilano Suspension Bridge and Park **4**
Grouse Mountain **2**
Jericho Beach Park **6**
Lighthouse Park **1**
Lynn Canyon Suspension Bridge & Park **5**
Nitobe Memorial Garden **9**

Museum of Anthropology **8**
Pacific Spirit Regional Park **11**
Queen Elizabeth Park **14**
Queen Elizabeth Pitch and Putt **14**
Spanish Banks Beach **7**
UBC Botanical Garden **9**
Van Dusen Botanical Garden **13**
Wreck Beach **10**

in the Greater Vancouver region. Locals, art students, and tourists flock here. People come for the fantastic Granville Island Public Market, with its fresh B.C.-grown fresh produce, exotic imported flavors, ready-to-eat ethnic and specialty foods — anything from French cuisine to sushi. Kids enjoy the Kids Only Market (see the "Finding More Cool Things to See and Do" section later in this chapter). You can find outdoor seating with pleasant views of False Creek and the West End — although eclectic street musicians and annoying seagulls also seem to like these tables, and on those days, you may actually hope for rain. Worthwhile indoor destinations include the Model Trains Museum and Sport Fishing Museum (see the "Finding More Cool Things to See and Do" section). Allow two or three hours if the weather's good; allow more time for visiting museums.

Don't even think of parking here during the weekend; instead, take the convenient False Creek Ferries, tiny boats that whisk you from the West End and trendy Yaletown.

See map p. 142. Information center at 1398 Cartwright St. ☎ *604-666-5784.* www.granvilleisland.com. *Admission: Free. Open: Daily late May–early Oct 9 a.m.–6 p.m.; late Oct–early May Tues–Sun 9 a.m.–6 p.m.*

Grouse Mountain
North Vancouver

If you arrive in Vancouver for the first time at dusk, you may see twinkling lights hovering about the night sky above the city. No, they're not UFOs left over from the days when *The X-Files* was filmed here. They're the lights of Grouse Mountain, tempting you from high above to come have a bird's-eye look from the 3,700-foot peak. With the hefty price of the eight-minute journey up the mountain, your best bet is to make a day of it. Up top, you find a bar that hops year-round, a decent restaurant, a movie theater, a playground, pony rides, hang gliders careening off the peak, lumberjack demonstrations, and — in winter — skiing, snowboarding, sledding, and ice skating, which are especially fun at night with the city lights below. You won't be bored, although you may be a little put off by the blatant commercialism of it all. Hikers and purists usually skip all that and do the very hip Grouse Grind, a near-vertical ascent of the peak. Allow two to six hours.

See map p. 145. 6400 Nancy Greene Way. ☎ *604-984-0661 or 604-984-9311.* www.grousemtn.com. *Admission: Adults C$26.95 (US$22), seniors C$24.95 (US$21), children 13–18 C$14.95 (US$12), children 5–12 C$9.95 (US$8). Open: Daily 9 a.m.–10 p.m.*

Jericho Beach Park
Point Grey

The first in a string of beaches that hug Point Grey, Jericho Beach is a quiet place to bring a Frisbee and dog, your fishing gear, or a good book. What used to be a military complex is now a premier beach destination for families and would-be anglers. The view from the park is of mist-covered mountains and freight ships moored in English Bay. Playing fields are nearby, as is a small playground and a youth hostel. Walk along the beach to sandswept Spanish Banks. In summer, the annual Folk Festival takes place here. Allow one to two hours.

See map p. 145. At the foot of Point Grey Rd. and 4th Ave. (West, 3 miles east of Granville Bridge.) ☎ *604-257-8400. Admission: Free. Open: Daily dawn to dusk.*

Kitsilano Beach
Kitsilano

The quintessential Vancouver beach experience is a trip over to Kitsilano Beach, called "Kits" by the locals. The beach offers fantastic views of the mountains and the city skyline, a host of activities (including a beachside heated outdoor pool), and a shell-filled beach — not to mention proximity to the beautiful people and trendy cafes that line Cornwall Avenue. Allow one to two hours.

See map p. 142. At the foot of Cornwall Ave. and Arbutus St. ☎ *604-257-8400. Admission: Free. Open: Daily dawn to dusk.*

Lynn Canyon Suspension Bridge & Park
Lynn Valley

If you like scary heights but don't want to pay for the experience, visit Lynn Canyon Suspension Bridge rather than its nearby cousin, Capilano Bridge (see its listing earlier in this section). This one's higher, although shorter, than Capilano. Here you're right in the thick of a beautiful rain forest of Douglas firs as you teeter more than 16 stories over a gorge. (Kayakers often run the river; no throwing stuff over the side to distract them.) You also find the Lynn Canyon Ecology Centre with films, slide shows, and displays, as well as tours to explain the ecosystem around you. Make sure to pack a lunch, sturdy hiking shoes, trail maps, and bear whistles (for scaring off bears) if you want to make a day of it and head down one of the surrounding trails. Allow one to four hours — one hour to cross the bridge and visit the Ecology Centre and up to four hours for hikes that radiate out from the park.

See map p. 145. Take Trans-Canada Hwy. (Hwy. 1) to the Lynn Valley Road exit. Continue north to Peters Rd. and make a right to the parking lot at the end of the road. ☎ *604-981-3103. Admission: Free. Open: Park daily dawn to dusk for cars and 24 hours for pedestrians and cyclists; Lynn Canyon Ecology Centre daily 10 a.m.–5 p.m.*

Museum of Anthropology
Point Grey

Located on the green campus of the University of British Columbia (UBC), this may be the city's top sight. In a building inspired by the longhouses of First Nations villages, the museum has carved front doors that open into a great hall where totem poles welcome you. With the aid of a free booklet, you can examine some 15,000 artifacts in glass drawers. Most of the holdings relate to Native-Canadian peoples, although you also find a wing of European ceramics. Highlights include carver Bill Reid's masterpiece *The Raven and the First Men*, which powerfully depicts a creation myth in which frightened humans emerge from a clamshell only to face a cackling raven. Scary stuff. Outside stand two Haida big houses and more totem poles. While in the area, check out the UBC Botanical Garden (see its listing in this section) and stroll through the university's campus, with its views of the mountains and sea. Allow one to two hours.

See map p. 145. 6393 Northwest Marine Dr. ☎ 604-822-5087. www.moa.ubc.ca. *Admission: Adults C$9 (US$7.50), seniors and students C$7 (US$5.80), children under 6 free; free Tues 5–9 p.m. Bring lots of small change for parking meters. Open: Late May–early Sept daily 10 a.m.–5 p.m. (Tues until 9 p.m.); early Sept–late May Tues–Sun 11 a.m.–5 p.m. (Tues until 9 p.m.). Closed December 25 and 26.*

Pacific Spirit Regional Park
Point Grey

Formerly called the University Endowment Lands, this huge park with towering trees and mysterious paths embodies the Canadian west: green, leafy, and vaguely spiritual. Located adjacent to the University of British Columbia, the park (which is even bigger than 1,000-acre Stanley Park and much less discovered) is a terrific place for a quiet stroll away from the madding crowds, amidst the enveloping and wonderful-smelling rain forest — just be sure not to get lost in the maze of trails. Allow two hours if you're planning to hike.

See map p. 145. Bordered by Southwest Marine Dr., 16th Ave. West, and Imperial Rd., about 3 miles west of Granville St. Admission: Free. Open: Daily dawn to dusk.

Science World British Columbia
Main Street Station

You don't have to be a science buff — or a kid — to appreciate this geodesic dome (which looks like a big golf ball) twinkling in the night sky across the street from Pacific Central Station in a forlorn industrial corner of downtown. The Matter and Forces gallery contains cool exhibits that fascinate young minds: The Plasma Ball (which tests your electrical conductivity) and the Shadow Wall (which holds your shadow in place using phosphorescent materials) are two of the more interesting ones. The mining exhibit is surprisingly pro-mining — well, this *is* Canada, after all — while natural science is tackled from a beaver lodge's point of view. Young kids (say, ages 3 to 6) enjoy the KidSpace Gallery with its brightly colored toys and over-sized building blocks. A giant-screen panoramic theater shows mostly science-themed films. Allow up to two hours.

See map p. 143. 1455 Quebec St. ☎ 604-443-7440. www.scienceworld.bc.ca. *Admission including exhibits, laser theater, and OMNIMAX: Adults C$18.75 (US$16); seniors, students, and children C$14.50 (US$12); children under 4 free. Admission including exhibits and laser theater: Adult C$13.75 (US$11); seniors, students, and children C$9.50 (US$7.90). Open: Mon–Fri, 10 a.m.–5 p.m., weekends and holidays 10 a.m.–6 p.m.*

Stanley Park
West End

Every city should be so lucky to have easy access to such a diverse and beautiful park. This 1,000-acre green space, a wonderful respite from downtown traffic, is the one truly must-see attraction in Vancouver. You can bike, in-line skate, or stroll on the miles of paths and seawall that ring and crisscross the park. The park also features lawn bowling (for the ultimate British experience) and a par-three golf course — bring decent shoes, the course can be a minefield of Canadian Goose poop. Begin at the park information booth near Lost Lagoon, the taking-off point for horse-drawn carriage tours (see the "Seeing Vancouver by Guided Tour" section later in this chapter) and bicycle rentals (see "Spokes Bicycle Rentals" near the end of the chapter). As you drive, bike, or walk the six-mile, one-way circuit, you pass Brockton Oval — a semicircle of native Kwakiutl totem poles — and two native canoes carved from a cedar log. This area has the largest concentration of tour buses and camera-toting tourists. If you continue beyond the children's farm and a miniature train, things quiet down again and you pass Deadman's Island, a former First Nations burial ground and quarantine during a late–19th century epidemic of smallpox; the Empress of Japan figurehead; and then remote Third Beach and Ferguson Point, home to The Teahouse Restaurant (see Chapter 10). Completing the circuit, you pass The Fish House restaurant in Stanley Park, positioned strategically near Denman Street and English Bay (see Chapter 10). Allow two to five hours.

When you descend the stairs to Third Beach, turn right and walk down to the end of the beach. Any of the benches along that walk are secluded and have a kissable view of the sunset. At Second Beach, you'll find a free, kid-friendly, outdoor, freshwater pool.

See map p. 142. 2099 Beach Ave. ☎ *604-257-8531.* www.city.vancouver.bc.ca/parks. *Admission: Park free, farmyard and train adults C$5 (US$4.15), seniors C$3.50 (US$2.90), children 13–18 C$3.75 (US$3.10), children 2–12 C$2.50 (US$2.10). Pitch & Putt Golf (☎ 604-681-8847), adult C$11 (US$9.15), senior C$7.25 (US$6.05), students C$8.25 (US$6.85). Tennis (☎ 604-605-8224), C$4.75 (US$3.95) for 30 minutes. Open: Park year-round; farmyard daily 11 a.m.–4 p.m.; train May–Sept daily 11 a.m.– 4 p.m.; tennis and golf May–Sept daily dawn to dusk.*

Storyeum
Gastown

This warehouse of a space — an area nearing six hockey rinks — combines state-of-the-art entertainment technology with live theater for a storytelling extravaganza. It chronicles British Columbia's history in nine separate vignettes, each with its own impressive set, walking you through time from First Nations settlements to the coming of the railroad to today's skyscraper city silhouettes. You're on your feet for most of the 70-minute production; childrens' strollers are welcome and the few seats that there are in each theater are for the elderly and those with a disability.

See map p. 143. 142 Water St. ☎ 604-687-8142. www.storyeum.com. *Admission: Adult C$21.95 (US$18), senior and student 13–18 C$18.95 (US$16), children 6–12 C$15.95 (US$13). Open: Daily 10 a.m.–5 p.m. (to 7 p.m. in summer).*

UBC Botanical Garden and Nitobe Memorial Garden
Point Grey

The University of British Columbia's (UBC's) eight botanical gardens and the separate (but sensational) Nitobe Garden ratchet up the green factor in a city that's already blessed with acres of green space. The UBC botanical circuit includes a 16th-century replica of a medicinal garden, native B.C. flowers and plants, and Alpine and food gardens. The Nitobe Memorial Garden, the most authentic Japanese garden in North America, consists of a large, informal Stroll Garden lined with a stone path bearing a passing resemblance to maps of the Milky Way — a subtle comment on the harmony running through nature, large and small. Here, graceful bridges span the streams, while colorful *koi* fish swim through a placid pool. The garden's other section, the Tea Garden, has a stone path leading to a teahouse, where tea ceremonies take place and where you find a Japanese garden planted with native Japanese maples, cherry trees, azaleas, and irises; come in spring to see the cherry trees blossom, or in fall to see the maples turning. Allow one to two hours.

See map p. 145. 6804 Southwest Marine Dr. ☎ 604-822-4186 or 604-822-6038. www.ubcbotanicalgarden.org. *Admission: Main garden adults C$6 (US$5), seniors C$4 (US$3.35), students C$3 (US$2.50), children under 6 free; Nitobe garden adults C$4 (US$3.35), seniors C$3 (US$2.50) and students C$2.50 (US$2.10), children under 6 free. Dual pass for both gardens C$8 (US$6.65). Open: daily mid-March–mid-Oct 10 a.m.–6 p.m.; Oct–Feb Mon–Fri 10 a.m.–5 p.m.*

Vancouver Aquarium Marine Science Centre
West End

You're instantly reminded that you are in the Pacific Northwest the moment you enter Vancouver's Aquarium and see the huge bronze killer whale looming. Highly interactive and education-oriented, the aquarium features a tropical gallery, which simulates an Indonesian reef and tidal pool teeming with piranhas and black-tip reef sharks, and an Amazon gallery with an hourly tropical computer-generated thunderstorm and an impressive collection of rain-forest fauna — three-toed sloths, scarlet ibis, toucans, boa constrictors, multi-eyed fish, and more. Another cool section — literally — highlights native Arctic species, such as beluga whales, which can be viewed above and below the water. Kids will also get of a kick out of the daily dolphin shows; the Steller sea lions in a nearby pool, who share their home with many a rescued harbor seal (they do a lot of marine rescue and rehabilitation here); and the lively sea otters. Other exhibits bring home the ecosystems of the Strait of Georgia and the Northern Pacific. Allow two hours.

See map p. 142. Stanley Park. ☎ **604-659-FISH (3474)**. www.vanaqua.org. *Admission: Adults C$17.50 (US$14.55); seniors, students, and children 13–18 C$12.95 (US$10.80); children 4–12 C$9.95 (US$8.30). Open: July–Sept daily 9:30 a.m.–7 p.m.; Oct–June daily 10 a.m.–5:30 p.m.*

Vancouver Maritime Museum
Kitsilano

This museum in Vanier Park isn't Vancouver's best known or biggest, but it's actually pretty interesting if you're a marine buff. Exhibits highlight the region's maritime heritage and include the restored Arctic exploring ship *St. Roch*, which is well worth the visit. Young visitors can also pilot a remote-controlled, deep-sea robot, drop by a boat-building workshop, and check out model ships. This being Vancouver, a totem pole stands guard, and — appropriately enough — you can get here using the False Creek ferries from downtown or Granville Island. Allow two hours.

See map p. 142. 1905 Ogden Ave. (in Vanier Park). ☎ **604-257-8300**. www.vmm.bc.ca. *Admission: Adults C$8 (US$6.65), seniors and children 6–19 C$5.50 (US$4.60). Family rate C$18 (US$15) for up to 2 adults and 4 children (max of 6 people). Open: Sept–late May Tues–Sat 10 a.m.–5 p.m., Sun noon–5 p.m.; late May–early Sept daily 10 a.m.– 5 p.m.*

Vancouver Museum
Kitsilano

The Vancouver Museum, Canada's biggest city museum, displays several Native-Canadian exhibits — the conical roof representing a Native cedar-bark hat, like the totem poles around town, is just another clue that you won't leave without learning plenty about its original inhabitants. The pioneer-era exhibits include a fur-trading post, a replica of an immigrant ship, a hundred-year-old home — and then, what's this? A mummified child from Egypt. What that has to do with Vancouver city history is beyond me. Anyhow, the Native-Canadian heritage is well depicted with ceremonial masks, baskets, blankets, and so on. Recent exhibitions explore the large Asian immigration to Vancouver.

See map p.142. 1100 Chestnut St. (in Vanier Park). ☎ **604-736-4431**. www.vanmuseum. bc.ca. *Admission: Adults C$10 (US$8.30), seniors C$8 (US$6.65), children 4–19, C$6 (US$5). Open: July–Aug daily 10 a.m.–5 p.m. (Thurs until 9 p.m.); Sept–June Tues–Sun 10 a.m.–5 p.m. (Thurs until 9 p.m.).*

Finding More Cool Things to See and Do

More to do? You bet! My recommendations in the "Discovering Vancouver's Top Sights from A to Z" section only scratch the surface. With its miles of beaches and sprawling green parks, Vancouver is paradise for kids of all ages — or anyone who's a kid at heart.

Kid-pleasing spots

Before hitting the attractions in this section, equip yourself by picking up the *Kids' Guide to Vancouver* at the **Tourist InfoCentre,** 200 Burrard St., Waterfront Centre (☎ **800-663-6000** or 604-683-2000), and log on to the Web site at www.kidfriendly.org, a not-for-profit organization that accredits and reviews businesses especially good for kids and families.

If you're in Vancouver with your kids at the end of May or early June, don't miss the **Vancouver International Children's Festival** (☎ **604-280-4444** tickets, **604-708-5655** information), a week-long event in Vanier Park.

Capilano Salmon Hatchery
North Vancouver

Come here to view the spawning of B.C.'s most famous fish. Along with tanks that contain tiny fry or baby salmon, kids can see the ladders that mature salmon climb to return to their streams of origin. Educational displays lay out the salmon's life cycle. Note that the best time to visit is from July to September (and sometimes later) when the adult fish return. Allow two hours, including travel.

See map p. 145. 4500 Capilano Park Rd. ☎ ***604-666-1790.** Admission: Free. Open: Daily June–Aug 8 a.m.–8 p.m.; Sept 8 a.m.–7 p.m.; Oct 8 a.m.–6 p.m., Nov–May 8 a.m.–4 p.m.*

CN IMAX Theatre at Canada Place
Downtown

Most visitors come here to see bigger-than-life movies on the five-story-high screens at the IMAX theatre, a kid-oriented adventure and probably not for people who frequent avant-garde film festivals. Expect cinematic views from mountaintops and deep space, to scenes from rock concerts and extreme sports. Allow one hour.

See map p. 143. 999 Canada Place. ☎ ***604-682-IMAX (4629).** www.imax.com/ vancouver. Admission: Adults C$11.50 (US$9.55), seniors C$10.50 (US$8.75), children under 12 C$9.50 (US$7.90). Show times: July–Aug daily 11 a.m.–10 p.m.; Sept–June daily noon to 10 p.m.*

Granville Island Model Trains Museum
Granville Island

Vancouver is a fitting spot for a museum dedicated to trains, because the city is about as far west as you can go on the Canadian National. (And Vancouver's original European and Asian population settled here to make a living building and working the rails.) In any event, kids and train fanatics alike enjoy the huge collections of model and toy trains — which is said to be the world's largest such collection on public display. The displays include trains running through a great set of miniature tunnels, trestles, mountains, and forests. Admission includes the Sport Fishing & Model Ships Museum next door. Allow one hour.

See map p. 142. 1502 Duranleau St. ☎ **604-683-1939.** www.modeltrainsmuseum. ca. Admission: Adults C$7.50 (US$6.25), seniors and students C$6 (US$5), children 6–18 C$4 (US$3.35), children under 4 free. Open: Tues–Sun 10 a.m.–5:30 p.m.

Granville Island Waterpark
Granville Island

Among the many kid-friendly spots on Granville Island is this park, a kind of supervised play area with large and small waterslides, whimsical fountains, and other waterworks, such as hydrants and hoses. Water sprays from anywhere at any time, which sends kids into fits of screaming glee. Volunteers supervise the action. This is said to be the continent's largest free waterpark, and in summer, it's a good cooling-off point after doing the shopping and museum thing on the island. You also find a playground with a swing, cool sandbox, and so on, along with washrooms at the adjacent community center. Bring bathing suits.

See map p. 142. In Sutcliffe Park at Cartwright and Old Bridge streets. ☎ **604-666-5784.** Open: Victoria Day (late May) to Labour Day (early Sept) daily 9 a.m.–6 p.m.

Kids Only Market
Granville Island

The Kids Only Market is a unique concept, although everyone knows that the parents' money keeps the place afloat. The two dozen or so stores — and not a chain among them — vend locally crafted products and toys. Older kids may be swayed by clothing stores that cater to their fickle tastes.

See map p. 142. 1496 Cartwright St. ☎ **604-689-8447.** Open: Daily 10 a.m.–6 p.m.

Kitsilano Pool
Kitsilano

The biggest outdoor swimming pool in Vancouver (and at 137 meters, it's Canada's longest), Kits Pool has a terrific beachside setting where stunning North Shore mountains gleam in the sun most summer days. The pool is graduated with a shallow end for kids.

See map p. 142. 2305 Cornwall Ave. (at Yew St.). ☎ **604-257-8400** or 604-257-8400. Admission: Adults C$4.50 (US$3.75), seniors C$3.20 (US$2.65), children C$2.25 (US$1.85). Open: Pool Victoria Day (late May) to Labour Day (early Sept), Mon–Fri 7 a.m.–8:30 p.m., Sat–Sun 10 a.m.–8:30 p.m.; park year-round.

Teen-tempting attractions

Teens aren't left out when looking for entertainment in Vancouver. Among the many highlights is the Kitsilano Space Centre, which has the right stuff when it comes to pleasing teens' finicky tastes. See also Chapter 12 for shopping options.

H.R. MacMillan Space Centre
Kitsilano

Also known as the Pacific Space Centre, this thrill-a-minute museum manages to capture most visitors' attention with interactive exhibits that highlight Canada's contributions to space exploration. The real show-stopper is the Virtual Voyages Simulator, where for five heart-pounding minutes you're jolted through space like a character in *Star Wars;* the Cosmic Courtyard contains a real rock from the moon; and the Gordon Southam Observatory houses huge telescopes — you can take snapshots of the moon for C$10 (US$8.30) a pop. The Vancouver Museum (see the listing earlier in this chapter) shares the same entrance and makes a good bookend trip with this attraction. Allow one to two hours.

See map p. 142. 1100 Chestnut St. ☎ *604-738-7827.* www.hrmacmillanspace centre.com. *Admission: Adults C$13.50 (US$11.25); seniors, students, and children 11–18 C$10.50 (US$8.75); children 5–10 C$9.50 (US$7.90). Evening laser shows C$10 (US$8.30). Open: Sept–June Tues–Sun 10 a.m.–5 p.m.; July–Aug daily 10 a.m.–5 p.m. Laser shows Sept–June Thurs–Sun 9 p.m. (second showing at 10:30 p.m. Fri–Sat); July–Aug daily 9:30 p.m. (second showing at 10:45 p.m. Thurs–Sat).*

Notable beaches, gardens, and parks

Vancouver's green space includes a lot more than just Stanley Park, as described in this section.

English Bay Beach
West End

English Bay Beach is a hectic swarm of well-heeled locals, all vying for a tiny plot of sand or driftwood log on which to savor nice weather or bring a takeout lunch from nearby Denman Street. You see it all here: Same-sex couples strolling arm in arm, blue-haired matrons walking their dogs, sun worshippers, Russian tourists, yuppies communing with their offspring, maybe even a movie star.

See map p. 142. Foot of Beach Ave. and Denman St. Admission: Free.

Lighthouse Park
West Vancouver

Named for Point Atkinson Lighthouse, this park is a popular family destination, especially on Sundays during the summer. The fir trees remain since the last logging in 1881, so you're getting an authentic look. Just don't expect any sandy beaches — this is strictly rocky shoreline, with great views of the Strait of Georgia and Stanley Park. My advice? Pack a lunch and come during the week when the crowds won't be as thick.

See map p. 145. Beacon Lane off Marine Dr. ☎ *604-925-7200. Admission: Free. Open: Daily year-round.*

Queen Elizabeth Park
Shaughnessy

Queen Elizabeth Park, notable for its Bloedel Floral Conservatory (see listing in the "Discovering Vancouver's Top Sights from A to Z" section earlier in this chapter), also boasts interesting sculptures, flower gardens, and walking trails and benches. Still not convinced? Check this out: The park is the highest natural point of land within Vancouver's city limits. It is also home to Nat Bailey Stadium, which hosts professional baseball affiliated with the Oakland Athletics, and has the best hot dogs around. In 2007, construction will start to transform it into the 2010 Winter Olympic curling arena.

See map p. 145. Cambie St. near 33rd Ave. Admission: Free. Open: Daily dawn to dusk.

Spanish Banks Beach
Point Grey

Extremely popular on summer weekends, this beach attracts families, and windsurfers, thanks to a lifeguard and occasional checks for alcoholic beverages and BC bud (a.k.a. marijuana). You find wide paths and views on clear days of the mountains that crown the North Shore.

See map p. 145. Northwest Marine Dr. (at the foot of Tolmie St.). ☎ ***604-257-8400.*** *Admission: Free. Open: Daily dawn to dusk.*

Van Dusen Botanical Garden
Shaughnessy

Located about 1½ miles from Queen Elizabeth Park in a wealthy neighborhood, this botanical garden occupies a former golf course. Consequently, the weaving concrete pathways once used by golf carts make this attraction particularly accessible for wheelchairs. You find beautifully groomed theme gardens, such as a topiary garden of whimsically designed "plant-imals," a rhododendron walk, a rose garden, a children's garden, a Mediterranean garden, and many other attractions. Perhaps the biggest draw for kids and teens is the hedge maze, which allows them to "get lost" — and eventually find their way out. Allow one hour or more.

See map p. 145. 5251 Oak St. ☎ ***604-261-0011.*** www.vandusengarden.org. *Admission: Adults C$5.50–C$7.75 (US$4.60–US$6.45), seniors C$3.75–C$5.50 (US$3.10–US$4.60), children 13–18 C$3.75–C$5.75 (US$3.10–US$4.80), children 6–12 C$2.25–C$4 (US$1.85–US$3.35). Open: Daily 10 a.m. to dusk.*

Vanier Park
Kitsilano

In an enviable location squeezed in between Granville Island and Kitsilano Beach, this park has a serious air about it with three classy museums gracing its green lawns. During the last week of May, the Vancouver Children's Festival kicks up its heels here. The Bard on the Beach Festival, held throughout summer, draws Shakespeare fans. This park is also a great place for flying kites.

See map p. 142. At the northern foot of Chestnut St. ☎ *604-257-8400. Admission: Free. Open: Daily dawn to dusk.*

Wreck Beach
Point Grey

North Americans are not typically associated with exhibitionism, but on the West Coast, rules are thrown to the wind — and Wreck Beach is a place without many rules. Clothing is entirely optional, and this beach gets *busy*. Some entrepreneurs have tapped into this unique market by vending a number of treats (tofu hot dogs anyone?). The beach is out of public sight but accessible via a steep trail off the western side of Marine Drive, near the University of British Columbia. Do bring an open mind. *Don't* bring binoculars, camcorders, or modesty.

See map p. 145. Off Southwest Marine Dr., near the University of British Columbia campus. ☎ *604-257-8400. Admission: Free. Open: Daily dusk to dawn.*

Intriguing museums

If you're a museum addict — or you just want to escape rainy weather — you'll be pleased with the specialty museums in this section.

Barclay Heritage Square and Roedde House Museum
West End

Barclay Heritage Square, a four-block area of nine restored heritage houses from the 19th century, provides a welcome counterpoint to all the glass and steel downtown. You can tour one of them, the Roedde House, which is a good example of Queen Anne architecture designed by Francis Rattenbury (who also designed The Fairmont Empress Hotel in Victoria). Period furnishings and gardens reflect the style of that time; teas and concerts frequently take place. Call for an events schedule.

See map p. 142. 1415 Barclay St. ☎ *604-684-7040.* www.roeddehouse.org. *Admission: Adults C$5 (US$4.15), C$4 seniors, students, and children (US$3.35). Open: Tours Sun 2–4 p.m. and by appointment.*

B.C. Golf Museum
Point Grey

Golf enthusiasts may want to combine a quick tour of this small museum near the University of British Columbia with a visit to the Museum of Anthropology and the UBC Botanical Garden and Nitobe Memorial Garden (see listings in the "Discovering Vancouver's Top Sights from A to Z" section earlier in this chapter). Located right at the university's golf course, the museum holds every manner of golfing paraphernalia, including an overload of clubs, trophies won by star B.C. golfers, and a reference library. Allow 30 to 45 minutes.

See map p. 145. 2545 Blanca St. (at the University Golf Course). ☎ 604-222-4653. Admission: By donation. Open: Tues–Sun noon to 4 p.m.

Granville Island Sport Fishing Museum
Granville Island

This museum is really only for fishing enthusiasts. Exhibits include a big collection of fishing rods, reels, paintings, and photographs — everything but the proverbial big one. You can also view the world's largest public display of fly-fishing plates and hardy reels, along with a fishing simulator to determine whether you have the right stuff to snag a big one in the near future; if you do, you'll land a virtual 35-pound salmon. (Tell fish stories later that it was 50 pounds.) There's also an impressive collection of model ships — submarines, warships, trawlers — as well as a 13-foot-long cast replica of the H.M.S. Hood. Allow 30 minutes.

See map p. 142. 1502 Duranleau St. ☎ 604-683-1939. www.sportfishing museum.ca. *Admission: Adults C$7.50 (US$6.25), seniors and students C$6 (US$5), children 6–18 C$4 (US$3.35), children under 4 free. Open: Tues–Sun 10 a.m.–5:30 p.m.*

Vancouver Police Centennial Museum
Gastown

As nice as Vancouver is generally considered, the city does have its steamy and seamy side. A sordid past is hung out like dirty laundry at this intriguing Gastown museum. (Appropriately enough, it's housed in a former morgue and near a fairly down-at-the-heels neighborhood.) Exhibits include tools used by crooks (such as lock picks), plus counterfeit money, surveillance equipment, and some interesting stories from the city's rough-and-tumble old days. Allow 30 to 45 minutes.

See map p. 143. 240 East Cordova St. ☎ 604-665-3346. www.city.vancouver. bc.ca/police/museum. *Admission: Adults C$7 (US$5.80); seniors, students, and children 4–13 C$5 (US$4.15); children under 4 free. Open: Daily Mon–Sat 9 a.m.–5 p.m.*

Recreation and spectator sports

Vancouver is nothing if not suited to active travelers: Literally hundreds of hikes, jogs, bikes, and walks are possible within or near the city limits. If you're feeling like a *'tator* — a spectator, that is, not a couch 'tator — you're still in luck: The city boasts professional football (well, CFL football) and hockey. See Chapter 7 for my advice on how to get tickets to major sporting events.

BC Place Stadium
Yaletown

Canada's version of football — on a bigger field than its U.S. counterpart, with slightly different rules and wild scoring — takes place in BC Place Stadium all summer and in the fall.

See map p. 142. 777 Pacific Blvd. ☎ **604-589-ROAR (7627)**. www.bclions.com. *Tickets: C$25–C$65 (US$21–US$54). Season: June–late Oct.*

Queen Elizabeth Pitch and Putt
Shaughnessy

This par-three course takes in sweeping views of the surrounding area (it's on the highest metropolitan point) and offers a short but beautifully undulating course. It's a great place to practice your short game. You'll be charmed by the weeping willows that line the green fairways even if you don't hit 'em straight enough. Allow 1½ to 2 hours.

See map p. 145. In Queen Elizabeth Park, on Cambie St. at 33rd Ave. ☎ **604-874-8336**. *Admission: Adults C$11 (US$9.15), children C$8 (US$6.65). Open Feb–Nov daily dawn to dusk.*

Art-lovers' sights

Vancouver's art scene is alive in both new and old artistic traditions.

Bau-Xi Gallery
South Granville

Bau-Xi (pronounced BOE-she and meaning "great gift") features work by Canadian artists like Jack Shadbolt. The gallery uses an open-storage concept much like that of the Museum of Anthropology at the University of British Columbia (see the "Discovering Vancouver's Top Sights from A to Z" section earlier in this chapter). You have better access to the art here than at many galleries because of smaller crowds. Allow one hour.

See map p. 142. 3045 Granville St. ☎ **604-733-7011**. www.bau-xi.com. *Admission: Free. Open Mon–Sat 10 a.m.–5:30 p.m., Sun noon to 4 p.m.*

Gallery of B.C. Ceramics
Granville Island

This small gallery highlights pottery designed by local artists, some with rather quirky takes on what's usually considered to be a pretty conservative art form. Allow 45 minutes and call ahead to confirm store hours.

See map p. 142. 1359 Cartwright St. ☎ **604-669-5645**. *Open Tues–Sun, hours vary.*

Vancouver Art Gallery
Downtown

If you're a big fan of British Columbia painter Emily Carr, you'll love this downtown museum, which holds a large collection of her work detailing the provincial landscape and the First Nations people who inhabit it. Even if you're not so crazy about Emily Carr, the permanent collections aren't short on big names. You can see a few 20th-century pieces by folks such as Andy Warhol and visit a children's gallery with a hands-on studio. Allow one hour.

*See map p. 143. 750 Hornby St. ☎ **604-662-4700**. www.vanartgallery.bc.ca.*
Admission: Adults C$15 (US$12), seniors C$11 (US$9), students C$10 (US$8), children
under 12 free; By donation on Thurs nights during low season. Open: Tues–Sun and
holidays 10 a.m.–5:30 p.m. (Thurs until 9 p.m.); Closed Dec 25 and Jan 1.

Stanley Park is a gathering place for local artists — all styles and talents
imaginable — on the weekend. Some paintings you love; others you
question. A great stroll if it's sunny weather — bring your wallet.

Seeing Vancouver by Guided Tour

If you're short on time, have a hard time getting around, or just want an
overview, then a guided tour may be a good idea. And because Vancouver
has so many specialty tours, from kayaking up the inlet to trekking
through rain forests, such activities offer a unique way to see the city that
you might not find on your own. I've listed some of my favorite, and the
best, tour operators. Note that prices and policies are always subject to
change, so check ahead to ensure that itineraries and prices are what you
expect — and that the outfit hasn't gone out of business.

To tour or not to tour?

In Vancouver, this isn't a dummies question because it's an easy city
to explore; I'd think hard before committing time and money to a tour
guide. I enjoy using my own feet, ears, and eyes to experience a new
place just like a local. And you may feel the same way. On another continent, sure, I'd take a tour. Here in North America? That's a tough sell.

Here's why: First, you can easily reach all of Vancouver's splendors
by car, foot, boat, or public transit. Second, with few historical sites,
Vancouver's main attractions — mountains, parks, beaches, views,
and neighborhoods — require little to no explanation. The mere sight
of the beach and mountains framing the skyscrapers is enough.

That said, however, I concede that you may enjoy a narrated tour,
whether it's a guided walk through Chinatown, a high-speed tour by
bicycle, or one of the many other options I list in this section.

Booking direct

Although I respect the humble hotel concierge who may offer to arrange
a tour for you, I always recommend booking a tour directly with the tour
company. Some hotels and/or their employees receive a discreet "cut" of
any tour business booked through their recommendations. In my opin-
ion, this slants their judgment. Plus, to ensure that a tour meets your
interests and budget, you really should talk with the company personally. Sure, doing so may require extra work, but think of it this way: A
tour can take up four or five hours of your trip, so you want to make a
wise decision.

Touring Vancouver

The varied topography that makes Vancouver such an interesting place means you can see it umpteen ways: by bus, boat, foot, horse-drawn carriage, mountain bike, airplane, floatplane, or ski.

 I leave airplane tours out of this book because they're mighty expensive, but the city's tourism office stocks plenty of information on the top providers if you want to go that route.

Most of the tours in this section run from spring (March, April, or May) through the summer (end of September), but be sure to check with the individual company or operator — you may be pleasantly surprised.

 Many of the tour companies that I list offer some form of a family rate that saves you money if you have two adults and two children. Inquire when making a booking.

On foot

Vancouver's a great city to tour on foot. The salt tang in the air, the smell of a Chinese restaurant, and the crowds of exuberant tourists can buoy you through hours of walking, if that's what you want. The central peninsula even has a gentle grade, so you get a low-impact workout at the same time. Here are some great tour companies to try:

- ✔ **Architectural Institute of British Columbia Tours** (☎ **604-683-8588** or 800-667-0753 in British Columbia only; www.aibc.bc.ca) offers free walking tours of the city highlighting — what else? — interesting architecture in various neighborhoods. Call ahead, because the schedule and focus change each year.

- ✔ **Chinese Cultural Centre Tours** (☎ **604-658-8850**; www.cccvan. com) provides a concentrated look at the history of Chinatown. Tour fees are C$4.50–C$6.50 (US$3.75–US$5.40) adults, C$4 (US$3.35) seniors and children.

- ✔ **Pacific Running Guides** (☎ **604-828-7690** or 604-684-6464; www.pacificrunningguides.com) caters to people who want to pick up the pace with a guided run or jog through the city (averaging about C$40 (US$33) per hour).

By boat

One of the most pleasurable ways to get a look at the city is by taking one of several boat tours. Consider the following:

- ✔ **AquaBus Tours** (☎ **604-689-5858**; www.aquabus.bc.ca) and **False Creek Ferries** (☎ **604-684-7781**; www.granvilleislandferries. bc.ca) are Vancouver's two short-hop ferry services, offering several tours of False Creek and the surrounding area. You can go anywhere from just out to Granville Island to all around the city waterfront — just don't feel silly in those bathtub-shaped boats. Fees are C$6 (US$5) adults, C$3 (US$2.50) children.

✔ **Harbour Ferries** (☎ **800-663-1500** or 604-688-7246; www.boat cruises.com) offers a more complete water tour than short-hop ferries do, and on a cooler boat, too — a paddle wheeler. You leave from the base of Denman Street, in the West End, and head for Stanley Park and other local points. A dinnertime sunset or starlight cruise, with meals and music, departs every night at 7 p.m. for about three hours; the cost is C$69.95 (US$58) adults, C$59.95 (US$50) children 2–11. Shorter, 75-minute tours of the waterfront depart three to four times daily; admission costs C$19 (US$16) adults, C$16 (US$13) seniors and children 12–17, C$7 (US$5.80) children 5–11.

By horse

Touring by horse-drawn carriage is incredibly romantic, but it's really possible in only one part of town — Stanley Park, whose green paths are relatively unsullied by the traffic that makes carriage travel so unpleasant elsewhere around town.

Stanley Park Horse-Drawn Tours (☎ **604-681-5115;** www.stanleypark tours.com) provides a romantic way to see the famous park in an hour without feeling rushed. From mid-March through October, the horses do the work and the driver-guide does the talking as you pass Deadman's Island, the Lions Gate Bridge, old-growth forests, totem poles, and lots more. As a bonus, you don't need to book this tour in advance; just show up at the carriage lineup near the tourism information kiosk on Park Drive and jump aboard (or hop the free bus from your downtown hotel). The rides, from 9:40 a.m. until 4 or 5 p.m. daily, cost C$20.55 (US$17) adults, C$18.65 (US$16) seniors and students, C$13.05 (US$11) children 3–12.

By bus and car

The following are a few operators using buses and cars to view the city's hot spots:

✔ **Early Motion Tours** (☎ **604-687-5088**) provides slightly corny, old-time tours in the back seat of a top-down Model A Ford. Call for current tour offers and prices. Seats must be reserved in advance.

✔ **Gray Line of Vancouver** (☎ **800-667-0882** or 604-879-3363; www.grayline.ca/vancouver), the huge bus tour company, weighs in with a huge selection of Vancouver itineraries, including ocean kayaking (C$49 (US$41) per 2.5-hour trip), a sea safari on powerful twin-hull inflatables (C$50–C$60 (US$42–US$50) per 2 hours), and a deluxe city coach tour (C$55 adult (US$46), C$53 (US$44) student and senior, C$37 (US$31) children under 12 years of age). I prefer the popular Decker/Trolley tour that uses both a bright-red, London-style bus and a green, gas-powered trolley to trundle you around Downtown, Chinatown, Stanley Park, Granville Island, and beyond. Other offerings include tours of Vancouver by night, a Native-Canadian dinner, and sunset cruises. There's also a full-day tour — nearly 12 hours — to Victoria, that includes a visit at Butchart Gardens.

✔ **Vancouver Trolley Company** (☎ 888-451-5581 or 604-801-5515; www.vancouvertrolley.com), a continuously narrated circuit of stops through Vancouver's chief must-see points, makes this a good option for hop-on, hop-off sight-seeing. (It's not an actual trolley running the rails but is more like a dolled-up bus.) Trolleys make 16 stops, spaced throughout Downtown, Gastown, Chinatown, Vanier Park, and Stanley Park, among other places; if you don't get off at all, it takes two hours to do the circle. The tour runs daily from April through October, then from Fridays through Sundays only the rest of the year. Tours cost C$28 (US$23) adults, C$14 (US$12) children 4 to 12.

By bike

A bike tour is truly in the spirit of Vancouver, seeing that many locals commute to work on their bikes and ride them regularly for leisure no matter what the weather.

✔ **Spokes Bicycle Rentals** (☎ 604-688-5141; www.vancouverbikerental.com) is down near Stanley Park and offers two bike tours: a 1 hour 30 minute seawall excursion (C$32.95 (US$27) per person) and a half-day cycle in and around the park, and on to Granville Island (C$65.95 (US$55) per person). If you prefer some independence, check out the range of rentals from city bikes at C$6.54 (US$5.45) per hour to tandem mountain bikes at C$13 (US$11) per hour.

Taking a special-interest tour

The following identifies a few tour operators who are known for their ability to pinpoint special interests and lead you to particular slices of Vancouver city life:

✔ **All-Terrain Adventures** (☎ 888-754-5601 or 604-984-2374; www.all-terrain.com) runs a variety of innovative hikes, bikes, and other adventure-type tours of Vancouver and the surrounding area. The Hummer Wilderness Adventure, for example, involves five hours of touring in a 4x4 vehicle. The C$125 (US$104) price per person includes pick-up from your hotel, snacks, and beverages. In winter, there's a nifty Snowshoe and Chocolate Fondue Under the Stars deal at C$95 (US$79) per person all inclusive.

✔ **A Wok Around Chinatown** (☎ 604-736-9508; www.awokaround.com) offers a meandering tour through colorful Chinatown. Tour host Robert Sung is a fourth-generation Chinese-Canadian who's spent 27 years in food education, so you're getting the real McCoy.

His tour highlights historical landmarks alongside all the culinary treasures and specialty shops, which feature products from barbequed crispy ducks and herbal medicines to cookware supplies. Tours are four hours and cost about C$90 (US$75) per person.

✔ **Asian Culinary Culture** (☎ **604-813-5169;** www.edible-vancouver. com) is another Chinese culinary adventure, led by Stephanie Yuen, a restaurant critic, food writer, and member of Les Dames d'Escoffier. Her tours incorporate the full enchilada of dining experiences, wine-paired dinners, cooking classes, and more. Prices vary.

✔ **LandSea Tours** (☎ **800-558-4955** or 604-662-7591; www.vancouver tours.com) is an active local operator. Its twice-daily, half-day tour of the city costs C$55 (US$46) for adults, C$52 (US$43) for seniors, and C$35 (US$29) for children.

✔ **Lotus Land Tours** (☎ **800-528-3531** or 604-684-4922; www.lotus landtours.com) offers four-hour kayak paddling tours of Indian Arm, a fjord. The tour breaks midway for an island picnic featuring barbecued salmon on an uninhabited island. Heartier offerings and tours for groups that combine paddling with motorboat cruising are also available. Prices vary.

✔ **Rockwood Adventures** (☎ **888-236-6606** or 604-980-7749; www.rockwoodadventures.com) runs daily walking tours of the city — rain gear provided when necessary — plus a range of tours of the surrounding mountains and islands. Rockwood specializes in environmental destinations: You see big trees, rain forests, and the like. The company also offers a Discover the Orient Tour of Chinatown and a Granville Island tour. Prices vary.

✔ **Silver Challenger Tours** (☎ **877-943-3343** or 604-943-3343; www. BCEcotours.com) operates multiple day fishing tours on a commercial fishing boat. Participants get to navigate using the boat's radar, locate fish with sonar equipment, watch the catch — and then dine on their own fresh-caught salmon and shellfish. If you have the time, this is quite the different adventure. Prices vary.

✔ **Sunsail Yacht Charters** (☎ **866-241-4111** or 250-758-5965; www. sunsail.ca) will appeal to those who want (and are qualified) to take to the seas under their own sail. With a small fleet of 6 10-berth Oceanis vessels, and a six-berth catamaran, these yachts are the ultimate way to explore some of the best sailing waters in the world. And there's always the option of taking along a Sunsail skipper. Sunsail usually caters only to multiple-day charters but if you call the local number, the local Sunsail folks are amazingly accommodating. If there's a boat in the dock, they'll grab a skipper and you'll be onto the water for as many hours as you want.

✔ **Takaya Tours** (☎ **604-904-7410;** www.takayatours.com) offers sea kayaking and canoe trips up Indian Arm; guides are First Nations and well informed on the region's history and mythology. Two-hour sampler tours are C$40 (US$33) per person; a five-hour adventure runs around C$75 (US$62) and a full moon paddle — very romantic — is C$40 (US$33).

✔ **The X Tour** (☎ **604-609-2770;** www.x-tour.com) offers a look at the local buildings that were used in *The X-Files* television program — Scully's apartment, FBI buildings, CIA buildings, the whole shebang. The show may no longer be filmed in Vancouver (it's in syndication now), but diehard fans may still want a brush with stardom. Prices vary.

Labyrinth secrets

And now for something completely different — the labyrinth at St. Paul's Anglican Church (1130 Jervis St. ☎ **604-685-6832;** www.stpaulsanglican.bc.ca/labyrinth). More than 4,500 spiritual pilgrims of all kinds walk, shuffle, dance, and skip along the path of this indoor labyrinth that has been painted onto an old gymnasium floor. There's no religious creed or expectation; it's simply there for all to enjoy and expereince. A place to come in from out of the rain. Call ahead to confirm opening hours.

Chapter 12

Shopping the Local Stores

● ●

In This Chapter

▶ Getting an overview of the shopping scene
▶ Reviewing the department stores and smaller boutiques
▶ Finding the best shopping neighborhoods

● ●

*I*f you believe the Monty Python skit, Canadians are a happy clan of lumberjacks who "drink all night and sleep all day." Thankfully, Canada — especially Vancouver — has a lot more to offer. Its size, multi-cultural make-up, and geographic location as a gateway to Asia (and Asian tourists) make for a pretty diverse shopping experience. There's no shortage of top designer names and high-quality as well as offbeat ethnic goods, hemp-related gear (Vancouver is North America's mari-juana capital), and one-of-a-kind finds. In fact, you may be surprised at how many internationally renowned labels originate from this fair city.

Surveying the Scene

But hold on. Before you set off on a Vancouver shopping spree, you need to know the basics of the local scene. This section includes a quick run-down on shopping hours, specialty items, customs, and taxes.

You need to get used to the general shopping hours in Vancouver, which are similar to those in the rest of Canada, but are a little different from standard hours in the United States. Stores usually open at 9:30 or 10 a.m. and close at 5 p.m. on Monday through Wednesday. On Thursdays and Fridays, however, stores stay open later, usually until 9 p.m. Then, on Saturday, it's 9 a.m. to 5 p.m. again. Sunday, as you might expect, is a short shopping day, with most stores opening at noon and closing at 5 p.m. (or even 4 p.m. in the case of smaller merchants).

Vancouver offers a few **specialty items** at great prices. Read on for the lowdown on the best-known stuff.

Vancouver Shopping

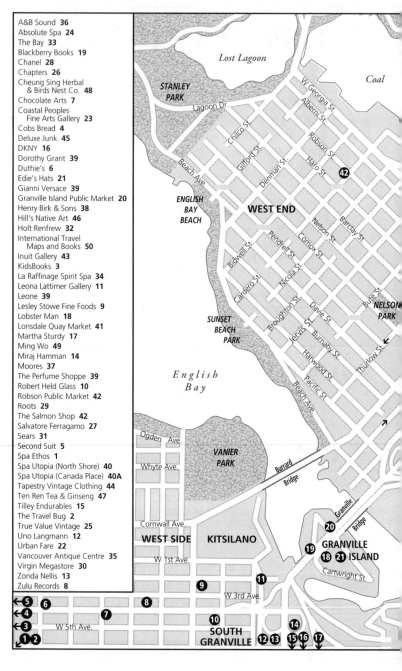

A&B Sound **36**
Absolute Spa **24**
The Bay **33**
Blackberry Books **19**
Chanel **28**
Chapters **26**
Cheung Sing Herbal
  & Birds Nest Co. **48**
Chocolate Arts **7**
Coastal Peoples
  Fine Arts Gallery **23**
Cobs Bread **4**
Deluxe Junk **45**
DKNY **16**
Dorothy Grant **39**
Duthie's **6**
Edie's Hats **21**
Gianni Versace **39**
Granville Island Public Market **20**
Henry Birk & Sons **38**
Hill's Native Art **46**
Holt Renfrew **32**
International Travel
  Maps and Books **50**
Inuit Gallery **43**
KidsBooks **3**
La Raffinage Spirit Spa **34**
Leona Lattimer Gallery **11**
Leone **39**
Lesley Stowe Fine Foods **9**
Lobster Man **18**
Lonsdale Quay Market **41**
Martha Sturdy **17**
Ming Wo **49**
Miraj Hamman **14**
Moores **37**
The Perfume Shoppe **39**
Robert Held Glass **10**
Robson Public Market **42**
Roots **29**
The Salmon Shop **42**
Salvatore Ferragamo **27**
Sears **31**
Second Suit **5**
Spa Ethos **1**
Spa Utopia (North Shore) **40**
Spa Utopia (Canada Place) **40A**
Tapestry Vintage Clothing **44**
Ten Ren Tea & Ginseng **47**
Tilley Endurables **15**
The Travel Bug **2**
True Value Vintage **25**
Uno Langmann **12**
Urban Fare **22**
Vancouver Antique Centre **35**
Virgin Megastore **30**
Zonda Nellis **13**
Zulu Records **8**

Lost Lagoon

Coal

STANLEY
PARK

W. Georgia St.
Alberni St.
Lagoon Dr.
Chilco St.
Gilford St.
Denman St.
Robson St.
Haro St.

42

Beach Ave.

ENGLISH
BAY
BEACH

WEST END

Nelson St.
Comox St.
Barclay St.
Pendrell St.
Bidwell St.
Nicola St.
Cardero St.
Broughton St.
Davie St.

NELSON
PARK

Bute St.

SUNSET
BEACH
PARK

Jervis St.
Burnaby St.
Harwood St.
Thurlow St.

Pacific St.

*English
Bay*

Beach Ave.

Ogden Ave.

VANIER
PARK

Whyte Ave.

Burrard
Bridge

Cornwall Ave.

WEST SIDE   KITSILANO

W 1st Ave.

Granville Bridge

20

19   **GRANVILLE**
18 **21** **ISLAND**
Cartwright St.

9

11

W 3rd Ave.

5 **6**

8

4

7

3

10
SOUTH
GRANVILLE

14

12 **13**   **15** **16** **17**

W 5th Ave.

1 **2**

✔ **Vintage clothing:** Vancouver really delivers in the vintage clothing department. Just head on down to Cordova Street (on the edge of Gastown) and troll through the lineup to get your very own hipster *Shaft*-era hat, granny glasses, bowling shirt, leather coat, or crinoline skirt. Or anything Elvis. Main Street, known as "Antique Row" between 15th and 30th, is another good bet for people's cast-offs.

✔ **Fine clothing:** The city has big bucks, and despite its casual West Coast groove, you can find an abundance of top-flight clothing on the downtown peninsula and occasionally elsewhere.

✔ **Native-Canadian arts, crafts, and woolens:** Native items are a big seller here, and quality selections are around downtown and out in politically correct Kitsilano. Look especially for Native-Canadian candy (a type of smoked salmon) and Cowichan sweaters, hand-woven in distinctively Native patterns. Begin looking along Water Street, at the foot of Gastown, which also has many touristy First Nations knick-knacks.

If you're going to be visiting the Museum of Anthropology at the University of British Columbia (see Chapter 11), pick up a brochure called *Publication #10: A Guide to Buying Contemporary Northwest Coast Indian Arts*; it explains the quality and pricing of Native-Canadian art and other crafts.

✔ **Asian and Indian items:** The city overflows with cheap, fun imported items from China, Hong Kong, Korea, and India — but also some higher-class stuff, too, from Japan and China. Chinatown is the obvious place to start; be prepared for crowds and confusion, and try to know what you're buying before paying big bucks.

South of the city center are several other Asian shopping areas. One, a string of Indian shops, is called the Punjabi Market (see "Going to Market" later in this chapter). An even larger — although harder-to-reach — area is located in Richmond, not so far from the Vancouver airport. This complex consists of four adjacent Asian shopping malls, all geared toward the well-heeled immigrant Asian. Here, you find quality, as opposed to sheer quantity in Chinatown, and don't be surprised if you suddenly think you're actually shopping in Hong Kong — the experience is that authentic! Also in Richmond lies the picturesque, and authentic, commercial fishing village of Steveston — first settled at the turn of the twentieth century — with its small antique shops, boutiques, and galleries.

✔ **Salmon:** Buying a cut of salmon is definitely *de rigueur* when visiting Vancouver, and it's better and cheaper (relatively speaking) here than anywhere else on the continent, except maybe Maine or Nova Scotia. Salmon is smoked in a number of different ways, and you can try them all. Many come gift-packaged in Native-inspired cedar boxes.

Foot fetish

As one of North America's most walkable cities, perhaps it shouldn't be a surprise to find that some very sought-after footwear originates here; check out **John Fluevog,** 839 Granville St. (☎ 604-688-2828), for over-the-top designs; **Dayton Shoes,** 2250 Hastings St. (☎ 604-253-6671), for the original, handmade biker boots that Hollywood has made so chic; and **David Gordon Boots,** 822 Granville St. (☎ 604-685-3784), for many one-of-a-kind Western boots to rival the best that Dolly Parton or Jimmy Buffet might ever have worn.

 Remember to keep careful track of whatever you buy in Canada. Customs regulations require an accounting of everything you bring home across the border, so keep those receipts and be honest when they question you. (For information on what you can take home with you, see Chapter 7.)

 And don't forget about taxes. You pay a surcharge totaling 14 percent for the privilege of shopping in Canada. For more information on taxes and how to receive a general sales tax refund, totaling half of that 14 percent, see Chapter 4.

Checking Out the Big Names

For such a large and prosperous city, surprisingly few big-name department stores are left in downtown Vancouver; in fact, now only three remain — and only two of 'em are Canadian:

- ✔ **The Bay,** 674 Granville St., Downtown (☎ 604-681-6211), also known as the **Hudson's Bay Company,** anchors the corner of Georgia and Granville Streets. The store contains a smattering from all the big-name fashion houses that you'd expect at any respectable big-league department store, plus a variety of other goods, too. You even find some Canadian items, such as its signature woolen blankets from the far north that recall the days when this was a rough-and-tumble, trapping-and-trading outfit. The store is open Monday to Wednesday, 9:30 a.m. to 7 p.m., Thursday and Friday until 9 p.m., Saturday 9:30 a.m. to 7 p.m., and Sunday 10 a.m. to 6 p.m.

- ✔ **Holt Renfrew,** 633 Granville St., Downtown (☎ 604-681-3121), is the other biggie still standing downtown, and it remains a classy (although not through-the-roof expensive) place to shop for fashions, particularly men's fashions, which are probably a cut above those you find across the street at The Bay. The store also has a very good shoe selection. Opening hours are the same as at the other two behemoths.

✔ **Sears,** 701 Granville St., Downtown (☎ 604-685-7112), on the third
level of Pacific Centre, where you can expect the usual sorts of
mid-priced cosmetics, men's and women's clothing, and housewares you would find in an American Sears. It's open Monday to
Wednesday, 9:30 a.m. to 7 p.m., Thursday and Friday until 9 p.m.,
Saturday 9:30 a.m. to 7 p.m., Sunday 10 a.m. to 6 p.m.

While visiting the big-name stores, don't panic if you don't recognize
some of the designer names, and don't feel tentative about buying the
house labels. Canada's fashion industry (based in Montreal) is going
strong, with a number of designers and tailors imported from France or
Italy. These are quality clothes.

You can also find outlet stores for many big-name designers downtown
and along Robson Street, including — but certainly not limited to —
Gianni Versace, 757 West Hastings, Downtown (☎ 604-683-1131);
Salvatore Ferragamo, 918 Robson St., Downtown (☎ 604-669-4495);
Chanel, 900 West Hastings, Downtown (☎ 604-682-0522); **DKNY,** 2625
Granville St., South Granville (☎ 604-733-2000), and **Betsey Johnson,**
1033 Alberni St., Downtown (☎ 603-488-0314).

Going to Market

Vancouver is blessed with an amazing concentration of urban markets —
with clothing, ethnic food, and more. They're so good that they may
actually provide you with more pleasure than the usual big-name and
big-street shopping described in this chapter. They are certain to supply
more cultural stimulation, because these are the places where Vancouver
locals shop, browse, and just generally hang out. To take just one example, dozens of Asian markets, dispersed throughout the city, provide
ample opportunity to pick up that exotic gift of ginseng jelly, lacquered
chopsticks, or that hard-to-find box of bonito flakes you've been dying to
find.

I highly recommend you make the time to explore at least one of the
markets described in this section.

Chinatown markets

The markets of Chinatown are a special case, because rather than finding one centralized Asian market, you'll discover a fascinating array of
individual merchants packed into the compact blocks within Powell,
Keefer, and Main Streets; seeing them is absolutely essential, even on a
short visit to the city. Thankfully, the area is fairly close to downtown, so
you can just dive in and sift through the mounds of straw mats and hats,
cotton slippers, candy, cookware, exotic spices, and veggies laid out in
barrels. The majority of these shops are inexpensive, chaotic, and pretty
similar to one another.

A few local favorites include **Ming Wo,** 23 East Pender St. (☎ **604-683-7268**), the flagship of the local cookware chain and a cut above the rest; **Ten Ren Tea & Ginseng,** 550 Main St. (☎ **604-684-1566**), a tea, herb, and spice shop; and **Cheung Sing Herbal & Birds Nest Co.,** 536 Main St. (☎ **604-899-1123**), a place of more epic contents that come with over-the-counter exotic medical remedies (optional, of course). Don't visit these places if you have a weak stomach, though, because many of the odder antidotes are, um, animal derived.

Although you may think so, bargaining isn't really kosher in the Chinatown markets.

One of the real joys of visiting Chinatown in summer is a chance to experience the so-called "night market," when several blocks centered around Keefer, Main, and East Pender Streets are closed to traffic on Friday, Saturday, and Sunday evenings from 6 p.m. until around midnight to allow pedestrians the full run of the area. That's when the good street food comes out, sold by the piece — no need to dine at a restaurant on one of these nights. If you don't mind a little jostling, you'll feel like you've penetrated the essential heart of Asian Vancouver.

Walking here from downtown or Gastown at night is certainly possible, logistically speaking, but the intervening area is a bit marginal in terms of safety. Take a cab after hours.

Granville Island Public Market

When the weather's good, the **Granville Island Public Market,** 1669 Johnston St. (www.granvilleisland.bc.ca), in a former factory complex, is by far the city's largest and most interesting market — a beautifully located concentration of produce, flower, and other markets rolled into one. The appealing waterside package also offers the bonus of a microbrewery on site. And the daily carnival of locals, tourists, performers, and panhandlers guarantees no people-watcher can possibly go home unsatisfied. The market is open daily from 9 a.m. to 6 p.m.; closed Mondays during January only.

With so much food from which to choose, sample takeout from several of a mind-boggling array of international offerings — and then pick up something for dessert and sit on the waterside benches. If the performers (who could be professional singers in training or basically panhandlers in disguise) bug you too much, rent a canoe from the kayak shop on Duranleau Street and paddle out of earshot.

Street parking is tight on the island, however, especially on weekends, in summer, or (egad!) on summer weekends. You can pay to park in the big garage, if there's room. It's probably more intelligent and less of a headache, though, to get here via the cute little AquaBus tugboats that run from the downtown peninsula, or by taking city bus #51 (see Chapter 8 for details on buses). If feasible, walking's a good option, too.

Lonsdale Quay Market

Across the water in North Vancouver, and conveniently right on the SeaBus ferry dock, the smaller **Lonsdale Quay Market,** 123 Carrie Cates Court (☎ **604-985-6261**), gives a good fix of food and scenery, especially if you're en route to or coming back from Grouse Mountain, the Capilano Bridge, the Horseshoe Bay ferry terminal, or Whistler. The market is open daily from 9:30 a.m. to 6:30 p.m. and until 9 p.m. on Fridays. Restaurants generally are open until 9 p.m. on weekdays, later on weekends.

The ground floor is dedicated to eats. Particularly good are the Chinese food stalls and fish and chips, and you can eat on the wharf. Don't miss the excellent produce too, which makes this market the perfect en-route stop for picnic planning. (You'll probably have to wait until you officially relocate to Vancouver to take advantage of the excellent fish market, however.) Upstairs, a collection of shops offers decent books, clothes, and knick-knacks. A special children's area called Kids' Alley is also here.

The evening rush hour can be a busy time here, as homeward-bound North Shore commuters scurry to pick up the evening's supper. Do your shopping before 4:30 p.m., if you can.

The easiest way to get to Lonsdale Quay Market is by taking the scenic SeaBus ride from the Vancouver waterfront to the North Vancouver landing; the market is right next to the landing.

Robson Public Market

The glass-enclosed **Robson Public Market,** 1610 Robson St. (☎ **604-682-2733**), up the street from the too-expensive shops along central Robson Street, is a real find. The market includes a tasteful collection of some of the city's better gourmet food offerings, all assembled under a long and airy roof that lets in the summer sunlight. Think trays of Okanagan cherries and apples, fresh-packed Pacific salmon, and just about anything else you could want — designer chocolate, good beer and wine, croissants, just-squeezed juice. And that's merely the bottom floor; upstairs, you find takeout fare of every stripe. This should be a locals' kind of place by now, and why they don't make better use of it beats me. The market's open daily from 9 a.m. to 9 p.m.

Punjabi Market

If you have the energy, the **Punjabi Market,** a hard-to-reach but visually interesting Indian market, is along four blocks of Main Street between 48th and 52nd Streets south of downtown, in an area sometimes called South Vancouver. As with Chinatown (discussed in the "Chinatown markets" section), this place isn't contained under one central roof but consists of a string of look-alike shops. Sure, the location is several miles south of the city, but nowhere else (save New York or Toronto, perhaps) can you find such an abundance of Indian fabrics, hot spices, Hindi hit tunes, and more at such amazing prices.

Aaaaah ... Spas in Vancouver

British Columbia has more spas per capita than anywhere else in Canada, and Vancouver's got the most spas in B.C. The range can be intoxicating, which also means the quality can fluctuate. Here are my recommendations for some top-notch spa experiences.

Absolute Spa at the Century (1015 Burrard St.; ☎ 604-684-2772; www.absolute spa.com) offers a slew of complimentary services with all its treatments such as light meals, eucalyptus steams, and a swim in its ozone-treated swimming pool — which means it's tough to get an appointment. Celebrities like Gwyneth Paltrow and Gillian Anderson have added to this spa's mystique. Absolute Spa is also at Vancouver Airport domestic (☎ 604-273-4772) and international (☎ 604-270-4772) departure gates, Fairmont Airport Hotel (☎ 604-248-2772), and Fairmont Hotel Vancouver (☎ 604-648-2909).

La Raffinage Spirit Spa (521 West Georgia St.; ☎ 604-681-9933; www.la raffinage.com) is a warm and inviting haven off the main drag, specializing in body work, facials, and treatments with a New Age — yet surprisingly mainstream — twist. It's the only place in town where you can combine a manicure or facial with Reiki, and an aura or tarot card reading. Cool!

Miraj Hammam (1495 West 6th Ave.; ☎ 604-733-5151; www.mirajhammam.com) is the only Turkish delight of its kind in Canada, and reportedly in North America. Akin to a Middle Eastern steam bath, or *hammam*, Miraj offers a luxurious steam and traditional body scrub with Moroccan black soap followed by an optional (and highly recommended) full-body massage. The entire experience, including the architecture and atmosphere, feels like something out of *The Arabian Nights*, save for the flying carpets.

Spa Ethos (2200 West 4th Ave.; ☎ 866-826-3838 or 604-733-5007; www.spa ethos.com), in yuppieville Kitsilano, is very, very nice. Although its dozen or so treatment rooms are on the small side, the tasteful, uncomplicated decor, well-trained staff, and range of services have made Spa Ethos a local favorite. A great interlude while exploring this neat neighborhood.

Spa Utopia (160–889 Harbourside Dr.; ☎ 866-980-3977 or 604-980-3977; www.spa utopia.ca), in North Vancouver, is likely the most over-the-top spa you'll find in these here parts — the ambiance is absolutely stunning, with Grecian columns, free-standing fountains, and floor-to-ceiling waterside views. Practitioners are highly skilled, and services are excellent. In April 2005, Spa Utopia opened another "wow" location at the Pan Pacific Hotel (☎ 604-641-1351).

Searching Out the Best Shopping Neighborhoods

The city is full of good shopping neighborhoods and specialty stores. This section includes my recommendations. If you're hunting for a particular item, jump to the index at the end of this chapter to find the store and neighborhood that fills your needs.

Downtown

Downtown is where most of the heavy hitters are concentrated, mostly in a series of malls with unexciting names like Pacific Centre, Sinclair Centre, and Harbour Centre. You also find several worthwhile shopping streets: Granville Street — with its too-urban mixture of department stores, record stores, and peep shows — and the much classier Robson Street, which has been taken over by chain stores like The Gap, but still offers great people-watching, cafes, and upscale merchandise. This section lays out the highlights of the downtown-shopping scene.

✔ Despite the tough competition around town, music store **A&B Sound,** 556 Seymour St. (☎ **604-687-5837**), succeeds by giving you a variety of experiences to keep you in the store. Pop music greets you as you enter, but A&B also has a book section upstairs, a small movie area where a film's always running, and classical music CDs and videos for sale. Periodic sales lower prices significantly.

✔ If you need a book title and need it fast, chances are excellent that huge **Chapters,** 788 Robson St. (☎ **604-682-4066**), will carry it when other bookstores may have to put in a special order. There's another branch at Granville Street and West Broadway (☎ **604-731-7822**).

✔ Located inside the upscale Sinclair Centre complex, **Dorothy Grant,** 757 West Hastings St. (☎ **604-681-0201;** www.dorothygrant.com), weaves her Haida heritage into Native-inspired fashions with appliqués onto suits, coats, vests, and jackets for men and women. While Grant's intricate button blankets and couture lines are considered collector's items, her off-the-rack styles are more affordable.

✔ Also in the Sinclair Centre is **The Perfume Shoppe (☎ 604-299-8463;** wwwtheperfumeshoppe.com), and its access to more than 750 scents. Here's where to sample all those hard-to-find and fine European parfumeurs' fragrances such as Serge Lutens, Carthusia, Creed, and Bellodgia. Since science tells us that smell tops the 0-zone barometer, dab it on, baby!

✔ **Henry Birk & Sons,** 698 West Hastings St. (☎ **800-682-2622** or 604-669-3333; www.birks.com), an upscale Canadian jeweler, is a good choice for reliable watches, engagement rings, and other traditional jewelry.

✔ **International Travel Maps and Books,** 530 West Broadway (☎ **604-687-3320**), is the place to come in town for topographic or other maps — the selection is fantastic — plus a huge array of specialty books you would never find anywhere else (because they were basically published in someone's kitchen). Need a hiking, skiing, or wildflower guide to some obscure B.C. mountain range? Come here first.

✔ When you shop for clothes at **Leone,** 757 West Hastings St. (☎ **604-683-1133**), you may want to dress your best even before you get here. A high-end and beautifully designed store, this shop offers every famous European designer you'd expect or want to find — each in its own carefully designated area. Head downstairs from Leone's main entrance to **A-Wear** for the 20-something crowd, and house-label clothes that don't have Italian names stitched on them but are still pretty good.

✔ The men's clothing store **Moores,** 524 Granville St. (☎ **604-669-1712**), is one of the better choices in the downtown district — not the most expensive in town, but stocked nevertheless with quality shirts, suits, neckties, and more.

✔ The Canadian clothing store of the moment is **Roots,** 1001 Robson St. (☎ **604-683-4305**). Not a new store, Roots transformed its look from post-hippie to simply hip (just as San Francisco's The Gap did). Everything here is casually cool, with an inclination toward clothes you can wear comfortably outdoors. Roots was the official outfitter for three Olympic teams in 2002, and are the folks who will dress the U.S. Olympians in 2008, 2010, and 2012.

✔ **The Salmon Shop,** 1610 Robson St. (☎ **604-688-3474**), is a convenient location to pick up smoked salmon before hopping back on your plane home. The Robson Street location means you may pay more than you should.

✔ You can find beads, leather, and odd garments galore at **True Value Vintage,** 710 Robson St. (☎ **604-685-5403**), a subterranean little showroom. Asian tourists love the place — I'm not sure why.

✔ For antiques hunting, hit the **Vancouver Antique Centre,** 422 Richards St. (☎ **604-669-7444**), a sprawling collection of shops and dealers in two unremarkable buildings. Some of the stuff for sale here is trash, some of it's treasure, but if it's pouring rain and you want to go a-hunting, this is the place to do it. Opening hours vary by dealer.

✔ **Virgin Megastore,** 788 Burrard St. (☎ **604-669-2289**), is a warehouse-like altar to recorded music (it was once a library). Dressed out in typically Virgin — that is to say, flamboyant — style, Vancouver's Virgin is located centrally in the city's poshest shopping district. Woe be to you, though, if the next-big-thing boy band should happen to be in the lobby signing T-shirts and body parts for hundreds of screaming teenaged girls. In that case, disappear to the basement, hook up some headphones, and listen to the latest CDs in relative obscurity. Open Monday through Thursday from 9:30 a.m. to 11 p.m., Friday and Saturday until midnight, and Sunday until 10 p.m.

Gastown

Gastown is the place to go for vintage clothing or modern art (not to mention camera-clicking tourists). Like Granville Street, this area is a blend of over-the-top tacky and gone-to-seed local characters. Cordova Street, in particular, serves up secondhand-clothing stores — including great leather coats and some wild '70s fashions — as well as a handful of topflight little avant-garde fashion shops and artsy galleries, too. This section gives you my top recommendations.

✔ Of all the joints along Cordova Street, **Deluxe Junk,** 310 West Cordova St. (☎ 604-685-4871), probably offers the best vintage clothing. There's a crazy-quilt of stuff to dig through, some of it truly deserving of the moniker "junk," and some of it just about to come back in vogue — maybe. Note that prices here, which can seem high at first glance, drop over time as an item awaits a home. Check the tag to see whether the shelf life of a knick-knack merits a markdown in price.

✔ **Hill's Native Art,** 165 Water St. (☎ 604-685-4249; www.hills nativeart.com), does resemble a former trading post, but get beyond the slightly campy look and you find quality items like Native-Canadian sweaters, totem poles, sculptured stone, masks, jewelry, and so on. Talking with the staff is an enjoyable lesson in First Nations culture and mythology.

✔ **Inuit Gallery,** 206 Water St. (☎ 604-688-7323), sells an amazing collection of Inuit art. The selection is top drawer, so don't come expecting a bargain-basement find. In fact, coming here is like going to a museum without actually having to buy a ticket, and for that alone — the exposure to such wonderful work — you want to make time for a visit.

✔ **Tapestry Vintage Clothing,** 321 Cambie St. (☎ 604-687-1719), a Gastown lowbrow option on grungified Cambie Street, seems to specialize in women's stuff (as many retro stores do). Think '40s, '50s, and '60s, for starters. This store has bell-bottoms, too, of course.

Chinatown

Chinatown is just what you'd expect, a concentration of shops, eateries, and produce markets, where nearly all the signs are in Chinese, the lampposts are elaborately Asian, and newspapers are in Chinese pictographs. The only real shopping you can do here is for exotic herbs, spices, and food, or for inexpensive souvenir-type items, such as bamboo flutes or chimes. See the "Chinatown markets" section earlier in this chapter for my recommended shops.

Granville Island

Granville Island is beloved by locals — it's just a fun place to hang out, eat, watch the water (and each other), and shop in the stalls, which purvey everything from organic produce to hand-knit clothing. Here are three of my favorite stores.

- ✔ Everyone raves about **Blackberry Books,** 1663 Duranlea St. (☎ 604-685-4113 or 604-685-6188), a good local favorite. It stocks upscale cookbooks — you know, the tomes with nice, glossy pictures throughout, not the ring-binder ones with grease stains — plus a selection of art, photography, and other titles.

- ✔ **Edie's Hats**, 1666 Johnston St. (☎ 604-683-4280), is all hats — but what fine (and expensive) hats these are, some designed by Edie and others selected from the best of Paris, London, and other fashion hot spots.

- ✔ **The Lobster Man**, 1807 Mast Tower Rd. (☎ 604-687-4531), has all manner of fresh lobster, clams, and Dungeness crabs snorkeling away in the oversized salt-water tanks, ready to be steamed (for free) while you wait or packed for travel. Open daily 9 a.m. to 6 p.m.

South Granville

Just south of Granville Island is the surprisingly upscale South Granville neighborhood, really a locals' kind of area but with some quality stores, if you know where to look.

- ✔ **Leona Lattimer Gallery,** 1590 West 2nd Ave. (☎ 604-732-4556), is where to come for higher-priced Native-Canadian goods — such as your very own totem pole. Don't forget your checkbook. This isn't the place for a stocking-stuffer, but rather a serious gift.

- ✔ **Martha Sturdy,** 3039 Granville St. (☎ 604-737-0037), is the doyenne of Canadian housewares, design furnishings, and some of the finest jewelry in North America. You're more likely to see her wares, though, in the pages of *Cosmo* or on the runways of Paris than about town. Sturdy's signature jewelry — twisted metal into eye-catching letters of the alphabet — is always popular, as are her chic earrings, necklaces, and pendants.

- ✔ Barbara and John Tilley have fostered their virtually indestructible travel hat into more than 65 varieties of headgear — a Tilley hat has become *the* signature of seasoned travelers. But you'll find much more really useful travel gear at their store, **Tilley Endurables,** 2401 Granville St. (☎ 604-732-4287) — you know, the kind that doesn't wrinkle, dries overnight, and repels dirt.

✔ You can tell right away from the short hours that antiques dealer **Uno Langmann,** 2117 Granville St. (☎ **604-736-8825**), deals in exclusive stuff. The high-priced antiques here run from European silver and porcelain to furniture and other items, all from way before you were born. Open Wednesday through Saturday only, 10 a.m. to 5 p.m.

✔ Designer **Zonda Nellis,** 2203 Granville St. (☎ **604-736-5668**) has dressed some of the world's most charismatic celebrities . . . Aretha Franklin, the queen of Morocco, and Bridget Fonda, to name just a few. Her uncreasable handwoven separates, with silks and knits to match, are as distinctive as they are sophisticated while her hand-painted velvet fashions are to die for, each piece coordinated with the other whether it's a long opera coat with pants and a short jacket, or a long skirt and blouse.

Kitsilano and Point Grey

Kitsilano is the place to come for gourmet foods: Every street corner has another cafe, coffee shop, sushi place, natural foods store, or chocolatier. The main shopping area extends west along West 4th Avenue from Granville Street. Only a few blocks south, **Broadway** runs parallel to the west and offers a somewhat more variable, alternative mix of businesses: dubious Chinese restaurants and junk shops, but then also a store selling excellent all-natural cosmetics. What follows are my picks for the neighborhood's best stores:

✔ **Chocolate Arts,** 2037 West 4th Ave. (☎ **604-739-0475**), is hands down the most interesting and best chocolate shop in a city that seems obsessed with the cocoa bean. Check out this recipe: Begin with one inventive chocolatier (that would be Greg Hook) who doesn't mess around with fillers in his product, using only organic fruits and the best cocoa butter. Then stir in one wonderful collaborating partner, Native-Canadian artist Robert Davidson. The result? High-quality chocolates formed into Native masks and other distinctively Pacific Northwestern shapes and patterns. Plus, they taste great.

✔ **Duthie's,** 2239 West 4th Ave. (☎ **604-732-5344**), is Vancouver's best-loved bookstore — heck, it may be *Canada's* best-loved bookstore — but apparently it's not being loved enough, because the cozy downtown location (big ladders and all) has closed, leaving only this Kits location as the last holdout. Still, it's well worth a stop if you're looking for Canadian history, travel titles, or books that were published abroad. The staff should be licensed as private detectives, they're so good at tracking down obscure or out-of-print stuff. *Generation X* author Douglas Coupland has been sighted working one shift a week here.

✔ One of the best bakeries in the city is **Cobs Breads,** 2320 West 4th Ave. (☎ **604-714-4070**) and 2837 West Broadway (☎ **604-714-0917**), a success story from down under that's come north with its delicious olive breads, focaccias, and similar artisanal breads. Knock yourself out with the fruity apricot loaf or the too-sinful chocolate cherry bread.

✔ **KidsBooks,** 3038 West Broadway (☎ **604-738-5335**), has the best selection of children's literature in the city by far. The store is totally geared to getting small folk into reading, what with its mobile displays, hand puppets, storytelling sessions, and staff that might even bring out your inner kid.

✔ There may be no better place to stock up for a luxurious picnic — from appetizer to finish — than at **Lesley Stowe Fine Foods,** 1780 West 3rd Ave. (☎ **604-731-3663**). The sweets are especially good.

✔ **Robert Held Glass,** 2130 Pine St. (☎ **604-737-2130**), is a warehouse-styled, glassblowing studio that showcases glassblowers at work alongside Held's collectible vases, paperweights, and goblets. While you might find some of his work unaffordable in galleries in the U.S., here you can find the big-ticket items as well as some great take-home pieces and too-good-to-be-true "seconds."

✔ The University of British Columbia's **Museum of Anthropology,** 6393 NW Marine Dr. (☎ **604-822-5087**), located just west of Kitsilano in Point Grey, has a very good store where you can stock up on books about the Native-Canadian arts and crafts you purchase while in Vancouver. The museum also sells assorted prints and jewelry, among other items. Staff members may even be able to give you some free advice on where to mount that totem pole that you're taking back to Milwaukee.

✔ **Second Suit,** 2306 West 4th Ave. (☎ **604-732-0338**), takes lightly used suits and fancy accessories — who knows, maybe they were worn by a mannequin one time — on consignment, and then marks them way down. Your eyes will pop at the big names and small prices, so don't be shy. It's not like you came all the way to Canada to pay top price on an Italian suit, is it?

✔ **The Travel Bug,** 2667 West Broadway (☎ **604-737-1122**), may not be the largest travel bookshop in Canada, but it's probably the most personable. Dwight Elliot runs a fabulous little place stocked with his choices of the big-name guidebook titles, plus some little-name ones, too, and a few travel supplies — including globes, although you're unlikely to take one of *those* to Europe in your backpack. If, like me, you're a fan of narrative travel books that make great reading on the train or plane, Dwight has lots of those, too.

✔ Just in case you happen to be after something really different and loud, come to **Zulu Records,** 1972 West 4th Ave. (☎ **604-738-3232**); they probably have it. Punk, hip hop, new wave, and all those other styles and tiny labels that don't fit neatly into a corporate-music bin — anything that's the opposite of wimpy music, basically — can be found here. The store sells used records, tapes, and CDs.

Yaletown

Yaletown is one of the hippest places to shop — a booming district of brewpubs, art galleries, and clubs that was once an industrial area but is now developing into a cool, creative, and high-tech neighborhood.

✔ **Coastal Peoples Fine Arts Gallery,** 1024 Mainland St. (☎ **604-685-9298;** www.coastalpeoples.com), specializes in Native-designed jewelry, especially pieces featuring whales, ravens, bears, and other animals and sea creatures related to Native oral traditions.

✔ **Urban Fare,** 1177 Davie St. (☎ **604-975-7550**), is one of Vancouver's most unique grocerias — a kind of West Coast version of Harrods's food floor! It combines everyday cornflakes with a host of international gourmet foods, and at last count had more than 220 varieties of cheese. A great place to stock up for a picnic.

Parking in Yaletown is hard to find and meters are C$4 (US$3.35) per hour, but park below Urban Fare and it's only C$1.50 (US$1.25) for an hour, the first of which is reimbursed to you upon proof of an Urban Fare purchase.

Index of Stores by Merchandise

Jewelry

Henry Birk & Sons (Downtown)
Martha Sturdy (South Granville)

Markets

Chinatown
Granville Island Public Market
(Granville Island)
Lonsdale Quay Market (North
Vancouver)
Punjabi Market (South Vancouver)
Robson Public Market (Downtown)

Music

A&B Sound (Downtown)
Virgin Megastore (Downtown)
Zulu Records (Kitsilano)

Native-Canadian items

Coastal Peoples Fine Arts Gallery
(Yaletown)
Dorothy Grant (Downtown)
Hill's Native Art (Gastown)
Inuit Gallery (Gastown)
Leona Lattimer Gallery (South
Granville)
Museum of Anthropology (Point Grey)

Specialty

The Perfume Shoppe (Downtown)
Robert Held Glass (West Side)

Chapter 13

Following an Itinerary: Four Great Options

*P*art of the fun of visiting Vancouver is that you can mix and match tastes and experiences all day and all night. You can go skiing in the morning and boating in the afternoon. You can feast on authentic dim sum in Chinatown for lunch and smoked salmon in a Native-Canadian longhouse for dinner. The following itineraries pull together some of the best experiences the city has to offer. I've grouped activities around themes so that you can more easily choose what's right for you.

Itinerary #1: Vancouver for Beer Lovers

Vancouver is a great place to fall in love with beer. In these parts, you may hear some quaffers saying, "Look at the head on her" or, "She's got legs" in reference to a glass of stout or India Pale Ale. If you're one of these people, this tour, which combines a sampling of the best imported beers with the finest local brews, is for you.

 If you tend to linger at a bar, you may want to do this tour in reverse, because the last stop involves a ferry ride across the inlet and you could get stuck on the North Shore if you miss the last ferry home. Or you can skip every other stop on the itinerary to ensure you're home by dinnertime.

 Because travel between some of these pubs is best done by car, rather than bus, make sure you have a designated driver. Choose a good friend . . . to whom you'll owe a big favor when this day is finished.

Itinerary #1: Vancouver for Beer Lovers

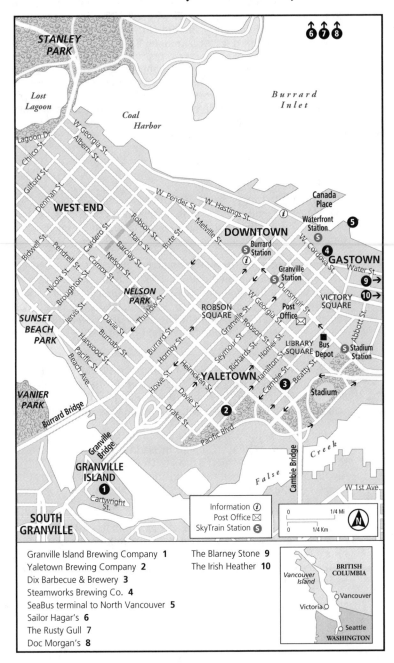

Granville Island Brewing Company **1**
Yaletown Brewing Company **2**
Dix Barbecue & Brewery **3**
Steamworks Brewing Co. **4**
SeaBus terminal to North Vancouver **5**
Sailor Hagar's **6**
The Rusty Gull **7**
Doc Morgan's **8**

The Blarney Stone **9**
The Irish Heather **10**

Begin on **Granville Island,** preferably at the market for a good breakfast or other repast. Then walk over to the **Granville Island Brewing Company** (1441 Cartwright St. ☎ **604-687-2739**) for a tour and taste. Most beers are high quality, middle of the road brews — nothing too adventurous, but perfect for a summer's sip.

Now either drive or hop on board a shuttle ferry that will take you into Yaletown. Here await two of the city's best brewpub experiences. The massive, handsome **Yaletown Brewing Company** (see Chapter 10) was one of the first brewpubs in town, and it's still the city's primary player in the biz. Despite the great beers and fun atmosphere, the place is pretty big and can feel a little impersonal at times. Oh, well, bottoms up.

The next microbrewery, which is actually a laid-back restaurant that brews beer on the premises, is just a short hop away. From Mainland Street, turn right (east) along Nelson or Smithe and continue two very short blocks to Beatty Street and **Dix Barbecue & Brewery** (see Chapter 15). This is a terrific spot to grab some much-needed barbecue to soak up the alcohol, while (naturally) sampling the house lagers at the same time.

Continue heading north on Beatty Street, turning left on Georgia Street, and then north again on Richards. This route bypasses a rather rummy part of town and directs you virtually into the front door of **Steamworks Brewing Co.** (see Chapter 15), in Gastown, where the beer's cold and the atmosphere is very English. The views of the water aren't half bad either — sweet temptation of your next libation over on the North Shore.

Any route east of Beatty, between Yaletown and Gastown, is still a bit seedy — a leftover from when it used to run with streetwalkers, drunks, and dope fiends. They've moved east a number of blocks but I would still take a cab or drive at night, and watch yourself during the day.

Having gazed at the water over a few brewskies, it's time to test your sea legs — hmmm . . . now *that* could prove interesting. Amble west (toward the building with the sails) a little to the SeaBus station (you've probably been watching the vessels shuttling to and fro for the last hour). Buy a ticket and take the SeaBus (see Chapter 8) across to North Vancouver.

Wander through the colorful market at Lonsdale Quay (where the boat docks) and then walk two short blocks uphill to find **Sailor Hagar's** (see Chapter 15). This place is a virtual temple to the brewed beer, with house beers and a vast, superb selection of imports, too. **The Rusty Gull** (see Chapter 15) is a few doors along — another emporium to the hallowed hop.

Now you've got two options, depending on whether you're driving or on foot:

✔ **If you're driving:** Take this neat island detour. Drive west along Highway 1 to the Horseshoe Bay ferry docks. Buy a ticket for Bowen Island, and then jump on the Queen of Capilano ferry boat to Bowen Island — the ride's normally pretty quick, unless the sea is choppy or they're repairing the Bowen docks.

Off the boat, all you need do is walk a few steps to **Doc Morgan's** (☎ **604-697-0707**). Owner Rondy Dike runs a classy, atmospheric place — and the Special Bitter is pretty darned good, too. Haven't eaten? Tuck into some pub grub. I warn you, though, you may like this island groove enough to want to stay over.

✔ **If you're walking:** I suggest you can catch the SeaBus back to Gastown for a little of the ol' Irish. **Blarney Stone** and **Irish Heather** (see Chapter 15) are party places until the wee hours, and the number of friends you can make in just a short time will astound you. The Guinness flows alongside the cacophony of the patrons. Enjoy.

Itinerary #2: Vancouver as Hollywood North

Vancouver is a popular spot for filming TV shows, feature films, and those dreaded TV movies. Celebrity spotting has become a common occurrence around town, particularly in Yaletown and the West End. Don't be surprised if you see Goldie Hawn or Kurt Russell hanging around South Granville — they've a place in nearby Shaughnessy. You, too, can play Hollywood movie mogul with this quick-and-dirty tour.

Begin by contacting the **British Columbia Film Commission** (☎ **604-660-2732**; Internet: www.bcfilmcommission.com). Its office, at 865 Hornby St., Suite 201 (open weekdays 8:30 a.m. to 4:30 p.m.), provides an updated list of current films in production around town. When you have the coordinates, simply head for the area and keep a sharp lookout for long, white trailers and lots of people with sneakers, baseball caps, and cell phones. Hang out, don't bug them, sneak a look inside the catering trailer (boy, do these guys eat well), and maybe you'll wind up as an extra in one of the numerous sci-fi shows that always seems to be filming in town. *Outer Limits* and *Stargate SG-1* are regulars. (Just don't blame me if your one shot at fame consists of being fried by alien goop or something equally glamorous.)

Done being a spectator? Now dig deeper into the city's tradition as a film (*Catwoman* with Halle Berry; *I Robot* with Will Smith; and *Fantastic Four* with Jessica Alba) and television (*Wiseguy, Smallville, The X-Files,* and many more) stand-in for other cities. The folks at **The X-Tour** (☎ **888-250-7211** or 604-609-2770; www.x-tour.com) have it all down to a science. They know where all the scenes in *The X-Files* television show were shot, and they know just about every other snippet of local movie and television trivia under the sun. Taking their tour should take up the better part of an afternoon.

The day wouldn't be complete, though, without a drink or a dinner at the **Alibi Room,** 157 Alexander St. (☎ 604-623-3383), in Gastown, the acknowledged hub of Vancouver's film community. (I can put it this way: The casual reading material here consists of a library of film scripts.)

Itinerary #3: Vancouver for Nature Lovers

When in Vancouver, you're practically falling over abundant natural splendors, which you can see from any point in town. This tour visits the major parks, canyons, and beaches around Greater Vancouver. Although I could have made this itinerary three times longer — countless parks fill the metro area — seeing these will certainly get your heart racing. You can tailor this tour to your personality. If you're a morning person, just do it in reverse.

Although many of Vancouver's natural areas are accessible by public transit, this itinerary is probably best done with a car if you're pressed for time. However, if you're in town for a few days, you can take the bus and follow one or two segments each day.

Start by driving to the western tip of the lower peninsula, which is known as **Point Grey** and is dominated by the '70s architecture of the University of British Columbia, or UBC for short. The UBC campus is surrounded by some of the most amazing landscapes any student could ever imagine. It's a wonder that they get any work done. Because UBC lies within what are called "endowment lands," they're open and free to the public.

A morning walk on the beach isn't a bad way to begin. Beaches run pretty much around the entire point, and most are public property (check for signs, however). **Wreck Beach,** near the base of University Boulevard off Marine Drive, is one of the most popular and controversial. That's because nudity is its claim to fame, and, at times, you feel like you've stepped into a time warp of hippie freedom — nude sunbathers, old guys peddling weird stuff from carts, and so on (see p. 187). My favorite stretch of beach, **Spanish Banks,** lies east of the campus on its north shore and leads right into **Jericho Beach** — one of the prettiest park-beaches in Vancouver, and party central for local dogs and their owners.

Next, make your way to **UBC Botanical Garden and Nitobe Memorial Garden** (see Chapter 11). Both spots sure look and smell good, and probably won't make for a long detour.

Travel east along 4th Avenue to the Burrard Bridge, which you should cross and continue straight into downtown, turning left onto Georgia Street. Follow signs to **Stanley Park** (see Chapter 11). You can spend hours (even days) here walking the trails, sunbathing, beachcombing, roller-blading your way around the seawall, and all that other stuff

Itinerary #3: Vancouver for Nature Lovers

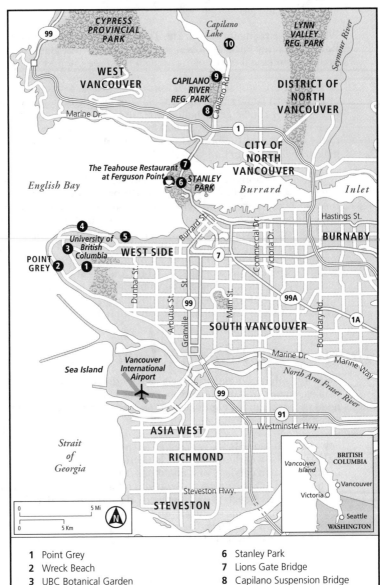

1 Point Grey
2 Wreck Beach
3 UBC Botanical Garden
   and Nitobe Memorial Garden
4 Spanish Banks
5 Jericho Beach

6 Stanley Park
7 Lions Gate Bridge
8 Capilano Suspension Bridge
   and Park
9 Capilano Salmon Hatchery
10 Grouse Mountain

you're supposed to be doing while on vacation. You can even play a round of pitch 'n' putt golf or just find a grassy verge near the open sea and catch a few zees.

When you're ready for lunch, **The Teahouse Restaurant at Ferguson Point** in Stanley Park is a lovely spot for a cup of tea, glass of wine, or a luxurious full meal overlooking English Bay (see Chapter 10).

Next, drive straight across the **Lions Gate Bridge,** a steeply pitched crossing with some rather spectacular (and vertiginous) views; it's definitely not for the heights-challenged. *Note:* Try to avoid the bridge at rush hour as traffic snarls can add an hour to your journey. As you come to the off-ramp on the other side, exit onto Marine Drive East, and then make the first left up Capilano Road.

You pass the **Capilano Suspension Bridge and Park** (see Chapter 11) — pricey, but worth a look if you like big drops — and eventually come to the **Capilano Salmon Hatchery** (see Chapter 11), a dandy spot to watch little salmons coming into being. But the granddaddy attraction lies a few hundred yards up this road: **Grouse Mountain** (see Chapter 11). Are you ready to tackle the nearly vertical Grouse Grind? Probably not on *this* itinerary — the climb takes a lot of huffing and puffing, and you have to be in excellent physical shape — but you can at least ride the gondola and check out the amazing geology on your way up. And once you're up top, there's a slew of activities to enjoy, plus a couple of eateries where you can watch the sun set against views that stretch forever.

Itinerary #4: Romantic Vancouver

Any city with mountains this big as a backdrop — not to mention whales, eagles, and crashing ocean waves at its doorstep — doesn't need to work hard to captivate and enchant. This romantic tour is best taken during warm weather.

Few places in downtown Vancouver are more romantic than **Stanley Park,** so if the weather's nice, begin there. Consider touring the park by horse-drawn carriage or a chauffeur-driven Model A Ford (see Chapter 11). Ask the driver to drop you off for a walk along one of the beaches. **Third Beach** is the most secluded and romantic. It's also a great spot for a picnic — check out Chapter 10 for suggestions for where to pick up picnic supplies. Or, you can always rent a tandem bicycle from **Spokes** (☎ 604-688-5141) and do the park under your own pedal-power.

All that exertion and you're probably ready for some pampering, and the new **Spa Utopia** at the **Pan Pacific Hotel** is, well, pampering personified (see Chapter 12). Book yourselves a massage for two.

Then head over to Granville Island, preferably via one of the **Harbour Ferries** (see Chapter 11), which can incorporate a romantic tour of the harbor before dropping you off for a meander through the island's artsy shops and studios. And if you're peckish, the market is always a hot spot for flavors. But don't eat too much, because the options for romantic dinners are numerous: **Bacchus** with its mood lighting, piano lounge, and excellent restaurant; **Villa del Lupo** for its heritage ambience and personal service; or over on the North Shore, **Salmon House on the Hill,** where you'll witness some of the best sunset views available. (See Chapter 10 for more suggestions.)

Finally, as a nightcap, here are three thoughts: a chocolate fondue under the stars (**All-Terrain Adventures** organizes this exquisite excursion; ☎ **604-984-2374**); a cognac at **Gerard Lounge** (see Chapter 15), where many of the glitterati snuggle up in the shadows, although by now you would probably prefer to snuggle up to each other, or a drink in the high-altitude, revolving **Cloud 9 Lounge** (see Chapter 15), where looking out at the twinkling lights of the city, boats, and Grouse Mountain, you can begin to plan your own private ending to the day.

Chapter 14

Going Beyond Vancouver: Three Great Day Trips

In This Chapter

▶ Traveling the Sea to Sky Highway
▶ Taking in the Sunshine Coast
▶ Discovering island havens beyond Nanaimo

*A*lthough Vancouver has plenty to offer, you may want to get out of town to experience the beautiful countryside. Those snow-capped mountains visible from downtown are one possibility, as is nearby Victoria (see Part IV), but a host of lesser-known day trips awaits, as well — all within an hour's drive or ferry ride from the city. This chapter presents three of my favorite trips, and they're so good that you may prefer one of them to staying an extra day in the city.

Day Trip #1: The Road to Whistler

One of the finest day trips you can do in Western Canada is a drive north up Highway 99 from North Vancouver to the ever-popular ski resort town of Whistler.

Getting there

Highway 99, mainly a two-lane road, is known as the Sea to Sky Highway, and sections are indeed spectacular — especially the first half, where you skirt the water of Howe Sound (a fjord) from atop cliffs. As the road begins climbing, you notice sturdy gates like those at a railroad crossing. These gates are closed when rock slides or sudden winter snowstorms close the route off. How to avoid these potential roadblocks? Go in summer or early in the day, although that said, you're still likely to encounter delays — not from the weather but from all the upgrades and roadwork that's happening in preparation for the 2010 Winter Olympics.

The route passes through tiny Britannia Beach — mostly just a handful of homes and a diner — although the BC Museum of Mining (☎ 800-896-4044) is a pretty neat spot, especially if you've kids in tow. It's open daily, 9 a.m. to 5:30 p.m.; admission is C$15 (US$12) adults, C$11.75 (US$10) seniors and children 6 to 18. The mines here were once the largest copper producers in the British Commonwealth.

Halfway to Whistler, you pass through Squamish, a logging community that's the only town of size en route; fast-food restaurants announce your brief return to civilization, where backpackers and other outdoorsy folks stock up on climbing gear and snacks before pressing onward. You may not think to linger or to climb the humongous granite monolith known as The Stawamus Chief, but a short detour west down an unmarked side road (ask locals how to find it) brings a surprising sight in winter: Brackendale, one of North America's finest eagle-viewing areas. The **West Coast Railway Heritage Park** (☎ 604-898-9336), also in Squamish, showcases a collection of train equipment and restored train compartments. The park is open daily from 10 a.m. to 5 p.m.; admission is C$19 (US$16) for adults and C$6.50 (US$5.40) for seniors and children 6 to 18.

 Just south of Squamish lies Shannon Falls, a Kodak-moment of raincoast waterfalls cascading amid Western hemlock, Douglas fir, and Western red cedar trees. Another photo spot, this time of the mountains, is just north of Squamish at the Tantalus pullover.

After another 30 or 35 miles of driving, you reach the highly developed town of Whistler. Internationally famous for its two ski mountains, Whistler and Blackcomb, and its world-class snowboarding, this resort shouldn't be overlooked during the summer months. It's a veritable cornucopia of outdoor adventure: horseback riding, alpine hiking, lake canoeing, white-water rafting, and paragliding to name a few.

If you want to explore further, continue driving north to Pemberton, a one-time logging town that has undergone a startling transformation into a hip West Coast outdoor playground. Cheaper than Whistler, Pemberton is far more pristine and authentic. Plenty of inns, B&Bs, and fine-dining establishments are here, as well as a winery (with suites on the premises) and various farms selling produce and baked goods.

Seeing the sights

This day trip is most convenient to do by car, because you have the freedom to turn off at various lookout points, trailheads, and shops. If you happen to drive through Squamish in winter, remember to get directions to the eagle lookout sights (best viewing time is December and January) at Easter Seal Camp, a few miles west of the downtown strip.

When in Whistler, hiking trails are the prime attraction. You can get information on the area's best hikes from the **Whistler Activity and Information Center** (☎ 800-944-7853 or 604-932-2394), in the main village, or from **Whistler Alpine Guides Bureau** (☎ 604-938-9242). Golf is another major attraction, with several good courses in the area, three of which are the acclaimed **Nicklaus North Golf Course,** 8080 Nicklaus North Blvd. (☎ 604-938-9898), an Arnold Palmer–designed course at

Whistler Golf Club, and the highly ranked Robert Trent Jones Jr.–designed course at **Fairmont Chateau Whistler,** 4612 Blackcomb Way (☎ **604-938-2092**). Courses are open from early May to mid-October.

You can also take a look at pretty Alta Lake, or canoe around Green Lake. And how about riding up the **Whistler Gondola** (☎ **800-766-0449** or 604-932-3434)? You may see bears roaming below. The gondola travels up Whistler Mountain from the center of town to the Roundhouse Lodge and operates from 8:30 a.m. to 8:00 p.m. Costs vary depending on whether you include The Peak, or a combination of mountains. The best value is an all-day adventure pass at C$35 (US$29) per person. To ride with a mountain bike — mountain bike trails are at the top and you must have a guide — costs C$75 (US$62) per person for the day. The gondola is wheelchair accessible.

If you simply want to linger in the village for a few hours, plenty of pubs, bistros, and very pricey stores are in the various Whistler complexes.

Where to stay

Along the Sea to Sky Highway, you encounter few lodgings, except campgrounds and Squamish hotels. Whistler, however, is another story — the town offers almost a glut of options, most geared toward a seasonal, well-heeled ski crowd. That means in summer, you can find deals on certain condominiums or resorts.

The **Fairmont Chateau Whistler,** 4599 Chateau Blvd. (☎ **800-606-8244** or 604-938-8000), is the town's luxurious grande dame — not the place to ask about discounts — while the somewhat remote **Durlacher Hof,** 7055 Nesters Rd. (☎ **604-932-1924**), is a more homey-feeling inn that's very alpine in flavor. One of the new kids in town is the **Four Seasons,** 4591 Blackcomb Way (☎ **604-935-3400**). **The Pan Pacific,** 4299 Blackcomb Way (☎ **604-905-2999**) opens in the village center this summer, joining its fairly new sister, the **Pan Pacific Whistler Mountainside,** 4320 Sundial Crescent (☎ **888-905-9995** or 604-905-2999). The **Chamber of Commerce** (☎ **604-932-5528**) or **Whistler Activity and Information Centre** (☎ **800-944-7853** or 604-932-2394), both in "downtown" at 4230 Gateway Drive, can quickly point you toward many rustic ski lodge–style accommodations, which are more mid-priced than super expensive. As can an accommodation service: **Whistler E-stays** (☎ **800-777-0185**). **Edelweiss,** 7162 Nancy Green Dr. (☎ **604-932-3641**), and the **Timberline Lodge,** 4122 Village Green (☎ **866-580-6649** or 604-932-5211), are two that get good reviews. Finally, you can find even less-expensive cabins scattered around town, although some cater to a younger, more boisterous crowd. **Swiss Cottage B&B,** 7321 Fitzsimmons Dr. (☎ **800-718-7822** or **604-932-6062**), is one of the quieter examples.

In Pemberton, I suggest checking first with the **Pemberton Valley Vineyard Inn** (☎ **877-444-5857** or 604-894-5857) about room availability and local restaurant recommendations — not to mention their current vintage.

Exploring Beyond Vancouver

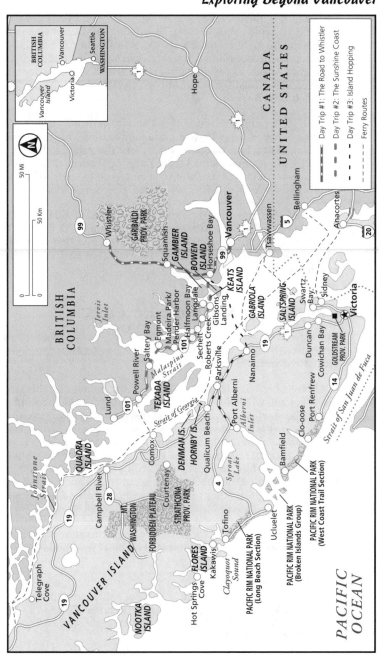

Where to dine

You can't possibly go hungry in Whistler, although you need to choose carefully to avoid overspending. Fine-dining establishments (with big-time prices to match) abound; try the **Wildflower** (☎ **604-938-2033**) in the Chateau Whistler hotel complex, **Joel's** (☎ **604-932-1240**) at the golf course, or **Araxi** (☎ **604-932-4540**) in Whistler Village Square to sample some nouveau West Coast cuisine, which is strong on Asian flavors and local fish and shellfish.

If you'd rather mix with locals than tourists, however, head for one of the many cozy pubs, delis, and pizza joints around town. You may have to search to find one, but persevere; these places are definitely a cut above greasy-spoon diners. **Auntie Em's,** 4340 Lorimer Rd. (☎ **604-932-1163**), serves a fine all-day breakfast and good lunches to Whistlerians and tourists alike. Or just ask a local for a recommendation.

You could also drop in at the **Roadhouse Diner** (☎ **604-892-5312**) at Shannon Falls, the **Britannia Beach Coffee House** (☎ **604-896-0272**) near the mines, or the small **Howe Sound Inn and Brewing Company** (☎ **604-892-2603**) in Squamish on the way up or back if you simply can't wait to eat.

Day Trip #2: The Sunshine Coast

Vancouverites call it the Sunshine Coast, and locals swear the weather's better here than in the city proper. Casting a skeptical eye skyward, I take their word for it.

But there's certainly no quibbling about the scenery on this stretch of the mainland, which follows the tortuous folds of Howe Sound as it twists and stretches in drop-dead-gorgeous curves west from Vancouver. These inlets are so indented and wild, in fact, that the entire region is cut off from Vancouver by road; you must fly in (prohibitively expensive for most people) or else take the regular ferries from Horseshoe Bay. The entire length of the Sunshine Coast (which is basically Highway 101) is 95 kilometers (60 miles). The closest town to Vancouver along this stretch is Langdale; other towns along the way are Gibsons Landing, Sechelt, Halfmoon Bay, Madeira Park, and Powell River.

If you're in the city for a week or more, try to find half a day to visit — this is small-town British Columbia at its most beautiful.

Getting there

The ferry from Horseshoe Bay, near West Vancouver, to Langdale runs on a variable schedule — check with **BC Ferries** (☎ **888-223-3779**; www.bcferries.com) for the latest schedules and fares. The trip takes about 40 minutes each way.

To get to Horseshoe Bay from downtown Vancouver, drive across the Lions Gate Bridge from the West End. Take the off-ramp to West Vancouver, which will swish-back you around to join Marine Drive. Turn left at your first opportunity, Taylor Way, and head up the hill for signs that will direct you west and onto the Trans-Canada Highway (Highways 1 and 99), and to Horseshoe Bay.

Seeing the sights

From the Langdale docking, most visitors choose to make the short drive of a mile or so over to **Gibsons Landing** (locals just call it "Gibsons"), a decent if overly precious first look at the coast. Canadians love visiting this town because a hotel here (**Molly's Reach**) was featured in a popular seaside television program for years; I understand that the show, *The Beachcombers*, is still in reruns in Japan and elsewhere. You may find the town worth a look, too — if only to stock up on essential supplies and gifts or to check out the **Sunshine Coast Museum & Archives** (☎ 604-886-8232), open Tuesday through Saturday, 10:30 a.m. to 4:30 p.m. year round.

There's only one main road (Highway 101) to speak of along the Sunshine Coast. Highway 101 goes west past **Roberts Creek Provincial Park** (about 7½ miles west of Gibsons), where you find good hiking trails and a beach, and on through the artsy hamlet of Roberts Creek and the larger Sechelt, a base for golf and other outdoor activities, such as kayaking, canoeing, boating, bicycling, mountain biking, fishing, diving, and cross-country skiing. The **Sunshine Coast Golf & Country Club** (☎ 877-661-2288 or 604-885-9212) in Sechelt is open year-round. Another Sechelt attraction, **House of Hewhiwus** (☎ 604-885-4592), showcases the culture and crafts of the local Sechelt tribe; its gift shop, **Tsain-ko Gifts,** is the place to pick up a souvenir.

Writers, musicians, and artists are thick on the ground in this part of the coast. From Sechelt, Highway 101 continues to Halfmoon Bay, with its authentically aging general store, and then finally to a series of settlements on Pender Harbour — the starting point for boating and fishing excursions, should you have the time, or a walk to the rapids at the interestingly named Skookumchuck Narrows. One company offering boat trips in the area is **Ketchalot Charters** (☎ 604-883-9351).

For more information on activities and tour operators along the Sunshine Coast, contact the Sechelt office of the **Sunshine Coast Regional District** (☎ 604-885-2261), the **Wilderness Tourism Association** in Gibsons (☎ 604-886-8755), or one of the local tourism posts such as the **Powell River Tourist InfoCentre** (☎ 604-485-4701) or the **Sechelt Tourist InfoCentre** (☎ 604-885-0662).

Where to stay

Because the coast is largely residential, few lodgings are available. Bed-and-breakfasts and off-the-beaten-track cabins predominate. However, there are a few truly outstanding accommodations available, so if you think that you might want to parlay a lo-ong day trip from Vancouver into an overnighter, the **West Coast Wilderness Lodge,** near Egmont at the north end of the coast, is a treat (☎ **877-988-3838** or 604-883-3667). At Powell River, **Desolation Resort** (☎ **604-483-3592**) is an adventure with its extraordinary tree-house cabins, and at Sechelt, I suggest you check out **Four Winds Beach House & Spa** (☎ **604-885-3144**).

Where to dine

This lightly populated area offers a surprising range of dining options, from country-store picnic fare to highfalutin gourmet meals.

Gibsons Landing offers the most possibilities. Go simple or fancy, burgers or French; you find the best choices on the main street. Farther down the road, everyone in Roberts Creek ends up, sooner or later, at **Gumboot Garden** (☎ **604-885-4218**), a plain-looking place concealing a terrific bakery and hearty grazing menu. In Sechelt, farther still, splurge at the widely renowned **Blue Heron** (☎ **800-818-8977** or 604-885-3847).

Day Trip #3: Island Hopping

You hear a lot of talk about the pastoral Southern Gulf Islands, the ones that lie between the mainland and Vancouver Island. Yes, they're lovely, but because of the ferries that connect one to the other, you can end up with an inordinate amount of time hanging around ferry terminals waiting for the next ship out. So, if you want a taste of island life, I'm suggesting that you head to the "other" Gulf Islands, the ones that lie just north of Nanaimo: Gabriola, Denman, and Hornby Islands.

Getting started in Nanaimo

You reach Nanaimo by one of two ferries, both operated by **BC Ferries** (☎ **888-223-3779;** www.bcferries.com). The **Horseshoe Bay–Nanaimo** ferry departs from the terminal at Horseshoe Bay, about 15 miles north and west of central Vancouver (take the Lions Gate Bridge from the West End and follow the Trans-Canada Highway to Horseshoe Bay). The ferry departs eight times daily for the 95-minute trip to Nanaimo. The **Mid-Island Express** departs about a half-dozen times daily from Tsawwassen for a two-hour crossing to Duke Point, just outside Nanaimo. The Tsawwassen docks are south of Vancouver on Highway 17. Contact BC Ferries for fares, schedules, and reservations.

Once you arrive in Nanaimo, most everything that's worth seeing is close to the docks. You can find a couple of worthwhile attractions, such as a fort on Front Street called the **Bastion** (☎ **250-753-1821**), complete with booming cannon, that's open mid-May to October daily from 10:30 a.m. to 4:30 p.m. Admission is only C$1 (US83¢) for adults and seniors; children enter free. You can also find the **Nanaimo District Museum,** 100 Cameron Rd. (☎ **250-753-1821**), a good little museum open May through

September, daily from 9 a.m. to 5 p.m. Admission is C$2 (US$1.65) for adults, C$1.75 (US$1.45) for senior citizens and students, C75¢ (US60¢) for children under 12. It closes Sunday and Monday in winter. Both the Bastion and the museum are wheelchair accessible. Additionally, Nanaimo's shopping district is compact, walkable, and reasonably quaint.

Gabriola Island

Stay in Nanaimo to catch the 20-minute ferry ride from Gabriola Ferry Wharf (right at the very end of Front Street) to **Gabriola Island.** The crossing costs C$6 (US$5) adults, and C$3 (US$2.50) children; ferries run roughly every hour (times vary) from 6:15 a.m. until 11 p.m.

Gabriola Island is a gathering point for artists, environmentalists, and other self-sufficient types. The island is full of beaches and parks and has a pub; a slew of galleries and studios are also on hand. But my favorite pick would be to play a round of golf at the island course, **Gabriola Golf and Country Club** (☎ 250-247-8822), or to stroll around the weird rocks known as the **Malaspina Galleries,** located roughly 6 miles north of the Taylor Bay Road turnoff. Once you've had your fill of what Gabriola Island has to offer, hop back on the ferry to Nanaimo for the next stage of your journey.

Setting out for more island adventure

Leaving Nanaimo, it's about a 20-mile drive to Parksville to the next stop (take Highway 19 north and then exit onto Highway 4, going west), where you find a mishmash of holiday homes, resorts, and budget motels. That's because it sits by **Rathtrevor Beach,** likely the safest swimming beaches for small children with miles of sand, and a shallow tide that's always warm and filled with sand dollars. You're also near excellent swimming at beaches like **Qualicum Beach,** and golf courses galore.

 At Parksville, you can detour inland on Highway 4 to Cathedral Grove, a magnificent forest of ancient Douglas fir, hemlock, and Western red cedar that are reminiscent of the California Redwoods.

Continue north, a short way up the highway, and it's only a 10-minute ferry crossing from Buckley Bay (north of Fanny Bay, the oyster haven) — lots of folks canoe or kayak across the narrow channel to Denman. A second ferry on the other side of the island takes you across on another 10-minute ride from Denman to Hornby. Each trip is C$5.50 (US$4.60) adult, C$3 (US$2.50) children, and ferries run roughly every hour at variable times from 8 a.m. to 6 p.m., with some later additional sailings on the weekend.

 The islands are a haven for aging flower children and have a distinct bohemian charm. Their beautiful landscapes have made them one of British Columbia's most popular beach vacations, so if you really want to appreciate the rural isolation of these islands, try to avoid the height of summer when the population of just over 1,000 can swell to ten times that number!

Denman Island

The beautiful sandstone on Denman is full of life: oysters, rock crabs, clams, eagles, and seabirds. There's good salmon fishing, particularly off the south end, and you can kayak across to Sandy Island Provincial Marine Park, a group of beautiful wooded islands with limited camping. **Denman Island Tourism** (☎ 604-335-0079) can tell you more, as can the Denman Grocery Store, a five-minute walk from the ferry in Denman Village.

Hornby Island

On Hornby, head for Tribune Bay Provincial Park. Here the sea has beaten the soft rock faces into dramatic hoodoo formations, which are stunning to explore. Helliwell Bay Provincial Park is also worth the trip, both for the trails along the bluff, and to see the thousands of nesting birds tucked into the cliffs. Hornby's two claims to fame are as the only spot in Canada where you find certain types of butterfly, including the Taylor's checkerspot, and the only place in the world where divers find primitive, deep-sea, six-gill sharks. Rent kayaks from **Hornby Ocean Kayaks** (☎ 250-335-2726) near the Central Road school building.

Where to stay

Nanaimo itself probably isn't interesting enough to warrant an overnight stay, but the surrounding area is. You can find plenty of farms, hills, and beaches within a short drive of this tiny city. A range of motels, inns, bed-and-breakfasts, and more luxurious options are both inside and outside the city. For information on accommodation choices, contact **Tourism Nanaimo,** 2290 Bowen Rd. (☎ 800-663-7337 or 250-756-0106). Contact the **Comox Valley Information Centre** for information on places north of Nanaimo (☎ 888-357-4471 or 250-334-3234).

Because of the popularity of the islands, accommodation on Gabriola, Denman, and Hornby can be hard to come by, so even if you're sleeping under canvas, book at least three months in advance. **Hornby Island Resort,** 4305 Shingle Spit Road (☎ 250-335-0136; www.hornbyisland. com/AllAccom/HornbyResort/HornbyResort.htm), is one option to try.

Where to dine

Nanaimo is decidedly gritty rather than flashy, and as such, many of the dining options are of the fried-seafood variety rather than gourmet. Still, the tourism traffic and the presence of a small university mean you can find good food with a little poking around. On Gabriola Island, a pub is right next to the ferry landing; it serves the pub food and English ales you'd expect in a place like this.

Although it won't make a meal, don't forget to try a so-called **Nanaimo bar,** a chocolate-and-butter confection invented by a local bakery and available everywhere around town.

And on Denman and Hornby Islands? Well, a handful of places exist. **Café on the Rock** (☎ **250-335-2999**) in Denman village is open for three meals daily, and on Hornby, the Thatch Pub at the Hornby Island Resort offers casual pub fare. It's the only waterside watering hole on the island and is a popular local night spot with live music Thursday through Saturday.

Chapter 15

Living It Up After Dark: Vancouver's Nightlife

In This Chapter

▶ Getting down with the music scene

▶ Visiting the best clubs and bars

▶ Discovering the city's performing arts

*L*et's get one thing straight from the start: Nightlife isn't hard to find in Vancouver, but it takes limited forms. Basically, I'm talking about a few true dance clubs — quite hip, mind you — plus a good supply of live music venues (where the city shines), and bars and pubs with character. You also find a decent slate of theater offerings. In fact, in an effort to support the performing arts, the tourism folks have developed an entire entertainment season (a.k.a. fall and winter), and Yaletown's been dubbed the city's "entertainment district" because of its proximity to many event venues.

Where should you go to find nightlife? Dance clubs increasingly litter the Yaletown, Robson Street, and downtown districts, while Kitsilano is more a place for an organic brew or a glass of wine. More upscale areas, such as South Granville and the West End, offer the sorts of bars where you may want to wear a jacket or at least shuck your sneakers — places where a drink can cost more than a meal sets you back in other parts of town. Finally, strip joints have long been fixtures on the fringes of downtown, Yaletown, and East Hastings — not that you were thinking of going to one of *those.*

Closing time for a Vancouver bar or club is usually 2 a.m. — earlier on Sundays — although exceptions exist.

Checking Out the Music Scene

The city's most popular music can be described by one of two R's: rootsy (blues, rock, Irish-tinged folk, acoustic folk, punk) or refined (in other words, classical). But the genres don't end there. The city's multicultural character (and its proximity to the U.S.) has spawned everything from Euro–dance clubs to jazz clubs to a hardcore punk scene. In other words, whatever you're looking for is probably already established in some pocket of town or another.

Most clubs in Vancouver charge a variable cover fee to see live music performances (better-known acts command higher cover charges), and the hipper dance clubs also require a C$5 to C$10 (US$4.15–US$8.30) cover charge to gain entrance — although women are often exempt from this.

To find out who or what's playing where, from nightclubs to theater productions, check the free weekly newspapers: *The Georgia Straight* (www.straight.com) is found in stores, bars, restaurants, and tourist offices; and *The West Ender* (www.westender.com). *Xtra West,* the city's gay and lesbian newspaper, publishes every two weeks and lists gay-oriented club events. *Vancouver Magazine* (www.vanmag.com) is put out once a month and provides in-depth coverage of the music scene, including clubs and bands. *Where Vancouver* (www.wherevancouver.ca) is another monthly, and although the tourist guide is a titch advertising-heavy, its event and restaurant reviews are independent and reliable. You can also call the **Talking Telus Pages (☎ 604-299-9000, ext. 2489**); for pre-recorded (although not comprehensive) club listings, press menu option 6.

Shaking your groove thing: The best dance clubs

Dance clubs are hotter than ever in Vancouver, and long lines will undoubtedly greet you on any weekend you try to get into one. My advice is to go either during the week or earlier than everyone else; sure, the dance floor may be a void, but at least you can wait inside, drinking and socializing, as opposed to freezing your tail off in the rain while arguing with some musclehead in a T-shirt and flak jacket. Here are my picks of the hottest spots:

- ✔ **Sonar,** 66 Water St., Gastown (☎ **604-683-6695**), probably the top dance club in British Columbia, established a name for itself far and wide by attracting top DJs to spin eclectic hip hop tunes and island rhythms — for once, much more than just droning, bass-fueled dance music — within a gorgeously designed space. Closed Sundays.

- ✔ **Stone Temple Cabaret,** 1082 Granville St., Downtown (☎ **604-488-1333**), a good old-fashioned disco, does everything — music, lighting — on a grand scale. Only the hairstyles have changed. Closed Sundays and Tuesdays.

- ✔ **The Urban Well,** 1516 Yew St., Kitsilano (☎ **604-737-7770**), delivers with a surprisingly good range of music and a top-notch drink selection. As with so many other popular Vancouver spots, though, the crowd may annoy with its perfection. The high-tone crowd jacks up drink prices, too. Mondays and Tuesdays usually involve improv nights and/or a stand-up comedy showcase.

Vancouver Nightlife

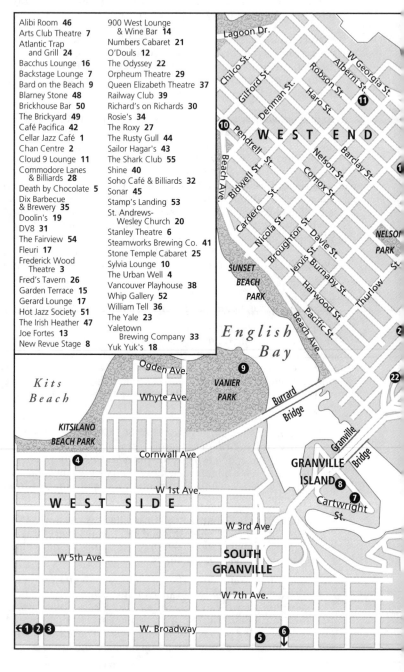

Alibi Room **46**
Arts Club Theatre **7**
Atlantic Trap and Grill **24**
Bacchus Lounge **16**
Backstage Lounge **7**
Bard on the Beach **9**
Blarney Stone **48**
Brickhouse Bar **50**
The Brickyard **49**
Café Pacifica **42**
Cellar Jazz Café **1**
Chan Centre **2**
Cloud 9 Lounge **11**
Commodore Lanes & Billiards **28**
Death by Chocolate **5**
Dix Barbecue & Brewery **35**
Doolin's **19**
DV8 **31**
The Fairview **54**
Fleuri **17**
Frederick Wood Theatre **3**
Fred's Tavern **26**
Garden Terrace **15**
Gerard Lounge **17**
Hot Jazz Society **51**
The Irish Heather **47**
Joe Fortes **13**
New Revue Stage **8**

900 West Lounge & Wine Bar **14**
Numbers Cabaret **21**
O'Douls **12**
The Odyssey **22**
Orpheum Theatre **29**
Queen Elizabeth Theatre **37**
Railway Club **39**
Richard's on Richards **30**
Rosie's **34**
The Roxy **27**
The Rusty Gull **44**
Sailor Hagar's **43**
The Shark Club **55**
Shine **40**
Soho Café & Billiards **32**
Sonar **45**
Stamp's Landing **53**
St. Andrews-Wesley Church **20**
Stanley Theatre **6**
Steamworks Brewing Co. **41**
Stone Temple Cabaret **25**
Sylvia Lounge **10**
The Urban Well **4**
Vancouver Playhouse **38**
Whip Gallery **52**
William Tell **36**
The Yale **23**
Yaletown Brewing Company **33**
Yuk Yuk's **18**

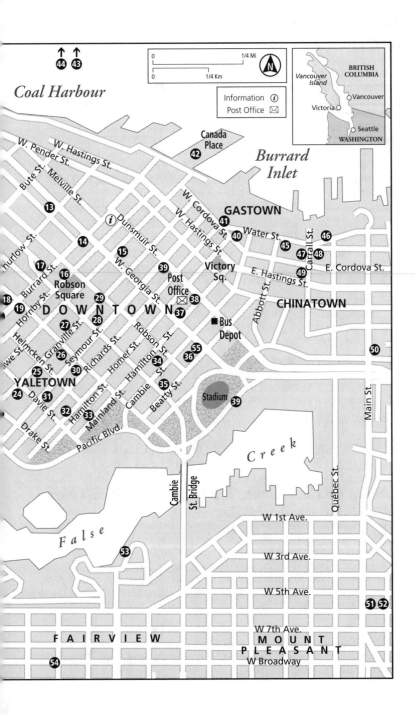

Focusing on the music: The best folk, jazz, and blues clubs

Jazz seems to be the cool thing around town these days — no doubt fuelled by aging baby-boomers mellowing their tastes. For up-to-date performance info, consult the **Jazz Hotline** (☎ 604-872-5200). If you're a real diehard fan, try to visit town during June as the annual **Vancouver Jazz Festival** is blowing full force. Blues and folk are harder to find, but it can be done. Here are my recommendations for enjoying all three styles:

✔ **Cellar Jazz Café,** 3611 West Broadway, Kitsilano (☎ 604-738-1959), presents musicians playing much more than top-quality jazz, although Sunday is reserved for its jazz brunch. You also hear blues, soul, funk, and related forms, all amid some wild decor (think red, seriously red) and the usual Kitsilano cooler-than-thou scene. Closed Mondays.

✔ **The Fairview,** 898 West Broadway, Fairview (☎ 604-872-1262), among the best blues bars in town, hides within a chain hotel. Sundays, various musicians play free-form with each other.

✔ **Hot Jazz Society,** 2120 Main St., Mount Pleasant (☎ 604-873-4131), a long-standing jazz joint, is authentic, which may explain its devoted following and staying power. Dixieland is big here, and so is dancing.

✔ **O'Doul's,** 1300 Robson St., Downtown ☎ 604-661-1400), is one of the few places in town offering live jazz seven nights a week. Because of its Robson Street location, the crowd is mixed — lots of out-of-town visitors, and locals enjoying a post-theater nightcap.

✔ **The Yale,** 1300 Granville St., Yaletown (☎ 604-681-9253) is a very good blues club stuck amid an otherwise down-at-the-heels stretch of Granville. Acoustics and sight lines aren't exactly top quality, but what do you expect? This *is* a blues dive, after all.

Turning up the volume: The best rock-and-roll bars

Rock-and-roll is alive and well, although it may not always seem so. You have to scout a bit to find its beating pulse in Vancouver, sometimes descending into grittier neighborhoods to hear up-and-coming stars. Frankly speaking, the town's just too politically correct and overly polite to appreciate hard rockers. (The biggest musical star ever to come out of here was Bryan Adams, after all, so maybe it's just not a hard rock town.) Here are a couple of places where you can really "r-a-w-k" — don't forget the earplugs:

✔ **The Brickyard,** 315 Carrall St., Gastown (☎ 604-685-3922), yet another gritty, down-to-earth joint in Gastown, rocks out part of the week and throbs to house and dance music the other. Definitely not for the beautiful people.

✔ **The Roxy,** 932 Granville St., Downtown (☎ **604-331-7999**), attracts a young, happy crowd with cover music and silly bartenders juggling hard liquor. The operative word is fun, and they do actually pull it off — hey, you just may win a trip to Cuba or something — but don't expect anything musically or culturally original.

✔ **Shine,** 364 Water St., Gastown (☎ **604-408-4321**), is one of the newest spaces in town, attracting the twenty- and thirtysomethings into its ultra-modern-yet-retro environment — it kind of conjures up "the Jetsons meet the new millennium." The dancing crowd gets to chill in the red room out back. Music is everything from '80s classics to rap to rock. Open nightly.

Hanging Out: Vancouver's Best Bars

If you don't care much for music but enjoy kicking back with a drink, you're in luck — this is definitely not a dry town. The central business core is home to a preponderance of hotel bars, most of them pretty good for atmosphere, local character, and a draft of something cold. Gastown, in particular, offers some grungy examples while Yaletown has more gentrified brewpubs; you feel well-nigh stupid ordering a brew that *wasn't* made in Vancouver. Sports bars do exist in the city, but they're mostly confined to the suburbs. And despite the city's English roots, the central city has surprisingly few authentic pubs — go to Victoria if you're craving true "bangers and mash" and a pint of some terrific but obscure English ale.

Pubs and bars normally don't charge a cover, unless some sort of event is going on, and then you may pay a small charge.

See-and-be-seen spots

Despite its laid-back charms, Vancouver certainly has its fair share — okay, maybe more than its share — of nightspots where patrons are simply there to make deals and connections, get noticed, and basically ignore anyone else who can't further their ends in life. That said, living like the other half for a night *can* be fun. And you may espy someone famous shooting a film or TV series in town; film stars are much more likely to hang out publicly here than in Los Angeles, because polite Canadians tend not to rush at them with popping flashbulbs, plastic grins, and boorish autograph requests. Here are the top places to get an eyeful:

✔ The **Alibi Room,** 157 Alexander St., Gastown (☎ **604-623-3383**), is ground zero for U.S. film industry types. Every wannabe Hollywood screenwriter and actor in town — a larger group than you'd guess — knows this place. Industry types drink upstairs in the restaurant section or, less frequently, downstairs in the lounge area.

✔ **Gerard Lounge,** 845 Burrard St., Downtown (☎ 604-682-5511), housed inside the Sutton Place Hotel (see Chapter 9), attracts a star-studded and blasé crowd to its posh surroundings. Try not to drop your drink when some mega–movie star saunters by on his/her way to the john. Tuesdays, a locally famous Chocoholic's Buffet lays out treats of a different kind.

✔ **Richard's on Richards,** 1036 Richards St., West End (☎ 604-687-6794) features various incarnations of dance and rock, sometimes played by local bands and sometimes by world-renowned acts. But you don't just come to listen: You come to look. This is *the* place to be seen in the city, so wildly popular among its surgically enhanced and overdressed clientele that it needs to open only two nights a week — Friday and Saturday, of course — plus additional days for concert performances.

English and Irish pubs

Finding an authentic pint being drawn in downtown Vancouver is amazingly hard. All the expatriate Brits and Irish appear to have headed for the 'burbs, and indeed several excellent pubs are in outlying areas. I don't assume that you're such a hardcore Anglophile that you'd head to the Canadian equivalent of Hoboken just for a beer. Bearing that in mind, here are the best of the central places, all somewhat geared to tourists, but nevertheless kind of fun:

✔ **Atlantic Trap and Gill,** 612 Davie St., West End (☎ 604-806-6393), is an Irish bar where the glass of stout reigns supreme and live Celtic music is almost a sure thing.

✔ **Blarney Stone,** 216 Carrall St., Gastown (☎ 604-687-4322), another Irish pub, sometimes features live fiddle players. Even without music, the pub stocks enough Harp and Guinness to make one teary for the Emerald Isle. It's closed Sunday through Tuesday, but open until 2 a.m. the rest of the week.

✔ **Doolin's,** 654 Nelson St., Downtown (☎ 604-605-4343), yet another pub of Irish persuasion blending rock and "kitchen ceilidh" with a sports flavor, especially on hockey nights. Open daily — until 4 a.m. Thursday through Saturday. **The Cellar** (☎ 604-605-4345) lies beneath the pub and is a popular underground dance club, so you can expect this corner of town to get mighty noisy on weekends.

✔ **The Irish Heather,** 217 Carrall St., Gastown (☎ 604-688-9779), one of several Irish pubs in this touristy part of town, nevertheless delivers famously — not too bright and clean. In other words, it's like a real Irish pub.

Neighborhood bars

Sometimes you really do want to go where everybody knows your name. Loads of neighborhood bars await in the residential neighborhoods of Vancouver, including these four for starters:

- **The Shark Club,** 180 West Georgia St., Downtown (☎ 604-687-4297), is the city's premier sports bar, and I don't just mean at the pool tables and musing over a beer at all the TV action. There's always a lot of serious shark action between mingling singles which gets especially rowdy if there's a sporting event in either General Motors Place or BC Place Stadium.

- **Brickhouse Bar,** 730 Main St., Main Street Station (☎ 604-689-8645), is a good neighborhood bar in what has long been a pretty rugged area. The area is gradually improving hereabouts, and kudos to the bar owners for leading the charge. This place has everything you want and more — good drinks, comfy seating, superlative snacks — and everyone remarks on the long fish tanks.

- **Stamp's Landing,** 610 Stamp's Landing, Kitsilano (☎ 604-879-0821), is an almost-authentic British pub — except with much better food — offering an array of draft beers that you normally find only in your dreams. Your fellow drinkers are wannabe boaters, however, so unless you enjoy boat talk and stock tips, you may want to cut out after a couple of pints. The location across False Creek from Yaletown is a bit hard to reach.

- **Sylvia Lounge,** 1154 Gilford St., West End (☎ 604-681-9321), a hotel bar, is loved by West Enders, and although the decor borders on tacky, the feeling is actually neighborhoody, and — thank goodness — no bad music is piped in to overwhelm attempts at conversation or matchmaking.

Hip alternative bars

I don't know what else to call this hodgepodge of a category, which simply denotes a place where the vibe is young, alternative, artsy . . . the kind of places where granny glasses, Gram Parsons, Elvis Costello, and Elvis Presley are still in.

- **Backstage Lounge,** 1585 Johnston St., Granville Island (☎ 604-687-1354), is frequented by young locals — and, yes, budding artists — for its water views, theater-company ties, and exceptionally happy atmosphere. The live music on weekends gets pretty good, too.

- **DV8,** 515 Davie St., West End (☎ 604-682-4388), a very late-night spot, attracts young, rich rebels busy rebelling on their parents' money. Dress like you're at a rave (or a prison break) and you're more likely to fit in than if you're sporting fancy threads. Seriously, though, the live music can be a cut above many other places.

- **Joe Fortes,** 777 Thurlow St., West End (☎ 604-669-1940), a hopping, healthy place named for a heroic Jamaican lifeguard, attracts a youthful, *St. Elmo's Fire*–type crowd flaunting some serious wealth.

- The **Railway Club,** 579 Dunsmuir St., Downtown (☎ 604-681-1625) is a nice spot thanks to a train theme, eclectic tunes, and famous musicians popping in. You pay a little extra to get inside if you're not already a member of the "club."

✔ **Whip Gallery,** 209 East 6th Ave., Mount Pleasant (☎ 604-874-4687), is hip, sure — hip enough to be a coffee shop or a design school graduate's crash pad. Instead, it's a bar with a decent (if limited) drink selection, light eats, occasional jazz, and funky art. The feeling is more laid-back and mature than you may expect from the living room–furniture motif. The freshly-baked pies are to die for!

Chic bars and lounges

If you like to feel right at home in a stylishly decorated lounge, sipping martinis and other shaken or stirred drinks, you'll find places aplenty around town. Here are some of the best:

✔ **Bacchus,** 845 Hornby St., Downtown (☎ 604-689-7777), a lounge in the plush Wedgewood Hotel (see Chapter 10), almost demands a dress code, it's so well appointed. Think of it as a potential pre- or post-dinner spot to snuggle over a drink. Quite expensive and trendy.

✔ **Cloud 9 Lounge,** 1400 Robson St., West End (☎ 604-687-0511), revolves high, high above the city's main shopping drag — and, no, the lounge doesn't whip around so fast that you'll get seasick. It's not as swish as you might expect from such a lofty location — it seems to rely on the incredible views of the mountains, the water, and even Washington State to lure people up. To find the club from street level, enter at the Empire Landmark Hotel and take the elevator.

✔ **Garden Terrace,** 791 West Georgia St., Downtown (☎ 604-602-0994), is the only place in town where you can sit beneath foliage imported from the African subcontinent. Housed within the ultra pricey Four Seasons hotel (see Chapter 9), it's an extremely refined place in which to sip a drink — save it for a special occasion. Closed Sundays.

✔ **900 West Lounge & Wine Bar,** 900 West Georgia St., Downtown (☎ 604-669-9378), the smartest wine bar in town, serves glasses, carafes, and bottles of some terrific vintages — plus great martinis if you don't feel like wine. Huge chandeliers and wingback chairs fill out the mood. Located in the Hotel Vancouver (see Chapter 9), it's a nice place for a snack with your drink, too, but wear your snazziest clothes and bring your wallet.

Thirst-quenching brewpubs

You may find no hotter trend, this moment, than the brewpub in Vancouver — and most of the action is tightly concentrated in Yaletown, although it's beginning to spread to other hip quarters of the city. I love sampling the freshly brewed products of a micro while chatting with the owners, and the atmosphere in such a place is almost always reliably affable, too. Here are my top picks:

✔ **Dix Barbecue & Brewery,** 871 Beatty St., Yaletown (☎ 604-682-2739), a microbrewery near BC Place Stadium, is as attractive as all the others in Yaletown, with good period photographs lining the walls. The crowd is pretty (although it morphs into Testosterone Central on hockey or hoops nights), and the beer isn't bad at all.

✔ **Steamworks Brewing Co.,** 375 Water St., Gastown (☎ 604-689-2739), brews such good drafts that you may not notice the sometimes-smarmy clientele. Explore several comfortable seating areas before settling down. This is one of Vancouver's original brewpubs.

✔ **Yaletown Brewing Company,** 1111 Mainland St., Yaletown (☎ 604-688-0064 or 604-681-2739), yet another Yaletown microbrewery, may be a bit of a scene, but the beer's the thing. You can drink outside when it's warm and dry, too, and the hip location for once doesn't preclude casual dress.

Beer joints

I love great beer, and I really like bar owners who know the huge difference between drinking a can of imported beer and savoring a hand-drawn pint of the same stuff. At the following places, you can count on a superb choice of beers and a staff that knows how to serve each and every one of 'em:

✔ **The Rusty Gull,** 175 East 1st St., North Vancouver (☎ 604-988-5585), is one of those bars that seems to exist simply for the pleasure of quaffing. Ownership has put together a knowledgeable beer list, and you'll want to sample as much of it as possible. Live music complements the atmosphere.

✔ **Sailor Hagar's,** 221 West 1st St., North Vancouver (☎ 604-984-3087 or 604-984-2567), seems to have everything under the sun. If you're a connoisseur of hard-to-find Bavarian dark beers, northern English ales, Irish cream stouts, or Belgian lambics, this is your place. They use authentic pub equipment to keep the beer fresh. Views of the city back across the water are astounding, and a restaurant is on the premises, too. Don't feel like driving to North Van? No problem — the bar's just a short walk from the SeaBus landing.

Cue-crackin' poolrooms

Sometimes you have to shoot some pool, and Vancouver's not short on places to do it. Here are two of the most fun:

✔ **Commodore Lanes & Billiards**, 838 Granville St. (☎ 604-681-1531), is tucked beneath the Commodore Ballroom, down a narrow stairwell that opens up to a humongous underground cavern of 8 lanes of bowling and 18 pool tables.

✔ **Soho Café & Billiards,** 1144 Homer St., Yaletown (☎ 604-688-1180), is a classy place to shoot some stick among the beautiful people. If you're looking for a dive in which to hustle some barflies, look elsewhere.

Laughing the night away: Comedy clubs

Vancouverites may take their West Coast–lifestyle pretty seriously, but when you consider this is improv comedy–champ Colin Mochrie's home base, you gotta believe this burgh has humor. Here are three ways to tickle your funny bone:

- ✔ **TheatreSports League,** New Revue Stage, 1601 Johnston St., Granville Island (☎ **604-738-8013**), has ongoing shows Wednesday through Saturday, although it's the late-night weekend gigs — appropriately called Improv Extreme — that can get really wildly funny.

- ✔ **Tony n' Tina's Wedding,** St. Andrew's-Wesley Church, Nelson St. at Burrard (☎ **604-258-4079** or TicketMaster ☎ 604-280-4444), is about as fun and interactive as comedy can get. As soon as you enter the church, you're a guest at a bizarre Italian wedding where the best man is dressed as Guido and the maid of honor? Well, I can't give too much away. The celebration continues at a downtown restaurant where members of the wedding party gradually start to unravel the family secrets. And you get to witness and live the drama.

- ✔ **Yuk Yuks Comedy Club,** Century Plaza Hotel, 1015 Burrard St. (☎ **604-696-YUKS**), is your traditional sit-back-and-be-entertained club, although the comics themselves may have plans to the contrary. Most of them are pretty good; many are on the Yuk Yuks circuit; one or two even end up on *The Tonight Show.*

Stepping out: The gay and lesbian scene

Vancouver is a very gay-friendly town, and a network of bars and clubs has emerged to bind together the area's growing gay and lesbian population. Here are two of the hottest places for gays and lesbians to meet:

- ✔ **Numbers Cabaret,** 1042 Davie St., West End (☎ **604-685-4077**), a multilevel complex of loud and quiet niches, is a prime spot for gay trawlers to sip beer, taste cocktails, cruise the scene, or just go nuts on one of several dance floors.

- ✔ **The Odyssey,** 1251 Howe St., Downtown (☎ **604-689-5256**), rages all night, every night, with everything from cultural events to disco DJs to some truly outrageous stuff, as well — I'll just say that showers and drag queens are involved. Not really a place for most straight folks.

Getting Artsy: The Performing Arts

Vancouver's sophisticates enjoy a major symphony orchestra, a world-class opera company, several large theater troupes, and an arena large enough to host such supergroups as U2 or the Rolling Stones.

To find out what's happening in venues big and small, just check the *Georgia Straight*, a free weekly newspaper. Its entertainment listings are beyond reproach. Or buy a copy of *Vancouver Magazine*, which does a good job of laying out each month's offerings.

Tickets for the performing arts and special productions or festivals are best bought in advance, either directly from the box office or via **TicketMaster** (☎ 604-280-4444; www.ticketmaster.ca). The latter is by far the easiest way to snag tickets for major events, although they'll come with the obligatory service charges — about C$5 (US$4.15) extra per ticket.

You can also call the **Vancouver Cultural Alliance's Arts Hotline** (☎ 604-684-2787; www.allianceforarts.com), which offers tickets sold by TicketMaster as well as for shows by independent producers throughout the region. Advance tickets can be purchased online or at the ticket booth at the Visitor Information Centre, 200 Burrard St.

If you're prepared for a catcher's catch-can choice, the Cultural Alliance also operates **Tickets Tonight** (☎ 604-684-2787; www.ticketstonight.ca), which sells same-day tickets at half price. Tickets Tonight is also at the Visitor Information Centre.

Raising the curtain on Vancouver's theaters

Vancouver's theater scene bumps along: It's usually pretty decent but occasionally a little rough for stretches of time. Current offerings include a mixture of retreads — which don't seem to do too well in this town — and original works, some of them locally penned. The city doesn't have a compact theater district, so plan well before heading out for the evening. The four major theater spaces to check out are

- ✔ The **Arts Club Theatre**, 1585 Johnston St., Granville Island (☎ 604-687-1644), the home of a big regional company, produces an interesting array of plays. The Backstage Lounge is here, too (see "Hip alternative bars" earlier in this chapter). Tickets start at C$15 (US$12) per performance.

- ✔ The **Frederick Wood Theatre**, 6354 Crescent Rd. at Gate 4 (☎ 604-822-2678), part of the University of British Columbia, offers student work at serious bargains (usually C$18 (US$15) per person).

- ✔ **Stanley Theatre**, 2750 Granville St., South Granville (☎ 604-687-1644), the best looking of these four theaters, is a renovated art deco–style movie house. The same company that performs at the Arts Club Theatre also performs here, but the shows are glitzier. Tickets generally run C$20 to C$45 (US$17–US$37) per show.

- ✔ The **Vancouver Playhouse**, 600 Hamilton St., Downtown (☎ 604-872-6622), is another place to see local and experimental work; sight lines are especially good. Tickets are C$21 to C$50 (US$17–US$42) depending on the night. The playhouse is adjacent to the Queen Elizabeth Theatre (see the opera section below).

If you happen to be in town during summer and like Shakespeare, the **Bard on the Beach** (☎ 604-737-0625) series is an absolute must-see. From mid-June to mid-September, actors perform Shakespeare's plays in Vanier Park inside three giant tents. Productions are fun and highly professional.

A similar series (without the Shakespearean focus) is the **Theatre Under the Stars** musical productions (☎ 604-257-0366; www.tuts.bc.ca) in Stanley Park during July and August. This popular open-air theater can be very romantic — although a brisk wind is usually blowing in from the ocean. Picnicking is encouraged.

If you're coming in September, be aware of the avant-garde **Fringe Festival** (☎ 604-237-0350; www.vancouverfringe.com), a spin-off from the popular Edinburgh festival, is held on and around Commercial Drive, east of downtown.

Tuning up for Vancouver's symphony

The **Vancouver Symphony Orchestra** (☎ 604-876-3434 for information, **604-280-4444** for tickets; www.vancouversymphony.com) gets classical — yet stays accessible with pops concerts, big-name guest soloists, and children's shows — at the venerable **Orpheum Theatre,** 800 Granville, Downtown (☎ 604-665-3030). Tickets run anywhere from C$20 to C$80 (US$17–US$67) per person.

Singing the praises of Vancouver's opera company

The talented **Vancouver Opera** (☎ 604-683-0222; www.vanopera.bc.ca) performs four or more times annually before gorgeous set pieces at the busy **Queen Elizabeth Theatre,** 600 Hamilton St., Downtown (☎ 604-665-3050), adjacent to the Vancouver Playhouse (see the theater section above). This venue is worth consulting for its other performances, too. Tickets generally cost from as little as C$25 (US$21) to as much as C$115 (US$96) per person — but, hey, you just may get to see one of those famous tenors you've only ever espied on PBS.

Et tutu, Vancouver? Dance in the city

For dance fans, **Ballet British Columbia** (☎ 604-732-5003; www.balletbc.com) stages a number of challenging performances around town, often at the Queen Elizabeth Theatre (see preceding listing). And some very good visiting companies often show up to join in the fun. Tickets for a performance usually cost between C$20 and C$70 (US$17–US$58) per person.

If you're tired of paying big bucks for nosebleed seats, head over to the University of British Columbia (UBC) in Point Grey. The university's **Chan Centre for the Performing Arts** (☎ 604-822-2697; www.chancentre.com) hosts a good bill of student and guest performances, sometimes free, sometimes at cost — but still at a better deal than in the big venues, and you definitely can hear better. (The venue is said to be world-renowned for its acoustics.) Performances happen year-round on weekends; more often in summer.

Part IV
Victoria

"...which reminds me — is your cousin's family still planning to visit us this summer?"

In this part . . .

Just a ferry ride away from Vancouver is picturesque Victoria, an English stronghold surrounded by beauty. In Chapter 16, I tell you what's where in Victoria and how to find information and get around. Then, I introduce you to the city's many charms and give you the lowdown on hotels (Chapter 17), restaurants (Chapter 18), attractions (Chapter 19), shopping (Chapter 20), and nightlife (Chapter 22). In Chapter 21, I also provide two itineraries: one for Anglophiles who want to enjoy the city's strong English heritage; the other for families.

Chapter 16

Arriving and Getting Oriented

. . . .

In This Chapter

▶ Getting your bearings
▶ Roaming the neighborhoods
▶ Finding information
▶ Traveling around the city

. . . .

*V*ictoria, being much more compact than Vancouver (see Part III), is even easier to get around. The airport and ferry terminals are a fair distance outside the city, but clearly marked roads and some public transit make getting into town relatively easy. In this chapter, I tell you how to get there, give you a quick outline of the city's layout, and point you toward the helpful tourist-information folks. Finally, I show you how best to get around Victoria by foot, car, or taxi.

Arriving in Victoria

Upon arrival in Canada, you first must pass through Customs and Immigration. See Chapter 7 for details on what to expect at these checkpoints — and what you need to get through them. Normally, U.S. citizens have little trouble at all, although the crossing is a bit more involved in the wake of September 11, 2001. My advice is to always bring your passport and, if you're from a country other than the United States, you may also need the appropriate visas.

Getting from Vancouver's airport to your hotel

En route to Victoria, you'll most likely fly into **Vancouver International Airport (YVR)** (☎ 604-207-7077). For information on what to expect at the airport and the location of information booths, see Chapter 8. To get to Victoria from this airport, you have several alternatives.

By ferry

Many travelers simply rent a car at the airport and drive straight to the Victoria ferry at Tsawwassen (pronounced SAH-WAH-sen, although you sometimes hear TAH-WAH-sen). This way is convenient, but if you go this route, you spend time driving to and from the ferry, waiting for the ferry, riding the ferry, and worrying about traffic and parking in Victoria. Then you need to reverse the process before leaving. Still, if you have to fly into Vancouver International and you have the need for a car, this may be your best option.

Several major rental car companies have representatives at the airport (see the Appendix for their toll-free numbers). After you pick up your car, drive out of the airport and turn onto Highway 99 South (*away* from Vancouver). Continue approximately 8 miles south to the junction with Highway 17, and then turn south on Highway 17. Then, you roll through suburbs and miles of peaceful farmland. After roughly 10 miles, the highway ends at the Tsawwassen dock of **BC Ferries** (☎ **888-223-3779;** www. bcferries.com). Drive right onto the dock and take a place in the lineup. If you're lucky, you won't face a huge backup; however, you may need to wait a while. The ferry ride across the Strait of Georgia and through several small channels to Swartz Bay takes about 90 minutes. (See Chapter 5 for ticket information for BC Ferries.)

From the Swartz Bay terminal, take Highway 17, the Patricia Bay Highway, directly south into downtown Victoria, where it becomes Blanshard Street. To reach Old Town and the Inner Harbour, turn right at Yates Street. To reach The Fairmont Empress Hotel, turn right at Burdett Avenue or Humboldt Street.

By plane or helicopter

Much easier — and cooler — is to fly from YVR straight to downtown Victoria via either a seaplane (also called a "floatplane") or a helicopter. Both land right in Victoria's Inner Harbour, steps from nearly all the major sights. The options include **Harbour Air, Helijet,** and **West Coast Air,** and costs range between C$99 (US$82) and C$105 (US$87) each way. Helijet trips are C$165 (US$137) one way. For details on these services, see Chapter 5.

By bus

You can even get to Victoria from the airport without lifting off *or* driving (yourself, that is). **Pacific Coach Lines** (☎ **800-661-1725** or **604-662-8074;** www.pacificcoach.com), known as PCL, runs three buses each day directly from Vancouver International to downtown Victoria — the bus drives right onto the ferry. Just remember that all departures tend to take place in the middle of the day, which is inconvenient if your flight arrives early or late. The bus ride costs C$36.25 to C$39 (US$30–US$32) one-way, and the trip takes about 3½ hours from the airport to Victoria's bus depot. Call or check the Web site for up-to-the-minute reservation, schedule, and fare information.

Getting from Victoria's airport to your hotel

In every situation I can think of, flying into Vancouver's airport is cheaper than flying into Victoria's. Assume, however, that you decide to value convenience over cost and fly into Victoria — either directly (which is actually possible from a handful of cities in the northwestern United States) or on a connecting flight from Vancouver.

Victoria International Airport (CYYJ) (☎ 250-953-7500; www.victoria airport.com) is a small facility located about 15 miles north of the city on Highway 17, up on the Saanich Peninsula. Several short-hop airlines, as well as various special charter flights, land here. Even with its current expansion, the facility is small enough that you won't get lost, and everything is clearly marked and signed. For a list of airlines that fly to Victoria International, see the Appendix.

Surprisingly, public transit does not connect the airport to Victoria. Therefore the quickest, although certainly not the cheapest, way to travel from the airport into the city is by cab. The 40-minute ride costs roughly C$38 to C$41 (US$32–US$34); a 15 percent tip is usually appropriate. The major cab companies include **Blue Bird** (☎ 800-665-7055), **Empress** (☎ 800-808-6881), and **Victoria Taxi** (☎ 888-842-7111). Empress usually has cabs waiting at the airport, but you can prearrange for any other cab company to pick you up if you call in advance.

Airporter (☎ 877-386-2525 or 250-386-2525), the privately operated shuttle bus, is also a good choice, because it leaves regularly from the terminal and makes stops at many of the key downtown hotels. You may have to wait a half-hour or more for a departure, however, depending on your timing. The fare is C$15 (US$12) for adults and the ride takes about an hour.

Although you won't need a car in Victoria, several rental car agencies are at the airport, including **Avis, Budget, Enterprise, Hertz,** and **National** (see the Appendix for their toll-free numbers). For directions from the airport into the city, see the following section.

Driving to Victoria

If you drive into Victoria, you'll either be coming from the U.S., arriving at the Inner Harbour ferry docks, the Swartz Bay terminal north of the city, the airport, or elsewhere on Vancouver Island.

- ✔ From the Inner Harbour ferry docks, simply drive two short blocks along Belleville Street to Douglas Street, just past the huge Fairmont Empress hotel; here, you turn left to reach the heart of the Old Town or right to reach Beacon Hill Park or the ocean loop through James Bay and Oak Bay.

- ✔ From the Swartz Bay terminal, drive off the ferry and onto Highway 17, the Patricia Bay Highway, which runs directly south into downtown Victoria, where it becomes Blanshard Street. To reach Old Town and the Inner Harbour, turn right at Yates Street. To reach The Fairmont Empress, turn right at Burdett Avenue or Humboldt Street.

✔ From the Victoria International Airport, you also drive Highway 17 south for about 15 miles into downtown Victoria, following the same directions as in the preceding paragraph.

✔ From elsewhere on Vancouver Island, simply proceed south on Highway 1, which becomes Douglas Street and runs right into the heart of town.

Getting to Know Victoria's Neighborhoods

Compact Victoria is less confusing than spread-out Vancouver. The city's three central neighborhoods are all connected, and as you walk or drive, they tend to blur into one another. Staying in one of these central areas is the best option if you're on a short visit, although you do pay extra. Victoria's suburbs tend to be almost exclusively residential, although one or two of these outlying areas have hotels. Finally, you can find chain motels and hotels on Highway 17 north of Victoria, but consider these only if you're strapped for cash or in a hurry to leave the following morning.

The **Inner Harbour** is the area surrounding the city's small inner harbor, where ferryboats, floatplanes, and whale-watching boats arrive and depart. Accommodations are plentiful and wonderfully situated. The views are splendid, and you're no more than a few minute's walk to important sights such as The Fairmont Empress Hotel, government buildings, and — of course — the waterfront and its ferries. This is, not very surprisingly, the most expensive place in town to bed down for the night.

The central portion of Victoria consists of an area along the waterfront, within five or so city blocks of it in any direction. This is the next-priciest location after the Inner Harbour, and it isn't a quiet place (except when bars shut down), but it does possess good atmosphere. Think of this area as two adjacent parts: **Old Town,** first up walking north from The Fairmont Empress and including Bastion and Market Squares, and then **Downtown,** which contains the bulk of the city's commerce — shopping, restaurants and bars, plus hotels.

 Downtown and Old Town are so interwoven that, for the purposes of this book, I combine them into a single area called "Downtown/ Old Town."

The adjacent neighborhoods are hit-or-miss when it comes to bedtime. The tiny and slightly grubby **Chinatown** (surprisingly, the continent's oldest in spite of its small size) occupies only a few narrow blocks north of Old Town, and I don't recommend any lodgings here. A few blocks

Victoria Neighborhoods

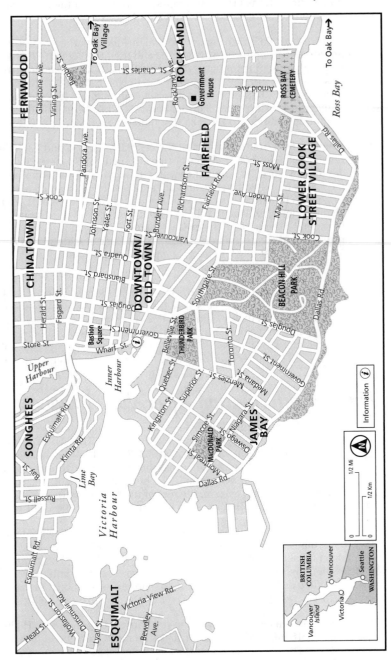

northeast lies **Fernwood,** a once down-at-heels area that has a new lease on life through the arts, restaurants, boutiques and the like; again, however, I don't recommend any accommodations here. Stay tuned.

Just west of Old Town, connected by a bridge, sits the neighborhood of **Songhees** (pronounced SONG-eeze) and then the separate municipality called **Esquimalt** (pronounced ess-KWHY-malt). Once an industrial area, this section is hot stuff today — home to North America's first microbrewery (see Chapter 18), but also several excellent lodgings, all with stupendous water views. Throughout this book, I combine these neighborhoods and refer to them as "Esquimalt/Songhees."

Finally, a little south and east of the central area, you find a number of residential neighborhoods harboring excellent, and quieter, lodgings. **James Bay,** directly south of downtown (to the right as you leave the ferries) is quietly attractive and offers a handful of distinctive lodgings to go with terrific views over water of islands and mountains. You can also wander nice Beacon Hill Park from your front door. The next neighborhood to the west is **Lower Cook Street Village,** a narrow strip that runs along the eastern side of Beacon Hill Park. **Rockland** and **Fairfield** are situated just north of here, composed of quiet and elegant streets and a handful of nice bed-and-breakfasts.

And **Oak Bay,** farther still to the east, is a friendly and British-feeling neighborhood with excellent beaches, golf courses, and a pleasant mixture of older and newer homes. You find surprisingly posh accommodations here. Think about staying in this neighborhood if you crave a quieter, more local experience. Reach the area by looping east and then north from the Inner Harbour along Dallas Road — a scenic drive.

Finding Information After You Arrive

Victoria has one central place for picking up comprehensive tourism information — thank goodness it's well stocked. The **Visitor InfoCentre,** 812 Wharf St. (☎ **250-953-2033; 800-663-3883** to book accommodations only), located right on the harbor at the corner of Government and Wharf Streets, is open daily year-round. The hours are 8:30 a.m. to 6:30 p.m. in summer and 9 a.m. to 5 p.m. the rest of the year. (And by the way, it looks sort of like a gas station because it *was* once a gas station. Fill 'er up!)

The friendly staff offers plenty of brochures and other printed material, covering nearly every aspect of Victoria. Beyond this, the InfoCentre can also find accommodations for you at no extra charge; book tours, boat excursions, and theater tickets; and offer recommendations. Note that the office distributes information for the rest of Vancouver Island, as well.

A smaller, seasonal InfoCentre on the Patricia Bay Highway (Highway 17) is about 16 miles north of town. This is a more convenient first stop if you're coming into town from the north — that is, from the Vancouver-to-Swartz Bay ferry or from Victoria International Airport. This office is open from March through the end of November every day from 9 a.m. to 5 p.m.

Getting Around Victoria

You're most likely to see Victoria by your own power, in a car, by private or public transportation, or as part of some sort of a tour. In this section, I let you know about each mode of transport.

On foot

You can reach many of the key sights — including all of the Inner Harbour, the Old Town, James Bay, and Chinatown — on foot. In fact, the vast majority of your fellow visitors will also be walking.

By bicycle

In a city possessing as many beaches, parks, and gardens as Victoria — without big-city traffic — bicycling turns out to be one of the best ways to see the local charms, if you have the energy. Bike lanes have been thoughtfully provided in key locations, and a day's rental costs only about C$35 (US$29), with an hour's rental about C$15 (US$12).

Some companies that rent cycles include **Harbour Rentals,** 811 Wharf St. (☎ 250-995-1661); and **Sports Rent,** 1950 Government St. (☎ 250-385-7368), which also offers rollerblades, camping gear, and other sports equipment.

A number of bike repair shops are in Victoria, as well, although they're almost all on the outskirts; the most central are **James Bay Bicycle Works,** 131 Menzies St. (☎ 250-380-1664), conveniently near the popular ocean loop, and the slightly hard-to-find but helpful **Fairfield Bicycle Shop,** 1275 Oscar St. (☎ 250-381-2453).

By car

Having a car in Victoria is convenient if you plan to get out into the countryside. But if you're concentrating on downtown, I recommend that you leave the wheels at home. If you do drive, you'll find that drivers here are exceptionally polite. You should drive — and act — in the same fashion.

Traffic rules are mostly the same as those of the United States: You drive on the right and stop at red lights. Plus, you can turn right on a red light if no traffic is coming. Blinking green arrows can be confusing — they simply mean "Proceed with caution" not "Go for it! (heh-heh)." Headlights must be on at all times, although on Canadian rental cars this happens automatically, and seat belts are always required. The speed limit within Victoria proper is generally 50 kilometers per hour (that's about 30 miles per hour), sometimes less.

Traffic backs up downtown at rush hour, which occurs from roughly 4 to 6 p.m. as downtown employees make an exodus for the northern, eastern, and western suburbs, and the one-way street system can be confounding. Parking is also often a hassle due to the compactness of the tourist area. On-street meters are expensive and nearly impossible to find during the high summer season — if you do manage to snag one, have plenty of change at the ready (a Canadian dollar gets you only a half-hour). Parking in a garage or lot is a better option than a meter. Several facilities are along Blanshard and View Streets, for example. For the locations of downtown parking lots, see the Cheat Sheet at the front of this book.

You should always find out whether your restaurant, hotel, or merchant can validate your parking slip.

Watch for parking spots that disappear at rush hour, when parking spaces become driving lanes; you'll be towed if you stay too long in these. Parking fines in Victoria run about C$35 (US$29) — you can pay online if you're nabbed, with discounts to C$15 (US$12) if you pay within 14 days.

By public transportation

BC Transit's Victoria arm, known as the **Victoria Regional Transit System** (☎ 250-385-2551; www.bctransit.com), consists almost solely of a bus network you may never use, but the agency still does a good job of collecting local maps and transportation information together in one package. You can pick up booklets such as *Victoria Rider's Guide* or *Explore Victoria by Bus* at the waterfront tourist information center. If you've already been to Vancouver, that city's transit guide also includes a section covering Victoria.

City buses do go to some tourist destinations, such as the ferry docks and Butchart Gardens. Buses are clean, but they're slow and make lots of stops.

Multiple fare zones determine prices: A ride costs either C$2 or C$2.75 (US$1.65 or US$2.30) per adult, depending on how far you go; less for seniors and children. Drivers don't carry change, so you need exact fare — a possible headache if you've just arrived. Day passes, available at both the tourist information center and certain stores, cost C$6 (US$5) for adults (C$4 (US$3.35) for children and seniors) and allow you to avoid the exact-change dance but otherwise aren't a good deal because you're unlikely to use the bus system enough to justify buying one.

You can get transfers for one-time use if you're continuing in the same direction on a different bus. If you venture out of zone one, which is downtown Victoria, you have between 30 to 45 minutes before a transfer becomes invalid. If you get off the bus and don't take the very next bus running the same direction, however, you have to purchase a new ticket. For a one-zone ticket, you have between 15 to 20 minutes to use the transfer, and the same rules apply. For more information on the zones, log on to www.bctransit.com.

By taxi

You probably won't need a cab in Victoria, but if you do here's the skinny. Taxis cost C$2.50 (US$2.10) to start the meter and C$1.45 (US$1.20) for each additional kilometer (which is a little more than half a mile). Downtown trips generally cost about C$6 to C$8 (US$5–US$6.65); from the airport, fares will run around C$40 (US$33). A 15 percent tip is appropriate. The major cab companies include **Blue Bird** (☎ **800-665-7055**), **Empress** (☎ **800-808-6881**), and **Victoria Taxi** (☎ **888-842-7111**). Call ahead if at all possible, rather than simply trying to hail a cab in the street — they may not stop.

Chapter 17

Checking In at Victoria's Best Hotels

. . . .

In This Chapter

▶ Looking at Victoria's best accommodations
▶ Glimpsing at your other options

. . . .

This chapter includes the best sleeps in Victoria from quaint B&Bs to luxury hotels . . . and this city has a number to choose from. The ones listed here are among my favorites, be it for price, ambiance, or service. Most of them include some form of breakfast in the room rate; are non-smoking — in keeping with the healthy West Coast lifestyle — so be sure to ask if you're needing to light up; and many provide free Internet access. Nearly all of them are within the downtown core, which means you can dump the car and enjoy the city at its best — by walking! Check out the additional listings in the "Runner-up Hotels" section toward the end of the chapter, if your first picks are booked.

See Chapter 9 for my strategies on how to get the best room and the best rate, how to surf the Web for hotel deals, and how to find a room at the last minute.

For a key to the dollar sign ratings used in each listing, see this book's Introduction.

 Look for the Kid Friendly icon to find hotels that are especially welcoming to families. These hotels usually offer plenty of room for families to spread out, and may also have kitchens, laundry services, or free breakfasts, along with special programs, rates, or facilities for kids.

Victoria's Best Hotels from A to Z

 Abigail's Hotel
$$$–$$$$ Downtown/Old Town

This Tudor mansion has been converted into one of the most romantic little hotels in the city in spite of its position off the water. The suites come

Victoria's Best Hotels

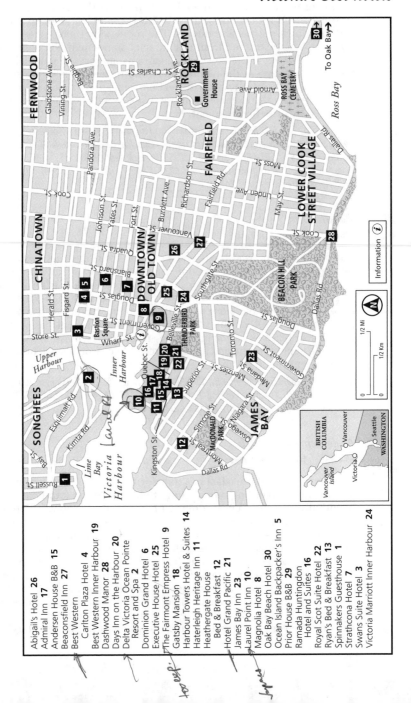

Abigail's Hotel **26**
Admiral Inn **17**
Andersen House B&B **15**
Beaconsfield Inn **27**
Best Western
  Carlton Plaza Hotel **4**
Best Western Inner Harbour **19**
Dashwood Manor **28**
Days Inn on the Harbour **20**
Delta Victoria Ocean Pointe
  Resort and Spa **2**
Dominion Grand Hotel **6**
Executive House Hotel **25**
The Fairmont Empress Hotel **9**
Gatsby Mansion **18**
Harbour Towers Hotel & Suites **14**
Haterleigh Heritage Inn **11**
Heathergate House
  Bed & Breakfast **12**
Hotel Grand Pacific **21**
James Bay Inn **23**
Laurel Point Inn **10**
Magnolia Hotel **8**
Oak Bay Beach Hotel **30**
Ocean Island Backpacker's Inn **5**
Prior House B&B **29**
Ramada Huntingdon
  Hotel and Suites **16**
Royal Scot Suite Hotel **22**
Ryan's Bed & Breakfast **13**
Spinnakers Guesthouse **1**
Strathcona Hotel **7**
Swans Suite Hotel **3**
Victoria Marriott Inner Harbour **24**

with extravagant touches, such as four-poster beds, leather loveseats, wood-burning fireplaces, and double-whirlpool baths, while the remaining pastel-colored rooms are outfitted with standard furnishings and comfortable down pillows and duvets. The rooms don't have televisions, so you won't be distracted from that special someone if you come for the romance. Marvel at the blossoming gardens and crystal chandeliers and meet fellow guests at the nightly sherry hour, when snacks are served in the library and sitting room. The next morning, don't rush out to sightsee without tasting the excellent full breakfast — which your hosts bring to your bed by prior arrangement.

See map p. 225. 906 McClure St. (from The Fairmont Empress Hotel, walk 2 blocks away from water along Burdett, turn right at Quadra, go 1 block to McClure, turn right again). ☎ *800-561-6565 or 250-388-5363. Fax: 250-388-7787.* www.abigails hotel.com. *Parking: Free. Rates: C$239–C$425 (US$199–US$354) double. Rates include full breakfast. AE, MC, V.*

Admiral Inn
$$–$$$ Inner Harbour

This family-run inn isn't the fanciest place in town, and that's exactly why people (especially families) come here, again and again. It's just plain amazing that you can spend this little for million-dollar harbor views. The larger rooms have fridges and microwaves for dining in, pull-out sofa beds on which tuckered-out kids can crash, and bonuses such as balconies and free local calls. Other thoughtful, almost youth hostel–like, amenities include free bikes — a boon in parking-strapped downtown — free Internet access, a laundry room, and loads of great advice from the friendly staff on what to see and do in the city.

See map p. 225. 257 Belleville St. ☎ *888-823-6472 or 250-388-6267. Fax: 250-388-6267.* www.admiral.bc.ca. *Parking: Free. Rates: C$149–C$249 (US$124–US$207) double. Rates include continental breakfast. AE, MC, V.*

Andersen House B&B
$$–$$$ Inner Harbour

This small bed-and-breakfast has transformed a turn-of-the-century house into a truly British Columbian kind of place, offering four spacious and beautifully decorated guest rooms with extras like CD players, interesting art, soaker tubs, and free Internet access. Their individual charms are pretty cool, too — from the Casablanca Room's private stairway, French doors, window seat, and views of the Parliament Buildings to the claw-foot tub, wet bar, and extra bedroom that come with the Captain's Apartment. The Southside Room is notable for its garden entrance, while the more luxurious Garden Studio features a hot tub and antiques. The full breakfast is truly sumptuous: You choose from entrees such as cheese soufflé, breakfast quesadillas, and Dutch apple pancakes, often with fruits and berries from the flower-laden garden. These folks also run the new **Baybreeze**

Manor (3930 Telegraph Bay Road; ☎ 250-721-3930; www.baybreeze manor.com), a restored — and very romantic — Victorian farmhouse that's about a 10-minute drive from downtown.

See map p. 225. 301 Kingston St. ☎ 250-388-4565. Fax 250-721-3938. www. andersenhouse.com. Parking: Street. Rates: C$195–C$275 (US$162–US$229) double. Rates include full breakfast. MC, V.

Beaconsfield Inn
$$–$$$ Downtown/Old Town

Located a few short blocks from the harbor, this nice bed-and-breakfast is well positioned and small enough to remain personable. Designed by famed local architect Samuel McClure in 1905, there's a pleasantly English feel to the place, as well. The Emily Carr Suite remains one of the show-piece rooms, with its romantic double hot tub in front of a fireplace, queen bed, and separate sitting area. Another suite features a flowery patio and similar double hot tub. As a bonus, the full breakfast, afternoon tea, and evening sherry in the sitting room are all complimentary.

See map p. 225. 998 Humboldt St. (from The Fairmont Empress Hotel, walk 2 blocks east away from the water along Humboldt). ☎ 888-884-4044 or 250-384-4044. Fax: 250-384-4052. www.beaconsfieldinn.com. Parking: Free. Rates: C$169–C$299 (US$141–US$249) double. Rates include full breakfast, tea, and evening sherry. MC, V.

Best Western Inner Harbour
$$–$$$ Inner Harbour

As long as you understand exactly what you're getting yourself into — an unspectacular chain motel — this is a good place to stay if you want to save some money and still get harbor views. The hotel's suites are a good choice for traveling families, with a queen bed and two pullout sofa beds apiece, plus full kitchen facilities, dual televisions, and big balconies, among other amenities. A laundromat, sauna, and pool are on the premises.

See map p. 225. 412 Quebec St. ☎ 888-383-2378 or 250-384-5122. Fax: 250-384-5113 www.victoriabestwestern.com. Parking: Free. Rates: C$119–C$269 (US$99–US$224) double. Rates include continental breakfast. AE, DC, DISC, MC, V.

Dashwood Manor
$$–$$$ Lower Cook Street Village

A pretty little Tudor inn with superb positioning on both a park and the ocean, this sleeper is outside the tourist bustle of downtown Victoria yet within a half-hour's walking distance of the Inner Harbour. Built in 1912, the inn features 14 rooms, many with close-up views of the bay and, 25 miles across the water, of Washington's Olympic Peninsula. The inn's gardens — and big Beacon Hill Park itself — are right outside your door, and you can make a fine day by cycling, walking, or driving around the water's edge through Oak Bay and beyond. For breakfast, you'll find the refrigerator stocked nightly so that you can cater to yourself the next morning. Some rooms also have whirlpools. If you're planning on an extended stay in Victoria, this might be the place for you — weekly and monthly rentals can reduce the nightly cost to as little as C$65 (US$54).

See map p. 225. 1 Cook St. (from back of The Fairmont Empress Hotel, travel south away from downtown along Douglas St. less than 1 mile to water; turn left, and continue north on Dallas Rd. ½ mile to corner of Cook St.). ☎ 800-667-5517 or 250-385-5517. Fax: 250-383-1760. www.dashwoodmanor.com. Parking: Free. Rates: C$125–C$325 (US$104–US$270) double. Rates include full breakfast. AE, DC, DISC, MC, V.

Delta Victoria Ocean Pointe Resort and Spa
$$–$$$ **Esquimalt/Songhees**

The OPR, as this hotel is known (even though it's in the Delta chain), makes for a great splurge, where you'll be pampered almost beyond belief with huge rooms and great bedding. You're not exactly right downtown — but you can see it spread out before you, and you're just a short ferry ride away from everything. There are very posh multi-room suites (with a very hefty price tag) as well as standard and deluxe rooms that are all very comfortable. Each has high-speed Internet access, a cordless phone, terry robes, and, for an extra fee, guests enjoy access to squash and tennis courts, a massage service, and the terrific in-house spa (see Chapter 20 for details). The hotel also offers child-care facilities. The excellent Spinnakers Brewpub (see Chapter 22) is a short walk from the front door. Note that off-season and low-demand-day promotional rates can cut your bill by up to 50 percent if you book in advance, although the availability of those rates is quite limited; be sure to ask. Oh yes, the OPR is Victoria's only resort to offer free pet stays, complete with personalized welcome!

See map p. 225. 45 Songhees Rd. (from downtown Victoria, proceed north to Johnson St. and cross Johnson St. bridge; hotel is on left, at corner of Songhees Rd.). ☎ 800-667-4677 or 250-360-2999. Fax: 250-360-1041. www.deltahotels.com. Parking: Valet, C$12 (US$10). Rack rates: C$185–C$295 (US$154–US$245) double. Suites are upwards from C$500 (US$416). AE, DC, DISC, MC, V.

Dominion Grand Hotel
$$–$$$ **Downtown/Old Town**

Built in 1876, this renovated heritage hotel is the oldest in the city and a good choice, considering its moderate rates and accessibility to downtown shops, restaurants, and tours. Upgrades have really cleaned up the place, polishing the copious marble, mahogany, etched glass, and crystal to something like its former glory. Standard hotel rooms aren't huge, but they're nicely decked out in vintage furnishings; the suites *are* big. Some rooms have yet to receive a facelift, so unless you're a real bargain hunter — these rooms are relatively inexpensive — be sure to ask. As if that weren't enough, several nearby family-style restaurants make this an attractive option for travelers with children. In fact, rates reflect this by including continental breakfast, to-go lunch, and dinner nearby. All in all, this hotel qualifies as a real find for the budget conscious.

See map p. 225. 759 Yates St. ☎ ***800-663-6101*** *or 250-384-4136. Fax: 250-382-6416.* www.dominion-hotel.com. *Parking: C$9 (US$7.50). Inclusive rates: C$149–C$249 (US$124–US$207) double. AE, DC, DISC, MC, V.*

Executive House Hotel
$$–$$$ Downtown/Old Town

The bland, highrise exterior of the Executive House conceals unbeatable luxuries, room to roam, and suites perfect for the traveling family that can afford one. The location is close to perfect, too — nearly across the street from the Empress hotel, a mere block from the Inner Harbour and the Royal B.C. Museum — while rooms are big and comfortable enough to satisfy even high rollers. All suites come with full kitchen facilities and pull-out beds, and if you don't feel like cooking, you'll find three restaurants on the premises, too. The suites on the 17th floor are beyond luxurious, with terraces, posh furnishings, and private hot tubs. Because this is primarily a business hotel (note the banquet room and upscale fitness center), ask about weekend discounts.

See map p. 225. 777 Douglas St. ☎ ***800-663-7001*** *or 250-388-5111. Fax: 250-385-1323.* www.executivehouse.com. *Parking: C$2 (US$1.65). Rates: C$195–C$210 (US$162–US$175) double. AE, DC, DISC, MC, V.*

The Fairmont Empress Hotel
$$$–$$$$ Inner Harbour

You don't necessarily have to be a "somebody" to stay here, but you do have to have somebody's mighty thick wallet. Formerly one of the crown jewels in the Canadian Pacific chain that once stretched across Canada, this huge hotel — now under the Fairmont name, but known locally as "the Empress" — is fancy in every possible way; you might feel stupid standing around in jeans (although tourists do it) trying to figure out how to get to the restaurants, pool, sauna room, spa, or business center. The Empress has more than 500 rooms and suites, and the cheaper ones can be considered spacious only by 1908 standards; if you have even a hint of claustrophobia, pay even more for an upgrade or stay somewhere else. Even if you can't afford to indulge, though, visit the topnotch shopping gallery attached to the hotel — see Chapter 20 for details — as well as the amazing Bengal Lounge (described in Chapter 22), good for a drink or a relatively inexpensive meal. Then there's always the "must-do-once" traditional afternoon tea that costs about the same in dollars as it does in calories. Services are doting, including buzzing valets, concierge service, the city's top spa (see Chapter 20), business facilities, a special children's pool, and much more.

See map p. 225. 721 Government St. ☎ ***800-441-1414*** *or 250-384-8111. Fax: 250-389-2747.* www.fairmont.com/empress. *Parking: Valet, $22 (US$18). Rates: C$239–C$569 (US$199–US$473) double. AE, DC, DISC, MC, V.*

Gatsby Mansion
$$–$$$ **Inner Harbour**

A rather quaint little B&B overlooking Victoria's harbor, the Gatsby probably gets less attention than it deserves. This place harks back to the roar-
ing '20s, certainly, with fine linens and a dashing hand throughout; they
don't skimp on the little things here. The design is full of clever exterior
and interior details — a pepper shaker tower, crystal chandeliers, stained-
glass windows, and frescoed ceilings. Although rooms have nice extras,
such as thick duvets, harbor views, and antique furnishings, they do vary
a good deal in size. (You can generally trade ocean views for extra space.)
Breakfasts are delicious, and the kitchen staff will even fashion picnic baskets to take out — or eat in bed — on request.

*See map p. 225. 309 Belleville St. ☎ **800-563-9656** or 250-388-9191. Fax: 250-920-5651.*
www.bellevillepark.com. *Parking: Free. Rates: C$179–C$289 (US$149–US$240)*
double. Rates include full breakfast. AE, DC, MC, V.

Haterleigh Heritage Inn
$$$–$$$$ **Inner Harbour**

One of the city's top bed-and-breakfast picks, with prices to match, this
restored mansion is located only two blocks from the harbor and the
action. Innkeepers Paul and Elizabeth Kelly have thought of everything:
sherry and chocolates at night, gourmet breakfasts each morning, extra
pillows, carefully refurbished leaded and stained-glass windows through-
out, and other touches that make for a *very* turn-of-the-20th-century
Victorian experience. It's a great place for honeymooners, too (every room
has a hot tub), with the Secret Garden and Day Dreams suites being espe-
cially decadent. Remember to book early; the place has only six rooms.

*See map p. 225. 243 Kingston St. ☎ **866-234-2244** or 250-384-9995. Fax: 250-384-1935.*
www.haterleigh.com. *Parking: Free. Rates: C$225–C$355 (US$187–US$295)*
double. Rates include full breakfast. MC, V.

Hotel Grand Pacific
$$$–$$$$ **Inner Harbour**

The Grand Pacific is one of the most comfortable upscale options around
the Inner Harbour. The more expensive rooms are worth the money, with
lots of little extras (a cordless phone to walk around with? Naturally!) and
guaranteed balconies; regular rooms are nice enough, but the suites really
pile on the luxury — think whirlpool tubs that fit two, plug-ins for laptop
modems, fireplaces, and multiple patios with views. The hotel is also very
child friendly, offering a kids' package that includes a disposable camera,
Nintendo games, cookies and milk, museum and theater tickets as well as
a kids' menu in the restaurant. The athletic club is pretty top notch, fea-
turing an impessive lap pool, workout machines, and even racquetball
courts. For a splashy night out, the hotel's fine dining room, The Mark, is
considered one of the city's ritziest.

See map p. 225. 450 Quebec St. (from The Fairmont Empress Hotel, walk south to Belleville St., turn right on Belleville and walk 2 blocks to Oswego St., turn left and continue to Quebec St.). ☎ *800-663-7550 or 250-380-4474. Fax: 250-386-8779.* www.hotelgrandpacific.com. *Parking: C$10 (US$8.30). Rates: C$189–C$359 (US$157–US$299) double. AE, DC, DISC, MC, V.*

James Bay Inn
$–$$ James Bay

Granted, this isn't the Ritz. But it *is* one of downtown Victoria's few budget steals, even without the off-season discounts that slash prices even more — don't mind the fading aura about the place, and you'll be fine. As a bonus, you can say you slept in Emily Carr's house. That's right. One of Canada's most beloved painters lived here for a time late in her life. You find few extras or amenities, but rooms are surprisingly large. Hotel guests get a discount at the on-premises restaurant and pub. The two-bedroom cottage, a five-minute walk down the road, is a good option for families, priced from C$222 (US$185) per night.

See map p. 225. 270 Government St. (from The Fairmont Empress Hotel, walk 4 blocks south on Government St.). ☎ *800-836-2649 or 250-384-7151. Fax: 250-385-2311.* www.jamesbayinn.bc.ca. *Parking: Free. Rates: C$84–C$151 (US$70–US$126) double. AE, MC, V.*

Laurel Point Inn
$$$–$$$$ Inner Harbour

Well-heeled Japanese tourists love this luxurious hotel sticking out into the Inner Harbour, and no wonder: The design touches, wall art, and even the robes are largely Japanese in style. The giant structure comes with tremendous, unencumbered views of the Inner Harbour and the Strait of Juan de Fuca. Suites are in a newer addition and are big and wonderful; rooms in the older building aren't, frankly, as large or modern, but everything here is well appointed. All the rooms — from the standard doubles to a wide assortment of suites with quickly escalating rack rates — feature scenic balconies, marble bathrooms, quality furniture, high-speed Internet access, down duvets, and Japanese kimonos. More expensive suites add soaker tubs, while the Panoramic Penthouse Suites (which cost a mint) also come with Italian linens, a double whirlpool tub, and wraparound balconies that offer 360-degree views of the city.

See map p. 225. 680 Montreal St. ☎ *800-663-7667 or 250-386-8721. Fax: 250-386-9547.* www.laurelpoint.com. *Parking: C$7 (US$5.80). Rates: C$239–C$319 (US$199–US$265) double. AE, DC, MC, V.*

Magnolia Hotel
$$–$$$$ Downtown/Old Town

Perhaps the most centrally located, this beautiful boutique hotel has plenty of touches — including one of the city's better spas. Most of the rooms, from the executive suites with fireplaces to standard rooms, have been outfitted with floor-to-ceiling windows, two-poster beds covered in duvets and feather pillows, wet bars, refrigerators, and — now *here's thoughtfulness* — umbrellas. Large desks come with two-line cordless phones, dataports, and speakerphone capability. Fine linens, terry-cloth bathrobes, and classy toiletries stock the marble bathrooms; some executive rooms are also equipped with soaker tubs and gas fireplaces. The Aveda spa is the real star, though, with a range of pampering services. **Hugo's Brewhouse** (adjoining a good bistro-styled restaurant) is a popular watering hole.

See map p. 225. 623 Courtney St. ☎ *877-624-6654 or 250-381-0999. Fax: 250-381-0988.* www.magnoliahotel.com. *Parking: Valet, C$12 (US$10). Rates: C$189–C$329 (US$157–US$274) double. AE, DC, DISC, MC, V.*

Oak Bay Beach Hotel
$$–$$$$ Oak Bay

Right on the ocean and directly across the street from a golf course, this Tudor-style resort hotel offers one of the most relaxing locations possible — although it's 3 to 4 miles from most of the main sights. Public rooms are furnished in elegant antiques and a baby grand piano, while the 51 rooms are each unique. Some rooms contain antiques and flower prints, and brass or canopy beds. Other rooms are more modern looking, with gas fireplaces, double soaker tubs, and balconies. A few rooms offer views of Haro Strait (and Washington State's mountains and islands beyond). I recommend an upstairs suite to get the best of all these things, although you pay quite a bit more for the privilege. The hotel takes full advantage of its beachside location: you can book dinner cruises, or kayaking or whale-watching outings at the front desk. If the weather's inclement, the little on-site pub is a treat.

See map p. 225. 1175 Beach Dr. (from The Fairmont Empress Hotel, follow Douglas St. south away from downtown to water; turn left and follow Dallas Rd. along the coast approximately 5 miles to golf course). ☎ *800-668-7758 or 250-598-4556. Fax: 250-598-6180.* www.oakbaybeachhotel.com. *Parking: Free. Rates: C$129–C$345 (US$107–US$287) double. Rates include continental buffet breakfast. AE, DC, MC, V.*

Ocean Island Backpacker's Inn
$ Downtown/Old Town

This is one of Victoria's best-kept secrets — a sort of youth hostel come historic apartment building come backpackers' layover, which attracts all ages and families. If you enjoy meeting other travelers, then this is the place since the lounges, bar, and dining room are hot gathering spots. Conversation is lively and multilingual. There are dorm accommodations for four to six people (co-ed and girls' dorms are available) as well as family rooms which are more hotel-styled with a private bathroom, multiple beds, and a fridge. If you're a twosome, rates are so reasonable that you might find it worthwhile to book a dorm all to yourselves. Laundry facilities and free Internet access are all part of the deal.

See map p. 225. 791 Pandora Ave. ☎ **888-888-4180**, *866-888-4180, or 250-385-1788. Fax: 250-385-1780.* www.oceanisland.com. *Parking: Free. Rates: C$18–C$24 (US$15–US$20) dorm; C$25–C$62 (US$21–US$52) private room; C$62–C$100 (US$52–US$83) family room. AE, MC, V.*

Prior House B&B
$$$–$$$$ Rockland

Out in the quiet and pretty Rockland neighborhood, this is one of the city's most luxurious B&Bs. The area's not the place for nightlife or a party, but rather a place for a contemplative stay. The oak-paneled rooms all come with goose-down comforters, duvets, pillows, and robes, but their individual character is quite different. You enter the Hobbit Garden Studios from a patio through a round-topped door to find a bar, queen bed, and fireplace; bathroom fixtures are all done in marble and there's a whirlpool tub. The Arbutus (sea views) and Linden Lea (which has a loveseat) rooms each include antiques, linens, fireplaces, and canopy beds, plus televisions and VCRs. The suites are even more luxurious. As a final nice touch, the hotel staff serves a complimentary afternoon tea daily in the public sitting rooms.

See map p. 225. 620 St. Charles St. (from downtown Victoria, follow Fort St. 1½ miles away from water to St. Charles, turn right, and continue 1 block to Rockland). ☎ **877-924-3300** *or 250-592-8847. Fax: 250-592-8223.* www.priorhouse.com. *Parking: Free. Rates: C$225–C$310 (US$187–US$258) double. Rates include gourmet breakfast and afternoon tea. MC, V.*

Royal Scot Suite Hotel
$$–$$$ Inner Harbour

This extremely kid-friendly and centrally located hotel is a favorite with families. You do find standard rooms, but most are spacious suites; the larger ones split between a living room, dining room, and a full kitchen — a great arrangement for large families. The Royal Scot is a good pick if you're traveling with little ones and don't care about impressing friends back home with tales of staying at the Empress Hotel. Other handy amenities include a do-it-yourself laundry, free parking, indoor pool, exercise room, and game room (with pool tables); although this isn't far from downtown, the hotel runs a courtesy shuttle to the central shopping and touring areas.

See map p. 225. 425 Quebec St. ☎ **800-663-7515** *or 250-388-5463. Fax: 250-388-5452.* www.royalscot.com. *Parking: Free. Rates: C$165–C$415 (US$137–US$345) double and suite. AE, DC, MC, V.*

Ryan's Bed and Breakfast
$–$$ Inner Harbour

This pretty Victorian home, only three blocks from the Inner Harbour and downtown, is a relative bargain. The renovated 1892 structure has been designated as a heritage property — you can easily see why. Oil paintings in gilded frames, china cabinets, and chaise lounges decorate the public areas. The six guest rooms, while not especially large, are certainly comfortable, and they're furnished in period antiques and rugs. The family serves breakfast in a dining room, which retains its original oak buffet and fir mantelpiece. Outside, the garden has plenty of sitting space. Fisherman's Wharf at Shoal Point (see Chapter 19) is minutes away on foot.

See map p. 225. 224 Superior St. ☎ *877-389-0012 or 250-389-0012. Fax: 250-389-2857.* www.ryansbb.com. *Parking: Free. Rates: C$139–C$229 (US$116–US$191) double. Rates include full breakfast. MC, V.*

Spinnakers Guesthouse
$$–$$$ Esquimalt/Songhees

This spot, with tremendous service and room options, is a good choice among Victoria's guesthouses. The complex has three handsomely renovated buildings, including the original 1884 home and the circa-1890 Lime Bay House. Most of the guest rooms have luxurious double whirlpool tubs, while some have fireplaces. The Garden Suites, added in 1998, include a queen bed, down duvets, a patio overlooking the garden and harbor, and a hot tub (with candles); two contain wood-burning fireplaces; use of kitchen facilities is also an option. Breakfast is served in the brewpub restaurant that made the place famous; it's also a great spot for lunch or dinner (see Chapters 18 and 22).

See map p. 225. 308 Catherine St. (from downtown Victoria, proceed north to Johnson St.; cross the Johnson St. bridge and continue ½ mile to Catherine St.). ☎ *877-838-2739 or 250-384-2739. Fax: 250-384-3246.* www.spinnakers.com. *Parking: Free. Rates: C$149–C$249 (US$124–US$207) double. Rates include full breakfast. AE, MC, V.*

Strathcona Hotel
$–$$ Downtown/Old Town

Possibly *the* cheapest recommendable hotel in downtown Victoria, the Strathcona is a city within itself. The rooms are clean and adequate, if rather plain and charmless — the sort you'd expect in a bland, mid-priced hotel in a European city, for example. The price is the reason you're staying here. Be aware, however, that the sprawling five-story complex also contains no less than nine hopping pubs, clubs, and restaurants — how do you think they make a profit? The offerings include a pool hall, a British pub, a divey bar, a roof-top patio for beach volleyball, and an off-track horse-betting parlor (see Chapter 22 for more on these). All this commotion means that "the Strath" attracts a younger crowd and that lower floors are quite noisy; try to stay on an upper floor if at all possible.

See map p. 225. 919 Douglas St. ☎ *800-663-7476 or 250-383-7137. Fax: 250-383-6893.* www.strathconahotel.com. *Parking: C$5 (US$4.15) Rates: C$95–C$120 (US$79–US$100) double. AE, DC, DISC, MC, V.*

Swans Suite Hotel
$$–$$$$ **Downtown/Old Town**

Once an ugly duckling, but now a swan — that's the story of this former grain warehouse, now a real winner in the Victoria accommodations game. An award-winning renovation of the building created 29 apartment suites — some of the biggest rooms for your dollar in the city — plus a luxurious penthouse. Each is decorated with original Pacific Northwestern art, derived from the hotel's private collection of nearly 1,600 paintings, sculptures, furniture, and antiques. On the top (third) floor, all nine rooms have skylights. Five rooms scattered throughout the property have private terraces. All rooms have kitchens, however, and either one or two bedrooms. No expense was spared in the renovation, which added chandeliers from the Empress Hotel, a jazz bar in the cellar, and beer engines imported from England in the excellent Swans Pub microbrewery on the main floor (see Chapter 22 for the pub listing).

See map p. 225. 506 Pandora Ave. (from downtown, walk north along harbor on Wharf St. ½ mile to Johnson St. and cross; hotel is at corner of Pandora and Store. ☎ *800-668-7926 or 250-361-3310. Fax: 250-361-3491.* www.swanshotel.com. *Parking: C$9 (US$7.50). Rates: C$189–C$359 (US$157–US$299) suites. AE, DC, MC, V.*

Victoria Marriott Inner Harbour
$$–$$$$ **Inner Harbour**

Although its modern and urban ambience feels as if it's geared more to the business executive than the casual visitor, rest assured that you'll get a warm welcome from the young and enthusiastic staff. Since this 236-room hotel opened in the spring of 2004, it has achieved number one status among Marriott hotels in Canada for guest satisfaction. The hotel's location is really central and although set behind the Empress, from the upper-floor guest rooms — all rooms are sumptuously decked out and have free high-speed Internet access — views stretch to the Olympic Mountain Range in Washington State. Hotel amenities include a cozy bar, full-size indoor pool, and a health club. Do give the hotel's restaurant, Fire and Water, a try; F&W is gaining quite a reputation for its barbecue grills and fish (hence the name), created by a chef who has cooked for the likes of the late Princess Diana.

See map p. 225. 728 Humboldt St. ☎ *877-333-8338 or 250-480-3800. Fax: 250-480-3838.* www.victoriamarriott.com. *Parking: Free. Rates: C$199 standard room–C$599 suites (US$166–US$498). AE, DC, MC, V.*

Runner-up Hotels

Best Western Carlton Plaza Hotel
$$ **Downtown/Old Town** This modern hotel, near several brew-pubs and clubs, is a surprisingly good deal — and rooms have kitchens or

kitchenettes. *See map p. 225. 642 Johnson St.* ☎ *800-663-7241 or 250-388-5513. Fax: 250-388-5343.* www.bestwesterncarlton.com.

Days Inn on the Harbour

$$ Inner Harbour   This pinkish property is blocky, predictable, and filled with tourists who appreciate both its centrality and the family-friendly amenities. *See map p. 225. 427 Belleville St.* ☎ *800-665-3024 or 250-386-3451. Fax: 250-386-6999.* www.daysinnvictoria.com.

Harbour Towers Hotel & Suites

$$–$$$ Inner Harbour   This Inner Harbour location offers a choice of nearly 200 rooms of varying styles and rates from plain to plush. *See map p. 225. 345 Quebec St.* ☎ *800-663-5896 or 250-385-2405. Fax: 205-360-2313.* www.harbourtowers.com.

Heathergate House Bed & Breakfast

$$ Inner Harbour   A typically simple yet elegant British-style B&B, this is one of the Inner Harbour's most affordable options — but it has only four rooms, so book early. *See map p. 225. 122 Simcoe St.* ☎ *888-683-0068 or 250-383-0068. Fax: 250-383-4320.* www.heathergatebb.com.

Ramada Huntingdon Hotel and Suites

$$–$$$ Inner Harbour   Close to the ferry docks, this hotel — owned by the same folks who own Gatsby Mansion (see the preceding section) — offers a choice of standard rooms, split-level suites, and small, apartment-style kitchenette units. *See map p. 225. 330 Quebec St.* ☎ *250-381-3456. Fax: 250-382-7666.* www.bellevillepark.com.

Index of Accommodations by Neighborhood

Ramada Huntingdon Manor and Suites ($$–$$$)
Royal Scot Suite Hotel ($$–$$$)
Ryan's Bed and Breakfast ($–$$)
Victoria Marriott Inner Harbour ($$–$$$$)

James Bay
James Bay Inn ($–$$)

Lower Cook Street Village
Dashwood Manor ($$–$$$)

Oak Bay
Oak Bay Beach Hotel ($$–$$$$)

Rockland
Prior House B&B ($$–$$$$)

Index of Accommodations by Price

$$$$
Abigail's Hotel (Downtown/Old Town)
The Fairmont Empress Hotel (Inner Harbour)
Haterleigh Heritage Inn (Inner Harbour)
Hotel Grand Pacific (Inner Harbour)
Laurel Point Inn (Inner Harbour)
Magnolia Hotel (Downtown/Old Town)
Oak Bay Beach Hotel (Oak Bay)
Prior House (Rockland)
Swans Suite Hotel (Downtown/Old Town)
Victoria Marriott Inner Harbour (Inner Harbour)

Haterleigh Heritage Inn (Inner Harbour)
Hotel Grand Pacific (Inner Harbour)
Laurel Point Inn (Inner Harbour)
Magnolia Hotel (Downtown/Old Town)
Oak Bay Beach Hotel (Oak Bay)
Prior House (Rockland)
Ramada Huntingdon Manor and Suites (Inner Harbour)
Royal Scot Suite Hotel (Inner Harbour)
Spinnakers Guesthouse (Esquimalt/Songhees)
Swans Suite Hotel (Downtown/Old Town)
Victoria Marriott Inner Harbour (Inner Harbour)

$$$
Abigail's Hotel (Downtown/Old Town)
Admiral Inn (Inner Harbour)
Andersen House B&B (Inner Harbour)
Beaconsfield Inn (Downtown/Old Town)
Best Western Inner Harbour (Inner Harbour)
Dashwood Manor (Lower Cook Street Village)
Delta Victoria Ocean Pointe Resort and Spa (Esquimalt/Songhees)
Dominion Grand Hotel (Downtown/Old Town)
Executive House Hotel (Downtown/Old Town)
The Fairmont Empress Hotel (Inner Harbour)
Gatsby Mansion (Inner Harbour)
Harbour Towers Hotel & Suites (Inner Harbour)

$$
Admiral Inn (Inner Harbour)
Andersen House B&B (Inner Harbour)
Beaconsfield Inn (Downtown/Old Town)
Best Western Carlton Plaza Hotel (Downtown/Old Town)
Best Western Inner Harbour (Inner Harbour)
Dashwood Manor (Lower Cook Street Village)
Days Inn on the Harbour (Inner Harbour)
Delta Victoria Ocean Pointe Resort and Spa (Esquimalt/Songhees)
Dominion Grand Hotel (Downtown/Old Town)
Executive House Hotel (Downtown/Old Town)
Gatsby Mansion (Inner Harbour)

Harbour Towers Hotel & Suites
(Inner Harbour)
Heathergate House Bed & Breakfast
(Inner Harbour)
James Bay Inn (James Bay)
Magnolia Hotel (Downtown/Old Town)
Oak Bay Beach Hotel (Oak Bay)
Ramada Huntingdon Manor and Suites
(Inner Harbour)
Royal Scot Suite Hotel (Inner Harbour
Ryan's Bed and Breakfast
(Inner Harbour)
Spinnakers Guesthouse (Esquimalt/
Songhees)

Strathcona Hotel (Downtown/
Old Town)
Swans Suite Hotel (Downtown/
Old Town)

$

James Bay Inn (James Bay)
Ocean Island Backpacker's Inn
Ryan's Bed and Breakfast
(Inner Harbour)
Strathcona Hotel (Downtown/
Old Town)

Chapter 18

Dining and Snacking in Victoria

. . . .

In This Chapter

▶ Scoping out the local scene
▶ Enjoying Victoria's best restaurants
▶ Eating on the run

. . . .

*T*he word "Victoria," doesn't carry the dining cachet of Paris, London, New Orleans, or San Francisco but don't be too quick to judge. The region's thriving tourist trade has boosted a larger choice of restaurants than you'd expect to find in a city this size. And that's good news — you can find *something* to eat no matter what you crave.

For the locations of most of the places mentioned in this chapter, see the "Victoria Dining and Snacking" map in this chapter. For a quick listing of restaurants by neighborhood, cuisine, and price, check out the index at the end of the chapter.

Chapter 10 offers tips on cutting your meal costs.

Getting the Dish on the Local Scene

Although it's taken awhile to shake up Victoria's distinctly British approach to cuisine, I'm glad — no, relieved — that nouvelle cuisine has arrived with gusto. As have a horde of ethnic flavors; in fact, today you're as spoiled for variety as you would be in any cosmopolitan city. Meals of Indian, Italian, Mexican, Greek, and Californian, among others, can easily be had. Chinese food is especially good, and less westernized than you might expect. You even find a flurry of activity on the health-food front — the popular **Re-bar Modern Food** serves up the best smoothies and vegetarian meals in British Columbia. (See "Victoria's Best Restaurants" later in this chapter for details on this restaurant.)

Is all that just a tad too adventurous for you? Well, you can always stick to seeking out and ordering what the Victorians themselves have long preferred to fancy foods: tea, high tea (which comes with loads of sweets and snacks), fish and chips, and pub food such as steak-and-kidney pie or "bangers and mash" (sausages and mashed potatoes).

As you might expect from the city's seaside position, with its constant supply of fresh finny, seafood is nearly always a good bet. And you can order it prepared every which way but loose: Anything from lowbrow (fried and stuck between two hamburger buns) at a dockside shack, to grilled or sautéed in the finest restaurants in town.

Searching Out Where the Locals Eat

Figuring out where to eat in Victoria is easy: Either read the listings in this chapter (see the "Victoria's Best Restaurants" section) and take copious notes, or simply track down a real Victorian, wait 'til he or she gets hungry, and then surreptitiously shadow this person to his/her favorite eatery. Where to begin hunting? Just pick a neighborhood.

Inner Harbour

Right on the Inner Harbour, places tend to fall into one or two categories: Very, very pricey (that is, hotel restaurants) or else dirt cheap (for example, **Barb's Place,** a fish-and-chips hole in the wall).

Downtown/Old Town

The eateries in the Old Town and Downtown districts are quite a mixture. You find a large number of overpriced tourist traps (often sporting oh-so-English spellings lyke thys: Yee Olde Drynkyng & Ryppyng-Offe Thee Custoumer Pubbe). But a number of extremely good restaurants are also in this area (such as **Camille's Fine West Coast Dining,** the **Herald Street Cafe,** and **Il Terrazzo Ristorante**), for which you pay more for the privilege of dining within, and a supply of middling eateries not worth mentioning.

Dressing to dine

Generally speaking, Victoria has loosened up its act since the colonial days. Years of sweatshirted, short-shorted U.S. tourists have helped soften up the locals, and you'll rarely be hassled about your attire except in the finest hotel restaurants and bistros. If a restaurant is very expensive, it probably operates some sort of official or unofficial dress code. Call if you're in doubt. Otherwise, though, don't sweat it.

Note: Although West Coast casual works in many places around town, it definitely doesn't work in the tearoom at The Fairmont Empress Hotel. Don't even think about wearing tennies, jeans, shorts, or other typically touristic garb. They'll escort you — politely, of course — back to the door.

Victoria Dining and Snacking

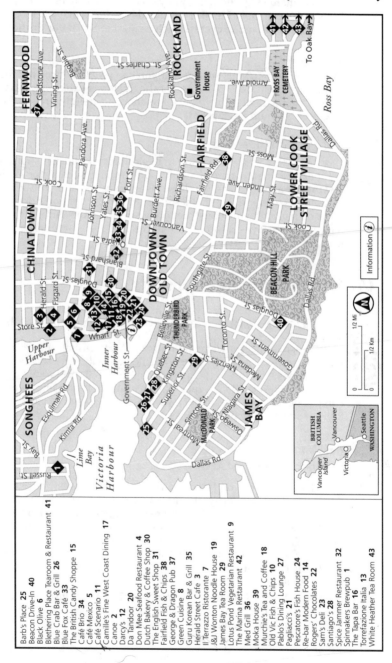

Barb's Place **25**
Beacon Drive-In **40**
Black Olive **6**
Blethering Place Tearoom & Restaurant **41**
Blue Crab Bar & Grill **26**
Blue Fox Café **33**
The British Candy Shoppe **15**
Café Brio **34**
Café Mexico **5**
Café Scenario **11**
Camille's Fine West Coast Dining **17**
Canoe **2**
Darcy's **12**
Da Tandoor **20**
Don Mee Seafood Restaurant **4**
Dutch Bakery & Coffee Shop **30**
The English Sweet Shop **31**
Fairfield Fish & Chips **38**
George & Dragon Pub **37**
Green Cuisine **8**
Guru Korean Bar & Grill **35**
Herald Street Cafe **3**
Il Terrazzo Ristorante **7**
J&J Wonton Noodle House **19**
James Bay Tea Room **29**
Lotus Pond Vegetarian Restaurant **9**
The Marina Restaurant **42**
Med Grill **36**
Moka House **39**
Murchie's Tea and Coffee **18**
Old Vic Fish & Chips **10**
Pablo's Dining Lounge **27**
Pagliacci's **21**
Pescatore's Fish House **24**
Re-bar Modern Food **14**
Rogers' Chocolates **22**
Sam's Deli **23**
Santiago's **28**
Spice Jammer Restaurant **32**
Spinnakers Brewpub **1**
The Tapa Bar **16**
Torrefazione Italia **13**
White Heather Tea Room **43**

Then there are the local haunts, which may not advertise with splashy signs or charge big prices, but they do the job nicely in a pinch for breakfast, brunch, or lunch. These kinds of places may even be tucked within larger shopping centers such as Market Square or Bastion Square.

Chinatown

Victoria's Chinatown is so tiny that you can practically log the total restaurant count on two hands. Yet the quality is extremely variable, so if you're going to dive in, you need to choose carefully. I recommend **Don Mee Seafood Restaurant.**

Outlying districts

Oak Bay is the district most worth mentioning, because it sports a number of authentic English pubs and tearooms, such as the **White Heather Tea Room.** Many of these also serve food and, thus, double as restaurants, despite their names. Plus, the neighborhood's oceanside position has led to the construction of several luxury hotels, and each has an exemplary — although not inexpensive — restaurant on the premises.

Victoria's Best Restaurants

This section includes my recommendations of the best places to dine. For a key to the dollar sign ratings, see the Introduction to this book.

The majority of Victoria's restaurants are fairly casual, and reservations won't be necessary. However, every rule naturally has exceptions — and so, too, does this one. In the listings, I note which restaurants require or recommend reservations year-round. During Victoria's high season (from June through September), you'll definitely want to call early for a table at some of the primo places.

Barb's Place
$ Inner Harbour   SEAFOOD

Actually located out on Fisherman's Wharf, the newest touristy destination, this little place (okay, shack) is Victoria's favorite lowbrow eatery — a place as famous as the city's gardens. You come for sandwiches of fried fish that was hauled onto the dock that very morning, just-cooked fries, or (if you're feeling fancy) maybe fried oysters. Don't expect linen napkins or candlelight. Although a bit off the downtown track, Barb's is right near one of the stops for those tiny ferries that constantly circle the Inner and Outer harbours.

See map p. 241. 310 St. Lawrence St. (from The Fairmont Empress Hotel, walk along Belleville St. to Kingston St., then continue to docks). ☎ *250-384-6515. Reservations not accepted. Main courses: C$4–C$9 (US$3.35–US$7.50). Credit cards not accepted. Open: Lunch and dinner daily. Closed in winter.*

Beacon Drive-In

$ Downtown/Old Town   BARBEQUE/BURGERS

Not a true drive-in in the sense that there isn't carhop service (this is right downtown, after all, where parking is a nightmare), the Beacon nevertheless captures the flavor of good ol' American burgers and fries. They also do rib-sticking breakfasts that will weigh you down all day, plus milkshakes, hot dogs, dinners of fried fish or chicken, and — naturally — soft-serve ice cream.

See map p. 241. 126 Douglas St. ☎ 250-385-7521. Reservations not accepted. Main courses: C$5–C$8 (US$4.15–US$6.65). Credit cards not accepted. Open: Lunch and dinner daily.

Black Olive

$$–$$$ Downtown/Old Town   CONTINENTAL

Family friendly and romantic — I know, it sounds impossible — makes this elegant restaurant a real pleasure but it seems to have something to do with the warmth of the welcome. Owner Paul Psyllakis has been in the restaurant biz for over 25 years and knows what good food and hospitality are all about. The menu is a Mediterranean–West Coast blend, including lots of local fare such as Fanny Bay oysters and Cowichan Bay duck. Obviously, not everything has an olive twist but let me tell you, the dishes that do (mmm . . . olive pesto pasta) are very, very yummy.

See map p. 241. 739 Pandora St. ☎ 250-384-6060. Reservations recommended. Main courses: C$15–C$26 (US$12–US$22). AE, DC, MC, V. Open: Lunch and dinner Mon.–Fri; dinner only Sat.

Blue Crab Bar & Grill

$$$–$$$$ Inner Harbour   SEAFOOD

If I were to pick one fancy restaurant for a piece of grilled salmon or something else from the sea, this place — located inside the Coast Harbourside Hotel — would be it. The kitchen is never short of daring, using the daily catch as its guide and then improvising wildly. Local oysters, prawns (basically, big shrimp), and salmon are the obvious stars, presented in a variety of interesting crusts, stir-fries, or bisques. For a real treat, try the signature platters for two (C$75–C$98 (US$62–US$82)), which serve up tasty morsels of several menu items. Wines, primarily from B.C. and the Pacific Northwest, are also top quality (earning *Wine Spectator*'s Awards of Excellence). Desserts are delicious, the view of the harbor is unbeatable, and — worth noting — the Blue Crab also offers daily breakfast and a Sunday brunch.

See map p. 241. 146 Kingston St. (inside Coast Harbourside Hotel; from The Fairmont Empress Hotel, walk along Belleville to Kingston). ☎ 250-480-1999. Reservations recommended. Main courses: C$22–C$45 (US$18–US$37). AE, DC, MC, V. Open: Breakfast, lunch, and dinner daily.

Café Brio

$$–$$$$ **Downtown/Old Town** **PACIFIC NORTHWEST/ITALIAN**

This place takes fusion to dizzying heights: Two chefs, one Italian and one Canadian, have put their heads together to create, well, a Pacific–Italian experience. In practice, that means anything from ale-braised mussels, smoked sablefish, or grilled sockeye salmon to upscale treatments of pastas, Italian sausages, proscuitto, and gnocchi. The more expensive — and expansive — chef's taster menu brings in potato and chive-blossom ravioli, olive oil–poached rare Albacore tuna, local lamb, polenta, and other surprises. Definitely one of the city's top bites. The three-course dinner is a good value at C$25 (US$21) per person.

See map p. 241. 944 Fort St. ☎ *250-383-0009. Reservations recommended. Main courses: C$19–C$36 (US$16–US$30). AE, MC, V. Open: Nightly from 5:30 p.m.*

Café Mexico

$–$$ **Downtown/Old Town** **MEXICAN**

There's nothing pretentious about this place; it's just bright, cheery, and fun with colorful Mexican knick-knacks and comfortable funky booths. The food's pretty good, too. At first glance, you see the same assortment of burritos, fajitas, nachos, and tacos as at a hundred other places, served with the usual order of refried beans, but it actually turns out to be prepared a tad classier than you'd expect. The kitchen even experiments a bit with Pacific Northwest fusion elements. The "not so grande" dishes are great for kids. Check the specials before ordering and wash it all down with sangria, margaritas, or Mexican beer.

See map p. 241. 1425 Store St. ☎ *250-386-1425 or 250-386-5454. Reservations not accepted. Main courses: C$10–C$15 (US$8–US$12). AE, DC, MC, V. Open: Lunch and dinner daily.*

Camille's Fine West Coast Dining

$$$–$$$$ **Downtown/Old Town** **PACIFIC NORTHWEST**

One of the city's most romantic fine restaurants, Camille's prides itself on using local ingredients, and, as such, the menu tends to abound with the highly seasonal: Tender fiddleheads in spring, blackberry desserts in summer, wild salmon and pumpkin in fall. The kitchen isn't afraid to use local wild mushrooms, Canadian bison, wild boar, or caribou when they're in season, either. In fact, they specialize in wild game, including pheasant, quail, and partridge. Start with pan-seared scallops, onion-and-Stilton-tart, jambalaya, or a ginger-lemon prawn bisque, and then move on to the daring entrees, like fillet of sole with garlic confit and fennel cakes in champagne sauce, a West Coast bouillabaisse, or ostrich with smoky creamed potatoes. The brick-walled room is lit with candles, softened with blues and jazz, and set with silver, linens, and fresh blossoms — all in all, a good honeymoon or anniversary choice. Samples from the wine cellar are laid out for tasting on Sunday evenings.

See map p. 241. 45 Bastion Sq. ☎ 250-381-3433. Reservations recommended. Main courses: C$22–C$34 (US$18–US$28). AE, MC, V. Open: Dinner Tues–Sun.

Canoe
$$–$$$ **Downtown/Old Town   PUB FARE**

A former warehouse now converted into a combination brewpub and restaurant space, this is a successful Victoria renovation story. It has the usual brick, timber, and skylights to set off the industrial look of the place, plus a menu that ranges from pizza and burgers to pasta, tuna, and more. My favorites are the tagines, classic North African stews served in traditional earthenware casseroles. The beers are every bit as good as the others around town.

See map p. 241. 450 Swift St. (walk north along Store St. to Swift, turn left, and continue to water). ☎ 250-361-1940. Reservations recommended. Main courses: C$14–C$32 (US$11.65–US$27). MC, V. Open: Lunch and dinner daily.

Da Tandoor
$$–$$$ **Downtown/Old Town   INDIAN**

The exotic interior invites you to take a seat and taste the best Indian food in town, with an East Indian slant and menu items such as biryani, tandoori, and chili chicken. Drawing on the city's maritime heritage and daily fishing catch, the restaurant also offers a small selection of seafood dishes. Several sampler plates give you the chance to try a little of everything, a good idea in a place this good; the chef's specials include small amounts of lamb, fish, chicken, beef, and vegetables, each prepared a different way. Desserts include typical offerings, such as Indian-style mango ice cream and fried cheese dunked in sugared rosewater.

See map p. 241. 1010 Fort St. ☎ 250-384-6333. Reservations recommended. Main courses: C$11–C$23 (US$9–US$19). MC, V. Open: Dinner daily.

Don Mee Seafood Restaurant
$–$$ **Chinatown   CHINESE**

In a town where the Chinese food varies tremendously in quality, everyone raves about this place. You come for seafood — fried, stir-fried, seasoned, or poached any number of ways — or for the classiest dim sum in town. Don Mee's also offers delivery and takeout from a much shorter, more touristy menu than in the restaurant, so takeout is heavy on chop suey, egg foo yong, and the like. But get a fixed-price combo meal for two to eight people, and you save money and get to sample and share lots of different menu items.

See map p. 241. 538 Fisgard St. ☎ 250-383-1032. Reservations accepted. Main courses: C$9–C$15 (US$7.50–US$12). AE, DC, MC, V. Open: Lunch and dinner daily.

Guru Korean Bar & Grill
$$–$$$ Downtown/Old Town KOREAN

It seems as if this restaurant opened just for the Korean tours that swing by in droves, but if you hit it right — as a late lunch or after 6 p.m. — then the food you'll experience is one for the books: Zucchini porridge, seafood pajun (like a pancake), wang kalbi, and various bulgogi (sliced meat on rice) are all very tasty. Dishes are small so go as a group and try multiple choices.

See map p. 241. 1015 Fort St. ☎ *250-384-5337. Reservations accepted. Main courses: C$10–C$18 (US$8–US$15). AE, MC, V. Open: Lunch and dinner daily.*

Herald Street Cafe
$$$–$$$$ Downtown/Old Town PACIFIC NORTHWEST

A fixture on the local scene for more than 20 years, owner Mark Finnigan cooks plenty of local seafood, pastas, and West Coast cuisine at this hopping bistro; it has that rare buzz that truly great bistros possess. Swirl in a super wine list that's acknowledged as one of the city's best, and you have a winner. You can find anything from British Columbian lamb to local salmon, shellfish, and fresh-picked berries on the menu, while Finnigan shows off influences from Italian to Asian. The Sunday brunch is especially interesting, delicious — and popular. Call to make a booking as early as possible.

See map p. 241. 546 Herald St. (from The Fairmont Empress Hotel, walk north along Wharf or Store St. ¾ mile to Herald and turn right). ☎ *250-381-1441. Reservations required. Main courses: C$15–C$34 (US$12–US$28). AE, MC, V. Open: Lunch and dinner Wed–Sat 11 a.m. until midnight; Sunday brunch 11 a.m.–3 p.m.*

Il Terrazzo Ristorante
$$$–$$$$ Downtown/Old Town ITALIAN

Actually down a cute little alley between Yates and Johnson Streets, this place has been voted Best Italian Restaurant in town by locals umpteen times by now, and not without reason. It's simply terrific, bursting with good pastas, risotto, seafood, steaks, osso bucco, and other mostly northern Italian specialties. The restaurant also boasts a solid wine list, specializing (no surprise here) in wines from Tuscany, Umbria, and the Veneto. If the weather's halfway decent, ask for a table on the patio, one of the city's better ones.

See map p. 241. 555 Johnson St. ☎ *250-361-0028.* www.ilterrazzo.com. *Reservations recommended. Main courses: C$17–C$37 (US$14–US$31). AE, MC, V. Open: Lunch Mon–Sat, dinner nightly from 5 p.m.*

J&J Wonton Noodle House
$–$$ Downtown/Old Town CHINESE

I'd eat Chinese a lot more often if more places were like this one. Fun, casual, visual — you get to see the noodle-makers in action — and a real bargain to boot, J&J's delivers a mix of Chinese and Asian specialties, such as wontons, hot pots, and stir-fries. Everything's very fresh and more inventive than at most Chinese restaurants in this or any other town.

See map p. 241. 1012 Fort St. ☎ **250-383-0680**. Reservations not accepted. Main courses: C$6–C$17 (US$5–US$14). MC, V. Open: Lunch and dinner Tues–Sat; closed Tues–Sat. 2–4:30 p.m.

James Bay Tearoom
$$ Inner Harbour   ENGLISH

Despite the name, this isn't the fanciest place in town; in fact, it's rather a quaint and tripped-up English version of a U.S. diner. Rather than being served dainty little sandwiches, most who stop by nosh on heavy, caloric foods, such as eggs, meats with Yorkshire pudding, and fried fish. Sure, _some_ of the diners will be sipping tea and eating light, but that doesn't mean _you_ have to. A special seniors' menu (as well as being kid- and family-friendly) makes this an especially busy place from 4:30 to 6 p.m. (This James Bay is not related to the James Bay Inn that's discussed in Chapter 17.)

See map p. 241. 332 Menzies St. (from The Fairmont Empress Hotel, walk south along Government St. to Belleville, go 1 block west on Belleville, then turn south on Menzies; continue 4 short blocks). ☎ **250-382-8282**. Reservations recommended. Main courses: C$12–C$16 (US$10–US$13). AE, MC, V. Open: Breakfast, lunch, and dinner Mon–Sat.

The Marina Restaurant
$$$–$$$$ Oak Bay   SEAFOOD

The panoramic water views from this hotel restaurant couldn't be finer, and although the seafood probably isn't the best in the city, it's good enough. Roasted salmon, steamed halibut, and grilled tuna are all typical dinner entrees, and the oyster and sushi bars are nice touches, too. But you come here for the sight of boats on water. The Sunday all-you-can-eat brunches _are_ something, though, an event in and of themselves — come if you want to gorge on oysters, eggs, and more.

See map p. 241. 1327 Beach Dr. (from downtown Victoria, drive along Fort St. away from the water about 1½ miles to Oak Bay Ave.; turn right and continue 1½ more miles to Beach Dr.). ☎ **250-598-8555**. Reservations recommended. Main courses: C$20–C$30 (US$17–US$25). AE, DC, MC, V. Open: Lunch daily, dinner Mon–Sat.

Med Grill
$$ Downtown/Old Town   PACIFIC

Hip and urban, you can choose to set yourself up at the really-nice-to-sit-at long bar or cozy up in a comfortable booth. Either way, you get to watch the antics of the open grill kitchen that pushes out tasty gourmet thin-crust pizzas as well as cedar roasted salmon and prime rib. "Tapatizers" draw in the after-work crowd, and many stay when the turntables start to spin — yes, turntables, in this day and age.

See map p. 241. 1063 Fort St. ☎ *250-381-3417. Reservations recommended. Main courses: C$11–C$15 (US$9–US$12). AE, MC, V. Open: Daily lunch and dinner.*

Pablo's Dining Lounge
$$$–$$$$ Inner Harbour CONTINENTAL

The feel is partly Spanish at this off-the-beaten-track place inside an attractive Edwardian-style house, but French food such as grilled lamb has been thrown into the mix, too, with good results — locals have been coming here for decades. Live music on weekends and other nights accentuates the mood, the Valenciana paella is just dynamite, and the desserts are suitably sweet.

See map p. 241. 225 Quebec St. (from The Fairmont Empress, walk about ½ mile down Belleville St. to Montreal St., turn left, and continue to Quebec St.). ☎ *250-388-4255. Reservations recommended. Main courses: C$24–C$38 (US$20–US$32). AE, MC, V. Open: Dinner nightly from 5 p.m.*

Pagliacci's
$$–$$$ Downtown/Old Town ITALIAN

There's nothing quiet or pretentious about this Italian place — no reservations are taken — so that means it's okay in my book. Apparently everyone in Victoria agrees, because the place has some of the longest pre-meal lineups (even in rainy weather) that you find in the city. The secret to this success? Elegant simplicity: Meals are fun, whether they're pasta, prawns, steak, or seafood. Menu items also include diet-conscious alternatives such as wheatless pasta and soya cheese. It's a great break from formality — and kids won't feel like they have to keep quiet, either. Live jazz and blues plays Sunday through Wednesday.

See map p. 241. 1011 Broad St. ☎ *250-386-1662. Reservations not accepted. Main courses: C$16–C$21 (US$13–US$17). AE, MC, V. Open: Lunch and dinner daily; snacks only 3–5 p.m.*

Pescatore's Fish House
$$–$$$$ Inner Harbour SEAFOOD

Superb seafood and shellfish in every guise is the draw here, in a room decorated with eye-catching and thought-provoking murals and artwork. Whether it's crab, clams, salmon, oysters on the half-shell at a raw bar, or thick soups and chowders, you'll find something from the sea to satiate. All items are well handled: The chefs know what they do best. The restaurant also serves some non-fish entrees — such as meat and lamb — and they're said to be very good, but I'd order those only if I were allergic to seafood.

See map p. 241. 614 Humboldt St. (across street from The Fairmont Empress Hotel). ☎ *250-385-4512. Reservations recommended. Main courses: C$17–C$33 (US$14–US$27). AE, DC, MC, V. Open: Lunch Mon–Sat, dinner daily.*

Re-bar Modern Food
$–$$ Downtown/Old Town   VEGETARIAN

King among a smattering of veggie restaurants in this town is Re-bar, a brightly painted throwback to the '70s. The fresh-squeezed vegetable and fruit juice combinations make an energizing, technicolor snack, but Re-bar also serves breakfast, lunch, and brunch meals, such as omelettes (which aren't strictly vegetarian, I must point out), sandwiches, Mexican, and more. A good variety of vegan dishes cater to vegetarian diehards.

See map p. 241. 50 Bastion Sq. (downstairs). ☎ *250-361-9223. Reservations not accepted. Main courses: C$9–C$16 (US$7.50–US$13). AE, MC, V. Open: Breakfast, lunch, and dinner Mon–Sat; brunch Sun.*

Sam's Deli
$–$$ Downtown/Old Town   DELI

This little delicatessen, which serves healthy sandwiches, tasty soups, and chili, is the most popular lunch nosh in town. And it's a mighty good deal, from the desserts to the snacks to the unusual prawn sandwich — just get there early, *really* early, because everyone in town eats lunch here at some point. No worries, though: If the tables are full (and it isn't pouring), get takeout and head for the waterfront.

See map p. 241. 805 Government St. ☎ *250-382-8424. Reservations not accepted. Main courses: C$4–C$10 (US$3.35–US$8.30). MC, V. Open: Breakfast, lunch, and dinner daily.*

Santiago's
$$ Inner Harbour   LATIN AMERICAN

Located just around the corner from Gatsby Mansion, you'll find this place because of its colorful ornamental lights, which seem to reflect its menu. Items are a glorious mix of tasty dishes from Argentina, Chile, Thailand, and Malaysia — creative enough for discerning palates yet with surprising appeal for the less adventurous. The breakfasts are great.

See map p. 241. 660 Oswego St. ☎ *250-388-7376. Reservations not accepted. Main courses: C$8–C$12 (US$6.65–US$10). MC, V. Open: Breakfast, lunch and dinner daily.*

Spice Jammer Restaurant
$$ Downtown/Old Town   INDIAN

Along with Da Tandoor (see earlier listing), this is the best Indian bite in town. The East Indian food is really good, everything from tandoori-oven specials to tasty curries, filling samosas, hot vindaloo dishes, and vegetarian dishes like coconut lentils. Stuffed naan is a house specialty. This place offers a few non-Indian dishes, too — concessions to tourist tastes, such as steak, grilled chicken, and stir-fried prawns — but also a couple surprises: Ever tried *mogo* (East African–style fried cassava root with chutney)? Probably not; here you can.

See map p. 241. 852 Fort St. ☎ 250-480-1055. Reservations not necessary. Main courses: C$10–C$17 (US$8–US$14). AE, MC, V. Open: Lunch Tues–Fri; dinner Tues–Sun.

Spinnakers Brewpub
$$–$$$ **Esquimalt/Songhees**   **PUB FARE**

This restaurant, housed in the same building as the award-winning (and original) North American brewery, serves plenty of pub grub meals of burgers, smoked sausage, fish and chips, pizza, ploughman's lunches, and steak sandwiches. But Spinnakers also offers more-upscale meals, as well, taking good advantage of the supply of locally raised beef, lamb, and chicken that's available on Vancouver Island — and combining these foods with the house ales, lagers, and stouts for flavoring.

See map p. 241. 308 Catherine St. (from downtown Victoria, proceed north to Johnson St.; cross the Johnson St. bridge and continue ½ mile to Catherine St.). ☎ 250-386-2739. Reservations recommended. Main courses: C$10–C$24 (US$8–US$20). AE, DC, MC, V. Open: Breakfast, lunch, and dinner daily.

On the Lighter Side: Snacks and Meals on the Go

As a tourist town, Victoria is necessarily loaded with on-the-fly snacking opportunities. Whether you crave a scone with tea, a fruit smoothie, or a chocolate truffle, your tank doesn't have to run too low while you're here.

The tea experience

When in Victoria, do as the Victorians do, right? And that means taking tea. You can eat as little as you like or go whole hog with high tea — almost a meal — and you pay accordingly, especially at the famed Empress Hotel. You can go easier on the wallet and still do the quintessential Victoria snack elsewhere. These spots will deliver a cuppa just right.

- ✔ **Blethering Place Tearoom & Restaurant,** 2250 Oak Bay Ave., Oak Bay (☎ 250-598-1413), is one of the grande dames of Victorian tea-osity, with all the decorations, pretensions, and nibbles you would expect. You need a car, bike, or bus to get here from downtown.

- ✔ **Murchie's Tea and Coffee,** 1110 Government St. (☎ 250-383-3112), offers the best selection of teas in the city, plus good coffee and everything from tea snacks to full-blown sandwiches and salads.

- ✔ **White Heather Tea Room,** 1885 Oak Bay Ave. (☎ 250-595-8020), is small, bright, unpretentious, and has a very loyal following, in part because of its lemon curd tartlets. The Big Muckle Giant Tea for Two is the grand slam of all teas. Lunches are also scrumptious, as is Saturday brunch.

The cafe connection

You don't need to cave into U.S. chain-coffee imperialism here, no sir. You're spoiled for choice and quality in Victoria; every new block seems to offer another take on the roasted bean.

- ✔ **Blue Fox Café,** 919 Fort St. (☎ 250-380-1683), is a pretty eclectic place and worth waiting through any lineup. Lunch is hearty, but breakfast is the show-stopper with eight types of eggs benny alone, homemade granola, and more. Watch the pancakes, they're humongous.

- ✔ **Café Scenario,** 506 Fort St. (☎ 250-480-5553), tucked a couple of steps down from street level, is a tiny treasure that serves up the best paninis in town and assorted homemade goodies. The granola bars and coffee aren't bad either.

- ✔ **Dutch Bakery & Coffee Shop,** 718 Fort St. (☎ 250-385-1012), is the epitome of good snacking, Victoria style: The shop makes its own chocolates, serves good coffee, and offers a range of other eats and treats, as well.

- ✔ **Moka House,** 345 Cook St. (☎ 250-388-7377), in Cook Village is a fair piece from downtown, but the walk is beautiful, and you're rewarded with trays of sweets and eats alongside the java.

- ✔ **Torrefazione Italia,** 1234 Government St. (☎ 250-920-7302), is among the classiest coffee shops in the city, with lots of street-side tables for people-watching. Stop by for a perfectly brewed cappuccino. Mineral water and Italian nibbles complement the atmosphere.

Burgers, fish, and pub grub

Without a doubt, the most plentiful quick food in Victoria is its pub grub. The only problem is that quality can be highly variable, and the grease factor is always a problem.

- ✔ **Darcy's,** 1127 Wharf St. (☎ 250-380-1322), one of the few authentic Irish pubs in town, goes nuts on St. Patty's Day. Besides the requisite Guinness and Harp, Darcy's does fish and chips and similar rib-sticking food.

- ✔ **Fairfield Fish & Chips,** 1275 Fairfield Rd. (☎ 250-380-6880), is a bit of a hike but is where all the locals gravitate for old-style fish and chips served in newspaper. It's a family business built from scratch, and *the* place for takeout.

- ✔ The **George & Dragon Pub,** 1302 Gladstone Ave. (☎ 250-388-4458), is much more eclectic than you'd expect — U.S., Asian, and other influences mingle with the usual English favorites.

- ✔ **Old Vic Fish & Chips,** 1316 Broad St. (☎ **250-383-4536**), an alternative to Barb's Place (see the "Victoria's Best Restaurants" section earlier in this chapter) in the very heart of the downtown area, offers a selection of fish, oysters, and chicken, all of which are very good.

- ✔ **The Tapa Bar,** 620 Trounce Alley (☎ **250-383-0013** or 250-383-0086), is a restaurant, a bar, and a snack stop all in one; load up on various kinds of Spanish tapas. *Note:* The price can escalate quickly as you pile on the chow.

Restaurant rescue for vegetarians

An English town is a meat-eating town, certainly, but this is also the West Coast: You're never too far from a plate of fresh fish, organic vegetables, and several restaurants that specialize in vegetarian or vegan dishes.

Even if you can't get to one of these places, always ask at any restaurant about veggie menu items. Some cafes — and *every* Asian restaurant — will gladly cook something meatless for you.

- ✔ **Green Cuisine,** 560 Johnson St. (☎ **250-385-1809**), the undisputed center of Victorian veggie life, is wildly popular for its good hot buffet, salad bar, and baked goods. The spot is tucked away from street activity on the courtyard level of the Market Square shopping complex.

- ✔ **Lotus Pond Vegetarian Restaurant,** 617 Johnson St. (☎ **250-380-9293**), is a newish vegan eatery — run by Buddhists, so this is the real deal — which stakes its claim on "mock" meats, a hot lunch buffet, and plenty of Chinese-influenced menu items.

Sweets to eat

This town has a sweet tooth, and you'll easily find chocolates, penny candy, and more. The central tourist area is the most abundant in sweets, but outlying neighborhoods have their own local candy shops, too.

- ✔ **The British Candy Shoppe,** 638 Yates St. (☎ **250-382-2634**), and **The English Sweet Shop,** 738 Yates St. (☎ **250-382-3325**), maintain that old-time candy store feel with shelves laden with jars of penny candies, lemon sherbets, toffee, jelly beans, and the like.

- ✔ **Rogers' Chocolates,** 913 Government St. (☎ **800-663-2220** or 250-384-7021), has been around for more than 100 years, making its own exquisite cream-filled chocolates in an old-candy-shop atmosphere. Delicious and not cheap.

Tastes beyond the norm

Victoria is small in stature but growing in ethnic flavors which says a lot about its growing cosmopolitan status, albeit with a very British stiff upper lip. In addition to the ethnic restaurants listed, there are a few others I suggest you try.

A happy choice for **Greek** food, especially if you've the kids in tow, is **Millos** (716 Burdett Ave. ☎ 250-382-4422) — just find the large, blue and white windmill behind The Fairmont Empress Hotel. Be prepared to smash a few plates. Sushi lovers might want to head for **Tamari** (509 Fisgard St. ☎ 250-382-3520). It's small and simple with good sushi plate combos from C$14 (US$11.60). With the Asian influence really gaining a foothold (the many dubious hole-in-the-wall eateries in Chinatown notwithstanding), **Saigon Harbour** (1012 Blanshard St. ☎ 250-386-3354) is a hot spot for **Vietnamese** serving up lots of Pho (beef noodle soups), vegetarian dishes, and more. Thai food, too, is worth seeking out at either **Siam Thai**, 512 Fort St. (☎ 250-383-9911) — a local favorite for authentic Thai food, prepared to your spice level of comfort — or **Sookjai Thai** (893 Fort St. ☎ 250-383-9945), which also offers takeout and delivery. And if you've not tried the latest Asian fad, bubble teas, head for the **Bubble Tea Place** (532 Fisgard St. ☎ 250-391-8960). It's a rather rinky-dink tea bar at the back of a trinket store but it does shake up some amazing multi-flavored, multi-colored tea concoctions.

Index of Restaurants by Neighborhood

Chinatown
Don Mee Seafood Restaurant (Chinese, $–$$)

Esquimalt/Songhees
Spinnakers Brewpub (Pub Fare, $$–$$$)

Inner Harbour
Barb's Place (Seafood, $)
Blue Crab Bar & Grill (Seafood, $$$–$$$$)
James Bay Tearoom (English, $$)
Pablo's Dining Lounge (Continental, $$$–$$$$)
Pescatore's Fish House (Seafood, $$–$$$$)
Santiago's (Latin American, $$)

Oak Bay
Blethering Place Tea Room ($–$$)
The Marina Restaurant (Seafood, $$$–$$$$)
White Heather Tea Room ($–$$)

Downtown/Old Town
Beacon Drive-In (Barbeque/Burgers, $)
Black Olive (Continental, $$–$$$)
Blue Fox Café ($–$$)
British Candy Store ($)
Café Brio (Pacific Northwest/Italian, $$–$$$$)
Café Mexico (Mexican, $–$$)
Café Scenario (Deli/Cafe, $)
Camille's Fine West Coast Dining (Pacific Northwest, $$$–$$$$)
Canoe (Pub Fare, $$–$$$)

Da Tandoor (Indian, $$–$$$)
Darcy's (Pub Fare, $–$$)
Dutch Bakery & Coffee Shop ($)
English Sweet Shop ($)
Fairfield Fish & Chips ($)
George & Dragon Pub ($–$$)
Green Cuisine ($–$$)
Guru Korean (Korean, $$–$$$)
Herald Street Cafe (Pacific Northwest, $$$–$$$$)
Il Terrazzo Ristorante (Italian, $$$–$$$$)
J&J Wonton Noodle House (Chinese, $–$$)

Lotus Pond Vegetarian Restaurant (Vegetarian, $–$$)
Med Grill (Pacific Northwest, $$)
Moka House (Sweets, $–$$)
Murchie's Tea & Coffee ($)
Old Vic Fish & Chips ($)
Pagliacci's (Italian, $$–$$$)
Re-bar Modern Food (Vegetarian, $–$$)
Rogers' Chocolates (Sweets, $)
Sam's Deli (Deli, $–$$)
Spice Jammer Restaurant (Indian, $$)
The Tapa Bar ($–$$)
Torrefazione Italia Café ($)

Index of Restaurants by Cuisine

Barbecue/Burgers
Beacon Drive-In (Downtown/Old Town, $)

Chinese
Don Mee Seafood Restaurant (Chinatown, $–$$)
J&J Wonton Noodle House (Downtown/Old Town, $–$$)

Continental
Black Olive (Downtown/Old Town, $$–$$$)
Pablo's Dining Lounge (Inner Harbour, $$$–$$$$)
Santiago's (Inner Harbour, $$)

Deli
Café Scenario (Downtown/Old Town, $)
Sam's Deli (Downtown/Old Town, $)

English
Bletherington Place Tea Room (Oak Bay, $–$$)
James Bay Tearoom (Inner Harbour, $$)
Murchie's Tea & Coffee (Downtown/Old Town, $)
White Heather Tea Room (Oak Bay, $–$$)

Indian
Da Tandoor (Downtown/Old Town, $$–$$$)
Spice Jammer Restaurant (Downtown/Old Town, $$)
Torrefazione Italia Café (Downtown/Old Town, $)

Spanish
The Tapa Bar (Downtown/Old Town, $–$$)

Italian
Café Brio (Downtown/Old Town, $$–$$$$)
Il Terrazzo Ristorante (Downtown/Old Town, $$$–$$$$)
Pagliacci's (Downtown/Old Town, $$–$$$)
Torrefazione Italia Café (Downtown/Old Town, $)

Latin American
Santiago's (Inner Harbour, $$)

Mexican
Café Mexico (Downtown/Old Town, $–$$)

Pacific Northwest

Blue Fox Café (Downtown/
Old Town $–$$)
Café Brio (Downtown/
Old Town, $$–$$$$)
Camille's Fine West Coast Dining
(Downtown/Old Town, $$$–$$$$)
Herald Street Cafe (Downtown/
Old Town, $$$–$$$$)
Med Grill (Downtown/Old Town, $$)

Pub Fare

Canoe (Downtown/Old Town, $$–$$$)
Darcy's (Downtown/Old Town, $–$$)
George & Dragon Pub (Downtown/
Old Town, $–$$)
Spinnakers Brewpub
(Esquimalt/Songhees, $$–$$$)

Seafood

Barb's Place (Inner Harbour, $)
Blue Crab Bar & Grill (Inner Harbour,
$$$–$$$$)
Fairfield Fish & Chips (Downtown/
Old Town, $)

The Marina Restaurant (Oak Bay,
$$$–$$$$)
Old Vic Fish & Chips (Downtown/
Old Town, $)
Pescatore's Fish House
(Inner Harbour, $$–$$$$)

Sweets

British Candy Store (Downtown/
Old Town, $)
Dutch Bakery & Coffee Shop
(Downtown/Old Town, $)
English Sweet Shop (Downtown/
Old Town, $)
Moka House(Downtown/Old Town, $)
Rogers' Chocolates (Downtown/
Old Town, $)

Vegetarian

Green Cuisine (Downtown/
Old Town, $–$$)
Lotus Pond Vegetarian Restaurant
($–$$)
Re-bar Modern Food (Downtown/
Old Town, $–$$)

Index of Restaurants by Price

The Marina Restaurant
(Seafood, Oak Bay)
Pablo's Dining Lounge (Continental,
Inner Harbour)
Pagliacci's (Italian, Downtown/
Old Town)
Pescatore's Fish House (Seafood,
Inner Harbour)
Spinnakers Brewpub (Pub Fare,
Esquimalt/Songhees)

$$

Black Olive (Continental,
Downtown/Old Town)
Blethering Place Tea Room
(English, Oak Bay)
Blue Fox Café (Pacific Northwest,
Downtown/Old Town)
Café Brio (Italian/Pacific Northwest,
Downtown/Old Town
Café Mexico (Mexican, Downtown/
Old Town)
Canoe (Pub Fare, Downtown/
Old Town)
Darcy's (Pub Fare, Downtown/
Old Town)
Da Tandoor (Indian, Downtown/
Old Town)
Don Mee Seafood Restaurant
(Chinese, Chinatown)
George & Dragon (Pub Fare,
Downtown/Old Town)
Green Cuisine (Vegetarian,
Downtown/Old Town)
Guru Korean Grill (Korean,
Downtown/Old Town)
J&J Wonton Noodle House
(Chinese, Downtown/Old Town)
James Bay Tearoom (English,
Inner Harbour)
Lotus Pond Vegetarian Restaurant
(Vegetarian, Downtown/Old Town)
Med Grill (Pacific Northwest,
Downtown/Old Town)
Moka House (Sweets, Downtown/
Old Town)
Pagliacci's (Italian, Downtown/
Old Town)
Pescatore's Fish House (Seafood,
Inner Harbour)

Re-bar Modern Food (Vegetarian,
Downtown/Old Town)
Sam's Deli (Deli, Downtown/Old Town)
Santiago's (Latin American, Inner
Harbour)
Spice Jammer Restaurant (Indian,
Downtown/Old Town)
Spinnakers Brewpub (Pub Fare,
Esquimalt/Songhees)
The Tapa Bar (Spanish, Downtown/
Old Town)
White Heather Tea Room (Oak Bay)

$

Barb's Place (Seafood, Inner Harbour)
Beacon Drive-In (Barbeque/
Burgers, Downtown/Old Town)
Blethering Place Tea Room
(English, Oak Bay)
Blue Fox Café (Pacific Northwest,
Downtown/Old Town)
British Candy Store (Sweets,
Downtown/Old Town)
Café Mexico (Mexican, Downtown/
Old Town)
Café Scenario (Deli/Cafe,
Downtown/Old Town)
Darcy's (Pub Fare, Downtown/
Old Town)
Don Mee Seafood Restaurant
(Chinese, Chinatown)
Dutch Bakery & Coffee Shop
(Sweets, Downtown/Old Town)
English Sweet Shop (Sweets,
Downtown/Old Town)
Fairfield Fish & Chips (Seafood,
Downtown/Old Town)
George & Dragon (Pub fare,
Downtown/Old Town)
Green Cuisine (Vegetarian,
Downtown/Old Town)
Guru Korean Grill (Korean,
Downtown/Old Town)
J&J Wonton Noodle House (Chinese,
Downtown/Old Town)
Lotus Pond Vegetarian Restaurant
(Vegetarian, Downtown/Old Town)
Murchie's Tea & Coffee (English,
Downtown/Old Town)

Moka House (Sweets, Downtown/
Old Town)

Re-bar Modern Food (Vegetarian,
Downtown/Old Town)

Rogers' Chocolates (Sweets,
Downtown/Old Town)

Sam's Deli (Deli, Downtown/Old Town)

The Tapa Bar (Spanish, Downtown/
Old Town)

Torrefazione Café (Italian,
Downtown/Old Town)

White Heather Tea Room (English,
Downtown/Old Town)

Chapter 19

Discovering Victoria's Best Attractions

In This Chapter

▶ Previewing Victoria's best attractions

▶ Exploring the city by guided tour

*Y*ou can easily cover the sights in Victoria's compact downtown in a day or two. In fact, downtown has fewer impressive sights than you may expect. As a result, several of my recommended must-sees lie on the fringes of the city, and two (Butchart Gardens and Victoria Butterfly Gardens) are located more than 15 miles northwest of it.

Discovering Victoria's Top Sights from A to Z

Art Gallery of Greater Victoria
Fairfield

Very near Craigdarroch Castle (see the listing later in this chapter), the AGGV — as it's known in shorthand — holds more than 15,000 pieces of art in its permanent collection, including a strong selection of local painter Emily Carr's works. Six wings of this museum feature more than 30 exhibitions each year; permanent exhibits include a life-size dollhouse and a genuine Shinto shrine, part of Canada's most extensive Japanese art collection. Allow 1 to 1½ hours.

See map p. 259. 1040 Moss St. (from downtown Victoria, walk along Fort St. away from downtown approximately 1¼ miles to Moss St. and turn right). ☎ *250-384-4101. Admission: C$6 (US$5) adults, C$4 (US$3.35) seniors. Open: Mon–Sun 10 a.m.–5 p.m., Thurs to 9 p.m.*

Beacon Hill Park
Inner Harbour

Without a doubt the top park in downtown Victoria, Beacon Hill Park does the city proud. It's a sprawling, green oasis of flowers, fields, trees, ponds,

Victoria Attractions

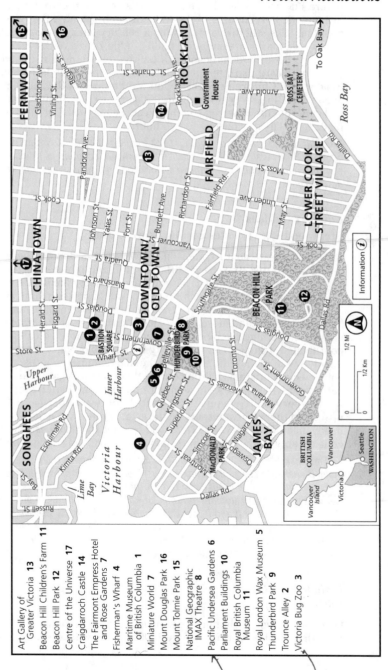

Art Gallery of
  Greater Victoria **13**
Beacon Hill Children's Farm **11**
Beacon Hill Park **12**
Centre of the Universe **17**
Craigdarroch Castle **14**
The Fairmont Empress Hotel
  and Rose Gardens **7**
Fisherman's Wharf **4**
Maritime Museum
  of British Columbia **1**
Miniature World **7**
Mount Douglas Park **16**
Mount Tolmie Park **15**
National Geographic
  IMAX Theatre **8**
Pacific Undersea Gardens **6**
Parliament Buildings **10**
Royal British Columbia
  Museum **11**
Royal London Wax Museum **5**
Thunderbird Park **9**
Trounce Alley **2**
Victoria Bug Zoo **3**

views, and totem poles — some of it very ordered, but some of it left to nature's devices. John Blair, a Scot, won a competition to design the park in 1889; the descendants of rhododendrons he planted that year around Fountain Lake still thrive more than a century later. One particularly tall totem pole marks the endpoint (called "Mile Zero") of the Trans-Canada Highway. Rose gardens, canals, a band shell, a small zoo, and even a cricket pitch are also interspersed throughout the grounds. Kids adore the **Beacon Hill Children's Farm;** if you want a taste of the salt air, you can even walk all the way through the 150-acre park — about a mile long — and come out the other side on the ocean, facing Washington State. A great place to fly kites. Allow one to two hours.

See map p. 259. Corner of Southgate St. and Douglas Blvd. (from The Fairmont Empress Hotel, walk south to Belleville St., turn left, continue to Thunderbird Park, and turn right on Douglas; continue 1 block to park). Admission: Free. Open: Daily dawn to dusk.

Butchart Gardens
Brentwood Bay (12 miles northwest of Victoria)

An amazing testament to one woman's love for gardening, these gardens are *the* top tourist draw to Victoria, despite their remoteness, and rightly so. Jenny Butchart planted 55 acres of gardens in her husband's exhausted marble quarry, stocking much of it with rare imported plants and showing a deft design touch as she created a rose garden, Japanese garden, "sunken garden," and more. Amazingly, thanks to the temperate maritime climate, something's in bloom 12 months of the year — all carefully color-coordinated, trimmed, and precisely timed to blossom — most of it illuminated with night lighting during the high summer months, then again with special Christmas lighting during that season. A gardening store and Saturday night fireworks in summer complete the experience, which is worth every pretty penny. Note that if you want to dine at the more upscale of the two restaurants on the estate grounds, you need to reserve in advance (☎ **250-652-8222**). Also know that after dark, the crowds thin considerably. Allow three hours, including travel time; longer if dining.

See map p. 259. 800 Benvenuto Ave. (from downtown Victoria, drive away from town along Blanshard St., which becomes Hwy. 17; after about 6 miles, exit onto Hwy. 17A and continue 5 miles to Wallace Dr. turnoff; then either follow Wallace Dr. 3 miles to Benvenuto, following signs to gardens, or continue 3 more miles on Hwy. 17A to Benvenuto Ave. turnoff and follow Benvenuto to gardens). ☎ 250-652-4422. www. butchartgardens.com. *Admission: C$18–C$22 (US$15–US$18) adults, C$9–C$11 (US$7.50–US$9.15) children 13–17, C$2–C$2.50 (US$1.65–US$2.10) children 5–12. Open: Daily at 9 a.m., closing times vary seasonally.*

Craigdarroch Castle
Fairfield

One-time British Columbia coal magnate Robert Dunsmuir built this Victorian "castle" during the late 1800s for his wife, decking it out with almost 40 rooms and plenty of eye-popping furniture, statuary, carpeting, and exotic wood. Dunsmuir passed away just before its completion, so he never lived in the house, but his wife did for years. The oak staircase is a real looker — and a real climb, at 87 stairs. (This attraction isn't fully wheelchair-accessible.) You have to show yourself around, because guided tours aren't available. Allow one to two hours.

See map p. 259. 1050 Joan Crescent (from downtown Victoria, follow Fort St. approximately 1½ miles away from the water to Joan Crescent turnoff). ☎ *250-592-5323.* www.craigdarrochcastle.com. *Admission: C$10 (US$8.30) adults, C$6.50 (US$5.40) students, C$3.50 (US$2.90) children 6–12. Open: Mid-June–Aug daily 9 a.m.–7 p.m., rest of the year daily 10 a.m.–4:30 p.m.*

The Fairmont Empress Hotel and Rose Gardens
Inner Harbour

The Fairmont Empress Hotel is, for all practical purposes, the hub of Victoria's substantial tourist trade. This rambling waterside hotel — now bearing the Fairmont name, but everyone still calls it the Empress — with its handsome mansard roofs, is the best, most obvious point to orient yourself on the Inner Harbour. It's the congregating point for every manner of double-decker tour bus, tour guide, and camera-clicking visitor; a must-see, inside and out. Designed by English architect Francis Rattenbury, this place is so big that is has three entrances — although the front stairs are no longer one of them. It's almost unnecessary to tell you that the wood, marble, stained glass, and crystal chandeliers are all of the highest quality. (Some of the hotel rooms *are* a bit on the small side, though.) There are no tours — not unless you're a paying guest, of course, in which case you get a *real* inside look — but most of the ground floors are open to the public, including a shopping gallery, a lush conservatory, lavish sitting rooms, two restaurants, and the wonderfully overdone Bengal Lounge (see Chapter 20), which serves tea, alcoholic drinks, and Indian meals. Outside, walk around to find the rose gardens, a fragrant and peaceful retreat from the touristy buzz of the harbor. Allow about one hour, two hours if taking tea. See Chapter 17 for information on staying here.

See map p. 259. 721 Government St. ☎ *800-441-1414* or *250-384-8111.* www.fairmont.com/empress. *Parking: Valet, C$22 (US$18) overnight guests; C$16.50 (US$14) day only.*

Fisherman's Wharf
Shoal Point, Inner Harbour

Walk along to the westernmost part of the harbour, near the Laurel Point Hotel, and you'll discover a delightful flotilla of working fishboats, houseboats, yachts, and other sailing vessels. Buy some fish and chips at wharfside, and savor the sights, sounds, and smells of this picturesque wharf.

See map p. 259. Runs along the water at Shoal Point; follow Bellville around to Erie Street.

Fort Rodd Hill and Fisgard Lighthouse
Colwood (8 miles west of Victoria)

As the crow flies, this lighthouse and fort practically overlook the twin peninsulas of Victoria and Esquimalt, and that's precisely why they were built during the late 19th century: to guard the strategic harbor from (primarily American) invaders. The lighthouse, constructed first, is the oldest on Canada's West Coast. Inside the keeper's house (everything is automated now), a small museum gives you some sense of what life was like here. The fort was added later, very close by, with three batteries of guns, barracks, underground magazines — the whole bit. And local volunteers help during summer to demonstrate the old blacksmithing ways. If you're not into all this history, you can still come for the oak meadows, blacktail deer, bobbing seals, and sea lions — it's a scenic place for a picnic. Allow two to three hours, including travel time.

See map p. 259. 603 Fort Rodd Hill Rd. (8 miles west of downtown Victoria; drive north on Douglas St. to Hwy. 1, continue 3 miles, take exit 10 for Colwood and follow Hwy. 1A another 1.2 miles. Turn left at Ocean Blvd. and follow signs.) ☎ **250-478-5849.** *Admission: C$4 (US$3.35) adults, C$3 (US$2.50) senior citizens, C$2 (US$1.65) children 6–16, Open: March–Oct daily 10 a.m.–5:30 p.m., Sept–Feb daily 9 a.m.–4:30 p.m.*

Maritime Museum of British Columbia
Downtown/Old Town

This museum, containing pretty much exactly what you would expect, is housed in the province's former courthouse. Various low-tech galleries explain the early history of marine exploration in the province, the story of Captain James Cook, naval history, and the role of BC Ferries in modern-day island life. Among the most interesting exhibits are a dugout canoe, marine charts, and ship bells. But the *really* interesting stuff has to do with the courthouse itself, a beautiful structure paneled in exotic woods that holds plenty of its own history. One especially tough judge made a name for himself in the oak chambers by sentencing dozens of criminals to death, ordering them hanged right out in front of the steps; the same judge designed the ornate elevator — Canada's oldest — supposedly because His Ampleness couldn't fit up the building's narrow stairway. Allow roughly one hour. *Note:* The Special Exhibition Gallery is not wheelchair accessible.

See map p. 259. 28 Bastion Sq. ☎ **250-385-4222.** www.mmbc.bc.ca. *Admission: C$8 (US$6.65) adults, C$5 (US$4.15) seniors, C$3 (US$2.50) children 11 and under. Open: Daily 9:30 a.m.–4:30 p.m.*

Parliament Buildings
Inner Harbour

Basically the Canadian equivalent of a state capitol building, Victoria's dual Parliament Buildings house the workings of its provincial legislators. A fresh-faced Englishman named Francis Rattenbury blew into town and somehow won the local design competition, overseeing the huge stone buildings' construction during the late 1890s; Rattenbury would go on to design nearly everything else of note in the city, including The Fairmont Empress Hotel. The exterior is notable for thousands of small light bulbs, which illuminate the facade at night, as well as a statue of early explorer Captain George Vancouver topping the centermost dome and another of Queen Victoria. Inside, it's all wood, marble, and stained glass. Free tours are given three times each hour during the summer, once an hour during the winter months. The chamber upstairs is chock-full of reminders of that not-so-bygone day when Canada was tied at the hip to England. If the legislature is in session, you can watch the lively give-and-take of parliamentary procedure, which peaks around 2:00 in the afternoon — probably too dull for the kids, but architecture and history buffs will certainly want a look. Otherwise, just wander through the halls looking like an important politician. Allow about one hour.

See map p. 259. 501 Belleville St. ☎ *250-387-3046. Admission: Free. Open: Daily 9 a.m.–5 p.m.*

Royal British Columbia Museum
Inner Harbour

Victoria's downtown tourist sites are sometimes a letdown, but this science, nature, and history museum isn't one of them — rather, it's a truly eye-opening experience, one of the highlights of a visit to the city. The displays include a *serious* collection of Native-Canadian artifacts, a re-created rain forest, a mini-train, actual seals, a mock-up of Chinatown, and much more. The attached National Geographic IMAX Theatre (see the "Finding More Cool Things to See and Do" section later in this chapter), with its panoramic screen and sound, is a must-visit if you're bringing kids. Almost everything here is lifelike, fascinating, and thought provoking for all ages — kids, teens, and adults. Allow 2 to 2½ hours hours.

See map p. 259. 675 Belleville St. ☎ *888-447-7977 or 250-356-7226.* www.royalbc museum.bc.ca. *Admission: C$12.50 (US$10.40) adults, C$8.70 (US$7.25) seniors, students, and children 6–18. Open: Daily 9 a.m.–5 p.m., Imax daily 9 a.m.– 8 p.m.*

Thunderbird Park
Inner Harbour

Free and absolutely fascinating, this park's collection of totem poles is a wonderful introduction to the island. Enhancing the experience in summer is the presence of carvers creating new poles. Sometimes the carvers even answer questions. A single carver revived the nearly lost art of making these poles right here in the park. Allow 30 minutes.

See map p. 259. Corner of Belleville and Douglas streets (from The Fairmont Empress Hotel, walk south a short distance to Belleville and turn left). Admission: Free. Open: Daily dusk to dawn.

Trounce Alley
Downtown/Old Town

There's not a lot to Trounce Alley, but it's still a quick and fun stroll into a bit of Victoria's past. Once the city's red-light district (okay, that's something the kids don't really need to know), this narrowest of streets — which you may still have a little trouble squeezing through — is today much scrubbed and polished up, lit with quaint lanterns. The alley now holds little nook-and-cranny shops, some of them among Victoria's most interesting, as well as a Spanish tapas restaurant, The Tapa Bar (see Chapter 18). Allow 30 minutes.

See map p. 259. Runs from Government St. to Broad St., between Yates and View streets. Admission: Free.

Victoria Bug Zoo
Downtown/Old Town

The squeamish won't want to visit this place; kids, not being squeamish, often get a kick out it, though. This zoo features live scorpions, tarantulas, centipedes, stick insects, exotic beetles, grasshoppers, and more. You can even — ugh — cradle some of these comely creatures, if you like. Not feeling up to it? Then you'll want to slide over to the gift shop and buy some chocolate-covered insects (maybe not) or local honey.

See map p. 259. 631 Courteney St. ☎ 250-384-2847. www.bugzoo.bc.ca. *Admission: C$7 (US$5.80) adults, C$5 (US$4.15) senior citizens, C$6 (US$5) students, C$4.50 (US$3.75) children 3–16. Open: Daily July–Aug 9:30 a.m.–9 p.m.; Sept–June 9:30 a.m.–5:30 p.m.*

Victoria Butterfly Gardens
Brentwood Bay (12 miles northwest of Victoria)

The motto here is, "Ever been kissed by a butterfly?" Well, have you? If not, it just may happen in this walk-through greenhouse full of specially selected tropical blossoms and exotic butterflies from all over the world. You won't believe the color and variety here, and some of the bigger critters approach a foot in length. Wanna kiss? Here's a sneaky inside tip: Women with bright lipsticks stand the best chance. This makes a good day trip when combined with nearby Butchart Gardens, which is less than 2 miles west. Allow roughly one hour.

See map p. 259. 1461 Benvenuto Ave., Brentwood Bay (from downtown Victoria, drive away from town along Blanshard St., which becomes Hwy. 17; after about 6 miles, exit onto Hwy. 17A and continue about 8 more miles to gardens on left). ☎ 250-652-3822. www.butterflygardens.com. *Admission: C$9.50 (US$7.90) adults, C$8.50 (US$7.05) seniors and students, C$5.50 (US$4.60) children 5–12. Open: Mid-May–Sept daily 9 a.m.–5 p.m., late Feb–mid-May and Oct daily 9:30 a.m.–4:30 p.m.*

Finding More Cool Things to See and Do

What? There's more?

Of course, although — frankly speaking — after you cover Victoria's central attractions and day-trip out to its gardens, you've hit everything major. But say you're staying in town for an extended period of time and want to see and do more. Well, you're in luck. What follows are a few more things you can pencil into your itinerary.

Kid-pleasing spots

If you have kids in tow, you may also want to check out the itinerary for families at the end of this chapter.

Beacon Hill Children's Farm
Inner Harbour

Kids love this little zoo-like corner of Beacon Hill Park, where they can ride, coddle, and otherwise get up-close and personal with farm animals. A small pool is on hand for cooling off during the hot weather, too, after riding the ponies; all things considered, the petting zoo is a great alternative to hot, boring (to kids) afternoons pounding the pavement doing the city walking-tour thing — and it's centrally located and practically free.

See map p. 259. Circle Dr. (in Beacon Hill Park). ☎ **250-381-2532.** *Admission: C$1 (US83¢) suggested. Open: Daily mid-March–Sept 10 a.m.–5 p.m.*

Miniature World
Inner Harbour

This openly corny attraction is, quite frankly, just a curiosity, with displays such as the smallest (supposedly) working sawmill, two very large doll-houses, and a very long model railway. The attractions are divided into sections with Disney-like names: Circus World, Space 2201, Frontierland, and Fantasyland. You get the picture.

See map p. 259. 649 Humboldt St. ☎ **250-385-9731.** www.miniatureworld.com. *Admission: C$9 (US$7.50) adults (seniors 10 percent discount), C$8 (US$6.65) children 12–17, C$7 (US$5.80) children 5–11. Open: Daily March–May 9 a.m.–7 p.m., June and Oct–Feb 9 a.m.–5 p.m., July–Sept 8:30 a.m.–9 p.m.*

Pacific Undersea Gardens
Inner Harbour

Extending more than 10 feet down to the floor of Victoria's Inner Harbour, the gardens offer a chance to view all sorts of sea life and a live scuba-diving show. You see live fish — salmon, sturgeon, snapper — swimming, eating, mating, and otherwise doing their thing amid the ruins of a sunken ship; not to mention brightly colored sea anemones, huge octopi, and other odd and carnivorous creatures in their natural environs. *Note:* This attraction is not wheelchair accessible.

See map p. 259. 490 Belleville St. ☎ *250-382-5717.* www.pacificundersea gardens.com. *Admission: C$8.50 (US$7.05) adults, C$7.50 (US$6.25) seniors, C$6 (US$5) children 12–17, C$3.50 (US$2.91) children 5–11. Open: Daily June–Aug 9:30 a.m.–9 p.m.; Sept–June 10 a.m.–5 p.m.*

Royal London Wax Museum
Inner Harbour

This collection of more than 300 wax figures shipped over from Madame Tussaud's original (and better) wax museum in London, England, is a bit schlocky. I don't find it worth the effort or money — but kids sometimes enjoy it, especially those unintentionally hilarious figures that are supposed to depict gruesome doings.

See map p. 259. 470 Belleville St. ☎ *250-388-4461.* www.waxmuseum.bc.ca. *Admission: C$10 (US$8.30) adults, C$9 (US$7.50) seniors, C$7 (US$5.80) children 13–17, C$5 (US$4.15) children 6–12. Open: Daily Jan–early May 9:30 a.m.–5 p.m., mid-May–Aug 9 a.m.–7:30 p.m., and Sept–Dec 9:30 a.m.–6 p.m.*

Teen-tempting attractions

Many teens seem to prefer shopping and hanging out at **The Bay Centre** or in **Market Square,** but the town has a few other teen-friendly attractions.

Centre of the Universe Dominion Astrophysical Observatory
Saanich (7 miles north of Victoria)

The white domes atop Little Saanich Mountain are visible from parts of Victoria, and the two large telescopes here — with 3½-foot and 5-foot mirrors — are used by professionals to stargaze on about 200 nights each year; the larger of the two, in fact, was once the largest telescope in the world. Tours take place Monday through Friday and last 75 minutes; you must have a reservation. Saturday night talks and public stargazing are also available on an irregular schedule. The facility is showing its age, but is still a fun excursion. Bring a light jacket, as the thick walls keep the inside temperature pretty cool.

See map p. 259. 5071 West Saanich Rd. (from downtown Victoria, drive north out Blanshard St. to Hwy. 17 and continue approximately 4.5 miles; exit onto Hwy. 17A north and continue 2½ more miles on West Saanich Rd. to observatory). ☎ *250-363-8262.* www.cu.hia.nrc.gc.ca. *Admission: C$7 (US$5.80) adults, C$5 (US$4.15) children 6–17, C$19 (US$16) family. Open: April–Oct daily 10 a.m.–6 p.m., Nov–March Tues–Sun 10 a.m.–4:30 p.m.*

National Geographic IMAX Theatre
Inner Harbour

One of the hippest, highest-tech attractions in Victoria is the six-story, panoramic IMAX movie screen housed inside the Royal British Columbia Museum (see the "Discovering Victoria's Top Sights from A to Z" section earlier in this chapter). Science, nature, and popular films screen every hour on the hour all day long; the pounding surround-sound brings another dimension to the huge wraparound images on the screen above.

See map p. 259. 675 Belleville St. (inside Royal British Columbia Museum). ☎ *250-480-4887.* www.imaxvictoria.com. *Admission: C$10.50 (US$8.75) adults, C$8.25 (US$6.85) seniors and children 6–18. Open: Daily 9 a.m.–8 p.m.*

Notable parks and gardens

Almost nothing is better in Victoria than wandering through one of the city's numerous parks, many snuggled into residential neighborhoods (discussed in the following section).

Horticulture Centre of the Pacific
Saanich (6 miles north of Victoria)

One of the better botanical gardens in the Greater Victoria region, this center is made up of more than 100 acres of property with hundreds of identified plants, trees, and flowers. The admission is a great deal less expensive than Butchart Gardens, if less spectacular.

See map p. 259. 505 Quayle Rd. (from downtown Victoria, drive north out Blanshard St. to Hwy. 17 and continue approximately 4½ miles; exit onto Hwy. 17A north and continue 1½ more miles and make a left on Beaver Rd., just after Beaver Lake Elementary school; at end of Beaver Rd., make a right on Quayle Rd.). ☎ *250-479-6162. Admission: C$7.50 (US$6.25) adults, C$5.25 (US$4.35) seniors. Open: Daily June–Aug 8 a.m.–8 p.m., Sept–May 9:30 a.m.–4:30 p.m.*

Mount Douglas Park
Saanich (3 miles north of Victoria)

Called "Mount Doug," this reclaimed copper-mining hill is perhaps the most impressive park of all in Victoria nowadays, although it does take a little finding — it's nestled within farms and suburbs a couple miles north of the city center. The 640-foot summit (to which you can walk or drive) has panoramic views of the city, the strait, and the mountains. The park has an ocean section with rocky tide pools and genuine cliffs, along with hiking trails that pass through fragrant ferns, wildflowers, Douglas firs, and cedar trees. This park makes a great spot to get away from the city for a few hours.

See map p. 259. Cordova Bay Rd. (from downtown Victoria, proceed to Johnson St. and turn right, traveling away from bridge; remain on main road for 3 miles — street changes name to Begbie, then Shelbourne, then Cordova Bay Rd.). Admission: Free. Open: Daily dawn to dusk.

Mount Tolmie Park
Mayfair

Several walking trails ascend the 350-foot summit in this small park — not a long climb, but high enough on this flat peninsula to reward the walker with good views of Victoria and the Olympic Mountain Range.

See map p. 259. Mayfair Dr. (from downtown Victoria, drive 2 miles east on Fort St. and turn left on Richmond Rd.; continue 1½ more miles north to Mayfair Dr., turn right onto Mayfair and continue ½ mile to park). Admission: Free. Open: Daily dawn to dusk.

Stroll-worthy neighborhoods

After you're done combing through the Inner Harbour, Old Town/ Downtown, and Antique Row (see Chapter 20), a few more areas await your inspection.

Chinatown is almost too small to explore for long, but Fan Tan Alley — a narrow passageway now filled with shops — is fun with the kids during the daytime. **Bastion Square,** on Government Street, was the original site of Fort Victoria, a fort constructed in 1843 by the Hudson's Bay Company but later torn down; it was also, for a time, a rough-and-tumble district of bars and houses of ill repute. Today, the square has mostly cafes and shops.

Beyond the central attractions, you can tour the nearby neighborhoods of **Lower Cook Street Village, James Bay, Oak Bay, Uplands,** and **Mayfair.** To do so, begin at Beacon Hill Park and cycle or drive along Dallas Road, which becomes Beach Drive and passes through gorgeous mansions and a golf course. The breakwater at **Ogden Point** is a good early respite spot on the journey, with seafood available to eat and a shore path for walking. This is a favorite location for scuba divers. Other recommended spots for breaks are (in succession) **Clover Point, Trafalgar Park, Willows Beach Park,** and big **Uplands Park,** all right on the same beach route. **Ross Bay Cemetery,** on the dry side of the road just after Clove Point, contains 27,000 graves, including those of notable locals Robert Dunsmuir, a Scottish mining baron, and Emily Carr, a painter. Turning inland at Cadboro Bay (site of the Royal Victoria Yacht Club), you pass the **University of Victoria** campus, which — in springtime — is ablaze with the blossoms of rhododendron gardens. From here, you can turn and follow Cadboro Bay Road south back into town, where it becomes Fort Street.

Seeing Victoria by Guided Tour

If you're pressed for time, a guided tour of Victoria may be a good idea. And for such a small city, you find a great variety of touring options — everything from walks through moonlit cemeteries to sailboat tours. Take note that almost all of them, however, operate only during the summer season, which here runs from roughly the beginning of June to the beginning of October. Some tour companies may also operate during spring and fall, as well, so it's always worth checking, but a winter visitor will find the tour offerings very much reduced.

Touring by foot

If you want to hoof it around Victoria, you have a few options. The cheapest tour is the one you make for free by yourself, using maps gleaned at the Visitor InfoCentre, 812 Wharf St. But even if you're a poor route-planner, you can take a free, guided tour, beginning at the InfoCentre, any afternoon during summer from the local chapter of the **Architectural Institute of British Columbia** (☎ 800-667-0753).

Several tours given by private companies point out Victoria's spookier side: **Ghostly Walks** (☎ 250-384-6698; www.discoverthepast.com) is one of the best, conducted by historian and storyteller John Adams — he's been on the TV series *Ghosts and Ghoulies* and Discovery Channel's *Creepy Canada*. The two-hour tour of reputedly haunted spots leaves nightly at 7:30 p.m. from the Visitor InfoCentre. The cost is C$12 (US$10) for adults and C$10 (US$8.30) for students and seniors, and C$6 (US$5) per child ages 6 to 12. His other neighborhood tours are not as spine-chilling, but no less interesting

Touring on wheels: Bus, carriage, pedicab, or limo

Gray Line of Victoria (☎ 800-663-8390 or 250-388-5248; www.grayline.ca/victoria) is the old standby. For overnight tours leaving from Vancouver to Victoria, call ☎ 800-667-0882. Among its offerings are the usual bus tours: A 90-minute Grand City tour costing C$19 (US$16) for adults and C$9.50 (US$7.90) for children, as well as more-expensive packages combining the standard city tour with destinations such as Butchart Gardens, Butterfly Gardens, and Craigdarroch Castle (see "Discovering Victoria's Top Sights from A to Z" for listings of these attractions). Call for details. Tours generally run from April through October, but check ahead to be certain.

Pacific Coach Lines Tours (☎ 800-661-1725 or 250-385-4411) offers several bus tours from Vancouver. The Royal Victorian & Butchart Gardens tour, for example, is for flower-lovers and includes two hours' time at Butchart Gardens; the Royal Victorian & Grand City Tour takes place on a London double-decker bus that drives through almost all of Victoria's neighborhoods; and the Royal Victorian Excursion is shorter and not narrated. Prices vary according to factors such as where your tour begins and how old you are, but all prices include ferry costs.

Horse-drawn tours are also an option in Victoria. **Tallyho Sightseeing** (☎ 866-383-5067 or 250-383-5067) provides an old-fashioned feeling in turn-of-the-20th-century carriages clip-clopping around town from March through October. Group tours in a carriage holding up to 20 strangers cost C$15 (US$12) per adult, C$13 (US$11) for seniors, and C$7 (US$5.80) for children. Or you can rent an entire, smaller carriage for somewhat more — a half-hour will cost you about C$80 (US$67), for example. You can find the carriages waiting in front of The Fairmont Empress or at Belleville and Menzies Streets, next to the ferry docks. **Carriage Tours** (☎ **250-383-2207**) offers a variety of carriage tours, starting at C$40 (US$33) per carriage for a 15-minute tour to C$160 (US$133) for an hour's ride; the carriage can seat four to six people at one time.

Perhaps the most fun and interesting way to see Victoria — although it isn't cheap — is inside a "pedicab," a kind of small rickshaw propelled by a cycling "driver" in front of you. These vehicles, operated by **Kabuki Kabs** (☎ **250-385-4243;** www.kabukikabs.com), are tiny, quick, and maneuverable. Expect to pay from C$60 to C$90 (US$50–US$75) per hour for a pedicab holding two to four people; shorter tours are certainly possible, charged at a rate of at least a dollar per minute. You can pick up a pedicab most easily in front of the Empress Hotel — or just hail any empty one you see returning to the waterfront.

More expensive limousine tours are also possible through **Heritage Tours Daimler Limousine** (☎ **250-474-4332**), but these cost approximately C$70 (US$58) per hour. One advantage of a limo rental, on the other hand, is that it holds up to six people at a time for the same price as the much smaller pedicab.

Going by other means

Victoria Harbour Ferries (☎ **250-708-0201**) runs touring boats around the waterfront from late spring until early autumn. A tour up the inlet known as "the Gorge" costs C$16 (US$13) for adults, C$14 (US$12) for seniors, C$8 (US$6.65) for children, and takes a little less than an hour. Harbour tours cost C$14 (US$12) for adults, C$12 (US$10) seniors, and C$7 (US$5.80) for children and last roughly 45 minutes each.

Wild Cat Adventures, 1234 Wharf St. (☎ **800-953-3345** or 250-384-9998; www.wildcat-adventure.com) offers whale watching from a 48-foot catamaran with an on-board naturalist who shares local history and anecdotes. The vessel's size means it can go farther out to sea than most other excursions; besides which it has two washrooms — to my mind, a real plus.

Great Pacific Adventures, 811 Wharf St. (☎ **877-733-6722** or 250-386-2277; wwwgreatpacificadventures.com) offers all manner of activities such as kayak, canoe, and boat rentals; wildlife viewing; and bicycle tours.

Chapter 20

Shopping the Local Stores

• •

In This Chapter

▶ Getting to know Victoria's shopping scene

▶ Visiting the big-name stores

▶ Checking out the neighborhoods

• •

*V*ictorians love to shop in any weather, and the handsome downtown buildings — once banks, warehouses, and offices — are now full of careful shopkeepers who ensure orderly stores. They also import a higher-than-usual level of quality goods, especially from the British Isles.

For a quick listing of Victoria's stores by merchandise, see the index at the end of this chapter.

Surveying the Scene

 In terms of specialty items to look for in Victoria, the city is probably best known for two things — **English** and **Native-Canadian goods.** Both are available, surprisingly, in more quantity and quality than in Vancouver, and often at bargain prices compared to elsewhere. Genuine Georgian pewter and similar British Empire antiques, not to mention tea sets, Aran sweaters, Celtic crests, kilts, shortbreads, and other Anglo items are easy to find. You can score deals on many of these items if you look hard enough. Given the city's English bent, the availability of English goods is not unexpected. However, the strong selection of Native-Canadian art and trade does come as a pleasant surprise. I'm always amazed by the number of Native galleries and shops within a small area of downtown. You may have a tough time visiting any of them without taking home at least a little bit of Native art, jewelry, clothing, or food. Some of these local goods are expensive, and some almost tacky, but for sheer concentration and choice, this is *the* place.

The store hours in Canada are different from those in the United States. Victoria's stores usually open at 9 a.m. and close at 5 p.m. or 6 p.m., Monday through Wednesday. On Thursdays and Fridays, however, they stay open much later than usual: until 9 p.m. Then, on Saturday, stores are open 9 a.m. to 5 p.m. again. Sunday is a short shopping day, with most stores opening at noon and closing at 5 p.m. (or even 4 p.m. at smaller stores).

Checking Out the Big Names

Victoria is a relatively small city and as such, the big-name department stores (Macy's, Bloomingdale's, and so on) simply don't exist here. For those stores, try Vancouver (see Part III) — or, actually, Seattle. But you can still find all the usual department store offerings at one long-time Canadian institution.

The Bay, 1150 Douglas St., Downtown/Old Town (☎ **250-385-1311;** www.thebay.ca), is the more streamlined name for what used to be known as the fur-trading Hudson's Bay Company. No longer a place of beaver pelts and rabbit furs, the store today carries the same upscale fashions, housewares, and perfumes that you would expect at any quality department store. But you do find some unique Canadian heritage items, such as the colorful wool blankets for which HBC is known. This particular outlet now anchors a beautiful shopping mall appropriately named **The Bay Centre.** See later in this chapter for details.

Aaaaah ... Spas in Victoria

Vancouver Island is recognized as one of the best spa destinations in the world and certainly, if you're prepared to travel, the rainforest wilderness delivers some exotic spa locations. That said, Victoria does have its share of urban spas — here are my top five:

Maria Manna Life Spa (714 View St. ☎ 250-385-6676; www.mariamannalifespa. com) has combined the Chinese principles of Feng Shui and an intimate Japanese-style decor with a blend of classic European and Ayurvedic spa therapies — there's even an Ayurvedic doctor on site.

Silk Road Natural Spa (1624 Government St. ☎ 250-704-2688; www.silkroadtea. com), in the heart of Chinatown, is tiny and rather offbeat, having parlayed the simple tea leaf into a tea emporium of tastings, spa treatments, aromatherapy workshops and tea paraphernalia. Green tea facial anyone?

The Spa at Delta Victoria, Ocean Pointe Resort, (45 Songhees Rd. ☎ 800-575-8882 or 250-360-5858; www.thespaatdeltavictoria.com), is an award-winner and consistently rated one of the city's best spas. And little wonder. This luxurious, European-inspired sanctuary has a wide range of services, and comes with a complete fitness facility, pool, sauna, and more.

Le Spa Sereine (1411 Government St. ☎ 866-388-4419 or 250-388-4419; www.laspa sereine.com), right downtown, has charm and capacity (it's on three levels) and offers steam rooms, Japanese soaker tubs, and extensive services as well as a lovely fireplace lounge — ideal for relaxing, or for drying your toes after a pedicure.

Willow Stream Spa at The Fairmont Empress Hotel (721 Government St. ☎ 866-854-7444 or 250-995-4650; www.willowstream.com) is elegantly chic and expensive, but when you consider that all treatments — and there's an excellent selection — include as much time as you'd like in the sauna, steam, and Hungarian mineral pool, a simple manicure can become quite the spa adventure. So, are you worth the investment?

Victoria Shopping

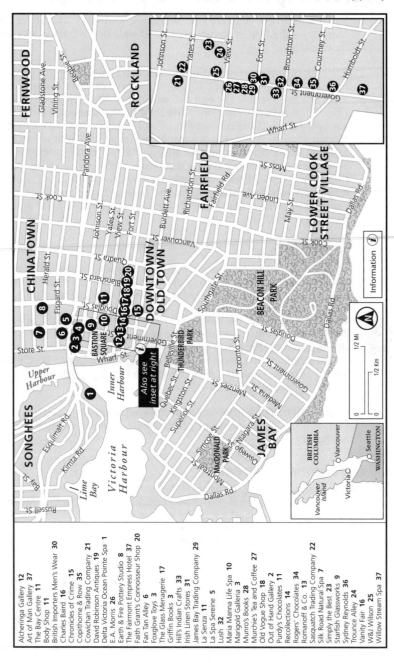

Alcheringa Gallery **12**
Art of Man Gallery **37**
The Bay Centre **11**
Body Shop **11**
British Importers Men's Wear **30**
Charles Baird **16**
Chronicles of Crime **15**
Copithorne & Row **35**
Cowichan Trading Company **21**
David Robinson Antiques **19**
Delta Victoria Ocean Pointe Spa **1**
E.A. Morris **26**
Earth & Fire Pottery Studio **8**
The Fairmont Empress Hotel **37**
Faith Grant's Connoisseur Shop **20**
Fan Tan Alley **6**
Foxglove Toys **3**
The Glass Menagerie **17**
Griffin Books **3**
Hill's Indian Crafts **33**
Irish Linen Stores **31**
James Bay Trading Company **29**
La Senza **11**
La Spa Sereine **5**
Lush **32**
Maria Manna Life Spa **10**
Marigold Galleria **3**
Munro's Books **28**
Murchie's Tea and Coffee **27**
Old Vogue Shop **18**
Out of Hand Gallery **2**
Purdy's Chocolates **11**
Recollections **14**
Rogers' Chocolates **34**
Romanoff & Co. **13**
Sasquatch Trading Company **22**
Silk Road Natural Spa **7**
Simply the Best **23**
Starfish Glassworks **9**
Sydney Reynolds **36**
Trounce Alley **24**
Vanity Fair **16**
W&J Wilson **25**
Willow Stream Spa **37**

Discovering the Best Shopping Neighborhoods

You'll want to concentrate your shopping in three or four areas, and — happily — all of them are within a short walk of the ferry docks on the Inner Harbour.

For ease of organization in this compact city, I describe the shopping options by region or street. If you're in search of a particular specialty item, see the index at the end of this chapter. The first shopping stop (The Fairmont Empress Hotel) sits right on the harbor. The next four shopping areas (Government Street, Antique Row, Yates/Douglas, and Market Square) may seem geographically separate, but they're actually all close to one another, and all are considered to be in Victoria's Old Town; I separate them here because each has a unique character. Chinatown, the last area, is attached to Old Town, but most people treat it as a separate and distinct area, and I do the same. Finally, I touch briefly on Oak Bay, an upscale residential area located a few miles from the harbor on Dallas Road.

Inner Harbour

You can't go wrong by starting right at Victoria's harbor, inside a hotel that's so interesting, it also qualifies as one of the city's best sights (see Chapter 19). Why not double your efficiency by doing two things at once?

The Fairmont Empress Hotel, 721 Government St. (☎ 800-441-1414 or 250-384-8111), offers several floors of displays and shopping spread throughout the hotel. You find expensive chocolate, clothing, porcelains, and much more; the real star is the **Art of Man Gallery** (☎ 250-383-3800), a Native-Canadian art gallery, with carvings, paintings, and masks, among other items.

Connected to The Fairmont Empress by a passageway, the Victoria Convention Centre maintains its own distinctive shops, as well as an art gallery.

Government Street

The first main shopping area off the harbor is along Government Street, a red-bricked road that runs from the Empress hotel to Chinatown and beyond. Here, you find a mixture of touristy shops stocking knick-knacks and truly fine goods, including one of Western Canada's best bookstores (read on for details); a little weeding out is necessary, so I show you where to look.

This street is one of the two best (also see the "Antique Row" section below) in North America to find anything you want that's English, Scottish, or Irish without actually buying a ticket to those fair islands. One of the best of these is **Sydney Reynolds,** 801 Government St. (☎ 250-383-3931), an elegant yet whimsical shop that sells wonderful china, British tea sets, porcelains, dolls, and more from the British Isles.

Ireland is well-represented, too, by classy **Irish Linen Stores,** 1019 Government St. (☎ 250-383-6812), a long-standing shop that sells fine Irish laces, sweaters, bow ties, and more; and **W&J Wilson,** 1221 Government St. (☎ 250-383-7177), an excellent men's clothing store that carries sweaters from Scotland and Ireland plus other European imports. Finally, **Copithorne & Row,** 901 Government St. (☎ 250-384-1722), is one of the city's top china and crystal shops.

Intermingling with this Anglo overload is an almost overwhelming concentration of Native-Canadian shops along the same stretch of Government Street — ironic, isn't it? The most popular Native shops offer a mixture of cheap souvenirs and pricier but authentic masks, carvings, jewelry, and more; you need to weed through the tawdry to get to the good stuff. These shops include the **Cowichan Trading Company,** 1328 Government St. (☎ 250-383-0321), **Sasquatch Trading Company,** 1233 Government St. (☎ 250-386-9033) across the road, and **Hill's Indian Crafts,** 1008 Government St. (☎ 250-385-3911), a spot for truly inspiring Native art (everything from kayak paddles to drums) from British Columbia's coastal peoples — with an emphasis on quality.

Also worth a visit is **British Importers Men's Wear,** 1125 Government St. (☎ 250-386-1496), with its continental imports of the highest quality in an exceptionally stylish showroom; think Armani suits, and you have the picture. This is the place to buy fine men's clothing in Victoria.

Some of the other unusual and interesting shops you find along this stretch of Government include the old, old **James Bay Trading Company,** 1102 Government St. (☎ 250-388-5477), which stocks Native-Canadian crafts and foods, along with thick maritime wool sweaters; **Earth & Fire Pottery Studio,** 1820 Government St. (☎ 250-380-7227), a working studio where you can watch the ocean-themed pots being thrown, fired, and glazed right on-site; **Rogers' Chocolates,** 913 Government St. (☎ 800-663-2220 or 250-384-7021), a wonderful, ye olde style candy shop that hand-concocts delicious cream-filled chocolates that are so good the Queen of England has ordered them; **Lush,** 1001 Government St. (☎ 250-384-5874), an all-natural cosmetics company based in Vancouver that sells bath soaps and other wholesome (and handmade) personal-care products in bulk; and **E.A. Morris,** 1116 Government St. (☎ 250-382-4811), the place to pick up hand-rolled cigars and pipe tobacco.

Finally, I'd be remiss if I didn't mention **Munro's Books,** 1108 Government St. (☎ 250-382-2464). Housed in a handsome old structure, packed with books amid elegant furnishings, Munro's is perhaps the province's best locally owned bookstore. The selection is strong on local history but offers plenty of everything else, too. And the staff is incredibly knowledgeable.

After a browse, head next door to **Murchie's Tea and Coffee,** 1110 Government St. (☎ 250-383-3112), for wonderful teas and coffees from around the world alongside eye-catching tea wares; Murchie's is somewhat of a local legend.

Two complexes just off Government Street also deserve a visit. Between Fort and View Streets (it can also be reached from Douglas Street), you find the **The Bay Centre** (☎ 250-952-5690, www.thebaycentre.ca). This modern shopping gallery — a four-story building with historic facades, a central atrium, and giant clock telling the time around the world — is anchored by **The Bay** (see "Shopping the Big Names" earlier in the chapter). But it also includes other merchants, such as **The Body Shop, La Senza** lingerie, locally made **Purdy's Chocolates** (☎ 250-361-1024) — this family-run chocolatier originally made its fortune by running liqueur chocolates across the border during Prohibition — and a host of other leather, gift, and apparel shops. In other words, everything you'd expect in an upscale retail destination. A second mall, the **Mayfair Shopping Centre** (☎ 250-386-3322), lies a few blocks east of the downtown core between Finlayson and Tolmie Streets (with two entrances off Douglas Street); it has about 50 stores to browse through, including another, albeit smaller, Bay.

Also just off Government Street is **Trounce Alley,** Victoria's former red-light district (although it's hard to believe now, given the current look of the area). The short alley holds all sorts of little stalls and shops, plus a few eateries, too. Nearby **Broad Street** is also a small and bustling spot, packed with gift shops, art galleries, clothing, and specialty stores.

A top favorite is **Simply the Best**, 1008 Broad St. (☎ 250-386-6661), which pretty much says it all. Looking for a C$32,000 (US$26,622) fountain pen that will give you something to write home about? This is the place!

Located in the centre of Canada's oldest Chinatown, **Fan Tan Alley** is barely four-feet wide. This narrow alleyway cuts through many of the original three-story, high-brick buildings that once housed gambling joints and opium dens, but today give way to curiosity and souvenir shops.

Antique Row (Fort Street)

Victoria's Antique Row is a sterling — pardon the pun — place to shop for antiques, especially those of British origin, such as porcelains, estate jewelry, and top-quality silver. It stretches about three blocks east along Fort Street. To get here, walk due east from The Bay Centre's south side along Fort Street two blocks until you reach Blanshard, where the district begins.

With so many choices here, I hardly know where to start. It's probably best just to wander at your leisure, popping in whenever a shop strikes your fancy.

Vanity Fair, 1044 Fort St. (☎ 250-380-7274), has roughly 40 dealer showcases under its roof — mostly small heirloom paraphernalia; next door, **Charles Baird,** 1044A Fort St. (☎ 250-384-8809), runs with good humor a skinny but well-stocked shop of antique furniture; **The Glass Menagerie,**

1036 Fort St. (☎ 250-475-2228), carefully shelves a huge array of collectible plates, plus china and pottery; **Romanoff & Co.**, 837–839 Fort St. (☎ 250-480-1543), run by a proprietor who comes from a family of dealers, is stronger in coins and jewelry than most, although it has a good selection of silverware, too; **David Robinson Antiques,** 1023 Fort St. (☎ 250-384-6425), deals classy (and pricey) furniture, silver, rugs, and other fine antiques; and the **Old Vogue Shop,** 1034 Fort St. (☎ 250-380-7751), is a good antiques shop for generalists, dealing in china, pottery, and a hodgepodge of other items.

Two more must-sees located along Fort Street, but outside Antique Row, are the **Alcheringa Gallery,** 665 Fort St. (☎ 250-383-8224), which features the work of many Native peoples from the world over — all of superior quality and expensive; and **Faith Grant's Connoisseur Shop,** 1156 Fort St. (☎ 250-383-0121), which is wonderfully stocked with antique furniture. Finally, don't miss **Recollections,** 817A Fort St. (☎ 250-385-1902), a sort of upscale flea market compressing together a mishmash of dealers and styles.

While you're strolling along Fort Street, be sure to step into **Chronicles of Crime,** 1067 Fort St. (☎ 250-721-2665), a terrific bookstore specializing in spy-, criminal-, and mystery-related titles. Owner Frances Thorsen is the mastermind who has made crime pay by securing more than 15,000 new and used books.

Yates and Douglas area

One of the largest shopping areas stretches north–south along big Douglas Street and east–west along the cross-street called Yates. Many restaurants, bars, and shops are packed into this area (which also includes a few other side streets, such as Broughton and Johnson), and you can easily spend hours here.

Perhaps the most intriguing of these stores is **Starfish Glassworks,** 630 Yates St. (☎ 250-388-7827), located in a former bank now containing its own kiln — you can watch the firing from an interesting viewpoint — and terrific pots and glassware. (Note that glass is blown during afternoons only, and not at all on Mondays and Tuesdays.)

Market Square

Market Square, a former warehouse and shipping-goods complex at 560 Johnson St. near the Esquimalt Bridge and Chinatown, is today one of the city's most interesting little shopping complexes. When it was legal, opium was once manufactured here; today many of the several dozen shops offer eclectic fare. (Two examples: a canine treats shop and a hilarious yet tasteful, er, condom shop.) Plus the central courtyard area often hosts music and other arts performances in summer. **Marigold Galleria** (☎ 250-386-5339), which sells ceramics and glasswork; **Foxglove Toys** (☎ 250-383-8852); and **Griffin Books** (☎ 250-383-0633) are three good examples of the more conventional stores in the complex. You can eat anything from wholesome vegetarian meals to typical fast food at the stalls.

Just outside the Market Square building, **Out of Hand Gallery,** 566 Johnson St. (☎ **250-384-5221**), purveys handcrafted home furnishings and art from mostly regional artists. If picturesque Victoria finally has you ditching your trusted SLR camera for a digital, **Camera Traders,** 560 Johnson St. (☎ **250-382-6838**), will take the old technology off your hands.

Index of Stores by Merchandise

Art and antiques

Alcheringa Gallery (Antique Row/Fort Street)
Charles Baird (Antique Row/Fort Street)
David Robinson Antiques (Antique Row/Fort Street)
Faith Grant's Connoisseur Shop (Antique Row/Fort Street)
The Glass Menagerie (Antique Row/Fort Street)
Old Vogue Shop (Antique Row/Fort Street)
Recollections (Antique Row/Fort Street)
Romanoff & Co. (Antique Row/Fort Street)
Vanity Fair (Antique Row/Fort Street)

Arts and crafts

Earth & Fire Pottery Studio (Government Street)
Out of Hand Gallery (Market Square)
Starfish Glassworks (Yates and Douglas)

Books

Chronicles of Crime (Antique Row/Fort Street)
Griffin Books (Market Square)
Munro's Books (Government Street)

British and Irish goods

Irish Linen Stores (Government Street)

Candy

Purdy's Chocolates (Government Street)
Rogers' Chocolates (Government Street)

China and glassware

Copithorne & Row (Government Street)
Marigold Galleria (Market Square)
Sydney Reynolds (Government Street)

Clothing and lingerie

British Importers Men's Wear (Government Street)
La Senza (Government Street)
W&J Wilson (Government Street)

Cosmetics

The Body Shop (Government Street)
Lush (Government Street)

Department stores

The Bay (Downtown/Old Town)

Malls

The Bay Centre (Downtown/Old Town)
Fairmont Empress Hotel (Inner Harbour)
Mayfair Shopping Centre (Douglas Street)

Native-Canadian items

Art of Man (Inner Harbour)
Cowichan Trading Company (Government Street)
Hill's Indian Crafts (Government Street)
Sasquatch Trading Company (Government Street)

Specialty stores

Camera Traders (Market Square)
James Bay Trading Company (Government Street)
Murchie's Tea and Coffee (Government Street)
Simply the Best (Broad Street)

Tobacco

E.A. Morris (Government Street)

Toys

Foxglove Toys (Market Square)

Chapter 21

Following an Itinerary: Two Great Options

● ●

In This Chapter

▶ "Anglo-cizing" your visit

▶ Having fun with the family

● ●

*T*he itineraries in this section showcase the best that Victoria and the surrounding area have to offer Anglophiles (lovers of all things English) and families.

Itinerary #1: Victoria for Anglophiles

This city is as English as they come in North America, as any stroll through town will attest. And if you just want to hit the Anglo highlights, the following itinerary is for you. Mix and match the sights in whatever order you choose. But no matter how you go about it, you're sure to have a *jolly* good time.

Your English day in Victoria must, at some point, pass through the doors of **The Fairmont Empress Hotel** (see Chapter 17). Its architecture inside and out oozes English gentry from the Victorian era — dark-stained oak paneling, richly patterned carpets (reminiscent of "Inja" — hey, what?), and over-the-top chandeliers. This is a particularly good spot for refreshments. A very touristy (but very good) high tea costs from C$36 to C$55 (US$30–US$46) — it's most expensive during the summer — and basically includes a full meal of sweets, treats, and finger sandwiches, plus, of course, a pot of special Empress Blend tea. Or you can stop by in the evening — it gets no more colonial than a drink or an Indian meal in the **Bengal Lounge** (see Chapter 22).

If that's too rich for your blood, pop into the nearby **James Bay Tearoom,** an Anglo stronghold near the Inner Harbour (see Chapter 18). The tearoom serves high tea at a fraction of what you'd pay at The Empress, although it's probably even better as a lunchtime stop for some fish and chips, "bangers and mash" (a.k.a. sausages and mashed potatoes), Yorkshire pudding, or a glass of bitters.

Some 12 miles north of Victoria, **Butchart Gardens,** with its very English landscaping and flower collections, is a must-see stop on this itinerary (see Chapter 19). You can enjoy afternoon tea here, too, for C$23.75 (US$20) per person.

English-style shopping is easy to find, beginning right outside the door of The Empress on Government Street. Whether it's a Scottish sweater from **W&J Wilson** or Irish linens from the **Irish Linen Stores,** you can't possibly go home empty-handed. (See Chapter 20 for these stores.)

Other Anglo shops of note are along Fort Street, also known as **Antique Row.** Here you find plenty of English silver, porcelain, and furniture dating from the 18th and 19th centuries. **David Robinson Antiques** and the **Old Vogue Shop** are two of the best. (See Chapter 20 for details.)

Take a #1 or #2 bus or an Oak Bay Explorer tour bus a few miles out to the **Oak Bay** neighborhood and you're in Victoria's most English of all enclaves (and home to many expat Brits, some of whom still wear plus-fours for their golfing constitutional). Walking, cycling, or driving along the main drag — simply called Oak Bay — you pass more than a half-dozen tearooms and a number of bookshops, British importers, candy shops, and antiques dealers, not to mention plenty of fine, turn-of-the-20th-century residential homes and gardens (which are off-limits to the public). You also find a long scenic beach and marina with fishing boats, yachts, seals, seagulls, and crashing waves — all, except the yachts, serving as additional reminders of Old England.

You can spend the better part of an afternoon just wandering around Oak Bay. Some of the high points include the **Blethering Place Tearoom,** where afternoon tea costs C$16.95 (US$14) (see Chapter 18), and the Tudor-style **Oak Bay Beach Hotel** (see Chapter 17). The resort has a pub, a water-view restaurant, a spacious library lounge (great for a game of checkers), and a nifty dinner theater package that's worth asking about.

 If you're a fan of English bitters, ales, and other beers — and that's a good bet if you're taking this Anglo-itinerary — swing by **Spinnakers Brewpub,** the first brewpub in Canada, or **Swans Pub,** which specializes in British ales (see Chapter 22).

Itinerary #2: Victoria for Families

Compact, attractive, and polite, Victoria is well suited to families. A number of tourist attractions — some more nutritious than others — are specifically geared to entertaining kids. This three-day itinerary guides you to your best options.

Weather permitting, spend the morning of Day 1 exploring the **Inner Harbour.** The causeway right in front of The Fairmont Empress Hotel is a charming spot to hang out with the family. Clowns perform here, cascading floral baskets and boats brighten up the scene, and the Tourism InfoCentre is just the place to load up on information for the remainder of your stay. For lunch, eat in or take out sandwiches from **Sam's Deli** (see Chapter 18). In the afternoon, depending on the age of your little ones, take either a **boat tour** of the harbor or a longer **whale-watching tour** of the waters offshore. (For tour companies, check out Chapter 19.) If the weather turns gray, head for the nearby **Pacific Undersea Gardens** or the adjacent **Royal London Wax Museum** (see Chapter 19 for both). Have dinner at a fun place near the waterfront such as **Pagliacci's** (see Chapter 18).

On the morning of **Day 2,** head to the fascinating **Royal British Columbia Museum** (see Chapter 19). Rain or shine, this is one of the must-sees. Easily distracted youngsters and curious teens alike will appreciate the creativity of this unstuffy museum — walk through dioramas, including an entire cobblestone street lined with shops, a train station, various natural history scenes (the woolly mammoth's a star), and lots of local history. You'll probably be ready to sit and eat for a spell afterward, so don't stray far for lunch; eat somewhere close to the museum, such as the buffet restaurant, **Kipling's** (☎ 250-389-2727), inside The Fairmont Empress Hotel. If you've the energy to walk a few blocks, **Barb's Place** at Fisherman's Wharf is always fun — kids don't have to put on any airs or haul out their social graces eating lunch out of newspaper.

Be sure to drop by **Thunderbird Park** next door and check out the totem pole carvers — ask and they're always pleased to explain their craft to you.

Pouring cats and dogs in the afternoon? Head back inside the museum and catch a flick at the six-story **National Geographic IMAX Theatre** (see Chapter 19). A family of four can watch a film here for about C$40 (US$33).

In the late afternoon, drop by the nearby **British Candy Shoppe** (see Chapter 18) for some sweets such as gumballs and sherbet fountains and then make your way up to **Bastion Square,** usually with lots of buskers and other outdoor entertainment. **Chinatown's** around the corner (be sure to include **Fan Tan Alley**), so why not try your hand at chopsticks? **J&J Wonton House** is especially fun (see Chapter 18).

On the morning of **Day 3,** make your way to the **Beacon Hill Children's Farm** (see Chapter 19) for a half-day in Beacon Hill Park — a great stop in good weather. The little ones can ride, pet, and get to know baby farm animals, and then soak in a pool afterward. For lunch, the **Beacon Drive-In,** across from the park, is ideal for a fun meal of burgers and shakes (see Chapter 18). In the evening, grab a meal at a lively place like **Millos** or **Café Mexico** (see Chapter 18) before heading out to the **Centre of the Universe Dominion Astrophysical Observatory** (see Chapter 19) — one last look at the starry skies above Victoria before you're homeward bound.

It's a full day's trip there and back, but what you'll find at the end of the road, **Botanical Beach** in **Juan de Fuca Provincial Park,** is one of the best tidal pool areas on the island — a fascinating adventure for youngsters. The drive there hugs the coast with many trailheads leading to the amazing Juan de Fuca Trail. Stock up with picnic fare and go for the gusto!

Two shorter diversions include **Sidney by the Sea,** a delightful seaside community that lies near the ferry terminal. After exploring the Marine Mammal Museum, marina, tiny museum and book stores, head over to the new **Brentwood Bay Lodge & Spa** for lunch. The spa is one of the Island's best — and if you care to stay a while, it's the only PADI dive resort in Canada.

If you just need to swing on a green, if only for a couple of hours, the other digression to your day could be the brand new **Fore! Bear Mountain Resort** and first Nicklaus-designed golf course on Vancouver Island.

Chapter 22

Living It Up After the Sun Goes Down: Victoria Nightlife

● ●

In This Chapter

▶ Getting into Victoria's music scene
▶ Swinging through the clubs and bars
▶ Stopping by the performing arts venues

● ●

*A*t first glance, the chief enjoyments around here would seem to be on the stodgy side — classical music, opera, theater . . . stuff like that. And it's true. Live contemporary music probably plays second fiddle here to tunes written during the Renaissance.

Nevertheless, Victoria does actually let its hair down at night. You find a thriving folk and jazz scene, for example, and more dance clubs in the downtown area than you would ever believe possible after walking the prim streets of the city by day. Hate music but like beer? Ah, you're in luck. The microbreweries here are world class; there may be no finer place in the hemisphere to do a mini-tour of local brewers while having so much fun. The pubs aren't bad, either, and there are even a few cocktail bars of some renown.

All the listings in this chapter are concentrated within a small area, close to the Inner Harbour or the Old Town. For convenience, I divide the listings into those clubs and bars where music is the primary draw and those spots where beer, cocktails, and socializing are the reasons to go. I follow these with my top recommendations for where to enjoy the performing arts, including theater, opera, and classical music venues.

The envelope, please . . .

Getting the Beat on the Music Scene

To find out who's playing where, check the weekly newspaper *Monday Magazine* (www.mondaymag.com), the best source for entertainment listings. The local daily paper *The Times-Colonist* (www.canada.com/victoria/timescolonist) is also good. Another option is to call the **Community Arts Council of Greater Victoria** (☎ 250-381-2787).

Some clubs in town charge a variable cover fee to see live music performances, and the hipper dance clubs also require a C$5 to C$10 (US$4.15–US$8) cover charge to gain entrance — although women are often exempt from a cover.

Listening to folk, jazz, or blues

As befits its strongly English heritage, this town loves a folk tune strummed away on something stringy — a disproportionate number of the English- and Irish-themed pubs here also offer live music, usually on weekends but sometimes during the week, as well.

This town also loves lots of other kinds of music, too. The **ICA Folkfest** (☎ 250-388-4728; www.icafolkfest.org), on the Inner Harbour from late June to early July, features folk music but also music and dance from all over the world.

Victorians also really like their jazz and blues. The biggest musical soiree of the season is probably the very experimental **Jazz Fest International** (☎ 250-388-4423), which includes more than just jazz and begins in late June. The other festival worth catching — this one blues-oriented — is the **Blues Bash** (☎ 250-388-4423), which wraps up the summer over Canada's Labour Day weekend in early September.

The local Jazz Society operates a recorded hot line (☎ 250-388-4423) to keep abreast of all local performances.

Here are some of the hot spots for blues and jazz music:

✔ **Hermann's Jazz Club,** 753 View St., Downtown/Old Town (☎ 250-388-9166), costs more than a hole-in-the-wall joint, because you have to buy dinner, but the music comes free and it's always good. You sometimes hear other kinds of music here, but it's mainly jazz. One of the few clubs that open Sundays; acts usually go on around the 4:30 p.m. cocktail hour and at 8 p.m.

✔ **Swans Pub,** 506 Pandora St., Downtown/Old Town (☎ 250-361-3310), a top-notch microbrewery with an amazing art collection, offers the added attraction of good rootsy musical performances on an ongoing basis. Among the top drafts is a dynamite Bavarian-style beer. Don't forget to catch some jazz in the basement nightclub or to try the superb restaurant food. Finally, if you're just too full of beer to move along, the operation has an excellent guesthouse (see Chapter 17).

- **Central Bar & Grill,** 708 View St., Downtown/Old Town (☎ 250-361-1700), dishes up some great memories with artists like Long John Baldry, Dr. Hook, and other jazz and blues greats. The house band isn't half bad, either.

- **Lucky Lounge,** 517 Yates St., Downtown/Old Town (☎ 250-382-LUCK), is a good place for a casual get together. Sit near the band for an up-close-and-personal music experience — Steve Lucky and his jump-swing band play all the great songs with gusto, and some of the band members might even step into the audience for some swing dancing. Also plays jazz and blues.

- **Steamers Pub,** 570 Yates St., Downtown/Old Town (☎ 250-381-4340) has undergone a somewhat surprising renaissance as a top-flight blues club (it was once a strip club). The visiting acts can be an eclectic lot, but they pack more talent than you'd expect to find in Victoria.

Shaking your groove thing

Now this is a real surprise: Young folks, dressed like they just got off planes from London or Milan, shaking their butts to house music? Omigawd! Surely this can't be Victoria? What would the Queen Mother have thought? But, yes, it is and they do. Two of the trendy dance clubs of the moment include:

- **Upstairs,** 15 Bastion Sq., Old Town/Bastion Square (☎ 250-385-LIVE), is one of the hottest new places in the city, playing top 40 music weekdays with live performances on weekends. The crowd leans towards the echo boomer generation and the kick-ass bartenders alone are worth the price of admission.

- **Uforia,** 1208 Wharf St., Downtown/Old Town (☎ 250-381-2331), beckons you to dance the night away. Whatever's popular is what's gonna be playing in this club near the water. Don't expect the latest experimental DJ to blow in; it ain't that kind of place. You're here to bow down to the pop music charts, past and present.

Rockin' the night away

Victoria isn't really a hard rocker's kind of town, although pockets of long-haired guys can be found in the 'burbs. If you really crave ear-splitting noise, go to Vancouver, instead. Stuck here? Try these places for size:

- **Legends,** 919 Douglas St., Old Town/Downtown (☎ 250-383-7137), once a slightly grotty and overly loud palace of Goth, has rounded out its tastes and now offers something for everyone in the basement floor of the huge Strathcona Hotel.

Victoria Nightlife

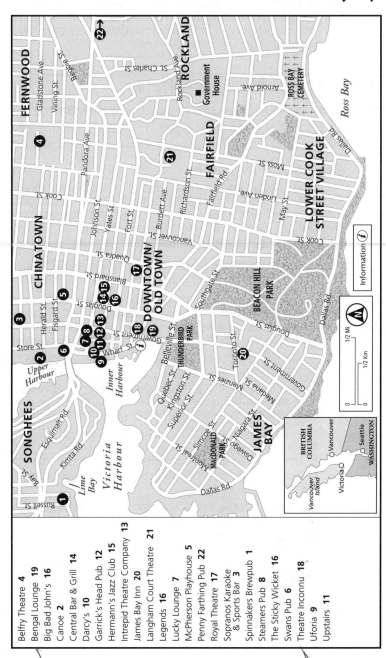

Belfry Theatre **4**
Bengal Lounge **19**
Big Bad John's **16**
Canoe **2**
Central Bar & Grill **14**
Darcy's **10**
Garrick's Head Pub **12**
Hermann's Jazz Club **15**
Intrepid Theatre Company **13**
James Bay Inn **20**
Langham Court Theatre **21**
Legends **16**
Lucky Lounge **7**
McPherson Playhouse **5**
Penny Farthing Pub **22**
Royal Theatre **17**
Sopranos Karaoke
  & Sports Bar **3**
Spinnakers Brewpub **1**
Steamers Pub **8**
The Sticky Wicket **16**
Swans Pub **6**
Theatre Inconnu **18**
Uforia **9**
Upstairs **11**

✔ **Sopranos Karaoke & Sports Bar,** 1961 Douglas St., Downtown/ Old Town (☎ 250-382-5853), tucked within the otherwise sedate Traveller's Inn, offers big-screen treatment of the usual sports-bar mixture of hockey, Canadian football, and other games, but karaoke warbling is the real entertainment.

Visiting the Watering Holes

You can find many fine spots to quench your thirst in Victoria, especially if you're in search of a cold brew. What follows are my favorite spots in a few different categories.

English and Irish pubs

This is no surprise at all: Pubs are thick on the ground in Victoria. Some of them are authentically Anglo or Celtic and others, well, basically consist of a veneer of Irishness (say, a few Harp posters and pictures of the Emerald Isle) pasted over watered-down, pricey drinks. Those places are for tourists. Head for one of the following places, instead:

✔ **Darcy's,** 1127 Wharf St., Old Town/Bastion Square (☎ 250-380-1322), awaits with pints of Irish beer and traditional Celtic music.

✔ **Garrick's Head Pub,** 69 Bastion Square, Old Town/Bastion Square (☎ 250-384-6835), in the Bedford Regency Hotel, is a pleasant place to get away from the faux-British pubs elsewhere around town. The food is authentically Brit and the beer is darned good.

✔ **James Bay Inn,** 270 Government St., Downtown (☎ 250-384-7151), another British pub, is attached to a decent hotel and quietly goes about the business of pulling good pints and maintaining a reasonably low profile. The Saturday-afternoon jam sessions get pretty lively, though.

✔ **Penny Farthing Pub,** 2280 Oak Bay Ave., Oak Bay Village (☎ 250-370-9008), is as picturesque as the village itself and a perfect stop if you're sightseeing outside of the downtown core. This is a quintessential English country pub complete with cosy fireplace, great brews, and pub grub.

✔ **The Sticky Wicket,** 919 Douglas St., Old Town/Downtown (☎ 250-383-7137), is one of many bars inside the Strathcona Hotel. Transplanted — and I mean piece by piece — from Ireland, it really scores with its basement-pub ambience.

Outstanding brewpubs

This is why you came to Victoria: To sip a tall cold one and marvel at the skill of the master brewer, while warming up your darts hand and looking out over the harbor.

✔ **Canoe,** 450 Swift St., Old Town/Downtown (☎ 250-361-1940), wasn't the first microbrewery in town, but it's one of the best. Live music, a pleasant atmosphere, and good — make that great — snacks entice you to stay as long as you can.

✔ **Spinnakers Brewpub,** 308 Catherine St., Esquimalt/Songhees (☎ 250-386-2739), is *it:* The very first brewpub in Canada, and one that continues to amaze with what are now dozens of home brews — almost every one of them delicious. That's to say nothing of the tremendous water views, the first-rate inn attached to the premises (see Chapter 17), or the active darts games. This is probably the most fun you can have in one place in town, and it's even walking distance — just — from the Old Town. Head across the Esquimalt Bridge to get here.

✔ **Swans Pub,** 506 Pandora Ave., Old Town/Downtown (☎ 250-361-3310), is as fun as Spinnakers; it's almost as if the two have a happy rivalry to be the best at everything. Well, I call it a tie. Terrific beers, a happy crowd, amazingly intriguing wall art, music downstairs, and plenty of different spaces and moods in which to relax all add up to a must-drink kind of place. Hard to believe this was once a warehouse.

Neighborhood bars

Sorry, although plenty of pubs and bars are tucked in outlying neighborhoods, Victoria has only one neighborhood bar that must be visited. And, although it's in a very good area, it sure acts like it's in Seed Central.

✔ **Big Bad John's,** 919 Douglas St., Old Town/Downtown (☎ 250-383-7137), located in the big Strathcona Hotel, attracts a lowbrow clientele. *Really* lowbrow — you may hear country music. A no-nonsense decor, wisecracking bartenders, and refreshingly unstarched ambience combine to make this the rowdiest place for miles around.

Chic bars and lounges

The Bengal Lounge quite simply is *the* place to sip a cocktail when in Victoria. Other lounges exist, but none can compare to this one.

✔ **Bengal Lounge,** 721 Government St., Inner Harbour (☎ 250-384-8111), inside The Fairmont Empress hotel, must be seen to be believed. Basically, you haven't been to the real Victoria until you've sipped a mixed drink here in an atmosphere of dark wood and lush plants designed to conjure up the British Empire's heyday in India. (The lounge also serves meals spiced with Indian curry, if you're hungry.) The exotic tiger pelt is either incredibly bad taste or incredibly cool, depending on your view of animal rights, but you can't deny that this is one the holdouts of the city's colonial past.

Raising the Curtain on the Performing Arts

Victoria does a great job of presenting the arts, given that it's a relatively small city. Several opera and theater companies, a small orchestra, and plenty of other diversions provide you with an arts fix while you're here. **Tourism Victoria** (☎ 250-953-2033) dispenses schedule, ticket, and venue information for all the offerings.

To get the skinny on what's happening, you can also consult the free weekly *Monday Magazine,* and phone the **Community Arts Council** (☎ 250-381-2787). You can access arts listings and calendars, too, at www.mondaymag.com or www.tourismvictoria.com.

Tickets for events are usually most easily purchased from the city's tourism center at 812 Wharf St. (☎ 800-663-3883 or 250-382-2127). The same helpful folks can also provide you with events calendars and lots of other information about the arts.

Calling all thespians: Victoria's theater scene

You may expect to find a decidedly Shakespearean bent here, but experimental companies remain strong, too, and you don't need to spend megabucks to enjoy theater as you do in nearby Seattle or Vancouver.

Don't miss the **Victoria Fringe Festival** (☎ 250-383-2663), a series of theatrical performances around town that runs from spring until the last two weeks of August, or the **Victoria Shakespeare Festival** (☎ 250-360-0234) — no surprise there — at St. Ann's Academy on Humboldt Street during August. Tickets for both events are cheap. The **UNO Festival** (☎ 250-383-2663) held around mid-May/early June, put on by the same folks who run the Fringe Festival, is also well worth catching if you're in town during that time.

Hereforth, a few of the city's top theater companies:

✔ The **Belfry Theatre,** 1291 Gladstone Ave., Fernwood (☎ 250-385-6815 box office), in a renovated church, is reason enough to come to town if you like small, local companies. Try to call ahead, because these performances are wildly popular with locals and Vancouverites alike. Tickets usually cost from C$17 to C$31 (US$14–US$26) per person.

✔ **Intrepid Theatre Company,** 110 Government St. #201 (☎ 250-383-2663), handles the organization and administration of the Fringe and UNO Festivals just mentioned.

✔ **Theatre Inconnu** (☎ 250-360-0234) is edgier and smaller than the other theaters mentioned in this list. Tickets run just C$10 to C$15 (US$8–US$12) per show.

✔ **Langham Court Theatre**, 805 Langham Court, Rockland (☎ 250-384-2142), is Canada's second oldest amateur theater company (it celebrated its 75th anniversary in 2004). The theater is actually a very handsomely converted barn and carriage house; sets and performances are a real pleasure, and tickets are all a flat C$15 (US$12). A great alternative with a terrific sense of community within the audience.

Locating high art: Opera, dance, and classical music

The city is well supplied with opera and classical offerings. However, you can find more variety than you may think — and there's nothing stodgy about it.

✔ The **Victoria Symphony** (☎ 250-385-6515 box office) performs a free waterside show called Symphony Splash from a stage floating on the Inner Harbour. The orchestra follows this event, which takes place on the first Sunday of August, with a full season of orchestral performances at the **Royal Theatre** at 805 Broughton St., Old Town/Downtown (☎ 888-717-6121 or 250-386-6121 for tickets). What the orchestra lacks in size, it makes up for in talent — and famous guests occasionally drop in. As orchestra prices go, tickets are amazingly low, usually no more than C$15, but can rise to C$60 (US$12–US$50). Tickets to the kids' concerts at the University of Victoria are C$11 (US$9)

✔ The **Pacific Opera Victoria** (☎ 250-385-0222) sings at the **McPherson Playhouse,** 3 Centennial Square (☎ 250-386-6121), an overwrought house from the early 20th century. The season comprises three different works, each presented about half a dozen times; you may hear classical or an operetta. Either way, ticket prices vary wildly — anywhere from C$24 to C$90 (US$20–US$75) per person — so check carefully before whipping out your credit card.

✔ The smaller **Victoria Operatic Society** (☎ 250-381-1021) isn't so much opera as musical theater and tends to perform extremely well-known works, probably those you sang back in high school. Performances are held at the McPherson Playhouse. Tickets cost from C$19 to C$35 (US$16–US$29).

Part V
The Part of Tens

The 5th Wave   By Rich Tennant

@RICHTENNANT

"Don't worry son. By the looks of it I imagine that cloud's headed straight for Vancouver."

In this part . . .

Here, I have a little fun. I share my insider tips on what you absolutely *must* have if you want to appreciate the personality of the two cities. Okay, so you may think twice about some of my suggestions — maybe you *could* do without the body piercings — but you also find some real advice: An umbrella *is* a must. Finally, I wrap up the section with a surprise rundown on some of the famous folks who hail from Vancouver and Victoria. Well, this is Hollywood North, dontcha know?

Chapter 23

Ten Things You *Can't* Live Without in Vancouver

. . . .

In This Chapter

▶ Preparing for the inevitable: Rain

▶ Dressing, eating, and drinking — Vancouver style

▶ Frolicking outdoors with bikes and Frisbees

. . . .

*O*kay, you're ready to go to Vancouver. You're psyched. You've put the mail on hold, the cat food in the dish, and the car in the garage. All that's left to do now is go, right? Not necessarily. Before you close the front door for the final time, make a last-minute check of that suitcase: Do you *really* have everything you'll need? Not sure? Check out these tips on how to fit in with Vancouverites, deflect raindrops, and otherwise equip yourself for the getaway of a lifetime.

Umbrella

After a few days here, the reminder chime for a 'brolly will become second nature to you. Granted, summers are generally bright and (relatively) dry, but the rest of the year? Well, think London, and you get the idea. David Duchovny from *The X-Files* famously remarked that it rains "400 inches a day" in Vancouver — a snarky comment which, although somewhat off base, quickly transformed him from a local icon to persona non grata. Besides, why do you think it's so green, anyway? You want a tan, go to the south of France.

With the Pacific air running up against the Coast Mountains, weather reports can be a bit iffy, too, unless they call for days of high pressure. Just because it isn't raining now doesn't mean it *won't* be in five minutes. I don't mean bucketsful, get-the-sandbags-and-head-for-the-levee kind of rain. No, Vancouver's rain is special. Imagine a fine mist, building itself up to an annoying drizzle and then, occasionally, spatterings of large drops. The kind that gets inside your shirtsleeves — and, after a while, your psyche. Vancouverites, however, are long-suffering when it comes to rain, likely because, given only one day of sunshine, they become so self-absorbed as to the beauty of the place, rain is quickly relegated to distant memory. Over and over again.

Bring an umbrella.

Coffee Cup

Have you ever seen people drink so much coffee, yet still remain relatively laid-back? I mean, in Vienna, they sit for hours over a single cup. That's because they're in Vienna. Here, though, coffee (and its growing rival, chai) is consumed as frequently as possible, in a wide variety of ways — iced, frozen, lattéd, mélanged, espressoed, double-decaf capped — whatever you want, really. Organic, shade-grown, handpicked by Ecuadorians? Yep, Vancouver's got that. Hawaiian? Arabica? No sweat. Soymilk instead of cream and organic raw turbinado sugar on the side? Come on, those are easy ones. (About the only thing you won't find here is instant coffee.)

To get your fill, pop into any of the dozens of local coffeehouses or, of course, the "cozy" little branches of those monster coffee chains whose names need no further free publicity with a mention here. Suffice to say that they've taken over the place. (One busy downtown corner even has *two* They-Shall-Remain-Nameless coffee shops facing off against each other across the traffic lights; both are always full. At last report, no price war has broken out between them.)

Ring/Stud/Tattoo

Actually, I'm going easy on you here. The true Vancouver slacker has at least one tongue, nose, eyebrow, or possibly another hidden body part pierced with a ring or stud. And usually a fascinating number rimming the ear. I'm giving you the tattoo as an out — there are some pretty cool skin artists here. For temporary cool, try a henna tattoo; it washes off.

Hiking Shoes

Very few cities in the world can boast a location that's at the base of a spectacular mountain range, *and* contains miles of beach within the city limits, *and* is a ferry ride away from even greener islands. Not to mention pristine, old-growth forests. But Vancouver can. And if you visit for more than a couple days, you owe it to yourself to explore these attributes like the locals.

If you're in excellent shape, make a point of heading over to Grouse Mountain (the one with the ski lift that's lit up at night, which seems to hover right over the city) and walk right up the side of it. It's called "the

Grouse Grind" for a reason, taking about an hour if you're super fit . . . a lot longer if you're not. That's too much? Okay, fine. Take the cable car up and walk back down — or vice versa. Still too tough? Fine. Drive up the neighboring mountains, Seymour and Cypress, and enjoy the trails through the woods. What? You want something easier? Well, then dump the hikers for a pair of runners and just walk the hilly parks, streets, and beaches of the West Side. Pacific Spirit Park and Camosun Bog are areas near the University of British Columbia that feel a lifetime away from the city-centre, not a 20-minute drive.

Chopsticks

Vancouver has long been considered North America's Gateway to the Pacific, so it's little wonder that it cooks with an amazing proliferation of Asian food. In some places, Asian cuisine has become quite pervasive. A virtual tidal wave of Japanese eateries has hit and multi-flavored bubble teas are all the rage, adding to an arsenal of Chinese places that may be second to none in North America.

Chopsticks: Get 'em, and figure out how to use 'em.

Jeans

This has to be one of the all-time casual-dressing towns. Of course, if you're dining at a place like, say, Chartwell or Diva at the Met (see Chapter 10), you'll want (and need) to break out the fancy duds. But in most other situations, cotton trousers (even jeans) and a designer T-shirt will get you by just fine. In Kitsilano, you could happily get away with a tie-dye.

Outside of eating, jeans seem to be a staple of travel, whether it's hopping on and off ferries, bellying up to the bar for a pint, or poking around in the gardens and parks.

Bike

Vancouver is an extremely bike-friendly town, in theory, although in practice the combination of lots of cars, high bridges, and wet roads doesn't always mean the biking is actually fun. Even on the designated "bike roads" (called "Greenways"), cycling can be a bit hairy. Think about it, though — would you rather drive to and around Stanley Park or bike there? That's a no-brainer. And, as a huge bonus, you can bring your bike onto the BC Ferries, and then use it to get around the islands at little financial — and no environmental — cost. Some hardbodies even bike up the side of Grouse Mountain, although I'm not ready to suggest that.

Part V: The Part of Tens _____

Sweater

Did I mention the weather? Summer nights are unlikely to get hot ever,
and if a fresh sea breeze is blowing they can indeed be a bit chilly. That's
when it's dry out. When it's wet, the temperature always feels colder
than it is (even though Vancouver rarely gets a hard freeze in winter). So
carry along a sweater no matter what time of year you choose to visit.
Look around and you'll see that the layered look is distinctly West Coast.

Organic Cotton/Hemp Mesh Bag

If you really want to live like a local, you must check out the city's markets at least one time. Start by getting an eco-correct bag — hemp and
other ethno-organic-type bags abound here. Then head for Granville
Market, just off the main peninsula, and stuff that politically correct bag
with all the (organic) fruits and veggies it can hold. Another time, take
the bus out to Broadway or to Main Street and find a little Asian food
market — then go wild. Vancouver is probably the best place on the continent to locate authentic, made-in-the-East bonito flakes, tofu, ginseng
royal jelly, and all the rest, not to mention plenty of spices, nuts, and
snacking materials in bulk.

Frisbees and Kites

So many parks are here that it would be a shame to neglect them. So
don't. Get yourself out to Kitsilano or Jericho Beach, borrow a local
dog (some hotels actually provide loaners), and go nuts with the flying
disc. The Spanish Banks and Vanier Park are your best bets for unfurling
kites (you can usually gauge the breeze by the number of windsurfers
zigzagging atop the whitecaps), and if you just want a frolic — no holds
barred — Wreck Beach is the place to bare all (just be careful with that
kite string — ouch!).

Chapter 24

Ten Things You *Can't* Live Without in Victoria

In This Chapter

▶ Acting like a proper wannabe Brit

▶ Celebrating beer and gadding about

▶ Capturing (and combating) the elements

Sure, you can be a tourist in Victoria, but why not try to blend in a little? All you need are a few props — and a little attitude adjustment.

Teacup

No place in North America is as English as Victoria (some say it is even more so than England), and tea is an integral part of the local wannabe ritual. Whether you're taking mid-morning tea (any Brits out there remember "elevenses"? — midmorning tea, it is), afternoon tea, or high (that is, with-the-works) tea, you need something to put it in, right? Just be sure to check your local lingo: MIF or MIL (see Chapter 2).

Malt Vinegar Shaker

All this English heritage also means you can find a surprising number of fish-and-chips (er, fish-and-french-fry?) shops here. Some serve up the fare in newspaper, just like in the ol' country. But remember, the English don't slather tartar sauce all over their fish and ketchup all over their chips. No, they use the one thing they always have plenty of — malted vinegar — on both. Then you realize why the newspaper's there; it acts as a kind of blotting paper!

Beer Stein

As you may guess if you've read the rest of this book, this town is loaded with better-than-avérage brewpubs. So make like a boy scout — always be prepared.

Golf Clubs

Vancouver Island contains some downright terrific golf courses in beautiful terrain, and whether you bring your own bag of sticks or rent 'em on the spot, any golfer will want to take advantage. And I'm talking about *any* time of the year. Believe it!

Camera or Camcorder

Rarely do you get a chance to film such lovely coastal scenery, maybe some whales or sails on the ferry over from Vancouver, fine architecture (hello, The Empress and Legislature Buildings), and cheesy gotta-show-the-family-later tourist sights (all those English pubs and double-decker buses) in one concentrated place while still in North America. Take full advantage.

Allergy Medication

Hey, they call this the city of roses, right? And for good reason — everybody and their cousin has a garden, and a climate in which flowers can bloom 12 months out of the year. And *that* means lots and lots of pollen at all times. Come prepared if pollen affects you.

Boat Shoes

Chances are pretty good that, at some point, you'll clamber onto a boat; perhaps a big Vancouver ferry, a smaller island vessel, or a whale-watching expedition boat. But bring waterproof shoes, for goodness' sake. You don't want to know what saltwater can do to fine shoes.

Cricket Wicket

Nah, just kiddin'. You may be surprised, though, how often this English theme keeps popping up in Victoria. A little cricket *pitch* (playing field) is in Beacon Hill Park, and who knows? Hang around long enough and some polite someone may actually volunteer to teach you the rules — after carefully explaining why the sport is so much more, well, civilized than baseball. Failing that, there are always any number of old codgers in the park ready for a game of chess (some play three or four games at a time) or, though doubtful, you might get pulled into an exciting (huh?) game of lawn bowls.

Bike Helmet

Victoria prides itself as being one of the top cycling cities in the world, and because it's smaller than Vancouver, it's been able to pull together some very impressive bike routes for the entire family. And if you're bringing the kids, all the more reason for helmets (which, incidentally, are mandatory in British Columbia).

Umbrella

Although Victoria proclaims itself to be British Columbia's sunniest spot, that's not saying much. Sure, the "rain shadow" of the Coastal Mountains keeps out a little rain. But it's still soggy as heck for much of the year. Don't forget the umbrella.

Chapter 25

Ten Celebrities You Didn't Realize Were from the Area

● ●

In This Chapter

▶ Gracing the big and small screens

▶ Cooking up with the best of 'em

▶ Cranking out Canadian rock: Ballads and spandex

● ●

*V*ancouver and Victoria rule! That's why so many people you meet here — Aussies, Ontarians, transplanted U.S. citizens — have abandoned their homelands for this watery paradise. At times, it seems as if nobody in the region actually grew up in these parts. So who knew that a handful of famous people actually did?

Bryan Adams

Perhaps the least edgy rocker in the history of pop music — wait a minute, is Michael Bolton still alive? — Bryan Adams grew up on Vancouver's North Shore and reportedly worked as a burger shop dishwasher during his teen years. Obviously he figured out a better way, and his soundtrack power ballads have moved millions of records (okay, make that millions of CDs and illegal downloads).

Pamela Anderson

The former Mrs. Tommy Lee was just a Vancouver Island teenybopper at a football game when she got caught on screen in the stands. Soon, she was the darling of Western Canadian beer ads; a local talent scout for a certain U.S. men's magazine — think bunny ears — got wind of her, her career then exploded with *Baywatch* and the rest is surgically enhanced (and then deflated) history.

Michael Bublé

Learn to say this name (pronounced Boo-BLAY), because this Vancouver crooner is touted to be the next Frank Sinatra. He's only in his mid-twenties but this lad swings, singing his versions of classics by Ella Fitzgerald, Keely Smith, Sarah Vaughan, Rosemary Clooney, and, of course, Old Blue Eyes himself. Appearances on David Letterman's *The Late Show*, *Today*, and overseas are rapidly making Bublé a household name.

Raymond Burr

Old Ironside a Canuck? Say it ain't so! Well, it *is* so. The portly actor who so brilliantly portrayed both Perry Mason and Robert Ironside — and, I'll be honest, I occasionally thought they were the same guy, but that's another matter — hailed from New Westminster, a Vancouver 'burb now but actually a fairly old part of the city just east of downtown. He passed away in 1993, but remains a solid television presence thanks to the magic of cable reruns.

Hayden Christensen

A few years back, he was an unknown Vancouver teen acting in Canadian TV; now he's world-famous as Anakin Skywalker, the focus of George Lucas's second and third *Star Wars* prequels, *Attack of the Clones* and *Revenge of the Sith*. (Anakin is the character who later fathers Luke Skywalker and eventually becomes Darth Vader.)

James Doohan

I'll wager that 99 out of 100 people who've seen the original *Star Trek* series thought the actor who played chief engineer "Scottie" actually was from Scotland. Wrong! He's from good old Vancouver, actually, and for a bit part, he sure made a pretty good career out of it, didn't he? He later reprised the role in several *Star Trek* films.

Rob Feenie

He's no slouch in the international culinary acclaim department and has earned himself enormous street cred to boot. *Iron Chef America*, a kind of WWF-meets-cooking, is the highest-rated series in Food Network history, and Feenie recently beat chef Masaharu Morimoto (who's taken 66 out of 75 Iron Chef battles) with a wasabi-infused knockout punch. See Chapter 10 for details if you want to sample his culinary prowess.

David Foster

A 14-time Grammy Award–winner with an unprecedented (to date, at least) 42 nominations, this homegrown Victoria talent is larger than life. As a musician, he's performed with musical titans such as John Lennon, Diana Ross, Barbra Streisand, and Rod Stewart, although today his claim to fame is in writing and producing. He has an eye for new talent, and has helped many a fellow Canuck, as Diana Krall, Michael Bublé, and Celine Dion will attest. Remember the soundtracks for *Ghostbusters*? *Footloose*? They're his.

Michael J. Fox

The charismatic Alberta native's family moved to the Vancouver 'burbs when he was still young, and Fox soon began starring on Canadian TV. Hollywood success — in *Family Ties*, *Teen Wolf*, *Back to the Future*, *Spin City*, and much more — soon followed. Fox is most famous today, however, for his advocacy for sufferers of Parkinson's disease, which afflicts him. Although Fox lives in Vermont and has changed citizenship, Vancouverites and Canadians are still proud to count him as one of their own.

Diana Krall and Nelly Furtado

All right, I'm using poetic license by wedging these two into one spot. But both these female crooners sport terrific voices, push at the boundaries of their form, have been widely acclaimed by critics and listeners alike — and hail from Vancouver Island! Krall, from little Nanaimo, is one of the world's top contemporary jazz singers; her silky voice is perfect for nighttime listening. Furtado, born in Victoria, makes an eclectic style of music that is difficult to categorize but draws on influences from the world over, including her family's native Portugal.

And More Bonus Celebs

And, finally, a cheer for all the rest — famous folks who weren't born either in Vancouver or on Vancouver Island, yet spent (or still spend) significant time here.

That includes everyone from members of the '80s spandex-rocker band **Loverboy** (am I the only one who remembers "Working for the Weekend"? "Hot Girls in Love"? Anybody?) to scary, black-and-white-era actor **Boris Karloff;** from au courant comedian **Colin Mochrie** (think Drew Carey's *Whose Line Is It Anyway?*) to *Generation X* novelist **Douglas Coupland;** from *Shoeless Joe* author **W.P. Kinsella** (his novel became the basis for the Hollywood smash film *Field of Dreams*) to the hard-rocking band **Nickelback;** from the undersized but big-hearted NBA All-Star point guard **Steve Nash** to *Sex and the City* bombshell **Kim Cattrall;** and from **Carrie-Ann Moss** of the *Matrix* trilogy to heartthrob actor and race-car driver **Jason Priestley,** who starred in *Beverly Hills 90210* when *People* magazine ranked him one of the 50 most beautiful people in the world. Oh, geez, gimme a break.

Appendix

Quick Concierge

Fast Facts

American Automobile Association (AAA)

In Vancouver, the British Columbia affiliate of AAA, known as BCAA, has an office at 999 West Broadway (☎ 800-663-1956 or 604-268-5600) that's open weekdays 9 a.m. to 5:30 p.m. and Saturdays 9 a.m. to 5 p.m. Members of AAA can pick up maps, tour books, and traveler's checks at no charge; and make travel arrangements here. Emergency road service and towing (☎ 604-293-2222) may also be free to members. Victoria's BCAA office is at 1075 Pandora St. (☎ 250-389-6700) and open Monday through Saturday, 9 a.m. to 5 p.m. The emergency road service number is ☎ 800-222-4357.

American Express

The main Vancouver office is located on the ground floor of the Park Place Building at 666 Burrard St. (☎ 604-669-2813). Open hours: Monday through Friday 8 a.m. to 5:30 p.m., Saturdays 10 a.m. to 4 p.m. AMEX cardholders can cash traveler's checks and pick up mail (envelopes only); there's also a travel agency. For lost or stolen credit cards, call ☎ 800-668-2639. For lost or stolen traveler's checks, call ☎ 800-221-7282. In Victoria, the American Express office and travel agency is located at 1213 Douglas St. (☎ 250-385-8731). It's open Monday through Friday, 8:30 a.m. to 5:30 p.m., Saturdays 10 a.m. to 4 p.m.

Area Code

The area code for Greater Vancouver and Whistler is **604**. For Victoria, Vancouver Island, and the Gulf Islands it's **250**.

ATMs

The most common places to find a major bank's machine in Vancouver and Victoria are the larger shopping and business districts. Major banks in Canada don't charge a user fee, even if you're not an account holder, but make sure the network logo on the back of your card matches that of the machine; Cirrus ☎ 800-424-7787 and Plus ☎ 800-843-7587 can tell you which ATMs work with their respective card systems.

Baby-sitters

Most hotels either have someone on staff who looks after children or can make arrangements to care for your child — just be certain to advise them of your child's special needs well in advance. In Vancouver, Moppet Minders (☎ 604-942-8167) have accredited sitters available throughout the city. Cribs & Carriages (☎ 604-988-2742) rents items like a car seat or crib and delivers them to your hotel, although many hotels may have these items on hand free of charge — ask first. In Victoria, try Wee Watch Private Home Daycare (☎ 250-382-5437) for baby-sitting.

Camera Supplies & Repair

With cameras getting more high tech, finding repair shops can be tough.

Camtex at 201-1855 Burrard St. (☎ 604-734-0242) is your best bet. For supplies and one-hour film processing, as well as digital transfer, try Lens & Shutter (☎ 604-684-4422), on the lower level of the Pacific Centre at 700 Dunsmuir St. in Vancouver. Another branch is in Kitsilano at 2912 West Broadway (☎ 604-736-3461). For less-expensive supplies and processing, pharmacies like the multi-branch Shopper's Drug Mart (☎ 800-363-1020) or London Drugs (☎ 604-272-7645) are usually well stocked. In Victoria, Lens & Shutter, 615 Fort St. (☎ 250-383-7443), provides one-hour film and digital-photo processing and supplies, while Broad Street Camera & Repairs, 1309 Broad St. (☎ 250-384-5510 or 250-384-5480), provides repairs and supplies.

Credit Cards

For lost or stolen cards, contact the following: Visa (☎ 800-847-2911), MasterCard (☎ 800-307-7309), or American Express (☎ 800-668-2639).

Currency Exchanges

Exchanges in Vancouver include American Express, 666 Burrard St. (☎ 604-669-2813); Custom House Currency Exchange, 375 Water St. (☎ 604-482-6006; www.custom house.com); Thomas Cook Foreign Exchange, 999 Canada Place, Suite #130 (☎ 604-641-1229) and 777 Dunsmuir St., in the Pacific Centre (☎ 604-687-6111); and Money Mart, 1195 Davie St. (☎ 604-606-9555). Exchanges in Victoria include American Express, 1213 Douglas (☎ 250-385-8731); Calforex, 724 Douglas St. (☎ 250-384-6631); Custom House Currency Exchange (☎ 250-389-6007), with locations at 815 Wharf St., Bastion Square, Eaton Centre, and the airport, among others; Money Mart, 1720 Douglas St. (☎ 250-386-3535), which charges high commissions; and Thomas Cook, 1001 Douglas St., Suite G-3 (☎ 250-385-0088).

Customs

Canada Revenue Agency (☎ 800-461-9999 or 204-983-3500) and U.S. Customs (☎ 604-278-1825) are both located at Vancouver International Airport. In Victoria, the office (☎ 800-461-9999 or 250-363-3531) is located at 816 Government St.

Dentists

In Vancouver, dental care is provided by the Vancouver Centre Dental Clinic (☎ 604-682-1601) at 650 West Georgia St., open Monday through Friday, 8:30 a.m. to 6 p.m. Don't expect to get in on an emergency basis, however; try to call ahead. For dental emergencies in Vancouver, call the College of Dental Surgeons of B.C. (☎ 604-736-3621) for help in locating a dentist near you. In Victoria, one clinic option — although it's far from downtown — is Cresta Dental Care, 3170 Tillicum Rd. (☎ 250-384-7711), in the Tillicum Mall (follow Douglas Street 2½ miles north away from town and turn left on Tillicum). It provides service Monday through Friday, 8 a.m. to 9 p.m., Saturday 9 a.m. to 5 p.m. and Sundays 11 a.m. to 5 p.m. Call ahead for an appointment. The Victoria District Dental Association (☎ 800-841-3504), can steer you to emergency on-call help.

Doctors

All major hotels should either have a doctor on call or be able to refer you to one. In Vancouver, Care Point Medical Centre, 1175 Denman St. (☎ 604-681-5338) and 1623 Commercial Drive (☎ 604-254-5554), offers walk-in services and accepts all major credit and debit cards. Open daily 9 a.m. to 9 p.m. Clinics in Victoria include the Downtown Medical Clinic, 622 Courtney St. (☎ 250-380-2210), open Monday through Friday 8:30 a.m. to 5:30 p.m., and James Bay Medical Treatment Centre, 230 Menzies St. (☎ 250-388-9934), open Monday through Friday 9 a.m. to 6 p.m., Saturdays 10 a.m. to

4 p.m. Appointments are taken until 30 minutes before closing.

Electricity

Canada's electrical outlets put out 110 volts AC (60 Hz) — same as those in the United States.

Emergencies

For fire, police, and ambulance, dial ☎ **911.** For non-emergencies in Vancouver, dial ☎ 604-717-3321 for police, ☎ 604-665-6000 for fire, and ☎ 604-872-5151 for ambulance. For non-emergencies in Victoria, call ☎ 250-380-6161. For questions about possible poisons, in Vancouver dial ☎ 604-682-5050 or ☎ 604-682-2344; in Victoria, dial ☎ 800-567-8911.

Hospitals

The closest hospital to downtown Vancouver is St. Paul's Hospital, 1081 Burrard St. (☎ 604-682-2344). You'll find the main city hospital, Vancouver Hospital, at 855 12th Ave. West (☎ 604-875-4111), just south and east of the Granville Bridge. The closest hospitals to downtown Victoria are Royal Jubilee Hospital, 1900 Fort St. (☎ 250-370-8000), 2 miles east of downtown, almost in Oak Bay; and Victoria General Hospital, 1 Hospital Way (☎ 250-727-4212), follow Douglas Street north out of town until it becomes Highway 1 (the hospital exit is about 3 miles from downtown).

Hotlines

See also "Emergencies" earlier in the Appendix. In Vancouver: If you see a crime happening, call Crime Stoppers ☎ 604-669-8477. For sexual assault, call the Rape Crisis Centre ☎ 604-255-6344 or Rape Relief ☎ 604-872-8612. In Victoria: Crime Stoppers is at ☎ 250-386-8477. For sexual assault, call the Victoria Women's Sexual Assault Centre ☎ 250-838-3232.

Information

In Vancouver, the Travel InfoCentre (☎ 604-683-2000; www.tourismvancouver.com) is located near Canada Place on the Plaza Level in the Waterfront Centre at 200 Burrard St. It's open daily 8:30 a.m. to 6 p.m., Monday through Friday; until 5 p.m. on Saturday. You can call toll-free (☎ 800-663-6000) for information prior to your arrival. Victoria's Travel InfoCentre, 812 Wharf St. (☎ 250-953-2033; www.tourismvictoria.com), near The Fairmont Empress Hotel, is the main information office, open Monday through Friday 9 a.m. to 5 p.m.

Internet Access

Most hotels have two-line telephones, and many have high-speed Internet access. Make sure to check the hotel's policy for in-room phone charges. Kinko's two Vancouver locations, 1900 West Broadway, Kitsilano (☎ 604-734-2679) and 789 West Pender St., downtown (☎ 604-685-3338) offer 24-hour computer access. Internet cafes are variable in quality, and you may have to order food or drink. But here are at least two good (and well-located) options in Vancouver: the Virtual Coffee Bean, 1595 West Broadway, Kitsilano (☎ 604-731-1011) and Webster's Internet Café, 340 Robson St., downtown (☎ 604-915-384-9327). In Victoria, the Greater Victoria Public Library, 735 Broughton St. (☎ 250-382-7241), provides 11 Internet terminals; and is open Monday, Wednesday, Friday, and Saturday 9 a.m. to 6 p.m. and to 9 p.m. Tuesday and Thursday. Web cruising and other business services can also be performed at J&L Copy Plus, 777 Fort St. (☎ 800-811-0333 or 250-386-3333).

Liquor Laws

You must be 19 years old to drink legally in British Columbia. You can purchase spirits at government-controlled LCBC (Liquor Control British Columbia) stores, found throughout both cities. The Yellow Pages listings under "Liquor Stores" will show one near you. Beer and wine are sold in restaurants, hotel lounges, taverns, nightclubs, and privately owned stores sporting a "Licensed Premises" sign on the door. LCBC stores are open Monday through Saturday from 10 a.m. to 6 p.m., some until 11 p.m.

Mail

Stamps for mailing letters within Canada cost C50¢, letters to the U.S. cost C85¢, and missives overseas cost C$1.45.

The Vancouver central post office, 349 West Georgia St., corner of Homer, is open weekdays 8 a.m. to 5:30 p.m. In Victoria, the central post office is located at 714 Yates St. (☎ 250-953-1352); a smaller branch is located at 1625 Fort St. (☎ 250-595-2552). You can also buy postage at any store with the red-and-white Canada Post logo, such as pharmacies and convenience stores.

Maps

Maps of Vancouver and Victoria are free from the Travel InfoCentres (see "Information" earlier in the Appendix). Maps are also in the respective city's Yellow Pages, as well as in the free visitor's guides you find in your hotel room. You can purchase useful and more detailed street maps such as the *Greater Vancouver Streetwise Map Book* (covers Vancouver and the surrounding area) at most gas stations and convenience and grocery stores.

Newspapers/Magazines

For mainstream news, try the *Vancouver Sun,* which is published Monday through Saturday, and *The Province,* published Sunday through Friday. On Thursdays, you may also want to pick up the free *Georgia Straight* at any coffeehouse, grocery store, or on-street newspaper box for entertainment and dining recommendations. For Victoria's daily news, check out the *Times Colonist.* For arts and entertainment, the alternative newspaper, *Monday Magazine,* comes out on Thursdays and can be found around town at the Travel InfoCentre, grocery stores, restaurants, and elsewhere.

Pharmacies

Shopper's Drug Mart has several locations throughout the Greater Vancouver Area. Call ☎ 800-363-1020 for store locations. There are three in the downtown district: inside the Denman Place Mall at 1020 Denman St. ☎ 604-681-3411; in Yaletown, 1006 Homer St. ☎ 604-669-0330; both are open until midnight; inside the Pacific Centre at 700 West Georgia St. ☎ 604-683-0358; and at 1125 Davie St. ☎ 604-669-2424, both are open 24 hours.

In Victoria, McGill & Orme, 649 Fort St. (☎ 250-384-1195), corner of Broad, is open Monday through Saturday 9 a.m. to 6 p.m., Sunday noon to 4 p.m. Shopper's Drug Mart is ubiquitous; one handy location is at 1222 Douglas St. (☎ 250-381-4321) open Monday through Friday 7 a.m. to 8 p.m., Saturday 9 a.m. to 7 p.m., and Sunday 9 a.m. to 6 p.m.

Police

Dial ☎ **911** for emergencies in Vancouver and Victoria.

For all other calls, dial the city police at ☎ 604-717-3321 in Vancouver or ☎ 250-380-6161 in Victoria.

Radio Stations

Filling the Vancouver airwaves are pop, alternative, and even country stations, including XFM (104.9 FM; alternative), JR-FM (93.7; new country), and The Fox (99.3 FM; pop). The public radio stations are CBC 1 (690 AM) and CBC 2 (105.7 FM). The most popular talk-radio station is probably CKNW (980 AM), which is heavy on news, sports, and commentary. CFUN (1410 AM) is mainly all talk, but geared to a younger, hipper audience. In Victoria, the CBC can be found at 90.5 FM for news, arts, and weather. CFAX, another news and sports source, is found at 1070 AM. Mainstream stations include The Ocean (98.5 FM), The Q (100.3 FM), HOT 103 (103.1 FM), and B107.3 (107.3 FM). For alternative music programming, tune in to CFUV, the University of Victoria's radio station at 102.0 FM.

Restrooms

You find clean restrooms in the following Vancouver locations: hotel lobbies; museums; the Public Markets (Granville Island, Robson Street, and Lonsdale Quay); malls including the Pacific Centre at 700 West Georgia St. and the Bentall Shopping Centre at 595 Burrard St. (on the ground level); supermarkets such as Safeway and Capers in Kitsilano; and department stores such as The Bay on Granville Street (restrooms are normally located on upper floors). In Victoria, try the Greater Victoria Public Library, 735 Broughton St. (☎ 250-382-7241), and bars, museums, restaurants, and service stations throughout town. The Victoria Bay Centre (anchored by The Bay) also has nice, newly renovated restrooms.

Safety

For the most part, Vancouver is much safer than its U.S. counterparts, such as Seattle. However, walking around at night in the following neighborhoods is not advised: the waning red-light district near Richards and Seymour streets, between Drake and Nelson; the unsavory area between Gastown and Chinatown called East Hastings; and the grunge neighborhood around and south of Pacific Central Station. Locals enthusiastically embrace

public transportation. You may witness occasional episodes of foul language or inappropriate behavior while using the system. Bus drivers have been trained to remove any person who is causing discomfort to passengers. Do not leave anything of value in your car or you may be a victim of a smash-and-grab — very prevalent east of Gastown. You should also never leave valuables in your hotel room. There's very little crime in Victoria of any sort at all — the occasional car break-in is about the worst of it. Of course, take the same care you would in any city: Avoid uninhabited and unlit areas at night and don't leave valuables in your car.

Smoking

Despite tight city anti-smoking laws, people continue to smoke — just no longer in public areas. Bars are about the only place where one can puff away without hassle, and hotels often have the majority of floors reserved for non-smokers. Always check signs before you light up; Vancouver and Victoria residents are sensitive about their right not to breathe smoke, and they won't hesitate to speak up about it.

Taxes

There is a 7 percent provincial sales tax (PST) on everything except food, restaurant meals, or children's apparel. There is also a goods and services tax (GST) of 7 percent levied by the federal government on everything but alcohol, which is subject to a 10 percent tax. Hotels charge an additional 10 percent lodging tax. The GST may be refunded to you if you fill out the paperwork properly and submit your original receipts; however, you won't be refunded on any purchases concerning car rentals, parking, restaurant meals, tobacco, or alcohol, and you must spend a minimum amount abroad in order to collect the refund. You can pick up a tax refund application from your hotel or the Travel

InfoCentres. There are also additional taxes on rental cars (a C$1.50 environmental fee, plus almost 15 percent of the rental amount if made from an airport) and hotels.

Taxis

Taxis line up for fares at downtown Vancouver hotels. You can also call a taxi company directly and have a ride within five to ten minutes, but you may have to wait longer when it's raining. Options include: Black Top Cabs (☎ 800-494-1111 or 604-731-1111); Yellow Cab (☎ 604-681-1111), or Vancouver Taxi (☎ 604-255-5111), which has wheelchair-accessible cabs. In Victoria, call ahead for a taxi, because you often can't find them cruising the streets. Popular companies include: Blue Bird Cabs (☎ 800-665-7055 or 250-382-1111), Victoria Taxi (☎ 250-383-7111), and Empress Taxi (☎ 800-808-6881 or 250-381-2222), which has some wheelchair-accessible cars.

Telephone

Pay phones are usually located in glass telephone booths in grocery stores, hotel lobbies, or on the street. To call, insert C25¢ in the slot, wait for a dial tone, and dial your local number. Most phones also take prepaid phone cards that can be purchased at postal outlets, pharmacies, and even tourist information offices. Local phone calls made from the phone in your hotel room can cost up to $1 or more per call, so check with your hotel on its policy.

Time Zone

Vancouver is in the Pacific time zone, the same one as Los Angeles and Seattle. Daylight saving time (one hour ahead) is observed from April to October.

Transit Information

In Vancouver, call ☎ 604-521-0400 for schedule and other information. In Victoria, call the BC Transit Bus Line (☎ 250-382-6161 or TTY 250-995-5622) for schedule information. For transit information online: www.translink.bc.ca (Vancouver); www.bctransit.com (Victoria); www.bcferries.com (major ferries).

Weather Updates

For Vancouver weather, call Talking Yellow Pages (☎ 604-299-9000) and punch extension #3501. On the Internet, www.cnn.com, www.weather.com, and www.weatheroffice.com provide free Vancouver forecasts. For Victoria-area weather reports, call ☎ 250-363-6717 and listen to the menu options for the city you want; Victoria is extension #3502. For marine conditions, call ☎ 250-363-6717.

Toll-Free Numbers and Web Sites

Major carriers flying into Vancouver and Victoria International Airports

Air Canada
☎ 800-663-3721
www.aircanada.com

Air New Zealand
☎ 800-262-1234
www.airnewzealand.com

Alaska Airlines
☎ 800-426-0333
www.alaskaair.com

Aloha Airlines
☎ 800-367-5250
www.alohaairlines.com

American Airlines
☎ 800-433-7300
www.aa.com

British Airways
☎ 800-247-9297
www.british-airways.com

Cathay Pacific
☎ 800-233-2742
www.cathay-pacific.com

Continental
☎ 800-525-0280
www.continental.com

Delta
☎ 800-221-1212
www.delta.com

EVAair
☎ 800-695-1188 (USA)
☎ 866-2-25011999 (international)
www.evaair.com

Harmony Airways
☎ 866-868-6789
www.harmonyairways.com

Japan Airlines
☎ 800-525-3663
www.jal.com/en

KLM/Northwest
☎ 800-225-2525
www.nwa.com

Korean Air
☎ 800-438-5000

Lufthansa
☎ 800-645-3880
www.lufthansa.com

Qantas
☎ 800-227-4500
www.qantas.com

Reno Air
☎ 800-736-6147
www.renoair.com

Singapore Airlines
☎ 800-742-3333
www.singaporeair.com

United
☎ 800-241-6522
www.united.com

Westjet Airlines
☎ 888-937-8538
www.westjet.com

Car rental agencies

Alamo
☎ 800-327-9633
www.goalamo.com

Avis
☎ 800-331-1212
☎ 800-TRY-AVIS in Canada
www.avis.com

Budget
☎ 800-527-0700
https://rent.drivebudget.com

Discount
☎ 800-263-2355
www.discountcar.com

Dollar
☎ 800-800-4000
www.dollar.com

Enterprise
☎ 800-325-8007
www.enterprise.com

Hertz
☎ 800-654-3131
www.hertz.com

Lo Cost Rent A Car
☎ 800-986-1266
www.locost.com

National/Tilden
☎ 800-CAR-RENT
www.nationalcar.com

Rent-A-Wreck
☎ 800-535-1391
rent-a-wreck.com

Thrifty
☎ 800-367-2277
www.thrifty.com

Major hotel and motel chains

Accent Inns
☎ 800-663-0298
www.accentinns.com

Best Western International
☎ 800-528-1234
www.bestwestern.com

Clarion Hotels
☎ 800-CLARION
www.hotelchoice.com

Comfort Inns
☎ 800-228-5150
www.hotelchoice.com

Days Inn
☎ 800-325-2525
www.daysinn.com

Hampton Inn
☎ 800-HAMPTON
www.hampton-inn.com

Hilton Hotels
☎ 800-HILTONS
www.hilton.com

Holiday Inn
☎ 800-HOLIDAY
www.basshotels.com

Howard Johnson
☎ 800-654-2000
www.hojo.com

Hyatt Hotels & Resorts
☎ 800-228-9000
www.hyatt.com

ITT Sheraton
☎ 800-325-3535
www.sheraton.com

Quality Inns
☎ 800-228-5151
www.hotelchoice.com

Radisson Hotels International
☎ 800-333-3333
www.radisson.com

Ramada Inns
☎ 800-2-RAMADA
www.ramada.com

Residence Inn by Marriott
☎ 800-331-3131
www.residenceinn.com

Sandman Hotels & Inns
☎ 800-SANDMAN
www.sandmanhotels.com

Super 8 Motels
☎ 800-800-8000
www.super8motels.com

Travelodge
☎ 800-255-3050
www.travelodge.com

Where to Get More Information

I like to think that you'll find most of what you need between the covers of this book, but if you're craving more, that's okay by me. To get more information about Vancouver and Victoria, contacting the respective tourism offices, all of which are exceptionally helpful, usually works best. Here's the contact info.

Tourist information offices

For regional information on British Columbia, your first stop should be **Tourism British Columbia,** Box 9830 Stn. Prov. Government, Victoria, BC VW8 9W5; (☎ **800-663-6000;** www.hellobc.com). Contact details for Vancouver and Victoria are under "Information" earlier in this appendix.

Newspapers, magazines, and books

In addition to the major dailies listed earlier, these publications are good event sources: Both the *Georgia Straight* (www.straight.com) and *The Westender* (www.westender.com) are freebie newspapers with lots of Vancouver entertainment listings; *Xtra West* (www.xtra.ca) has a gay and lesbian focus; *Vancouver Magazine* (www.vanmag.com) has a more sophisticated emphasis on the arts, dining, and entertainment. In Victoria, *Monday Magazine* (www.mondaymag.com) is the best for that city's entertainment happenings.

Finally, a book worth checking out is *Frommer's Vancouver & Victoria* (Wiley Publishing, Inc.), an easy-to-use guide with more nightlife, accommodations, and dining choices.

Index

See also separate Accommodations and Restaurant indexes at the end of this index.

General Index

• A •

AARP, 51
Above and Beyond Tours, 55
Absolute Spa at the Century, 173
Access Canada, 53
Access-Able Travel Source, 52
Accessible Journeys, 52
accommodations. *See also*
    Accommodations Index
arrival without reservations, 90–91
best hotels (Vancouver), 9–10, 91–104
best hotels (Victoria), 13, 224–235
best rates, 88–90
and children, 36
costs, 31–32
direct bookings, 88–89
five-diamond status (Vancouver), 10
gay-friendly, 56
Internet deals, 89–90
islands, 198
by neighborhood (Vancouver),
    105–106
by neighborhood (Victoria), 236–237
options, 87–88
by price (Vancouver), 106–107
by price (Victoria), 237–238
reservations, 90
runner-up hotels (Vancouver),
    104–105
runner-up hotels (Victoria), 235–236
Sunshine Coast, 195–196
toll-free numbers and web sites, 314
travel agents, 88
Whistler, 192
Adams, Bryan, 302
Adams, John, 15
AFB, 52
Air Canada Vacations, 47
Air Tickets Direct, 42
airfare deals, 41–42

airline security measures, 68–69
airlines, 40–43, 47, 312–313
Airport Improvement Fee, 41
airport recovery fee, 62
Airporter, 53, 74, 217
airports, 73–74
Alaska Airlines, 47
Alcan Dragon Boat Festival, 27
Alibi Room, 205
All-Terrain Adventures, 162
allergy medication, 300
alternative bars, 207–208
American Automobile Association
    (AAA), 307
Amtrak, 43
Anderson, Pamela, 302
Anglophiles itinerary, 280–281
Antique Row, 15, 276–277
antiques, 15
AquaBus ferry, 84
AquaBus Tours, 160–161
Aquarium and Marine Science
    Centre, 12
Architectural Institute of British
    Columbia Tours, 160
architecture, 19, 21
area code, 307
arriving in Vancouver, 73–75
arriving in Victoria, 215–218
Art Gallery of Greater Victoria, 258
arts
    First Nations art, 12
    performing arts, 210–212, 290–291
    Vancouver, 19, 158–159
Arts Club Theatre, 211
Asian Culinary Culture, 163
Asian food, 128
Asian shopping items, 168
ATMs (automated teller machines),
    37–38, 307
attractions. *See also* children's
    attractions
    Art Gallery of Greater Victoria, 258
    arts (Vancouver), 158–159

Accommodations Index

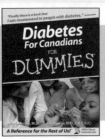

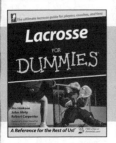

FOR DUMMIES®

A world of resources to help you grow

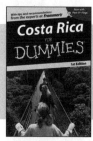
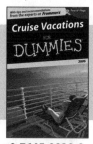
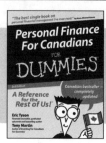

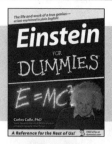
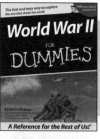